WHY DAVID SOMETIMES WINS

MARSHALL GANZ

WHY DAVID SOMETIMES WINS

Leadership, Organization, and Strategy in the California Farm Worker Movement

OXFORD
UNIVERSITY PRESS

OXFORD
UNIVERSITY PRESS

Oxford University Press, Inc., publishes works that further
Oxford University's objective of excellence
in research, scholarship, and education.

Oxford   New York
Auckland   Cape Town   Dar es Salaam   Hong Kong   Karachi
Kuala Lumpur   Madrid   Melbourne   Mexico City   Nairobi
New Delhi   Shanghai   Taipei   Toronto

With offices in
Argentina   Austria   Brazil   Chile   Czech Republic   France   Greece
Guatemala   Hungary   Italy   Japan   Poland   Portugal   Singapore
South Korea   Switzerland   Thailand   Turkey   Ukraine   Vietnam

Copyright © 2009 by Marshall Ganz

Published by Oxford University Press, Inc.
198 Madison Avenue, New York, New York 10016

www.oup.com

First issued as an Oxford University Press paperback, 2010

Oxford is a registered trademark of Oxford University Press

Library of Congress Cataloging-in-Publication Data
Ganz, Marshall, 1943–
Why David sometimes wins : leadership, organization, and strategy in the California
farm worker movement / Marshall Ganz.
p.   cm.
Includes bibliographical references.
ISBN 978-0-19-975785-5
1. Agricultural laborers—Labor unions—California—History.   2. United Farm Workers—
History.   3. Migrant agricultural laborers—Labor unions—California—History.
4. Agricultural laborers—California—History.   I. Title.
HD6515.A29G36   2009
331.88'1309794—dc22   2008027860

Printed in the United States of America
on acid-free paper

To the organizers who,
with hopeful heart,
critical eye,
and skillful hand,
bring us together
to change ourselves,
our communities,
and our world.

Preface

WHY I WROTE THIS BOOK

Why can the powerless sometimes challenge the powerful successfully? And how can strategic resourcefulness sometimes compensate for lack of resources? In this book, I respond to these questions—a mission to which I've devoted a lifetime of practice, scholarship, and teaching.

I grew up in Bakersfield, California, where my father was a rabbi and my mother, a teacher. Bakersfield is an oil and agriculture town at the southern end of the San Joaquin Valley, terminus of the "dustbowl" migration memorialized by John Steinbeck in *Grapes of Wrath*, a book banned in the county's high schools for many years. Graduating from high school in 1960, the year John F. Kennedy was elected president, I traveled east to enter Harvard College, where I became active in civil rights work.

I felt myself called to the civil rights movement for several reasons. For three years following World War II, my family had lived in Germany, where my father served as an army chaplain. He worked with "displaced persons," survivors of the Holocaust, whom I met as a child as they passed through our home. Although I was too young to grasp the full horror of what had occurred, the people whom I'd met had clearly survived a catastrophe. My parents, especially my mother, who had grown up in Virginia, taught me that the Holocaust was the result not only of anti-Semitism, but also of racism—and that racism could kill. It was an evil. And that was what civil rights was fighting.

I had also grown up on years of Passover *seders*—that celebration of an ancient journey from slavery to freedom. This was a journey, I was told as a child, that was my journey, that I had been a slave in Egypt. Although it took me a while to figure this out, I came to see that this is a journey that passes from generation to generation. Explicitly evoking the Exodus narrative, the civil rights struggle proclaimed itself the "freedom movement."

It was also a movement of young people: Dr. King had been only 25 when he led the Montgomery bus boycott, and many leaders of the sit-ins, freedom rides, and voter registration drives were even younger. This was no accident. Often, young people see the world with what some call a "prophetic imagination" that combines a critical view of *what is* with a hopeful view of *what could be.*[1] And because I shared their values, I found myself challenged and called by their spirit of commitment, courage, and hope. So, in the summer of 1964, I volunteered for the Mississippi Summer Project, and when the time came to return to school for my senior year, I went to work for SNCC (the Student Non-Violent Coordinating Committee) instead.

In the fall of 1965, I returned home to Bakersfield, just 30 miles south of Delano, California, where Cesar Chavez had just begun a grape strike. Although I had grown up in the midst of the farm worker world, I had never really seen it. But Mississippi had taught many of us that it was not an exception, but rather a clearly drawn example of how race, politics, and power work in America. This gave me the "Mississippi eyes" to see where I had grown up in a new way. I now saw farm workers who faced challenges not unlike those faced by their southern counterparts: no voting power, low wages, and, as people of color, subjected to California's own legacy of racial discrimination, which began with the Chinese immigrants. Now, they too were fighting back with their own movement. In October 1965, my friends LeRoy Chatfield, a Christian brother, and Mike Miller, the Bay Area SNCC organizer, introduced me to Cesar. After a weekend driving him around on one of his Bay Area fundraising trips, he asked me to join him. So I began working with the farm workers, a calling I would pursue for the next 16 years. During the brief period covered in this book, I served as the Bakersfield organizer; march to Sacramento coordinator; organizer on the Arvin DiGiorgio campaign; Lamont field office director; and assistant negotiator at DiGiorgio, Christian Brothers, and Almaden. During the following 14 years, I served in a wide range of positions, including boycott director, organizing director, and national Executive Board member from 1973 to 1981, when I resigned.

In 1991, after 10 years of electoral, union, and community organizing, mostly in California, I returned to Harvard College to complete my undergraduate degree in history and government, graduating class of 1964–1992. The following year, my wife, Susan Eaton, and I entered the Kennedy School of Government as midcareer students, earning M.P.A. degrees in 1993. We then began work on our PhDs, my own in sociology at Harvard and Susan's in management at MIT. While working on my doctorate, I was asked to teach organizing at the Kennedy School and, upon completing our doctorates in 2000, Susan and I both joined the faculty there—where we remained until her untimely death from leukemia in December 2003.

I am blessed to have had the opportunity to participate in the farm worker movement, to contribute to its development, and now to be possessed of the energy, time, and support to revisit it from a fresh perspective. Just as my experience as an organizer in Mississippi had given me new eyes through which to see the farm worker world in which I had grown up, so my experience as a scholar gave me new eyes to see the farm worker world in which I worked for 16 years. From a purely academic point of view, my participation in this conflict could raise a problem of bias, due to my interest in controversial events and my personal relationships with participants on all sides. However, I believe that the benefits far outweigh the costs. My experience has equipped me with a deep understanding of the context in which events unfolded, direct information as to what took place, and access to important research resources. It has infused my work with a deep desire to understand not only what happened, but also why things happened as they did, and thus equip others to learn from this experience. One lesson I learned is that things don't have to be the way they are, but they don't change by themselves. Challenging the status quo takes commitment, courage, imagination, and, above all, dedication to learning.

ACKNOWLEDGMENTS

This book—and the dissertation that preceded it—has been a long time coming. I am deeply grateful to the people who made it possible for me to write it. I thank the members of my dissertation committee for their mentoring, support, and confidence in me. I thank Theda Skocpol, my committee chair, advisor, and friend, for her love of the craft of scholarship, her example of a committed public intellectual, and her patient persistence in making sure I "got it done." I thank Richard Hackman for sharing his love of learning and his clarity of mind, and Mark Moore for his love of ideas, willingness to take risks, and constant support. To Kenneth Andrews, I am grateful for his engagement with my questions, his care in reading my work, his reliability, and the years of subsequent collaboration on other projects.

I appreciate my teachers, colleagues, and students who read my work, commented on it, and helped me to improve it. I thank John Campbell, Mark Warren, Robert Putnam, David Hart, Doug McAdam, Bill Gamson, Paul Osterman, Mary Jo Bane, Katherine Newman, Jim Jasper, Francesca Polletta, Ziad Munson, Gzergorz Ekiert, Marion Fourcade-Gourinchas, David John Frank, Lani Guinier, Jason Kaufman, Irene Bloemraad, and Michael Jones-Correa. Robert Brandfon helped me to recognize the value of reflection on my experience. Tom Kochan reviewed my labor history chapter, and David Montgomery contributed thoughtful responses to my queries. Don Villarejo, Phil Martin, and Paul Rhode helped me to understand the mysteries of agricultural economics. Andy Molinsky shared the culture and cognition literature so important for this work. George Strauss tracked down elusive data at the University of California. And Richard Parker bicycled his way with me through the first half of the twentieth century and gave me valuable advice on how to deal with publishers. I am also grateful to the seminar members who discussed my work in progress: the MIT Industrial Relations Seminar, the Kennedy School Junior Faculty Research Workshop, the Sawyer Seminar on Democratic Performance, the American Political Development Workshop, the Social Movements Workshop, the Hauser Center Workshop, and the MIT DUSP Seminar.

Fellow researchers provided valuable feedback and, in some cases, original data. Bill Friedland, Craig Jenkins, Theo Majka and Linda Majka, and Cletus Daniel were all helpful. Dick Meister shared his research files for his book (written with Anne Loftis), *Long Time Coming*. Frank Bardacke shared his thinking, insight, and data from his forthcoming UFW history, *Beneath the California Sun*. And Don Watson, ILWU leader emeritus, shared his original research into the agricultural labor politics that were critical to key periods of this conflict.

The documentary history of the UFW is housed principally at the Walter Reuther Library, Wayne State University, Detroit. I could not have completed this book without the dedicated, imaginative, and reliable support of Kathy Schmelling, curator of the UFW Archives. Archivists of Stanford University Special Collections and the Southern

Indiana University Collection also helped. Sandy Chung facilitated the time-consuming work of gathering documents, making copies, and remembering where they are. During the last two years of this project, I benefited from Jenny Oser's wonderful gift of making things appear just when I needed them. I also thank Dick Chandler, the guard at William James Hall, who in many a late-night conversation helped to keep things in perspective.

A crucial source of inspiration and insight for this work has been my students at Harvard College, the Kennedy School of Government, the Harvard Divinity School, and the Harvard Graduate School of Education, who gave me the opportunity to develop my theory of strategic capacity in practice. I could not have won my book campaign without the support of teaching fellows Dina Abad, Liz Steinhauser, Tony Mack, Julia Greene, Devon Anderson, Metta McGarvey, Sue Crawford, Mary Hannah Henderson, Heather Harker, Andrea Sheppard, Carlos Diaz, Lisa Boes, Jack Pan, Aimee Carevich, and Jenny Oser.

Although some of the learning that enabled me to write this book has been recent, much of it also goes back to my years of work with the farm workers. I thank Fred Ross and Cesar Chavez for mentoring me in the craft of organizing. I hope this book does them justice. I thank Jessica Govea for all she taught me and shared with me: her caring, her understanding, and her family. I thank my collaborators, from whom I learned so much and many of whom I interviewed for this project: Gilbert Padilla, Jerry Cohen, LeRoy Chatfield, Chris Hartmire, Eliseo Medina, Jim Drake, and others. I also thank other participants who gave interviews: Henry Anderson, Hermann "Blackie" Levitt, Ron Taylor, Al Brundage, Albert Rojas, Kevin Grami, Tom Kircher, and Don Garnel. Paul Schrade and Peter Edelman helped with timely and thoughtful responses to my questions.

Clearly presenting what you want to say can be as challenging as figuring out what you want to say in the first place. Chris Campbell, who believes all dragons can be slain, thoughtfully translated many a turgid sentence into more readable prose. Stuart Allen, with whom I shared a cell in Mississippi, designed the beautiful maps. Rhea Wilson contributed her editing skills, good humor, and persistence to bring this project home. Tamar Miller helped to wrap it up.

Writing a book takes time, money, and encouragement. I am grateful for the institutional support of the Civic Engagement Project, Sawyer Fellowship in Democratic Performance, Hauser Center Doctoral Fellows Program, Hauser Center Director's Fund, Harvard Department of Sociology, and Kennedy School of Government. I appreciate the commitment of my colleagues to support me in completing this project—protecting my time, attending to my motivation, and making certain I had the wherewithal. I specifically thank Theda Skocpol, Mark Moore, Fred Schauer, Dutch Leonard, Kathleen Fox, Sue Williamson, Shawn Bohen, and Derek Bok. Ben Presskreischer helped me to find the inner resources to make this happen.

The central metaphor for this book, the story of David and Goliath, emerged in a conversation with Andy Molinsky. Richard Hackman "got it" right away, formulating the question as "why David sometimes wins." And the Reverend William Barnwell of Trinity Episcopal Church encouraged me to "preach on it" at a meeting of the professional ministers caucus of the Greater Boston Interfaith Organization. Their reaction, and that of Jim Wallis, convinced me there was really something there.

This whole undertaking never would have happened without the loving support of my wife, Susan Eaton. She enabled me to take this journey, shared it with me, and, for 13 years of marriage, joined her journey to my own.

Returning to this work in the last three years has been challenging. I am grateful to Mark Moore and Derek Bok at the Hauser Center for their support; to Dedi Felman, at Oxford University Press, for her patient encouragement; to Jessica Mele, my assistant, who with her great good humor helped me to manage my time to get this done; to Marion Fourcade-Gourinchas for getting me reenergized to work on it at UC Berkeley; to Adam Reich, now studying for his doctorate in sociology at UC Berkeley; to Hahrie Han, now assistant professor of political science at Wellesley, for their careful reading of the manuscript. I thank Margaret Weir for her thoughtful reviews, constancy of support, and friendship. And for the inspiration, hopefulness, and energy to complete this project, I thank my good friend Tracy Powell, who, for a time, brought new light into my life.

Contents

Abbreviations

CIO	Congress of Industrial Organizations
CMM	California Migrant Ministry
CORE	Congress of Racial Equality
CRLA	California Rural Legal Assistance
CSFL	California State Federation of Labor
CSO	Community Service Organization
ECAFW	Emergency Committee to Aid Farm Workers
FALA	Filipino Agricultural Labor Association
FAW	Federation of Agricultural Workers
FSA	Farm Security Administration
FTA	Food, Tobacco, and Agricultural Workers Union, CIO
FWA	Farm Workers Association
FWO	Farm Workers Organization
IBT	International Brotherhood of Teamsters
ILA	International Longshoremen's Association, AFL
ILGWU	International Ladies' Garment Workers' Union
ILWU	International Longshoremen and Warehousemen's Union
IUD	Industrial Union Department, AFL-CIO
IWW	Industrial Workers of the World
MAPA	Mexican-American Political Association
NAACP	National Association for the Advancement of Colored People
NACFL	National Advisory Committee on Farm Labor
NAWU	National Agricultural Workers Union
NFLU	National Farm Labor Union
NFWA	National Farm Workers Association
NFWSC	National Farm Workers Service Center, Inc.
NIRA	National Industrial Recovery Act (1933)
NLB	National Labor Board (1933)
NLRA	National Labor Relations Act (1935)

NLRB	National Labor Relations Board
NRA	National Recovery Administration
NWLB	National War Labor Board (1942)
OEO	Office of Economic Opportunity
SCAL	Student Committee for Agricultural Labor
SCLC	Southern Christian Leadership Conference
SDS	Students for a Democratic Society
SNCC	Student Non-Violent Coordinating Committee
STFU	Southern Tenant Farmers Union
TUUL	Trade Union Unity League
UAW	United Automobile Workers
UCAPWA	United Cannery, Agricultural, and Packinghouse Workers of America, CIO
UFW	United Farm Workers of America, AFL-CIO
UFWOC	United Farm Workers Organizing Committee, AFL-CIO
UPWA	United Packing House Workers, CIO
UTS	Union Theological Seminary
WCT	Western Conference of Teamsters

WHY DAVID SOMETIMES WINS

ONE

Introduction

How David Beat Goliath

O N EASTER SUNDAY morning, April 10, 1966, Roberto Roman, walking barefoot, bore his heavy wooden cross triumphantly over the Sacramento River Bridge, down the Capitol Mall, and up the steps of the state capitol of California. Roman, an immigrant Mexican farm worker, was accompanied by 51 other *originales*— striking grape workers who had walked 300 miles in their *perigrinación*, or pilgrimage, from Delano to Sacramento. They were met by a crowd of 10,000 people who had come from throughout the state to share in their unexpected victory.

For seven months, striking grape workers organized by the fledgling National Farm Workers Association (NFWA) had endured picket lines, strike breakers, arrests, economic uncertainty, and, at times, despair. But they had also been buoyed by the support of religious leaders, students, civil rights groups, and trade unionists. Many supporters had traveled to Delano to bring food, clothing, money, and messages of solidarity, and they had begun to respond to the farm workers' call for a nationwide consumer boycott of Schenley Industries, a national liquor distributor and major Delano grape grower. In the winter of 1966, as the new grape season approached, NFWA leaders decided to conduct the 300-mile *perigrinación* from Delano to Sacramento in order to mobilize fresh support for the strike among farm workers, to call attention to the boycott among the public, and to observe Lent.

The farm workers began the *perigrinación* on March 17, carrying banners of Our Lady of Guadalupe, patron saint of Mexico, portraits of the Mexican *campesino* leader Emiliano Zapata, and placards proclaiming *peregrinación, penitencia, revolución*—pilgrimage, penance, revolution. They also carried signs calling on supporters to boycott Schenley. Roberto Roman carried his six-foot-tall wooden cross, constructed with two-by-fours and draped in black cloth. Of the strikers selected to march the full distance, William King, the oldest, was 63, and Augustine Hernandez, the youngest, was 17. Nearly one-quarter were women.

Launched the day after Senator Robert Kennedy had visited Delano to take part in hearings being conducted by the U.S. Senate Subcommittee on Migratory Labor, the march attracted wide public attention from the start. Televised images of a line of helmeted police blocking the marchers' departure—calling it a "parade without a permit"—evoked images of police lines in Selma, Alabama, just the year before. As the marchers progressed up the valley from town to town, public interest grew. A crowd of more than 1,000 welcomed the marchers to Fresno at the end of the first week. Daily bulletins began to appear in the San Francisco Bay Area press, chronicling the progress of the march. Reporters profiled the strikers, discussed why they would walk 300 miles, and analyzed what the strike was all about. Roman Catholic and Episcopal bishops urged the faithful to join the pilgrimage, and the Northern California Board of Rabbis came to share Passover matzo. The march powerfully expressed not only the farm workers' call for justice, but also the Mexican-American community's claims for a voice in public life. As Cesar Chavez, the NFWA's leader, later described it, the march was also a way, at an individual level, of "training ourselves to endure the long, long struggle, which by this time had become evident...would be required. We wanted to be fit not only physically but also spiritually."[1]

On the afternoon of April 3, as the marchers arrived in Stockton, still a week's march south of Sacramento, Schenley's lawyer reached Chavez on the phone. Schenley had little interest in remaining the object of a boycott, especially as the marchers' arrival in Sacramento promised to become a national anti-Schenley rally. Schenley wanted to settle. Three days of hurried negotiations followed. The result was the first real union contract in California farm labor history—a multi-year agreement providing immediate improvements in wages, hours, and working conditions and, perhaps most important, formal recognition of the NFWA. Chavez announced the breakthrough on Thursday. By Saturday afternoon, some 2,000 marchers had gathered on the grounds of Our Lady of Grace School in West Sacramento, which was on a hill looking across the Sacramento River to the capital city that they would enter the next morning. During the prayer service that evening, more than one speaker compared them to the ancient Israelites camped across the River Jordan from the Promised Land. That night, Roberto Roman carefully redraped his cross in white and decorated it with spring flowers. The next morning, barefoot, he carried it triumphantly into the city.

How did California farm workers achieve this remarkable breakthrough? And why did a fledgling association of farm workers achieve it rather than the AFL-CIO or the Teamsters, its far more powerful rivals?

Since 1900, repeated attempts to organize a farm workers' union in California had failed because the farm owners—or "growers"—had vigorously resisted farm labor organizing, often violently. Their large-scale, specialized, and integrated agricultural enterprises required large numbers of seasonal workers to be available whenever and wherever they were needed.[2] At harvest time, these workers held the economic well-being of these enterprises literally in their hands. So the growers protected themselves—and held labor costs down—by recruiting a particularly powerless workforce of impoverished new immigrants who lacked the political rights of other Americans and who, as people of color, faced racial barriers in all spheres of life. For farm workers, the result was low wages, poor living and working conditions, and a lack of security for themselves and their families.

At three junctures, however, between 1901 and 1951, a tight farm labor market created a brief opportunity for workers to turn their labor resource into economic power. At each of these junctures, ethnic labor associations, networks of radical organizers,[3] and the American Federation of Labor (AFL) attempted to seize the opportunity to create a union. Indeed, their strikes often won short-term gains for specific groups of farm workers, as well as some degree of outside support. But each effort failed before a farm workers' union could be established. At each juncture, a wartime mobilization afforded growers the political support they needed to suppress the organizing and once again flood local farm labor markets with new immigrants.

A fourth major wave of organizing activity, which began in the late 1950s, seemed unlikely to end any differently. It was prompted by erosion in political support for the *bracero* program, which supplied California growers with workers from Mexico. Yet, as the civil rights movement got under way, farm worker advocates found they could stir public concern for the plight of migrant workers of color. In addition, political rivalries within organized labor rekindled interest in unionizing the 250,000 workers employed in California's $3.5 billion agricultural industry. Once again, the AFL (by then merged with the CIO) launched an organizing drive. Two years later, the International Brotherhood of Teamsters—at the time the largest union in the United States, already representing 50,000 California cannery, packinghouse, and food-processing workers—launched its own effort. In 1962, the FWA, a small, independent, and uncertainly funded ethnic community association, entered the fray. So when the *bracero* program finally came to an end in 1965, each group was poised for a new round of organizing in the fields.

Leaders of Filipino grape workers persuaded the AFL-CIO's farm worker organizing committee to authorize a strike by 800 workers to raise their wages to $1.40 an hour. It was a strike much like those of the past. But one week later, the NFWA led 2,000 Mexican workers out of the fields to join the strike, and the game began to change. The NFWA began turning the strike into a kind of civil rights struggle, which engaged in civil disobedience, mobilized support from churches and students, boycotted growers who recruited strike breakers, and transformed itself into La Causa, a farm workers' "movement."[4] On Easter Sunday morning of 1966, it was not the AFL but the NFWA that marched into Sacramento to celebrate a breakthrough union contract with Schenley Industries, the owner of 4,000 acres of grapes and the employer of 300 farm workers.[5]

But the struggle had only begun. When the NFWA tried to build on its success at Schenley by boycotting another major Delano grower, it found itself in a far more complex and threatening world. The powerful DiGiorgio Fruit Corporation, which had defeated three earlier organizing attempts in the 1930s and 1940s, launched a major counterattack in concert with the Teamsters union. Nevertheless, within a year, the NFWA regained the initiative, winning the first union representation election in the history of California agriculture. It reorganized as the United Farm Workers Organizing Committee, absorbed the AFL-CIO group into itself, and drove the Teamsters from the fields. These successes cleared the way for an international grape boycott, which brought the entire table grape industry under union contract in July 1970.

Ups and downs continued after that, including another seven-year battle with the Teamsters. But by 1977 the United Farm Workers—the UFW, as the union was now called—had successfully negotiated more than 100 union contracts, recruited a dues-paying membership of more than 50,000, and secured enactment of the California Agricultural Labor Relations Act, the only legislative guarantee of farm workers' collective bargaining rights in the continental United States. The UFW also played a major role in the emergence of a Chicano movement in the southwestern United States, recruited and trained hundreds of community activists, and became a significant player in California politics. And although the UFW would suffer decline during the 1980s and 1990s, it had already made a far greater difference in the lives of farm workers than any earlier organizing effort had.

Why did the UFW succeed at such a daunting task—a task at which other far more powerful organizations had repeatedly failed? To some, the answer seems obvious: the favorable political environment of the 1960s weakened the growers and gave organizers access to new resources. A national liberal coalition had formed to end the *bracero* program, while the civil rights movement effectively mobilized urban support for claims based on racial justice.[6] But that explanation doesn't answer the question of why it was the UFW, and not the AFL-CIO or the Teamsters, each with far more resources, which translated these opportunities into success.

Some observers point to the distinctive framing of the UFW "message." Farm workers, they say, responded to a call rooted in their religious, ethnic, and political culture more readily than to a "straight trade union" approach. And the general public responded more positively to the portrayal of the grape strike as an extension of the civil rights movement than as a routine conflict over wages, hours, and working conditions. While true, this observation too offers no insight into why it was only the UFW that articulated its message in this way.[7]

Students of strategy point to the UFW's innovative redefinition of the arena of conflict, which linked farm workers to supporters through consumer boycotts.[8] But why did the UFW alone employ this strategy? The AFL-CIO and the Teamsters could have done the same. They were well established in urban areas where agricultural produce was sold, and their members served as key links in the distribution chain. Moreover, although the Taft-Hartley Act banned secondary boycotts by these unions, no legal constraint kept them from organizing *consumer* boycotts as the UFW did.

Most popular accounts attribute the UFW's success to the charismatic leadership of Cesar Chavez.[9] It is true that, in times of crisis, particularly talented leaders may become symbols of hope, sources of inspiration for their constituents. But this is not the same thing as achieving successful outcomes.[10] And although the effects attributed to charismatic leaders—attracting followers, enhancing their sense of self-esteem, and inspiring them to exert extra effort—can be invaluable organizational resources, they are not the same as outcomes either.[11] As scholars of religion have found, many groups have charismatic leaders, but few achieve stability, much less become successful social movement organizations.[12]

So why *did* the UFW succeed? In this book, I will argue that the UFW succeeded, while the rival AFL-CIO and Teamsters failed, because the UFW's leadership devised more effective strategy, in fact a stream of effective strategy. The UFW was able to do this because the motivation of its leaders was greater than that of their rivals; they had better access to salient knowledge; and their deliberations became venues for learning. These are the three elements of what I call *strategic capacity*—the ability to devise good strategy. While I do not claim that strategic capacity guarantees success, I do argue that it makes success more probable. The greater an organization's strategic capacity, the more informed, creative, and responsive its strategic choices can be and the better able it is to take advantage of moments of unique opportunity to reconfigure itself for effective action.[13] An organization's strategic capacity, I argue further, is a function of who its leaders are—their identities, networks, and tactical experiences—and how they structure their interactions with each other and their environment with respect to resource flows, accountability, and deliberation.

UNDERSTANDING STRATEGY

Strategy is how we turn what we have into what we need to get what we want. Strategy is intentional—a pathway that we shape by making a series of choices about how to use resources in the present to achieve goals in the future. Strategy, thus, requires the courage to venture into the unknown, risk failure, say no to current demands, and commit to a course of action that we can only hypothesize will yield the desired outcome.

Why do we have to strategize? In our world of competition and cooperation, achieving our goals usually requires power.[14] To act on our interests successfully, we must mobilize and deploy our own political, economic, or cultural resources to influence the interests of others who hold the resources we need. In 1955, for example, in Montgomery, Alabama, the site of the bus boycott that launched the modern civil rights movement, black community members held few resources. But everyone who rode the bus to work, most of whom were black, had the resource of bus fare. As long as each person used this resource individually, it gave its holder a ride on the bus, but no power. By mobilizing this resource collectively—and withholding it—community leaders found that they could make the bus company dependent on the community, thus transforming its resources into the power to require the company to desegregate its buses.

Three critical elements of strategy are targeting, tactics, and timing. *Targeting* requires a focused choice to commit resources to specific outcomes that have been judged likely to move one closer to one's goal. By focusing on desegregating the buses, leaders avoided spreading their resources too thinly and chose a target that could engage the resources of the entire community. One chooses *tactics* that can make the most of one's own resources and, at the same time, limit the value of the opponent's resources. As recounted by Herodotus, for example, when the Athenians drew the Persians into the narrows of Salamis, they could take advantage of their greater seamanship and limit the value of the Persian advantages of numbers of men and vessels.[15] *Timing* matters because some moments, often fleeting, promise greater opportunity than others.[16] Opportunities occur when environmental change increases the value of one's resources, the way an impending election increases the value of a swing voter's vote. Opportunities arise not because we acquire more resources, but because resources that we already have acquire more value. A full granary acquires greater value in a famine, for example, thus creating opportunity for its owner. Opportunities often occur at moments of unusual structural fluidity, such as the beginning of a project or at times of "role transition" in the lives of individuals or communities.[17] At these moments—which combine uncertainty with significance—we have a great deal of choice, and our choices have a great deal of consequence. A breakthrough event, such as the Schenley contract, creates just such an opportunity. Although it appears to be an end point, a simple victory, its occurrence may so alter the environment that prior expectations are thrown up for grabs, creating an opportunity to reconfigure the whole struggle. Opportunities thus are critical—but in themselves do not create outcomes. One strategizes to turn opportunities into outcomes. So timing, recognizing opportunity and acting on it quickly, is often at the heart of good strategy.

Strategy is a verb—something you do, not something you have. An ongoing interactive process of experimentation, learning, and adaptation, we strategize as we act. Because the unknown is almost by definition such a big factor in social movements, we often can't get the information we need to make good strategic choices until we begin to act. As community organizer Saul Alinsky put it, most often the "action is in the reaction."[18] Any single tactic thus has limited influence. So, in discussing effective strategy, I refer not to a single tactic, but to a whole series of tactics through which strategists may turn short-term opportunity into long-term gain. And long-term gain is most securely won when one not only acquires more resources (higher wages, for instance), but also generates new institutional rules that govern future conflicts in ways that privilege one's interests.[19] Effective labor strategy, for example, can turn short-term labor market advantages into long-term gains if they are institutionalized as formal organizations, collective bargaining agreements, and/or legislation.

STRATEGIC CAPACITY

Although strategy is the work of leaders, it is neither random nor a mere reflection of the environment. Leaders do make strategic choices, but these choices are situated within a biographical and organizational context.[20] The biographical context includes who the members of a leadership team are, whom they know, and what they know—their identities, social networks, and tactical repertoires. The organizational context includes the organization's deliberative process, the sources of its resources, and its accountability structure. Furthermore, although we tend to think of leadership as individual, strategy is the output of a leadership team far more often than organizational myths acknowledge.[21] The individual leading the team plays a uniquely important role, especially in forming, coaching, and sustaining the team.[22] But strategy—like innovation—is often a result of interactions among the individuals authorized to strategize on behalf of the organization.[23] Indeed, in complex, changing environments, devising strategy requires team members to synthesize skills and information beyond the ken of any one individual, like a good jazz ensemble.[24] And good strategy, like good jazz, is an ongoing creative process of learning to achieve a desired outcome by interacting with others to adapt to constantly changing circumstances.

So why should one strategic team outperform another, especially when the latter enjoys an advantage in resources? Because strategists, especially social movement strategists, operate in highly uncertain conditions, I answer this question by focusing on factors shown by social psychologists to foster creativity: motivation, salient knowledge, and learning—or heuristic—practices.[25] A comment from a friend reminded me, however, that my question had been addressed long before the beginning of modern social science. When I mentioned that California farm workers were not the only unlikely group that had won a major victory against great odds, that social movement history offered many such examples, my friend responded, "Oh, sure, just like David and Goliath." So, I wondered, what did the Bible actually say about how David, a mere shepherd boy, could defeat such a powerful warrior? The account is remarkable:

> And there went out a champion out of the camp of the Philistines, named Goliath...whose height was six cubits and a span. And he had a helmet of brass upon his head, and he was armed with a coat of mail...and he had greaves of brass upon his legs...and the staff of his spear was like a weaver's beam; and his spear's head weights six hundred shekels of iron....And he stood and cried to the armies of Israel..."Choose you a man for you....If he be able to fight with me, and to kill me, then will we be your servants; but if I prevail against him, and kill him, then shall ye be our servants....Give me a man that we may fight together." When Saul and all Israel heard those words of the Philistine, they were dismayed and greatly afraid.
>
> And David said unto Saul,...[I] will go and fight with this Philistine. And Saul said to David, Thou art not able to go against this Philistine to fight with him: for thou art but a youth, and he a man of war from his youth....David said...The Lord that delivered me out of the lion, and out of the paw of the bear, he will deliver me out of the hand of this Philistine. And Saul said unto David, Go, and the Lord be with thee.
>
> And Saul armed David with his armour, and he put an helmet of brass upon his head; also he armed him with a coat of mail. And David girded his sword upon his armour, and he assayed to go....[But then] David said unto Saul, I cannot go with these; for I have not proved them. And David put them off him. And he took his staff in his hand, and chose him five smooth stones out of the brook, and put them in a

shepherd's bag which he had...; and his sling was in his hand, and he drew near unto the Philistine....

And [when] the Philistine looked about and saw David, he disdained him: for he was but a youth, and ruddy, and of a fair countenance....And then said David to the Philistine, Thou comest to me with a sword, and with a spear, and with a shield; but I come to thee in the name of the Lord of hosts....and David put his hand in his bag, and took thence a stone, and slang it, and smote the Philistine in his forehead...and he fell upon his face to the earth. (Samuel 17:4–49, King James Bible)

Plainly, David is courageous. But it takes more than courage to defeat Goliath. David wins the battle because he thinks about it differently. At first, he accepts the shield, sword, and helmet that conventional wisdom deems necessary. He then realizes, however, that he cannot use these weapons effectively against a master of them. Instead, he conceives a plan of battle—a strategy—based on the five stones he notices in a creek bed, his skill with a slingshot, and the giant's underestimation of him.

Why is he, unlike everyone else on the battlefield, so strategically resourceful? First of all, because he is more *motivated*. Angered that no one will respond to Goliath's insults to the "ranks of the living God," he feels "called" to act and commits to the outcome before he knows how he will achieve it. Unlike the frightened soldiers, his commitment to act does not depend on his knowledge of a feasible strategy. Rather he devises a feasible strategy based on his commitment to act. His decision to fight moves him to figure out how he can do so successfully.

Researchers have found much the same thing: motivation enhances creativity by inspiring concentration, enthusiasm, risk taking, persistence, and learning. We think more critically when intensely interested in a problem, dissatisfied with the status quo, or experiencing a breach in our expectations.[26] And when we have small successes, they can enhance our creativity, in part because they generate greater motivation.[27]

The research also shows that the intrinsic rewards associated with doing work one loves to do, work one finds inherently meaningful, are far more motivating than extrinsic rewards.[28] For social movement leaders, whose work is deeply rooted in what moral philosopher Charles Taylor calls their "moral sources,"[29] their work is not a job but a "vocation" or a "calling."[30] As such, its rewards are intrinsic and highly motivating. Motivational differences can account in no small part for differences in resourcefulness among leadership teams. As I will show in this book, a key difference between the UFW's leaders and those of the Teamsters and the AFL-CIO was in the depth of each team's collective commitment to the enterprise.

In the story of David and Goliath, a second key to the shepherd boy's strategic resourcefulness is his access to salient knowledge, both of both skills and information. When David notices the five smooth stones, he recognizes them as something he knows how to use—and use well—and his competence frees him to consider novel applications of this skill.

Similarly, scholars find that creativity in a craft is linked to mastery of its tools[31]—that is, to the craftsperson's relevant knowledge and skill. Comparable organizational elements are the leadership team members' tactical skills and their knowledge of domains within which the organization acts. In the volatile circumstances of a social movement, in which the environment changes as a result of one's strategic initiatives, quick access to both kinds of knowledge can be critical.[32] In this light, the links of UFW leaders to the worlds of farm workers, churches, students, unions, and others gave them far more—and far quicker—access to salient knowledge than their rivals, who were largely limited to their own union world.

A third element of creativity is learning how to solve novel problems by reflecting on the results of one's own experience—what researchers call a "heuristic process." David's salient knowledge, his skill with sling and stones, proves useful because he can reimagine the battlefield. But he comes to this solution only after he has tried the conventional wisdom of the sword and shield and found that he cannot use them. An outsider to battle, he sees resources others do not see and opportunities they do not grasp. In contrast, Goliath, military insider that he is, fails to recognize that a novel problem has even presented itself. He can't imagine that a shepherd boy could be a threat.

Creativity scholars make much of just such a difference. Key to solving a novel problem is recognizing that the problem *is* a new one, at least to us, and thus requires a new solution. Creative thinkers find ways to turn the problem around and reconsider it from different angles—to "recontextualize" it.[33] They use their capacity for analogy to conceive novel interpretations and new pathways, often employing a kind of bricolage to combine familiar elements in new ways.[34]

Furthermore, encounters with diverse perspectives—whether within one's own life experience (David's perspective as a shepherd among soldiers) or within the combined experience of team members (the UFW team's capacity to see things through the eyes of farm workers, religious leaders, political activists, and so on)—facilitate innovative thinking.[35] Such encounters contribute a "mindfulness" that multiple solutions are possible.[36] The variety of solutions proffered in such circumstances can have its own value: the more ideas a creative individual or team generates, the greater the chance there will be good ones among them.[37]

The effective strategy of the UFW leadership team can be traced to its realization, largely unshared by its rivals, that it had to come up with a new way to organize farm workers. At the same time, the diverse but highly relevant backgrounds of team members facilitated recontextualization, bricolage, and an unusually unconstrained approach to learning—in part, because they were highly accustomed to learning from experience.

In sum, I argue that the likelihood that a leadership team will devise effective strategy depends on the depth of its motivation, the breadth of its salient knowledge, and the robustness of its reflective practice—on the extent, that is, of its strategic capacity. Differences in strategic capacity can explain not just why one tactic is more effective than another, but why one organization is more likely than another to develop a whole stream of effective tactics.[38]

SOURCES OF STRATEGIC CAPACITY

A leadership team's strategic capacity derives from two sources: biographical and organizational. As shown in table 1.1, the biographical sources lie in the identities, social networks, and tactical repertoires of team members. The organizational sources are deliberative processes, resource flows, and accountability mechanisms.[39]

Biographical Sources

The motivation, knowledge, and learning practices of a leadership team grow in part out of the combined *identities* of its individual members. By identity, I mean the way each person has learned to reflect on the past, attend to the present, and anticipate the future—his or her "story."[40] Demographic categories, such as ethnicity, gender, religion, occupation, age, marital status, etc., are useful indicators of the life experiences that shape a team member's way of thinking. In turn, members' ways of thinking influence each aspect of the team's strategic capacity. For example, the more team members see themselves as "called" to their

TABLE 1.1. Sources of Strategic Capacity

Sources of Strategic Capacity	Elements of Strategic Capacity		
	Motivation	Salient Information	Learning Practices
Identities			
Insiders and Outsiders Personal, Vocational Commitment	Intrinsic Rewards Personal, Vocational Commitment	Diverse Local Knowledge	Broad Contextualization
Social Networks			
Strong and Weak Ties	Personal Commitment Reputation	Diverse Local Knowledge Feedback	Broad Contextualization
Tactical Repertoires			
Diverse Repertoires	Competence Feedback	Diverse Local Knowledge	Sources of Bricolage or Analogy
Organizational Deliberation			
Regular, Open, and Authoritative	Commitment Autonomy	Diverse Local Knowledge	Heterogeneous Perspectives Periodic Assessment

(Continued)

TABLE 1.1 (Continued)

Sources of Strategic Capacity	Elements of Strategic Capacity		
	Motivation	Salient Information	Learning Practices
Resource Flows			
Multiple Constituencies	Autonomy		
Task Generated	Feedback	Feedback	Heterogeneous Alternatives
Reliance on People	Commitment		
Accountability			
Constituency Based	Commitment		
Elective or Entrepreneurial	Intrinsic Rewards Feedback	Diverse Local Knowledge Feedback	

Note: This chart illustrates the leadership and organizational sources (left column) of strategic capacity (right three columns). The influence is meant to be simultaneous not sequential.

joint project, the greater their collective commitment—and therefore the greater the team's motivation—will be. The more diverse the team members' life experiences, the greater the range of relevant knowledge from which the team can draw. And the greater the diversity of identities, the more innovative the team's approach to problem solving can be. In particular, teams composed of individuals who are insiders to some constituencies and outsiders to other constituencies can approach their undertakings with both an insider's motivation and deep knowledge of local circumstances and an outsider's ability to recontextualize those circumstances within broader frames of reference.[41]

The leaders' *social networks* can similarly feed the team's strategic capacity. Strong ties to people whose lives one affects and whose regard one wishes to earn can be powerfully motivating.[42] And the more diverse the relevant social networks with which members of the leadership team interact, the broader the range of useful information and feedback to which the team has access. This too increases the team's salient knowledge and enhances its approach to problem solving.[43]

The same benefits accrue when team members have access to a diversity of *tactical repertoires*.[44] When different team members know how to get things done in different settings and by different methods, they add to the whole team's skills, its flexibility, and its capacity for bricolage. One result, as community organizer Saul Alinsky saw many years ago, is a team that can transport tactics familiar to its own constituency into other realms—a church-style vigil into a courtroom, for instance. Such a team enjoys an advantage over its opposition. At the same time, when leaders use tactics familiar to their constituency, they are likely to receive affirming feedback, which enhances their motivation. In all of these ways, a leadership team's strategic capacity grows out of who its members are.

Organizational Sources

Organizational sources of strategic capacity are perhaps less obvious, but they exist in the structures of legitimacy, power, and deliberation established by founders. These structures shape leaders' interactions with each other and with their constituents, supporters, opponents, and the public.[45] Whatever the founders' intentions, once established, these structures have a profound influence on subsequent behavior.[46]

In terms of strategic capacity, leadership teams that conduct regular, open, and authoritative *deliberations* to devise strategy benefit synergistically from team members' knowledge and motivation in ways that organizations in which a "lone ranger" decides strategy cannot. The participation of a variety of team members linked to a diversity of constituencies contributes feedback that enables a team to evaluate changing circumstances swiftly, enhancing its facility in recognizing and solving novel problems.[47] Furthermore, team motivation is enhanced when members can contribute to making strategic choices upon which they then act.[48]

Sustaining a creative deliberative process, however, is challenging and requires leadership with a high tolerance for ambiguity.[49] We know that deliberation that is open to "deviant"—that is, contrary—perspectives enhances learning, innovation, and the performance of cognitive tasks in general.[50] But because minorities tend to conform to majorities, and persons with less authority tend to conform to those with more authority, a group's tendency over time is to lose its diversity. Particular organizational practices are thus required to preserve diverse perspectives. For brainstorming to give way to decision making, deliberative practices that encourage divergent thinking must also allow for convergent thinking. Conflict resolution by negotiation accompanied by voting is thus preferable to decision making by either fiat or consensus, because negotiation and voting make collective action possible while preserving the differences that are so useful in deliberation.[51] Moreover, if a leadership team strategizes and acts at the same time, as is the case in a rapidly unfolding social movement, managing these two deliberative modalities—divergent and convergent—poses a special challenge.[52]

A second important structural influence on strategic capacity derives from the kind of *resources* on which the organization relies.[53] For example, organizations that depend on constituency-based, task-generated resources (e.g., members' dues) must devise strategies to which their constituents respond. By contrast, organizations that rely on outside resources (e.g., grants) can be less responsive to the constituencies that are critical to their strategic success. It is often the case, for example, that reliance on outside resources can discourage learning—in fact, as long as the bills keep getting paid, leaders of such organizations can keep doing the same things wrong.[54] An organization generates the most strategic capacity, however, by drawing resources from multiple salient constituencies. This arrangement allows leaders the most room to maneuver while at the same time affording them the benefits of feedback from a diversity of constituencies.[55]

Finally, *accountability structures* can affect strategic capacity. Self-selected leadership teams and those elected by their constituencies are likely to be more motivated, enjoy greater access to salient information, and possess greater political skills than those chosen bureaucratically.[56] Similarly, leaders chosen bureaucratically—such as those fielded by the AFL-CIO—are more likely to possess skills and motivations compatible with bureaucratic success than with strategic innovation. Bureaucratic accountability, especially to superiors only remotely connected to the constituency of interest, insulates leaders from a particularly important source of motivation and salient new ideas.[57]

CHANGE

Attending to the sources of strategic capacity suggests how an organization might cultivate it, and also how it can erode. Organizations can grow more strategic capacity if they reconfigure participation in their leadership team to reflect changes in the environment. For example, should churches become relevant to the project, organizations might add people with ties to the church world to their leadership team. Multiplying the venues for strategic deliberation as an organization grows in scale and scope can generate more strategic capacity. Continued accountability to key constituencies, as the organization continues to derive resources from them, can also grow capacity. Moreover, an organization that relies more on people than on money as a source of power—and which therefore must develop more leaders as it grows and must teach them how to strategize—will increase its strategic capacity as its leadership circle expands.[58] Finally, as strategy teams continue to work together over time, they can become more effective problem solvers as they learn more about each other, determine how they can best work together, and become more attuned to the commonalities and differences in the pattern of problems they are trying to solve.[59]

On the other hand, as I will show in the epilogue, organizational changes that increase homogeneity, reduce accountability to constituents, suppress deliberative dissent, and disrupt cycles of learning can diminish strategic capacity, even as an organization's resources grow. But because organizations tend to institutionalize resources upon which they rely for power, their loss of resourcefulness may only become apparent when faced with new challenges. This helps to explain not only why David can sometimes win but also why Goliath can sometimes lose.

When faced with the crisis created by a grape strike called at the initiative of the rival AFL-CIO, the NFWA's leaders transformed their association into a social movement. This deepened their own motivation and that of farm workers and supporters, expanded their access to a diversity of relevant information, and expanded opportunities for them to learn from experience. Leaders of the AFL-CIO's farm worker organizing committee, on the other hand, proved unable to change and, as a result, their organization ended up absorbed by the UFW. For their part, the Teamsters were well financed, well situated with respect to the industry, and persistent. They eventually tried to copy the UFW strategy, but never understood it and could not replicate the underlying strategic capacity that produced this strategy, adapted it, and sustained its effectiveness.

METHODOLOGY

To explain why, of the three organizations trying to organize farm workers at the same time, the one with the least resources turned its effort into a historic success, I compared a sequence of concurrent choices made by the UFW, the AFL-CIO, and the Teamsters at the same critical junctures between 1959 and 1967. This research design allowed me to control for the environment while comparing outcomes, the strategies that produced those outcomes, and the contributions of leadership and organization to the development of those strategies. Moreover, by observing the organizations over time, I learned about the mechanisms that generate strategy and not just the effect of specific strategic choices on specific outcomes.

I did not test the influence of any single variable or set of variables on good strategy. Instead, I offer a grounded, theoretically informed, analytic framework to explain observed differences in outcomes, a framework that can be tested in other settings. As shown in figure 1.1, the result is the theory presented here: strategic capacity, strategy, and outcomes are all links in a probabilistic causal chain. It is my argument that over the long haul, greater strategic capacity is likely to yield better strategy, and better strategy is likely to yield better outcomes.[60] While more traditional studies of how the environment influences actors are important, studying how actors influence the environment helps us to understand not only how the world works, but how to change it.

In the course of this book, I will name many individuals who played various roles in a rich variety of ways. I ask readers' indulgence because one of the key points I hope to make is that particular people, their life stories, their relationships, and the choices they make in interactions with their social context make a big difference. I also will provide

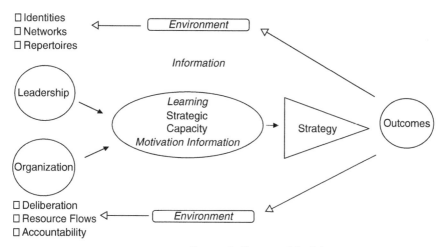

FIGURE 1.1. Strategic Process Model

readers with the details I believe are required to offer a finely tuned feel for the texture of contingency in the emergence of particular outcomes; that is, what turned out one way could have surely turned out otherwise. The telling of the layered stories of people, timing, choices, and events is an effort to portray the intricacies of a social movement as it unfolded with its many moving parts that created new opportunities, challenges, and outcomes with which purposeful actors interacted.

I will conclude this book with a brief account of more recent events. Their lesson is one that neither analysts nor organizers of social movements can afford to ignore. Understanding the sources of strategic capacity can help to explain why the powerful do not always stay powerful—and thus why David sometimes wins. But remaining David can be even more challenging than becoming David in the first place.

MAP 1.1. California Agricultural Valleys, Towns, and Cities; Irrigated Acreage; and Grapes. *Source:* Ravon Maps, Medford, Oregon

TWO

Beginnings

Immigrants, Radicals, and the AFL (1900–1959)

At the edge of your cities you'll see us and then
We come with the dust and go with the wind.

—*Woody Guthrie, "Pastures of Plenty," 1941*

THE STRIKES AND boycotts of the 1960s were not the first attempt to unionize California farm workers. Three waves of farm labor organizing had come and gone since 1900. In fact, farm workers tried to organize almost every time a labor shortage created an opportunity for them to make demands on their employers. At each of those moments, ethnic labor associations, radical networks, and the American Federation of Labor (AFL) were involved, but in competition rather than collaboration. And—until the 1960s—each effort failed before a union could establish itself.

The first attempt to organize farm workers was in the early 1900s, at the virtual founding of California's agricultural industry, with its large-scale enterprises dependent on large numbers of seasonal workers. Carey McWilliams memorably described these agricultural enterprises as "factories in the field." From the beginning, there was no mistaking them for family farms. The Durst ranch, for example, where the Industrial Workers of the World (IWW) tried to organize in 1913, required 1,500 farm workers just to harvest its hops. DiGiorgio Farms, organized by the National Farm Workers Association in 1966, hired a peak workforce of more than 3,000 on its 15,000 acres of grapes, tree fruit, and other crops.

Large-scale farming was a legacy of the way public lands were privatized after California became a state in 1850. Because they were exempted from the Homestead Act, which would have broken the land into family farms of no more than 160 acres, some 35 million acres—one-third of the state's total area—had been sold off in large units by 1880.[1]

At first, much of this land was used for raising cattle. But the completion of the transcontinental railroad in 1869 and an expansion of irrigation facilities, induced by drought in 1871, created new opportunities for large landowners who had access to preferred railroad rates and the capital to invest in threshing equipment. With a large migrant labor force, landowners found that raising wheat on these "bonanza" farms, as they were called at the time, could be far more lucrative than raising cattle.[2] For their workforce, they turned to some 12,000 Chinese immigrants who had been imported to build the Central Pacific Railroad and were now mostly unemployed.[3]

Because these immigrants were not "white," these racially segregated, single men were barred from most urban employment and were ineligible for U.S. citizenship.[4] Denied access to the political influence that could have improved their condition, they were willing to work at wages low enough to make large-scale wheat farming profitable. Moreover, the Chinese laborers returned to San Francisco, Stockton, and Sacramento during the off-season, relieving growers of the indirect costs of maintaining unemployed workers.[5] Growers, in other words, learned how to recruit a workforce too powerless to give them much trouble—a workforce of impoverished new immigrants, noncitizens, and people of color who would "come with the dust and go with the wind."[6]

The same labor market strategy that made wheat farming profitable soon opened the door to the even more profitable transformation of California agriculture into a major producer of fresh fruits and vegetables. By 1900, wheat farming had given way to the fruit and vegetable growing for which the state's climate, topography, and soil were uniquely suited.[7] Falling wheat prices, reduced yields, and a long drought in the 1890s had again stimulated investment in irrigation, which created new possibilities for intensive farming. When refrigerated railcars and new food-processing technologies gave California access to East Coast markets, growers found ways to coordinate which crop to grow, in which region, during which growing season, and for which market, creating the most complex farming regime in the country. They even commercialized production on very small plots of land, while at the same time integrating them into large enterprises. Since shipping to distant markets required careful packing, packinghouses began to appear alongside the farms. Since point-of-production food-processing technologies could reduce shipping costs, mills, wineries, and canneries began to dot the rural landscape as well.[8] Between 1890 and 1920, irrigated farmland quadrupled from 1 million to 4.2 million acres as intensive farming came to account for two-thirds of California's crop value.[9] All of it depended on a large, cheap, seasonal labor force.

Continued access to such a workforce, however, turned out to be a matter of politics. Even as the labor demand of California's specialty agriculture was growing rapidly, anti-immigrant groups won legislation restricting the supply. A populist coalition of small farmers and urban workers secured legislation to expel the Chinese in 1882, 1892, and 1902.[10] When sugar beet growers, who had employed Japanese workers on their Hawaiian sugar cane plantations, responded by initiating the import of some 40,000 Japanese laborers between 1890 and 1909, similar racial politics slowed Japanese immigration.[11]

The growers were persistent. They recruited several thousand Sikhs from the Punjab, turned to Mexico, and hired Southern European men who had settled in farm communities but lacked the capital to become growers.[12] Many of the wives and daughters of these European men worked in the packing sheds and processing plants. Finally, the growers recruited from the army of "bindle stiffs"—white, single men searching for work and driven west by downturns in the business cycle.[13] Despite these efforts, the rapid growth of intensive farming meant that local labor shortages persisted, and three different sets of organizers mobilized to take advantage of them.

THE FIRST WAVE OF FARM WORKER ORGANIZING: THE JAPANESE, THE IWW, AND THE AFL (1900–1919)

The most effective early farm worker organizers were the leaders of the Japanese labor associations. Japanese immigrants had introduced methods of intense cultivation to the growing of cantaloupes, tomatoes, onions, asparagus, celery, berries, and sugar beets in California. Taking advantage of the demand for their specialized skills, they used collective action aggressively. Although the Japanese, like the Chinese, were ineligible for citizenship, they could root their collective action in ethnic solidarity, the organizing experience they had acquired in Hawaii, and some modest backing from the government of Japan.[14] They organized a system in which crew bosses served not as agents of the employers but as intermediaries between workers and growers. Their strategy was to accept wages below standard, gain control of a local labor market, wait until crops reached a critical stage, and then threaten to strike unless wages were raised.[15] To a limited extent, this strategy worked. They won many seasonal contracts and boosted wages by as much as 50 percent between 1900 and 1910.[16] They might well have established a formidable base for organized labor in California agriculture, as they had in Hawaii, had they enjoyed the support of the AFL with its far greater economic and political resources. But it was not to be.

The California State Federation of Labor, an AFL affiliate, did show interest in organizing migrant farm workers—if only to keep them from "scabbing on white people," in the words of the Los Angeles Labor Council.[17] The CSFL backed strikes by Anglo raisin, prune, sugar, and citrus packinghouse workers,[18] and in 1902, it called on the national AFL to ask other state federations to organize migrants as well. Yet the CSFL organizers, mostly Anglo building tradesmen, knew little of how to organize the farm workforce. The national AFL, committed as it was to Asian exclusion, refused to establish links with the Japanese associations that were the real organized base among farm workers.

In 1903, for example, a Japanese-Mexican labor association won a signed contract with Oxnard sugar beet growers by leading 1,800 workers in a strike. Wishing to affiliate with the U.S. labor movement, they applied for an AFL charter as the Sugar Beet Laborers Union of Oxnard. The request was signed by "Y. Yamaguchi (Japanese Secretary) and J. M. Lizarraga (Mexican Secretary)." Yet AFL president Samuel Gompers replied only to Lizarraga. He would grant a charter, he said, but on the condition that "your union will under no circumstances accept membership of any Chinese or Japanese." The Mexican workers returned the charter unsigned, and their union later dissolved.[19]

Rebuffed by the AFL, Japanese workers continued their self-help unionism and ultimately achieved some degree of economic security,

FIGURE 2.1. Japanese and Filipino Sugar Beet Strikers, Oxnard, 1903. *Source:* Bill Rodgers

but as growers, not as workers. By pooling their earnings, negotiating sharecropping arrangements, and winning financial support from Japanese banks in San Francisco, they became farmers. This route, too, was a difficult one. The combination of their large numbers, economic success, and political impotence revived the old anti-Asian coalition of urban workers and smaller farmers, who secured passage of the 1913 Alien Land Law. The law barred immigrants who were ineligible for naturalized citizenship from owning land. Because they were not white, this included the Japanese. But Japanese farmers learned to circumvent the law's restrictions by placing land titles in the names of their children or American agents. The farm land that they or their agents owned grew from 83,000 acres in 1909 to 427,000 acres in 1919,[20] while the number of Japanese farm workers employed by Anglo growers declined by nearly half.

The third group of organizers responsible for this first wave of farm labor organizing was the radicals of the IWW. While the AFL's leaders saw unorganized farm workers primarily as a threat to urban labor, the IWW saw them as "likely recruits into the advance guard of a revolutionary cadre" necessary to "deliver the working class from wage slavery."[21] The IWW was founded in Chicago in 1905 with the specific intention of organizing immigrants, laborers, and migrants in whom the AFL had little interest.[22] Its most successful California local was in Fresno, the unofficial capital of the San Joaquin Valley.

But because it was committed to a strategy of raising revolutionary consciousness rather than to workplace organizing, the IWW at first focused on free speech fights with local authorities who had banned public meetings, arrested organizers, and collaborated with vigilantes. When IWW supporters from around the United States converged on San Diego in 1912 in support of one such free speech fight, and a small war erupted between vigilantes and demonstrators, IWW leaders Emma Goldman and Benjamin Reitman narrowly escaped lynching.[23]

The California State Federation of Labor, largely in response to the IWW, did try its hand at farm worker organizing again in 1908 and 1909, but the experience of the two men hired for the job was in the skilled trades, and their tactics were limited to "talking to [farm workers] when they were in town on Sunday."[24] By 1913, although the CSFL claimed 3,000 members in a united laborers union, it had no contracts to show for its efforts.[25]

That same year, when the IWW finally turned to a strategy of workplace organizing to improve wages, hours, and working conditions, it found itself in the midst of what Carey McWilliams called the "first California labor *cause celebre*."[26] In late July, when 2,800 men, women, and children had been recruited for only 1,500 jobs at the Durst hops ranch near the town of Wheatland in Yuba County, IWW organizer Richard Ford saw an opportunity. When the workers began arriving to find no housing, little work, and low wages, Ford formed a committee to protest working and living conditions, formulate demands, and submit them to Durst. The grower acceded to some demands, but refused to raise wages and threatened to have Ford arrested. The Yuba County sheriff, deputies, and district attorney arrived, fired shots, and in the ensuing battle four persons died: the district attorney, a deputy sheriff, a young English worker, and the Puerto Rican worker who had killed the district attorney and the deputy. Six companies of National Guardsmen dispatched by Governor Hiram Johnson arrived early the next morning to find the ranch deserted. A manhunt netted Ford and three others, and despite a nationwide campaign launched by the IWW, Ford and one other participant were convicted and given life sentences.[27]

Although the radicals knew how to rally a strong public response to these events, it was the policy makers who put it to use. They interpreted the miserable conditions at Wheatland as evidence of a social problem, not a labor problem, so no real improvement in farm workers' lives resulted. Governor Johnson assigned his new California

Commission on Immigration and Housing to investigate, and although it further publicized the farm workers' miseries, it proposed solving the problem with a Camp Sanitation Act, which was duly enacted but not enforced.[28] This call for better housing—backed by unenforced regulation—would become typical, a seemingly enlightened response to farm worker organizing, which turned public concern into policies which did little to alter the power inequalities that were responsible for the problem in the first place.

The IWW might have turned public concern into a useful resource for farm workers, but its California organizers were focused on trying to free the Wheatland defendants. When they resumed organizing two years later—using a multipronged strategy that IWW organizers had developed in the Midwest—it was too late. The new approach was to mobilize a network of traveling "job delegates" to offer protection against thugs on freight trains, organize job actions to raise wages, and establish local union halls where migrants could congregate.[29] In February 1917, the IWW organizers led 2,000 mostly Italian vineyard workers on strike near Fresno and won a wage increase for the season and an eight-hour day. In April, they led orange-picking crews on strike near Redlands. They opened halls in Fresno, Sacramento, San Francisco, Stockton, and Los Angeles.[30] But in April 1917, America entered World War I, and that put a stop to further farm worker organizing.

Mobilization for World War I ushered in the period of greatest growth in urban union membership in AFL history, but it had just the opposite effect in the countryside. Mobilization drew rural white workers to jobs in a thriving urban economy just as Japanese workers were moving into farm ownership. As a result, the local farm labor supply once again became constricted enough to provide farm worker organizers with an opportunity to act. But it was the growers, not the workers, who had the economic and political resources to take advantage of the labor shortage created by the national emergency, and they used the opportunity to rebuild their workforces and suppress the organizing.

Shortly after the declaration of war, California growers secured exemption from key provisions of the federal Immigration Act that had passed just two months earlier.[31] They had only to assert that American labor was unavailable, announce what they would pay, and report available housing, and they were permitted to contract as many workers as they wanted in Mexico. Furthermore, upon entering the United States, these workers were excused from an $8 head tax and the literacy test required by the new law. Between May 1917 and June 1921, 71,000 Mexicans entered the United States under wartime exemptions, most to do farm work.[32] Contracted Mexican workers faced deportation if they quit and were supposed to be returned to Mexico at the end of the year. Few, however, did return.[33] Most of those who stayed remained politically powerless. Although Mexicans could become citizens because they were legally "white," their ambiguous immigration status, their intent to return home, and the fact that they would lose the minimal protection they were getting from the Mexican consul, inhibited any rush to citizenship.[34]

Not only did the war enable the growers to reconstruct their workforce with the help of federal immigration policy, but wartime antisubversive policies also crippled farm worker organizing. In September 1917, the U.S. Justice Department conducted nationwide raids of IWW offices, often in collaboration with local vigilantes. In one horrific example, the organizer of the Fresno free speech fight was hanged by vigilantes from a railroad trellis in Butte, Montana.[35] According to one U.S. attorney, the aim was "very largely to put the IWW out of business."[36] By late 1918, 51 IWW activists in California had been arrested, held, and tried for violations of the 1917 Espionage Act. Despite the crippling impact of these arrests, IWW organizers led a citrus strike in the San Gabriel Valley. The end finally came with the 1919 "red scare," when California passed the Criminal Syndicalism Act, under which more than 500 IWW activists were arrested, prosecuted, and jailed.[37] The AFL, too, came under attack in the years of the red scare; and with the election of a post-war Republican administration in 1920 and the launching of anti-union "open shop" campaigns by business groups throughout the country, it soon lost more than a quarter of its membership. The labor movement was effectively demoralized until the 1930s.[38]

The IWW organizers were far more committed and imaginative than those of the AFL and had found ways to bring the farm workers' plight to the attention of a somewhat sympathetic public. Unlike the AFL, the IWW also welcomed collaboration with the Japanese. As one IWW organizer declared, "[A] yellow skin is to be preferred a thousand times to a yellow heart."[39] But Japanese leaders had little to gain from an alliance with revolutionary socialists, especially when their goals lay more in the direction of landownership than revolution. The AFL wanted nothing to do with either the radicals or the Japanese. In the end, each set of organizers targeted different workers, devised different strategy, and, acting separately, proved incapable of countering the growers' power.

THE GROWERS ORGANIZE: MEXICAN AND FILIPINO IMMIGRATION (1920–1930)

With the war over, California growers concentrated on stabilizing a workforce of 200,000 people, whom they needed to work their 4.7 million acres. They succeeded. The farm labor supply ran an average of 5 percent ahead of demand for the next decade.[40] In 1921, Congress established immigration quotas, but under pressure from California growers and others, it exempted Western Hemisphere nations from those quotas.[41] The number of persons born in Mexico who lived in California thus grew from 33,694 in 1910 to 86,610 in 1920 to 199,994 in 1930.[42] Of the 128,092 Mexicans employed in any California occupation in 1930, 41,191 worked as farm workers. Mexicans made up about 25 percent of the entire California farm labor force[43] and 70–80 percent of the seasonal workforce, dominating crops such as cotton, sugar beets, and grapes.[44]

Many Mexicans immigrated in extended families that worked together, a mode of migration the automobile made possible. Some families, like that of future United Farm Workers leader Gilbert Padilla, moved into the cotton camps on the west side of the San Joaquin Valley. Others, like that of Cesar Chavez's wife, Helen Fabella, settled in towns on the east side, where grapes and tree fruit were grown. Segregated *barrios* emerged in Fresno, Bakersfield, Visalia, Delano, and other towns. Families that did not settle worked for six months on cotton ranches in the San Joaquin Valley and returned for the rest of the year to the new Mexican communities growing up around Los Angeles.[45] And in more stable communities, such as Brawley, they formed mutual benefit associations, such as the Benito Juarez Society, which charged members $2 per month, entitling them to emergency food, $7 per week of medical assistance when needed, funeral benefits, and even some legal aid.[46]

Like the Japanese before them, Mexican workers formed crews as their basic unit of production and social life, especially within the camps.[47] But unlike the Japanese, the Mexican crews were led by labor contractors: Mexican and Mexican-American middlemen employed by growers to recruit, hire, and supervise workers. The Japanese crew leader made his living by forming a skilled, disciplined work crew on whose behalf he could negotiate good pay rates. By contrast, the new labor contractors were brokers. Paid by the unit of work—a field harvested or bushel picked—they could increase their own earnings by holding farm workers' hourly wages down. The fact that the contractors competed with each other to get jobs from the shippers and processors further depressed wages. Organizing was inhibited by the fact that workers usually had no idea for whom they were actually working as they moved from job to job. The growers, on the other hand, benefited from the arrangement, which allowed them to deal with a few contractors to set wages and working conditions for all.[48]

To hedge their bets on the outcome of the immigration debates, growers also began to recruit Filipino workers from Hawaii and the Philippines, both of which were U.S. territories.[49] Since Filipinos were thus American nationals, they were not subject to the immigration restrictions that applied to other Asians. From 1923 to 1929, 31,092 Filipinos were admitted to the United States, of whom 16,100 became farm workers. The rest, such as future AFL organizer Larry Itliong, entered service work or the canneries.[50] Of this total, 84 percent were men under 30. Most were unmarried when they arrived, and many remained so.[51] When the United States declared independence for the Philippines in 1934, these men found that they could no longer send for countrywomen to marry. To make matters worse, a number of Filipinos were prosecuted under the 1880 California antimiscegenation law barring marriage between white women and "Negroes, mulattos, or Mongolians." A bachelor culture developed within the Filipino community, and the growers' camps often became their permanent homes.[52]

Filipino workers organized crews like those of the Japanese, in which crew bosses acted as representatives.[53] They negotiated wages on behalf of their workers, ran the camps, and provided meals and transportation. The Filipinos also found an agricultural niche similar to that of the Japanese, working specialized crops that required skill and consistency, such as asparagus, lettuce, celery, and table grapes.[54]

Eventually, the growers integrated this system of labor contractors and crew bosses into an overarching network of centralized labor bureaus. By setting wages for almost every major crop and growing area in the state, the bureaus cut labor costs by 10–30 percent over the decade.[55] At the same time, the growers were organizing their firms, cooperatives, and associations horizontally by product—crop, region, and industry—and vertically by process: growing, packing, shipping, processing, and marketing.[56] By 1930, the Sunk-ist cooperative, for example, picked, packed, and marketed 75 percent of the fresh citrus in California and Arizona, owned refrigerator cars, offered discount supplies, owned a lumber mill, managed pest control, coordinated irrigation, and loaned money.[57] In addition, growers organized dozens of umbrella groups, often with state sponsorship[58]—from crop-by-crop marketing associations to the powerful California Farm Bureau Federation initiated by the University of California's Agricultural Extension Service.[59] Ethnic, commercial, and political ties linked growers to the urban business establishment, with coordination formally vested in the Agriculture Committee of the California Chamber of Commerce.

To close the loop, California growers institutionalized their grip on state politics through a reapportionment plan adopted by the state's voters in 1926. The plan, promoted by a coalition of northern California and rural legislators in response to the rapid growth of Los Angeles, provided that no county could be represented by more than one state senator and no more than three counties could be combined into a single senate district. This meant that 6 percent of the voters would elect a majority of 40 senators, while Los Angeles County, with 39 percent of the electorate, would elect one.[60]

By 1930, then, California growers were, to cite Carey McWilliams again, the "most highly organized" farmers in the United States.[61] They had again constructed a workforce composed largely of new immigrants, with Mexicans replacing the white migrants of the prewar years and Filipinos replacing the Japanese. The better-paying packing shed and cannery jobs went to white workers, many of whom were female members of families in which men worked as "hired hands" in the local community.[62] From the growers' point of view, the arrangement was ideal. But with the onset of the Depression, it fractured.

THE SECOND WAVE OF FARM WORKER ORGANIZING: CAIWU, UCAIWA, AND UCAPAWA (1933–1942)

The Depression created turmoil in the California farm labor market. In response to massive unemployment, federal, state, and even local governments started repatriating Mexican workers.[63] As a result, the number of farm workers whom California growers hired fell from

206,000 in 1929 to just 163,000 in 1932—even as wages fell to 10 cents per hour. As shown in figure 2.2, there were fewer hired workers per acre of irrigated land than at any time since 1910. Meanwhile, union organizing revived across the country, spurred by the enactment of President Franklin D. Roosevelt's National Industrial Recovery Act in June 1933. Some union leaders, most notably John L. Lewis of the United Mine Workers, interpreted passage of this law as public affirmation of the right to form unions, and they committed major resources to organizing. A newly defiant spirit of resistance to wage cuts among working people matched their efforts. On California's farms, the opportunity created by a tight labor market once again presented itself; once again, radical organizers, leaders of ethnic labor associations, and the official American labor movement—both the AFL and the CIO (the newly formed Congress of Industrial Organizations)—took advantage of this opportunity to try to organize California farm workers.

This time, radicals came from the Communist Party's Trade Union Unity League (TUUL), who learned early on to focus on workplace organizing. Like those of the prewar IWW, many of these organizers were outsiders, deeply committed to a mission to which they had been called.[64] Unlike the IWW organizers, though, they moved quickly to recruit leadership from among farm worker insiders. The Communists' Cannery, Agricultural, and Industrial Workers Union (CAIWU) was the first white-led farm union to incorporate Mexican and Filipino

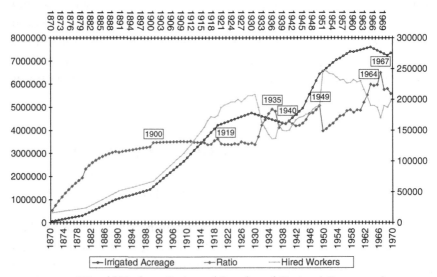

FIGURE 2.2. Hired Workers, Irrigated Land, and Ratios (1870–1970)

leadership. This gave it both a better understanding of the workforce than previous white unions and the opportunity to mobilize around ethnic solidarity.

CAIWU organizers also enjoyed access, as the earlier radicals had, to a national network of legal, political, and financial support—a network that CAIWU used to harness unprecedented political resources.[65] The NIRA was ambiguous about its coverage of agricultural workers, and CAIWU was able to use that ambiguity—along with the large scale of its strikes—to win greater state and federal intervention in support of its organizing than the law actually required. The CAIWU got the U.S. Department of Labor, the National Labor Board, and the California Labor Commission to push growers to negotiate.[66] Mexican workers found they could also bring Mexican consuls and vice consuls into the picture.

As a result, at a time of general labor resurgence, the CAIWU led the most effective farm worker organizing in the country. Of the 87,364 farm workers who took part in 61 strikes in 17 states in 1933 and 1934, those in California accounted for 49 of the strikes and 67,887 of the workers.[67] Of the 48,000 California farm workers who took part in strikes in 1933, 40,000 participated in strikes organized by the CAIWU.[68]

The high point of the CAIWU's strike wave was the Pixley cotton strike from October 4 to October 26, 1933. Mobilized across a 100-mile-long front from Bakersfield to Fresno, between 12,000 and 18,000 workers from 200 ranches walked off the job at the height of the cotton-picking season. The CAIWU had organized a network of delegates from each of the crews, and together they demanded a pay raise to $1 per hundredweight of cotton picked. When the growers would not improve upon their offer of 60 cents, the strike began. Immediately, the growers evicted strikers from labor camps and organized "protective associations," which launched violent assaults on union meetings and picket lines. Just one week into the strike, on Tuesday, October 10, vigilantes attacked striker meetings in Pixley and in nearby Arvin. They fired into the crowd and killed three strikers: Delfino Davila, 58; Dolores Hernandez, 50; and Pedro Subia, age unknown.

In response to calls for assistance from the CAIWU's support network, George Creel, the western director of the National Recovery Administration and an aspiring candidate for the Democratic gubernatorial nomination in California, argued that the strike was a "threat to recovery." Creel urged incumbent Republican governor James Rolph to intervene. Furthermore, a director of the NRA's mediation board,

FIGURE 2.3. Mexican and "Okie" cotton strikers, Pixley, 1933. *Source:* Ralph H. Powell, permission from Bancroft Library

Rabbi Irving F. Reichert, claimed that economic aid provided to growers by the Agriculture Adjustment Act entitled the striking workers to government intervention on their behalf. Following the three deaths, Rolph responded by making federal emergency relief funds available to the strikers—the first time the state had ever provided strike aid—and by appointing a fact-finding board that consisted of the Roman Catholic archbishop of San Francisco, Edward Hanna, and two academics. Ten days after they were appointed, the mediation board recommended a compromise of 75 cents per hundredweight. When Creel threatened to deny the growers access to federal crop loans if they failed to cooperate, they accepted. Threatened with losing relief funds, the CAIWU accepted as well.

The Pixley victory, however, was not to be repeated. The cotton growers had been taken by surprise, especially by the willingness of federal officials to intervene. So when the CAIWU moved south to the Imperial Valley to organize a winter lettuce strike, growers there were ready. When some 5,000 workers walked out of the lettuce fields on January 8, 1934, the growers responded with arrests, assaults, and beatings that were so severe that the union called off the strike in four days.

The CAIWU once again turned to its national network. When an American Civil Liberties Union lawyer who went to El Centro to represent the strikers was abducted, beaten, and run out of town—and Senator Robert Wagner, chair of the NLB, dispatched a committee to investigate—it looked as if it could mobilize the same kind of government intervention as before. Within two weeks, Wagner's committee issued a report citing massive civil liberties violations and arguing that the problem was a lack of collective bargaining rights for farm workers. When Senator Wagner appointed Creel to mediate, based on his record in resolving the cotton strike, the CAIWU seemed to be on its way to a second victory.

But this time, the growers, too, had mobilized their political resources. Senator Wagner suddenly withdrew from the fray, just two days after introducing the National Labor Relations Act. The swiftness, brutality, and effectiveness of the repression were followed by the formation of the Imperial Valley Grower and Shipper Protective Association, the Imperial Valley Anti-Communist Association, and the Mexican Association of Imperial Valley, a company union that all workers had to join to work in the valley.[69]

Fighting to regain the initiative after the strikes, with the backing of the Chamber of Commerce and the Farm Bureau, the growers also formed the Associated Farmers, a vigilante organization that won the cooperation of state and local law enforcement in a decade-long campaign of union repression statewide. That campaign began on July 20, 1934, when police raided the CAIWU's Sacramento headquarters and arrested 24 organizers, charging 17 with criminal syndicalism. Eight were eventually convicted and sentenced to from one to five years. The CAIWU suspended operations. By 1936, in contrast, the Associated Farmers had established chapters in 42 counties.[70]

Nonetheless, the Depression era organizing continued. Over the next few years, independent Mexican and Filipino unions remained active. These ethnic associations were effective in settings similar to those in which the Japanese unions had prospered: when specialty work required skilled and disciplined crews and when there was a local labor shortage. They led strikes in Santa Maria (1934), Santa Ana (1935), and Venice (1936) and won seasonal contracts providing for union recognition, hiring agreements, and grievance procedures. In early 1936, inspired by former CAIWU organizers, many came together to form the multiethnic Federation of Agricultural Workers, affiliated with the AFL. Reflecting the shift in Communist Party strategy from one of "dual unionism" to one of a "popular front," CAIWU organizers encouraged leaders of the Mexican and Filipino associations with whom they were working to link up with white packinghouse and cannery workers in which the AFL had more interest. For the first time, it seemed possible that the diverse efforts of the radicals, the ethnic associations, and the traditional labor movement might be combined to the benefit of California farm workers. The new FAW led strikes throughout southern California that summer.[71]

At the same time, major changes in the national labor picture—the enactment of federal legislation and competition within the labor movement—pushed Depression era agricultural organizing in a different direction. On July 5, 1935, Congress enacted the National Labor Relations Act (NLRA), which provided industrial workers with a set of powerful new organizing tools and protections. Four months later, the president of the United Mine Workers, John L. Lewis, walked out of the AFL convention, formed the CIO, and initiated 21 years of competitive organizing between the two labor groups. Both developments were a boon for urban labor. During the first 11 years of competition between the AFL and the CIO, union membership tripled from 4,140,700 in 1936 to 14,067,100 in 1947.[72]

For California farm workers, however, these two developments had the opposite effect. A coalition of southern and western senators had succeeded in excluding "agricultural workers" from the NLRA. As it became clearer that the statutory exclusion applied to field workers, who were mostly of color—but not to the mostly white men and women working in canneries and commercial packinghouses—both the AFL and the CIO came to see their organizing interests as also excluding field workers. Moreover, the new law strengthened two powerful transport unions, the International Longshoremen's Association (ILA) and the International Brotherhood of Teamsters, which unleashed a struggle between them that further institutionalized divisions among farm workers along racial and ideological lines. Both of these unions had been built by the use of the recently legalized "secondary boycott," a refusal to perform services for a company doing business with another company where the employees are in a labor dispute.[73] This tactic allowed unions to use strength in one labor market to compensate for weakness in other labor markets. It was used by the ILA, led by Harry Bridges on the West Coast, to leverage control over the port of San Francisco, which was won in the 1934 general strike, into the unionization of ports along the entire West Coast.[74] Dave Beck, the Seattle Teamsters leader, learned from Bridges' example and used secondary boycotts to leapfrog from control over Seattle and San Francisco trucking terminals to control of over-the-road trucking throughout California, Washington, and Oregon.[75] By 1937, both unions had achieved their initial goals and turned their attention to warehouses, which were central to their secondary boycott strategy and over which they both claimed jurisdiction.[76]

These warehouses housed the products of California's largest industry: agriculture. In 1937, when the ILA launched a march inland to organize warehouses and the AFL granted jurisdiction over warehouses to the Teamsters, the two major transport unions joined in a struggle over which would organize in agriculture. The Teamsters had a toehold in northern California dairies. Furthermore, because most over-the-road trucking into San Francisco carried produce, their leapfrog campaign yielded locals in farming centers throughout rural California. The ILA, on the other hand, established a base among cotton compresses, fish canneries, and packing and processing enterprises up and down the coast.[77]

Their conflict was not only jurisdictional. The West Coast longshoremen's union was radical, close to the Communist Party, committed to social unionism, and aligned with the CIO. The Teamsters' leaders were business unionists, Republicans or conservative Democrats, and the cornerstone of AFL opposition to the CIO. These differences were evident even in the way Bridges and Beck operated within their own unions. Bridges, who was 37 in 1937, rose inside the ILA by challenging its president. Beck, 43, rose within the Teamsters in alliance with its president.[78] To Beck, a union was "a marketing agency for the sale of labor services, totally devoid of ideological goals and reformist aspirations."[79] He warned the business community that it had to choose between the "responsible, conservative AFL and the radical, violent CIO."[80]

The ILA was friendly with the radical organizers in California who wanted to see all agricultural workers in a single union. They hoped to unionize field workers by leveraging the power of workers in commercial packinghouses and canneries, who could be organized under the NLRA. The Teamsters, on the other hand, wanted to sever the more easily organized cannery and packinghouse workers from field workers, most of whom were people of color and more closely tied to the radicals.[81]

The leader of the California State Federation of Labor, Secretary-Treasurer Edward Vandeleur, became a central player in this conflict. Vandeleur, 50, was hostile to the radical politics of Bridges and his allies.[82] In early 1937, Vandeleur refused to fund the latest version of his federation's own agricultural union—a grouping of 14 AFL locals,

15 Mexican locals, 4 Filipino locals, and a Japanese labor group—because it united field and processing workers in an "unholy alliance" of Communists, immigrants, and the ILA.[83] When the group's Stockton local led a strike of several hundred cannery workers, Vandeleur, with the support of the Teamsters, went a step further. An attack on the Stockton picket line by 1,200 special "deputies" led local union leaders to threaten to call out field workers as well. The canning companies refused to negotiate, claiming that a union that included field workers could not represent cannery workers. Rather than back the local, Vandeleur exercised his authority to take it over and purge it of field workers. He settled with the employers the next day.[84]

Shortly afterward, Vandeleur won authority from AFL president William Green to field 18 organizers in a joint drive with the Teamsters to organize food-processing workers statewide. By July, this alliance had reorganized 10 locals that had been associated with the ILA, excluded field workers from them, and signed contracts on their behalf with the California Processors and Growers Association, which represented northern California cannery owners. By the following spring, when Vandeleur regrouped these locals and two others as the state Council of Agricultural and Cannery Workers, chaired by a Teamster, he claimed that they held contracts representing 50,000 workers.

In the first enactment of a strategy that remained unchanged for the next 40 years, the Teamsters won control of the canning industry by appealing not to workers so much as to anxious employers. The cannery owners watched the U.S. Supreme Court affirm the constitutionality of Roosevelt's NLRA and saw U.S. Steel voluntarily recognize the CIO. They understood that it would be harder to use traditional, brutal means to prevent organizing among cannery workers—many of them white women—than among field workers. Sooner or later, the owners expected that they would have to negotiate with a cannery union. The only question was, which one? In a choice between the radical unionists backed by the ILA and the CIO and the AFL's businesslike Teamsters, who also could threaten their shipping, there was no contest.[85] The owners signed on.

So in July 1937, giving up on the AFL, the radicals decided to join in launching the CIO's new United Cannery, Packing House, and Agricultural Workers Union (UCAPAWA). The UCAPAWA thus inherited various California field worker locals that the Teamsters did not want, along with those processing locals that the Teamsters could not reorganize. Nonetheless, like the Teamsters, the new CIO union also chose to focus on the more easily organized workers covered by the

NLRA. A month later, Bridges too left the AFL and joined the CIO. In return for an appointment as western CIO director, he formed his West Coast longshoremen's locals into a new, CIO-affiliated union, the International Longshoremen and Warehousemen's Union (ILWU)— thereby continuing the competition between himself and Beck.[86] By 1938, both the AFL and the CIO had major agricultural unions active in California. Meanwhile, abandoned by both radicals and the AFL, efforts to organize field workers passed into the hands of those with the strongest motivation to continue: the Mexicans and the Filipinos.

At that moment, an unexpected transformation of the California farm workforce gave field workers temporary access to new political and cultural resources, even as their labor market power hit its lowest ebb. The 1937 dustbowl migration and 1938 recession had inundated rural California towns with Anglo families from Texas, Oklahoma, Arkansas, and Missouri, creating a labor surplus which persisted in some areas until 1942.

Ironically, the dustbowl migration proved to be a boon to the farm worker cause when the farm workers suddenly "became white." This transformation, though it lasted only briefly, gave field workers access to political and cultural resources they never had before. Conditions that had remained hidden as long as Japanese, Mexican, Filipino, or other workers of color endured them came into public view. By 1939, the nation was listening to stories of the white migrants as told by John Steinbeck in *Grapes of Wrath*, Carey McWilliams in *Factories in the Field*, and Dorothea Lange and Paul Taylor in *American Exodus*. These graphic accounts helped to mobilize public sympathy for the plight of migrant farm workers across the country.[87]

At the state level, the fact that the dustbowl migrants were citizens who could vote contributed to a sea change in farm labor politics. In 1938, their votes helped to put a New Deal Democrat, Culbert Olson, in the California governor's chair and contributed to defeating a statewide ballot initiative intended to restrict secondary boycotts, picketing, and strikes in agriculture. An attempt to legislate collective bargaining rights for California farm workers, a "little Wagner Act," even passed the California assembly, although the growers' lock on the state senate killed it.[88] At the urging of Governor Olson and others, Wisconsin senator Robert La Follette brought his Senate Civil Liberties Committee to California in December 1939, to take testimony from over 400 witnesses over the course of 28 days of hearings. It was the first time that anyone had held California growers accountable for a decade of violent repression of farm workers' attempts to organize.

Federal response to the new public concern about farm workers, however, took a course quite similar to that of Governor Johnson's administration in 1913. Instead of enfranchising farm workers economically by extending collective bargaining rights, the Roosevelt administration focused only on their housing. Beginning in 1937, the Farm Security Administration (FSA), the federal agricultural agency most oriented toward the rural poor, established a chain of 17 model migrant camps across California. Attention to the dustbowlers, however, was the first time the federal government acted on the farm labor issue as anything other than a labor supply problem that required adjusting immigration laws or a special case that required exclusion from labor laws. Although defined as a social problem, not a labor problem, the fact that migrant workers became a national issue of any kind would be a legacy of the brief moment when farm workers became white.[89]

Meanwhile, the ethnic unions continued to organize and win seasonal contracts in specialty crops. Most successful was the Filipino Agricultural Labor Association (FALA), which won strikes in asparagus, tomatoes, and other crops in 1939 and 1940.[90] In some cases, it had support from the UCAPAWA cannery locals. The FALA's success and the possibility that it might ally with UCAPAWA were not lost on Vandeleur, who decided it was finally time to add farm workers to his Council of Agricultural and Cannery Workers. The council now claimed 64 locals in agriculture, canneries, and citrus packing and had a core membership of 21,305.[91]

When the FALA launched a major celery strike near Stockton in December 1939 in alliance with the CIO's UCAPAWA, Vandeleur enlisted the Teamsters' support for a secondary boycott backing the FALA. In return, he required the FALA to sever its relationship with UCAPAWA by threatening to boycott growers who signed their shed workers into the CIO. As a result, the FALA won a seasonal contract. They won another the next year, when Vandeleur threatened "hot celery" action against growers,[92] and the Filipino association affiliated with the California State Federation of Labor. In January 1941, Vandeleur authorized support for a citrus strike that then spread to 4,000 lemon pickers. He announced another secondary boycott, this one of Ventura County lemons, in which the Teamsters began to refuse loads. As the strike expanded to other southern California citrus regions, the secondary boycott was a threat that previous struggles over trucking, warehouses, and canneries had taught growers to take seriously.[93] The AFL at last seemed to be developing an effective strategy for organizing a viable farm workers union, based on alliances with ethnic associations and use of the secondary boycott.

Unfortunately, before farm worker organizers could consolidate this promising new alliance, the wartime emergency created an opportunity for the growers to fatally undermine it. When mobilization for World War II got under way, the increased demand for labor in California seemed likely to further enhance the leverage of farm worker organizers. However, the Associated Farmers and the Farm Bureau launched a public relations campaign, arguing that the "efficacy of defense activities" and "the protection of agriculture's endeavors to that end"[94] had to be kept free from "union molestation."[95] With the support of the California Chamber of Commerce, they won a statewide legislative ban on secondary boycotts in May 1941.[96] Governor Olson vetoed the ban, but the state legislature overrode him. A few months later, the California State Federation of Labor narrowly lost a hard-fought referendum on the measure. The Associated Farmers also won anti-union ordinances to ban picketing, ban secondary boycott activity, and/or require the licensing of union organizers in 34 of California's 56 counties and 19 of its municipalities.[97] Unfortunately, the lesson that leaders of the California State Federation of Labor seemed to take from all this was that trying to unionize farm workers could precipitate legislation which could cripple the entire labor movement.[98]

Furthermore, World War II created an opportunity for growers to regain control of the labor market by importing *braceros* from Mexico.[99] The federal government treated the wartime mobilization of industrial workers as a labor problem to be managed by the War Manpower Commission. At the same time, farm worker mobilization was consigned to the Department of Agriculture, where once again it was seen only as a question of supply[100]—a supply over which growers now established firm command. Although the 1941 *bracero* legislation enacted by Congress required growers to offer work to domestic workers at a prevailing wage before they could bring in Mexican workers, the responsibility for determining the prevailing wage was vested in a grower-dominated agency as was the procurement and distribution of the *braceros*.[101] The fox—or, in the version better known in the Southwest, the coyote—had won control of the hen house.

The results shaped California agriculture for the following 25 years. By 1941, with America's entry into the war, a decade of serious attempts to organize farm workers was over. And although the number of *braceros* imported to California during the war was not so large, Mexican recruiting stimulated a demand for opportunities to work in the United States that far exceeded the supply of jobs, resulting in a dramatic increase in illegal immigration.[102] By the end of World War II, the growers had transformed a workforce which in 1941 had consisted of immigrant Mexican families, Filipinos, and dustbowl migrants, into one in which resident Mexicans and Filipinos competed with *braceros* and undocumented workers, who had no rights of citizenship or economic organization. Moreover, the new workers, like California's first large farm labor force, were mostly single men. In the words of historian Erasmo Gamboa, these men were "on call on a daily basis, including Sundays, [and] could be transferred at a moment's notice to meet labor shortages elsewhere."[103] California growers had reestablished their ideal workforce.

THE THIRD WAVE OF FARM WORKER ORGANIZING: THE NFLU (1946–1951)

In the three years after the Second World War ended, California growers greatly expanded their acreage in production. This created a tight farm labor market because their ideal labor force grew more gradually (see figure 2.2). To the dismay of the growers, however, expansion of the immigrant labor supply depended on public policy. This fact, in conjunction with the continuing competition between the AFL and CIO, created the next opportunity for farm worker organizing.

When World War II was over, contention over the domestic impact of imported labor again turned migrant workers into a national issue. A federal Interagency Committee on Migrant Labor in 1947 called for "justice for Americans equal to that afforded to foreign workers in the United States" and made proposals to limit immigration and to improve living and working conditions in agriculture.[104] Growers, as a result, were threatened not only by a tight labor market, but even more so by uncertainty over the future farm labor supply. The threat did not last long. By 1951, the growers had prevailed in the policy arena and had achieved an almost unlimited flow of labor, which would last for another decade.[105] But for a few years, a temporarily tight labor market and the growers' political vulnerability encouraged organizers once again to try to build a farm workers union, especially when the competition might do the job if they didn't.

Both the AFL and the CIO made attempts in this period. Both emerged from the war greatly strengthened in membership and financial resources. In the canneries and packing sheds, they picked up their prewar competition where they had left off. In May 1945, the California State Federation of Labor acceded to a demand by the Teamsters for jurisdiction over the canneries and packing sheds, which they had helped to organize before the war—and which AFL leaders believed "were about to be overrun by subversives." This move split the leadership of the cannery workers' council of local unions that had been established by the California Federation of Labor before the war, prompting the CIO's new Food, Tobacco, and Agricultural Workers Union (FTA) to enter the fray.

At first, the CIO seemed poised to recoup its prewar losses; in October 1945, UCAPWA's CIO successor, the FTA, petitioned for a statewide National Labor Relations Board (NLRB) election among cannery workers and won it. But by February 1946, the Teamsters had successfully lobbied the NLRB to throw out the results of that election and schedule another. In the interim, the Teamsters signed a contract with the cannery owners that required cannery employees to become Teamsters, in what the NLRB called a "flagrant violation" of its orders. The NLRB, however, did nothing to stop the collusion of the cannery owners and the Teamsters. Together, the owners and Teamsters conducted an intense campaign of strikes, lockouts, violence, and intimidation, led by Dave Beck's protégé, Einar Mohn. Mohn made "red baiting" of the FTA the Teamsters' main campaign theme.[106] When the second election was held in August 1946, the Teamsters won all but a handful of independent canneries in southern California, settling one of the major organizing conflicts dating from the 1930s. This result left the canneries firmly within Teamster control.

AFL leaders, nonetheless, remained wary of the CIO. The ILWU, stymied by the Teamsters in its attempt to march inland, had shifted its focus to Hawaii, where it won legislation that extended collective bargaining rights to farm workers in 1946. In the ensuing representation election and strike, the ILWU brought 30,000 sugar and pineapple workers under union contract by the end of 1946—the first such contracts in the United States.[107] Given the CIO success and the status that migrant workers had acquired as a national issue, AFL president Green chose to put some effort and money, perhaps preemptively, into farm workers. In August 1946, the AFL, for the first time, chartered a farm workers' union: the National Farm Labor Union (NFLU). To lead it, Green selected H. L. Mitchell, 41, a native of Tennessee and head of the Southern Tenant Farmers Union (STFU). Mitchell, who had broken with his Communist Party associates over ideological issues in the late 1930s, combined the impeccable anti-Communist credentials important to the AFL with a real commitment to advocacy for the rural poor. His STFU was a widely respected advocacy group, especially among Washington liberals, with a formally organized national support network, the National Sharecroppers Fund. When the STFU became part of the National Farm Labor Union, Mitchell retained these resources while refocusing his attention on California, where many of his old constituents had settled during the dustbowl years.[108]

Mitchell, who worked mainly from Washington, hired two lead organizers for California, white Socialist Party activists from New York who had met at Columbia University in the 1930s. Hank Hasiwar, 30, became a union organizer and served in World War II. William Becker, 28, was a party organizer who had managed the 1944 and 1948 Norman Thomas presidential campaigns.[109] Like Mitchell and like the radicals of the 1930s, both saw labor organizing as their calling. Yet the NFLU leaders differed from the 1930s radicals in their distance from the Mexicans and Filipinos who made up so much of the California farm workforce. They tried to rectify this problem by bringing Ernesto Galarza, 42, onto their leadership team. Galarza, the talented son of Mexican immigrants, had earned a Ph.D. in economics at Columbia and served as research director for the Pan-American Union. The NFLU leadership was thus composed of men with some complementary experience: Mitchell as an advocate, Hasiwar and Becker as organizers, and Galarza as a researcher. This combination of experience, however, did not equip them with the networks or the understanding of how to connect to the world of Mexican and Filipino farm workers. Moreover, the way they were organized internally insulated their deliberations from the influence of ethnic leaders and local union members. Because the NFLU was funded entirely by the AFL, its leaders were accountable primarily to themselves and Green, not to their constituency. This proved to be a serious limitation when it came to developing strategy.

Scholars of social movements, such as Craig Jenkins and Charles Perrow, have tried to explain the NFLU's failure in the 1950s and the United Farm Workers' success in the 1960s by citing differences in public support during the two eras. In fact, the NFLU did enjoy substantial outside support. However, they faltered because its leaders did not develop a strategy to turn that support into economic power in the few years before the next war once again gave growers the upper hand. The NFLU strategy for winning contracts did develop in some ways over those years, but its two key elements remained unchanged, despite the fact that changing circumstances limited their usefulness.

First, the NFLU leaders counted on secondary boycotts to provide them with key leverage, even after the Taft-Hartley Act of 1947 made them illegal. As Mitchell saw it, "The key to successful organization of agricultural labor is working out cooperative arrangements with the Teamsters Union which has strong organization among the cannery and packing shed workers."[110] Second, the NFLU leaders thought they could use their political influence with the federal government to constrict local labor market supplies enough to compel growers to sign contracts. They stuck to this strategy even after it was clear that the Truman administration was not going to provide that support.

The NFLU's campaign against the DiGiorgio Fruit Corporation was the first failure of this strategy. Mitchell targeted DiGiorgio with the eye for political drama that he had developed as a Washington advocate for southern sharecroppers. The company had been a symbol of California agribusiness ever since Steinbeck had caricatured it as "DiGregorio" in *Grapes of Wrath*. DiGiorgio was the largest private distributor of deciduous and citrus fruits in the nation and the second largest private winemaker. Its diversified operations included 11 packing facilities; interests in Baltimore, Chicago, New York, Cincinnati, and Pittsburgh fruit exchanges; an Oregon shipping crate company; and 33 percent of the stock of Italian Swiss Colony, the third largest winery in the United States.[111]

The 12,000-acre Arvin ranch in the southern San Joaquin Valley was the largest DiGiorgio holding. It hired a peak of 2,000 workers: 1,500 Anglos who lived in town, 500 Mexicans who lived on the ranch, and a few Filipinos.[112] That is where the NFLU struck on October 1, 1947, with less than a month of harvest work remaining.

The campaign had gotten under way in June with assurances of support from the Kern County Labor Council, a promise from the California State Federation of Labor to pay for two full-time organizers, and an agreement with Teamsters Local 87 to conduct a joint organizing drive. It was not too difficult to convince the Anglo workers that a union might be a good idea. Within a month, the organizers had recruited 1,000 members, who paid a $2 initiation fee and monthly dues of $1, and set up a local.

Although Hasiwar had intended to organize until spring to prepare for the plum harvest, DiGiorgio changed Hasiwar's plans. In late September, with most of the season over, DiGiorgio seized the initiative by firing several NFLU leaders. When the company declined to meet with the union, despite the union's claim to represent 1,200 of DiGiorgio's employees, 800 of the workers voted to strike for a wage increase of 10 cents and the institution of grievance procedures, a seniority system, and union recognition.

DiGiorgio lost much of the remaining crop, but the strike did not shut the ranch down since some 200 employees kept working: 70 Mexican and Filipino seasonal workers, a few discouraged Anglo strikers, and 130 *braceros*. The *braceros* walked out on the first day of the strike. Soon thereafter, they were instructed by Mexican and U.S. officials to fulfill their contracts or be deported. Unable to speak with the Mexicans because he had no Spanish-speaking organizers, Hasiwar hired Louis de Anda, a Mexican-American former air force officer whose sister ran a popular Spanish-language radio program. A month later, as a result of AFL protests to the Labor Department, the *braceros* were finally removed—just as the harvest ended. By then, however, DiGiorgio had recruited 600 strike breakers to do the winter pruning. The picket line settled down to a core of 100–200 strikers. By spring, work resumed with almost a full complement of workers, many of them Mexicans.[113]

The NFLU maintained its picket lines, which Mitchell knew was critical not because it kept out strike breakers, but because it attracted the money and publicity needed to keep the organizing effort alive.[114] He had learned this lesson organizing southern tenant farmers whose strikes had been more effective as protests inspiring political mobilization in the North than as economic weapons in the South. At DiGiorgio, he once again mobilized public backing, this time to support the strikers and to pressure the government to remove the *braceros*. The *New York Times* gave surprising coverage to an event far away in rural California. In November, U.S. representative Helen Gahagan Douglas visited the picket line. At Christmas, a delegation of Los Angeles religious leaders arrived and a 200-car caravan of supporters drove up from the Los Angeles Labor Federation. The Hollywood Movie Council produced a film called *Poverty in the Valley of Plenty*, which Mitchell showed to the House Labor and Education Committee in Washington. It caused such a stir that DiGiorgio filed a libel suit to keep it from being shown elsewhere. The California State Federation of Labor provided monthly financial support,[115] while other labor, religious, and liberal groups raised substantial additional funding.[116]

Despite considerable public support for the farm workers, the federal government came to the aid of the employers rather than the union. The *bracero* program, which the NFLU organizers had expected would end in December 1947 when congressional authority for it lapsed, was instead continued under the executive authority of President Harry S Truman. Although the sheer political power of southwestern growers partly accounts for that unexpected turn of events, the growers were also learning how to turn mounting concerns about undocumented workers—or "wetbacks," as they were called—to their own long-term advantage. Truman was also under pressure from the Mexican government, which objected that unregulated emigration was taking control over its borders out of its hands, exposing its citizens to gross exploitation at the hands of U.S. employers, and driving down the wages being paid to legal immigrants in the United States as well as domestic workers. The administration's answer was to try to reduce illegal immigration by increasing the number of *braceros*, a solution the growers found quite agreeable. The Truman administration reached an agreement with Mexico to repatriate undocumented workers, certify them as *braceros*, and return them rapidly to the United States.[117]

The effect on the farm labor force was not trivial. While the 1947 figures report that only 19,632 *braceros* were recruited that year, in truth 50,000 more undocumented workers were legalized, or "dried out" as it was called. The U.S. government also set up recruiting sites near the border to help growers contract *braceros*. And although only employers who did not hire undocumented workers were deemed "eligible" to contract *braceros*, undocumented workers continued to pour into the country.[118]

Secondary boycotts, the other prong of the NFLU's strategy for compelling employer concessions, also fizzled. Growers once again got them banned—this time nationally, as part of the Taft-Hartley Act passed by the conservative 80th Congress before the DiGiorgio strike began. When unionized winery workers at Italian Swiss Colony and Teamsters at Safeway's Los Angeles produce terminal refused to handle DiGiorgio products, the grower filed charges against all of the unions involved.[119] Although farm workers, exempt from the protections of federal labor law, remained free to conduct secondary boycotts on their own, the workers to whom they turned for support were barred from doing so.[120] The Teamsters and winery workers thus found themselves enjoined from boycotting and embroiled in costly litigation in their own defense.

DiGiorgio, meanwhile, escalated pressure on the picket line. A group of 40 strike breakers led by the ranch supervisor and armed with chains and farm tools attacked the pickets. Three strikers were hospitalized, and a riot of some 1,000 union supporters ensued. Then, in mid-May 1948, in tactics reminiscent of the 1930s, a failed attempt to assassinate the strike's chief organizer resulted in the shooting of NFLU local union president James Price. California governor Earl

Warren sent investigators in and offered a $5,000 reward for information, but the strike was effectively over.[121]

After their disappointment at DiGiorgio in 1948, Hasiwar, Galarza, and Becker regrouped. In the fall of 1949, they revived the tactics of the 1930s radicals, organizing Mexican seasonal workers on a crop-wide basis, rather than those of a single employer. The strikes the NFLU led that season did have a short-term impact on wages in cotton, tomatoes, and other summer crops. (Although Filipino unions tried to pick up where they had left off before the war, leading a major asparagus strike near Stockton in 1948, the NFLU, perhaps concerned with their radical affiliations, had no contact with them.)[122]

The union's central strategy for achieving longer-term results remained pressuring the federal government to constrict the farm labor force. Mitchell and his allies lobbied for a Presidential Commission on Migratory Labor, which they hoped would provide the political impetus to end the *bracero* program.[123] The lobbying worked. In June 1950, Truman formed the commission; he appointed government, civic, academic, and religious leaders, many of whom had long been supporters of the NFLU.[124] They did not allow themselves to be derailed, even when North Korea invaded South Korea just three weeks after the commission was appointed. Once again, the growers could claim that a national emergency required reestablishment of the *bracero* program on an even larger scale. Nonetheless, the commission held hearings throughout that summer, and in April 1951, it issued a report that challenged the existence of the labor shortages that were the premise of the *bracero* program. The report documented the devastating effect that importation of foreign labor had on domestic workers, urged penalizing employers who hired undocumented workers, called for tougher enforcement of immigration laws, and the extension of collective bargaining guarantees to farm workers. This, the commission said, was the only way to remove farm work from a low-wage "ghetto."[125]

In California, meanwhile, NFLU organizers targeted Imperial Valley *meloneros*, the skilled crews of legally resident Mexican workers who followed the melons up and down the state, returning to their families in the valley each winter. Despite secondary boycott concerns and past rivalries, the NFLU won cooperation in this organizing drive from the Teamsters, which represented Imperial Valley produce truckers, and the United Packinghouse Workers (CIO), which represented melon shed packers. The *meloneros* demanded a wage increase and preferential hiring for legal residents. When the growers refused and began firing them, 500 *meloneros* voted to go on strike. On May 24, a month after the Commission on Migratory Labor issued its report, the NFLU set up picket lines throughout the Imperial Valley and closed the Mexican border to commuters, a task accomplished with the help of a baseball bat brigade. As for the undocumented workers living on the U.S. side of the border in grower-supplied housing, Hasiwar hit upon the idea of making citizens' arrests and turning them over to the Border Patrol. This campaign largely stopped melon production, even though the Teamsters and the United Packinghouse Workers went back to work after only three days.[126] Mitchell was even called to a meeting in Washington, DC, with the Border Patrol, which wanted to get a similar program going all along the border.

The larger strategy, however, once again failed. The growers bused in 7,500 *braceros* and housed them in their own camps. Since *braceros* could not legally be used for strike breaking, Hasiwar tried to pressure the Mexican consul in Calexico to remove them, while Mitchell worked the Department of Labor in Washington. But the Mexican government did not act and the Truman administration stalled. On June 25, when the U.S. Labor Department finally agreed to remove the *braceros*, Mitchell was elated and telephoned Galarza. Galarza informed him that the melon season had just ended, and they called off the strike that morning.

The next month, on July 12, 1951, Congress passed Public Law 78, which put the *bracero* program back on solid footing for the next 14 years. This new labor pool inhibited unionization and facilitated bringing 1.4 million new acres into production. The growers had once again stabilized their hired workforce, at a new high of 230,000.[127] NFLU organizing ground to a halt. In Washington, the NFLU organizers had again been outflanked; after the secondary boycott was outlawed, they never found another way to turn their urban support into economic power. The NFLU's most significant contribution turned out to be keeping the issue of migrant workers alive through the 1950s.

CONCLUSION

From 1900 to 1950, three waves of farm worker organizing attempts failed to win a single multiyear contract, establish a sustainable farm workers union, or reform the rules governing the farm labor market. Recognizing their limited ability to challenge growers on their turf, labor leaders quickly learned that no matter how well organized they were locally, they often had to win outside support to make even short-term gains. Typically, leaders from new immigrant groups made use of the modest support available from the governments of their countries of origin. Radicals drew on national networks for as much legal, financial, and political support as they could muster. And the AFL, while most often found organizing farm workers in reaction to the radicals, backed up its efforts with union support, at times in the form of secondary boycotts. Yet none of them got very far before the growers were able to take advantage of war mobilization to suppress organizing, rebuild their workforce, and strengthen their control of labor market institutions. Although three different groups of organizers—each with different kinds of resources—were involved in each wave of organizing, they never came together in such a way that they could succeed in breaking this cycle.

It was not until the 1960s that another tight labor market, this time a result of the end of the *bracero* program, created the next opportunity to organize farm workers. This time, however, ethnic community leaders, radical organizers, and the AFL-CIO came to play roles in a common endeavor. One reason they could do so was that racial justice claims—which challenged barriers that had inhibited earlier efforts to join forces—could now enhance economic justice claims as a basis for public support. At the same time, the state institutions through which the growers had consolidated their earlier successes now offered farm worker organizers new venues for the mobilization of public support. These opportunities, however, like David's stones, would be of little value to those who could not see them. It is to the story of those who could see—and those who could not—that we now turn.

THREE

New Opportunities, New Initiatives

AWOC, Teamsters, and the FWA (1959–1962)

Our goal is "organizing farm workers to improve their wages, hours and working conditions... [and] to mobilize our full resources" in a "well planned realistic organizing drive with affiliates having appropriate jurisdiction."

—Resolution Establishing Agricultural Workers Organizing Committee, AFL-CIO
Executive Council, San Juan, Puerto Rico, February 23, 1959

You know, this is almost going to be a losing proposition.... every year you've got different workers coming in...so even if you organize the group the prior year, they are not going to be there next year.

—Einar Mohn, president, Western Conference of Teamsters, 1974

A union is not simply getting enough workers to stage a strike. A union is building a group with a spirit and an existence all its own...built around the idea that people must do things by themselves, in order to help themselves.

—Cesar Chavez, director, National Farm Workers Association, April 1964

IN THE LATE 1950s and early 1960s, changes in American political, economic, and social life—and the expectation that the *bracero* program was in its final days—once again opened a door for organizers bold enough to try unionizing farm workers. This time, the newly merged AFL-CIO acted first by launching the Agricultural Workers Organizing Committee (AWOC) in 1959. The Teamsters, recently expelled from the AFL-CIO, initiated their attempt in 1961. The fledgling Farm Workers Association (FWA) launched in 1962.

The strategies that the leaders of these efforts devised to challenge the power of California growers could hardly have differed more. These strategic differences were not arbitrary. They grew out of real differences among the people who devised the strategy of each organization and how they worked together to do so. Table 3.1, "Comparative Strategic Capacity," shows how the leaders' identities, social networks, and organizing experience varied across the three organizations—as did their deliberative processes, the resources they mobilized, and the constituencies to which they were accountable (see table A.2 for details). The result was systematic differences in the "strategic capacity" of each group's leadership team: disparities in the strength of their motivation, the salience of the knowledge they brought to the project, and their ways of learning from new experience. In the years 1959 to 1962, these differences in people and processes influenced the launching of three very different organizing attempts, thus shaping their subsequent development.

NEW OPPORTUNITIES: THE TWILIGHT OF THE *BRACERO* PROGRAM

By the end of the 1950s, opposition to the *bracero* program was mounting in Washington. President Dwight D. Eisenhower's labor secretary, James Mitchell, a New York Republican and active Roman Catholic with a positive labor record since the New Deal, was calling the "conditions of farm worker life…an affront to the conscience of the American people":

> [America] has a large surplus of underemployed domestic farm workers, workers not only without social protections but whom foreign workers deprive of the benefits of market competition for labor.…Foreign labor programs…often permit employers to evade the necessity to pay the wages and to do the many other things needed to attract and retain domestic farm workers.[1]

Support for the *bracero* program was eroding in Congress, too, as the interests of growers outside California changed. In the upper

TABLE 3.1. Comparative Strategic Capacity: AWOC, the UFW, and the Teamsters

	AWOC	UFW	Teamsters
Biographical	Homogeneous Outsiders Occupational Commitment	Heterogeneous Insiders and Outsiders Personal and Vocational Commitment	Homogeneous Outsiders Occupational Commitment
Networks	Strong Ties	Strong Ties and Weak Ties	Strong Ties
Repertoires	Applying What Knew How to Do Labor Market Repertoire	Learning to Do Something New Diverse Repertoires	Applying What Knew How to Do Responsible Union Repertoire
Deliberation	No Regular, Open, Authoritative Deliberation	Regular, Open, Authoritative Deliberation	No Regular, Open, Authoritative Deliberation
Resource Flows	Outside Politically Generated Based on Money	Inside and Outside Task Generated Based on People	Outside Politically Generated Based on Money
Accountability	No Constituency Accountability Bureaucratic Leadership Selection	Constituency Accountability Elective, Entrepreneurial Leadership Selection	No Constituency Accountability Bureaucratic Leadership Selection

Midwest, family farmers increasingly resented privileges granted to California agriculture as a cost-price squeeze placed their own farms at risk. Among southwestern cotton growers, the rapid spread of mechanized harvesting was eliminating demand for *braceros*. California fruit and vegetable growers thus found themselves increasingly isolated. By 1962, they would be using 60 percent of the *braceros* who entered the country. In fact, by then, less than 2 percent of U.S. farms, located in just five states, were driving the entire *bracero* policy.[2] As agricultural support for the program weakened, the opposition grew stronger: urban congressional representatives; farm leaders fearful of losing support for other agricultural programs; and labor, religious, and farm worker advocacy groups.

Meanwhile, cold war politics created pressure to correct the discriminatory treatment of U.S. racial minorities, drawing attention to the plight of African-American migrants on the East Coast and Mexican migrants in the Midwest and West. In 1957, H. L. Mitchell formed the National Advisory Committee on Farm Labor, a successor to his earlier advocacy groups, which was also stirring debate about migrant workers, the *bracero* program, and agricultural policy in general.[4] Chaired by Eleanor Roosevelt, the NACFL included an impressive array of national figures: Senator Frank P. Graham, former president of the University of North Carolina; A. Philip Randolph, president of the Sleeping Car Porters; the Reverend Eugene Carson Blake, president of the National Council of Churches; Rabbi Eugene J. Kipman, director of social action for the Union of American Hebrew Congregations; and Father James L. Vizzard, S.J., vice president of the national Catholic Rural Life Conference.

The 1958 congressional election, held in the midst of the Eisenhower recession, transformed these developments into political opportunity. A sharp increase in domestic unemployment no doubt evoked painful memories for those who had lived through the Great Depression and made it hard to explain "the incredible anomaly," in author Ellis Hawley's words, "of importing foreign workers to produce farm surpluses at a time when several million American laborers were looking for work."[5] These elections returned the most liberal House of Representatives since 1936.[6] In California, Democrats swept the state, with voters electing Edmund G. "Pat" Brown as governor and rejecting an anti-union "right to work" initiative.[7] In the words of Lyndon Johnson, majority leader of the U.S. Senate, "It was time to do something..." about the migrant farm workers.[8] Labor Secretary Mitchell concurred. "The problem of farm labor in America," he declared, "is one of the two or three most important and most difficult manpower problems with which the Nation is confronted."[9]

The days of the *bracero* program seemed to be numbered; national support for farm workers was building. People hoping to seize this opportunity to improve the lot of farm labor began to appear in California's valleys.

THE NEW RADICALS

While demands for economic justice had provided the moral energy that drove earlier public concern for farm workers, demands for racial justice became the nation's new source of moral energy. Like labor radicals whose moral outrage called them to organize farm workers in earlier periods, the civil rights radicals became key actors in the new era.

Although discussion of the civil rights movement of the 1950s and 1960s is usually limited to the consideration of African-American claims to racial justice, the children of the Mexican immigrants of the 1920s had come of age and begun organizing to make claims of their own in the Southwest.[10] In 1949, for example, young men who had served in World War II founded the American GI Forum to seek redress for discrimination against Mexican-American veterans.[11] The new organizations moved into the vacuum that had been created by the Depression era collapse of many Mexican mutual benefit lodges formed in the 1920s. *[margin note: civil rights movement]*

In California, the first major Mexican-American advocacy organization—the Community Service Organization, or CSO—was initiated in 1947 by white Los Angeles liberals who enlisted Chicago community organizer Saul Alinsky to mount a challenge to racial discrimination against Mexican Americans. Inspired by John L. Lewis's organizing of the CIO in the 1930s, Alinsky had developed a collective-bargaining model for community organizing which won support from liberals and churches because it used democratic, nonviolent means to bring about greater social equality.[12] *[margin note: Mex-Amer advocacy]*

The man Alinsky tapped to build the CSO in 1947 was a 37-year-old organizer named Fred Ross. Ross had grown up in Los Angeles and graduated from USC with a degree in social work in 1937. He found work with the Farm Security Administration, was assigned to the Arvin Farm Labor Camp, and served with the War Relocation Authority during World War II. Afterward, he became an organizer for the American Council on Race Relations, a Chicago-based civil rights group led by Alinsky's friend sociologist Louis Wirth, which had begun to organize in southern California in response to the post-war race riots. In this way, Ross learned to organize voter registration drives and campaigns to desegregate schools and public accommodations in Los Angeles, San Bernardino, and Orange counties.[13] Once hired to form the new organization, Ross quickly linked up with supporters of Edward Roybal, a community leader who had just lost a bid to become the first Mexican American on the Los Angeles City Council. Together, they developed the CSO, a community-based membership association that led voter registration drives, conducted citizenship classes, and engaged in advocacy.

After registering 14,000 new voters, the CSO succeeded in breaking the color bar to elect Roybal to the Los Angeles City Council in 1949. Two years later, the CSO secured the imprisonment of five Los Angeles police officers in the "bloody Christmas" case. On Christmas Eve, the officers had beaten seven young Latino men in the back of the police station throughout the night. The CSO documented complaints, demanded court action, and collaborated with Roybal to mobilize public opinion until the police were convicted.[14] As Chavez later said, it was "the first time any one could remember" police being jailed for beating up young Mexicans.[15] In 1953, with the financial support of the Emil Schwartzhaupt Foundation, Ross began to organize CSO chapters across the state.[16] When he arrived in San Jose, he turned for leads to Father Donald McDonnell, the pastor of a Mexican-American parish. McDonnell referred Ross to a young Mexican American active in the parish, whom he thought had "potential": Cesar Chavez.[17]

Chavez, only 26 years old at the time, was married and was raising a family that would grow to include eight children. He grew up in a Mexican immigrant family that lost its small Arizona farm and became migrants in California when he was 10. After serving in the U.S. Navy, Chavez settled with his wife, Helen Fabela, also from a Mexican immigrant family, in San Jose. There, he found work in a lumberyard.[18] Inspired by Ross, he volunteered to help organize a CSO chapter; within a year, he joined the CSO staff full time and eventually became its lead organizer. By 1959, Ross and Chavez had built an organization of 35 chapters across California and Arizona, recruited 30,000 members, and registered upward of 200,000 new voters. Perhaps most importantly, they trained a network of organizers who were rooted in the farm worker community and committed to improving its lot. This network included Dolores Huerta, Gilbert Padilla, and others who would go on to become leaders of the

FWA—as, of course, would Chavez.[19] For perhaps the first time, the *importance of leadership* [handwritten margin note] ethnic community leaders and the radical organizers who hoped to organize farm workers were the same people.

Churches, a key arena of the civil rights movement, became another source of new radicals, who were pressing racial justice claims on behalf of immigrant farm laborers. The fact that the Cold War followed quickly after World War II—a war in which racial ideology had figured so prominently—challenged activist religious leaders such as Reinhold Niebuhr to articulate a faith-based political agenda that was explicitly liberal in terms of race. At the same time, urban churches were struggling to meet the needs of cities transformed by black migration and Hispanic immigration. Simultaneously, in the country's new white suburbs, church membership was growing rapidly, generating unprecedented financial resources.[20]

Among mainline Protestant denominations, these developments converged in the 1950 founding of the National Council of Churches. The staff the council hired was drawn from the younger clergy who were strongly oriented toward social action—many of them recruited from Niebuhr's base, Union Theological Seminary.[21] At the local level, Union also contributed to launching the urban ministry movement with projects such as the East Harlem Protestant Parish, a cooperative ministry of three young clergymen and their families who were committed to working with the residents of this inner-city community.[22] Influenced by Niebuhr, the civil rights movement, and Alinsky, the younger religious activists' approach to social service ministry was to organize those in need. It was a major departure from older forms of charity.

In rural California, the signs of change appeared gradually. Since 1956, the American Friends Service Committee led self-help housing, community development, and cooperative labor projects in a number of San Joaquin Valley towns.[23] In 1957, the national Migrant Ministry, an affiliate of the National Council of Churches, received a $123,000 grant from the Schwartzhaupt Foundation for organizer training by Alinsky. And Doug Stills, the new, Alinsky-trained director of the California Migrant Ministry (CMM), began to send his staff for regular training by the CSO's Ross, Chavez, Huerta, and Padilla. Among Stills' staffers was a young Presbyterian minister, the Reverend Wayne C. "Chris" Hartmire, who had graduated from Princeton, served three years in the U.S. Navy, and was attending Union Theological Seminary when Stills recruited him. Hartmire served with the seminary's East Harlem ministry for a year and then

natural change [handwritten margin note]

became Stills' successor in California.[24] He, too, would play a critical role in the FWA.[25]

The Catholic Church was less directly challenged than the Protestants were by the African-American civil rights movement; nonetheless, it had to address the needs of a burgeoning Hispanic constituency, including many farm workers. Historically, it regarded its Mexican adherents as objects of mission rather than as full participants in parish life, but that now had to change. Church activists drew on a tradition of social ministry developed during waves of European immigration. This ministry included parish organizing, the Association of Catholic Trade Unionists, the public policy advocacy of the national Catholic Welfare Conference, and the call of prophetic communities such as Dorothy Day's Catholic Worker movement. Lay apostolic movements begun in Europe also encouraged a new generation of lay leaders eager to share mission and ministry with the clergy, especially in the quest for social and racial justice.[26]

Catholic initiatives emerged at parish, diocesan, and national levels. National Roman Catholic leaders, such as Monsignor George Higgins of the National Catholic Welfare Conference and Father James Vizzard, S.J., of the Catholic Rural Life Conference, became forceful advocates for migrant workers. At the diocesan level, the Chicago Archdiocesan Office of Urban Affairs developed a close collaboration with community organizer Alinsky. This collaboration yielded a Chicago organizing model of training "priests as organizing partners," which began in 1959.[27] And at the local level, younger clergy took initiatives. For example, four young priests who met at St. Patrick's Seminary in California in 1950 and discerned a calling to serve farm workers formed themselves as the Missionary Apostolate of the San Francisco Diocese (informally, the California mission band). One of them, Father Donald McDonnell, was the priest who introduced Chavez to organizing. Another member of the Missionary Apostolate, Father Thomas McCullough, organized a mutual benefit association among Stockton farm worker parishioners, which became a model for the early FWA.[28]

NEW INITIATIVES: LAUNCHING AWOC

By 1959, growing opposition to the *bracero* program, a renewed concern with migrants in the context of urban unemployment, the new legitimacy of racial justice claims, and new activism in the Mexican-American and religious communities provided farm worker advocates with means to pressure AFL-CIO president George Meany to do something about migrant workers. He complained that he "got tired of going to international conventions and being needled by labor people from smaller, poorer foreign countries, who could point out that at least they had organized farm workers, while the American labor movement hadn't."[29] Also spurring Meany to action were union leaders who believed that organizing agricultural workers could curb the political power of agribusiness, "some of the most reactionary forces in the United States."[30] Most important, however, was Meany's rivalry with former CIO president Walter Reuther. Reuther was now vice president of the AFL-CIO and a critic of Meany's failure to act on the new federation's widely proclaimed intent to "organize the unorganized."[31] Reuther had already begun working with other unions to encourage farm worker organizing.

In 1959, Reuther was 52 years old. For 10 years, he had been president of the United Auto Workers (UAW), the most powerful industrial union in America. He was president of the CIO for 4 years. A former socialist union organizer and the son of a German Lutheran immigrant brewery worker, he now enjoyed extensive national and international connections. He was a co-founder of Americans for Democratic Action and the chief public spokesman for social unionism.[32] In negotiating the AFL-CIO merger, he had agreed to put Meany at the helm not only because the AFL had grown to twice the size of the CIO, but also because he anticipated that Meany, who was 14 years older than Reuther, would soon retire. Meanwhile, according to historian Nelson Lichtenstein, "Reuther remained an alien presence [in the AFL-CIO] who wanted to transform a College of Cardinals into a combat organization."[33]

Meany, on the other hand, exemplified the traditional "business unionism" of the AFL.[34] In 1959, he was 66 years old, an Irish-American lifelong leader in the plumbers' union, the building trades, and the New York AFL—as his father had been before him. He had little interest and no experience in organizing and was suspicious of the civil rights movement. He once asked, "Why should we worry about organizing groups of people who do not appear to want to be organized?"[35] This, he thought, was the job of individual unions, not the federation. He excelled at insider politics among other union chiefs and within the halls of Congress—and this experience gave him a strong preference for legislative strategy.[36] Yet he found himself responsible for a new farm worker organizing project begun in 1959.

The AFL-CIO director of organizing would also be a key player in the attempt to form a farm worker union, and the politics of the AFL-CIO merger slated this position for someone from the CIO. But the selection of UAW vice president John Livingston, 52, did little to advance the cause of organizing. Livingston, a Missouri auto worker, had risen within the UAW not as an organizer, but as a negotiator and as a Reuther rival. By appointing Livingston, Meany got a CIO person whose politics he didn't have to worry about and Reuther got rid of some internal opposition. It was a fine political solution yet did little to address the needs of a new organizing department.[37] Livingston was shut off from both Meany's inner councils and those of the UAW.

Nonetheless, he proceeded to design an organizational vehicle for unionizing farm workers. In the jurisdiction-minded AFL-CIO, this was no easy task. H. L. Mitchell's old NFLU, now calling itself the National Agricultural Workers Union (NAWU), still held the charter to organize farm workers, although it had had no real resources since Meany revoked its subsidy back in 1954. The former CIO's United Packinghouse Workers of America (UPWA), however, became very interested in organizing shed and field workers, because the former UCAPAWA locals that had affiliated with it now gave it a base in most California vegetable production regions. Ralph Helstein, a labor lawyer and former socialist who led the UPWA, wanted to "follow the jobs" that employers were moving out of unionized sheds and into non-union fields. He wanted to organize unorganized citrus packinghouse workers in Oxnard. And he wanted to court public support by exposing the lack of sanitary facilities in the fields. When his Oxnard citrus drive bogged down, Helstein consulted with his Chicago friend Saul Alinsky, who persuaded him that an organized Mexican community might strengthen his union's ability to get contracts.[38] At Alinsky's suggestion, Helstein made a $20,000 grant to the CSO for Cesar Chavez to do a one-year pilot project in Oxnard.[39] At the same time, he was working with Mitchell and Livingston to devise a joint farm labor organizing plan to present to the AFL-CIO Executive Council. For a time, it appeared that the UPWA would pick up the farm worker organizing challenge and run with it.

But when Meany finally agreed to fund such an undertaking, he would allow neither the NAWU nor the UPWA lead it.[40] Instead, he created an organizing committee directly accountable to the AFL-CIO. This allowed him to postpone the politically tricky question of which union would get which members until there were members to get.

[margin handwritten note: Helstein (worked in industry)]

So, on February 23, 1959, AWOC, the Agricultural Workers Organizing Committee, was born. It was charged with the dual mission of "organizing farm workers to improve their wages, hours and working conditions" and "supporting efforts [to be undertaken by AFL-CIO lobbyists] to repeal the *bracero* program."[41] It was allocated a substantial budget of $200,000 a year for a two-year organizing drive.[42]

AWOC failed to launch a farm workers union. It failed despite leading a major strike wave, raising farm wages across the state, and focusing a national spotlight on the *bracero* program. It failed not for a lack of opportunity or of resources, but because of its limited strategic capacity. From the beginning, AWOC strategy reflected political compromises among labor leaders who knew nothing of farm labor, relied on familiar organizing models, and had a very modest commitment to the whole enterprise. By choosing the leaders it did and embedding them in an organizational structure in which farm workers had no role, AWOC succeeded neither at organizing a base among farm workers nor at devising a way to strengthen the limited local labor market power that had crippled earlier organizing attempts.

To choose a director for AWOC, Meany and Livingston followed the same political logic that Reuther and Meany had used in appointing Livingston. To avoid choosing between the UPWA's California organizer, Clive Knowles, and NAWU's Ernesto Galarza—both reasonable candidates, but aligned with opposing political camps—they reached outside the labor movement to select Norman Smith, a supervisor with the Kaiser Steel Company in Fontana, California. Smith, 62, had no California agricultural experience, spoke no Spanish, and had no ties to the farm worker world. However, he did have ties to Livingston that went back to the St. Louis UAW plant where Smith had recruited Livingston into the union. Standing 5 feet 8 inches tall, Smith weighed almost 300 pounds and loved to reminisce. "His life," according to his colleague Henry Anderson, "was centered, single-mindedly, on the ideals and dynamics of the labor movement as he had known it in the 1930s."[43] But he was so close to retirement that his selection would offend no one, and his lack of a union political base kept him beholden to Livingston.

As assistant director, Meany and Livingston appointed Galarza from the NAWU. Galarza, the son of Mexican immigrants, was a researcher and author. In 1956, he had published *Strangers in Our Fields*, an influential exposé of the *bracero* program. For the only Mexican with a leadership role in AWOC, the AFL-CIO had selected a scholar, not an organizer. In any case, it was Meany, Livingston, and Smith—not Galarza—who developed AWOC strategy. And all three were white men, over 50 years of age, with a strong sense of the "legitimate" way to do union work. For them, organizing farm workers was not a calling; it was a job—although for Smith it may also have been an opportunity to relive his glory days with the UAW in the 1930s. It was a job for which they were ill-prepared. Of the three, only Smith had ever learned organizing tactics, but he had not used them for 18 years, and when he did it was in a radically different setting.[44] Their plan was to mobilize workers to join the union, support them in making demands on their employers, and get contracts. They targeted California because of the size of its hired farm workforce, its organizing history, the strength of its labor movement, and the fact that, in the 1958 elections, the Democrats had swept the state. They planned to develop eight local branches of 200 members each within a year and later expand to Oregon, Washington, Arizona, Texas, and New Jersey.[45] While the struggle over the *bracero* program would unfold in the national political arena, AWOC's focus would remain local, work-centered, and short-term.

On the advice of many, including Galarza, Smith decided to head-quarter AWOC in Stockton, a traditional farm worker center.[46] Located where the San Joaquin and Sacramento valleys meet, Stockton was the heart of the canning industry and was the site of many past labor struggles. But in 1959, it was also one of the few remaining centers for Anglo "fruit tramps" and one of a handful of places in which Filipino workers had established a strategic niche. And it was the county seat of San Joaquin County, the largest *bracero*-using county in the state. The area's highly seasonal work in tree fruits, asparagus, and tomatoes both created the demand for *braceros* and crippled the development of a stable local workforce. These conditions posed formidable obstacles to organizing farm workers.

Despite this, two local groups had tried their hand at it: the Filipino Farm Labor Union and Father Tom McCullough's Agricultural Workers Association. Smith hired Larry Itliong, the leader of the Filipino group, as an AWOC organizer. He also hired several staffers recommended by McCullough, including Dolores Huerta of the CSO. Unfortunately, Smith did not include them in AWOC's strategic decision making. The combination of motivation, relationships, and experience that could have greatly enhanced AWOC's strategic capacity was thus available, but AWOC strategists failed to take advantage of it.

Itliong, who was 46 in 1959, had immigrated from the Philippines to the United States at age 15 and found his calling as a union organizer in the 1930s. He had worked with UCAIWA, UCAPAWA, and the ILWU, organizing fields, canneries, and fisheries as far north as Alaska. In 1956, he had formed the Filipino Farm Labor Union and in 1959 was serving as president of the Filipino community of Stockton and as vice chair of the Council of United Filipino Organizations of Northern and Central California.[47]

McCullough, 37, one of the California mission band and the son of a San Francisco Bay Area trade unionist, started the Agricultural Workers Association when he could elicit no interest from national labor leaders in Stockton farm laborers.[48] For organizers, McCullough recruited Huerta and other CSO members, as well as Filipino union organizer Cipriano Delvo. He targeted the resident farm worker families who lived in the fringe communities around Stockton, the so-called home guard. The association held house meetings, collected dues of $2 per month, elected a board of directors, and began to develop mutual benefit and service programs.[49] Due to the *bracero* program, many local farm workers could not be organized on the job. So McCullough tried to organize them where they were, in the community, to demand the jobs.

But AWOC never understood this strategy. It focused on the workplace and tried to bring the workers who held jobs into the union—even though, in farm labor, there was far more continuity among workers found in the community than on the job. For strategic advice, Smith turned not to McCullough, Itliong, or Huerta—with their organizing experience—but to Galarza. And Galarza based his strategy on what he knew how to do—research and advocacy—and documented the abuses of the *bracero* program, in order to lobby for legislative reform.

Not Productive

At the same time, Chavez was developing a very different organizing strategy in Oxnard. His idea was to mobilize workers to take actions targeted at those responsible for their problems, just as CSO had done in Los Angeles. By contrast, one participant recalled, "Galarza ran weekly staff meetings that consisted of instructing people as to the wording of Public Law 78 [the *bracero* law] and how to look up violations of the law and report them."[50] Huerta wanted Smith to phone Chavez and hear about the Oxnard campaign. When she asked Father McCullough to help her persuade Smith to listen, however, McCullough deferred to the AFL-CIO's "experienced organizers."[51]

Smith did hire people with useful experience, but he didn't listen to them. By November 1959, he had recruited a staff of 23, including 16 organizers: 10 Anglos, 4 Mexicans, and 2 Filipinos.[52] On his staff were Raul Aguilar, a Mexican-American former NAWU organizer;[53] Lou Krainok from the UPWA; and Itliong and Delvo from the Filipino associations. For AWOC's research director, on McCullough's recommendation, Smith had hired Henry Anderson. A 32-year-old Anglo whose doctoral research in public health had led him to El Centro, Anderson became an expert on abuses of the *bracero* program.[54] And there was Dolores Huerta, 30, hired for a brief stint in 1959. Huerta was a native of New Mexico, where her mineworker father had served in the state legislature. She grew up in Stockton, where her mother operated a boarding house. Huerta was herself a mother of six and a graduate of the College of the Pacific. She had been a teacher until 1956, when she was recruited by Ross to work for the CSO. Interestingly, all of these people—whose life experiences, networks, and tactical repertoires tied them not only to the farm worker community but to religious, student, and liberal groups as well—remained outside the circle of AWOC decision makers.

Smith deployed his organizers to farm worker towns like Marysville, Yuba City, Stockton, Sacramento, Modesto, Fresno, Strathmore, San Jose, and Oxnard. But because farm employment was unstable—and because Smith had shunned the community organizing approach advocated by Huerta and McCullough—local AWOC branches never took root outside Stockton.[55] AWOC's leadership made its strategic choices within constraints decided by George Meany, in consultation with his AFL-CIO Executive Council, discussions that even Livingston was not permitted to attend. The national AFL-CIO stayed on top of things through reports from Livingston or his assistant, who met monthly with Smith,[56] but Livingston and Smith collectively provided themselves with few opportunities to consider perspectives other than their own. Although farm workers were asked to pay $2 per month dues to get the backing of the union, AWOC held no membership meetings. When AWOC's Stockton branch elected officers, including Dolores Huerta as secretary, Livingston, back at AFL-CIO headquarters, nullified the election as inappropriate for an organizing committee.[57] As for AWOC staff meetings, they were irregular and lacked agendas; they were venues for announcements rather than strategic discussion. The organizer's job was to do what he or she was told.

Furthermore, since AWOC's resources flowed from the top down, maintaining the flow was a matter of satisfying those at the top. The money with which AWOC paid its staff, covered expenses, and maintained offices was provided by the AFL-CIO as an annual operating budget. (The AWOC director and his assistant were paid

FIGURE 3.1. AWOC's AFL-CIO office, Stockton, 1960. *Source:* © 1978
Ernest Lowe / Take Stock

$1,000 per month, the research director $90 per week, and the organizers $75 per week. And they were reimbursed 5 cents per mile
for gas.)[58] In AWOC's first year, the AFL-CIO impounded all dues
money, making AWOC wholly dependent on AFL-CIO funds. But
even afterward, dues were not a significant source of revenue, and
this limited AWOC's need to create a financial base among workers.
Because AWOC relied on paid staff to do the organizing, it also had
little motivation to recruit volunteers from among farm workers or
supporters.[59]

AWOC's accountability structure thus consisted of a chain of command insulated from claims from below. Meany appointed the director, with input from Livingston, and the director hired the staff. There
was no advisory board of supporters, no mechanism of accountability
to farm workers, nor was there any role for farm worker leadership at
all. The top-down structure muted the urgency of thinking strategically about how to organize farm workers, because farm workers were
neither the source of funds nor of legitimacy. Instead, Meany's concerns would always carry the day. In this way, AWOC leaders could

count on the resources they needed to keep making the same mistakes over and over again, as long as the people at the top were satisfied.

Meanwhile in Washington

While Smith was assembling a staff in California, Washington was buzzing. In August 1959, the Senate Subcommittee on Migratory Labor began work, with energetic leadership from New Jersey senator Harrison Williams. Eager to make a name for himself and his committee, he launched a series of hearings across the United States to draw attention to the farm worker problem. For the first time, the issue was to be considered in a legislative venue outside the strongholds of support for the *bracero* program: the House and Senate Agriculture committees.[60]

In October, a report commissioned by Labor Secretary Mitchell delivered a powerful indictment of the *bracero* program.[61] The use of *braceros*, the report concluded, had an adverse effect on domestic wages. Furthermore, the domestic labor shortages used to justify the use of *braceros*, to the extent they existed at all, were due to bad employment conditions. Most employers had not even tried to recruit domestic workers, and many were using *braceros* as regular skilled workers in violation of the law. The report recommended that the secretary of labor establish a prevailing wage that employers would have to offer domestic workers before they could apply for *braceros*. It also recommended that a tripartite advisory committee representing workers, growers, and the public should be established to oversee the *bracero* program.[62] Mitchell then shocked growers by reaching back to the 1933 Wagner-Peyser Act. This act gave the authority to mandate those using the U.S. Farm Labor Service to recruit interstate workers to comply with the minimum wages and working conditions set by the Labor Department.[63]

The growers' supporters in Congress reacted forcefully to Mitchell's activism by introducing bills that attacked his authority to regulate wages. They proposed returning the *bracero* program to the Department of Agriculture, where Ezra Taft Benson, former president of the American Farm Bureau Federation, was in charge. And the battle was joined. South Dakota representative George McGovern countered with a measure to phase out the *bracero* program. When the House instead passed a simple two-year extension of it, Minnesota senator Eugene McCarthy led a strong challenge in the Senate. In September 1960, the program was extended—but for only six months, until December 1961.[64]

AWOC Strikes

The timing was therefore excellent when AWOC began organizing in earnest in the spring of 1960. For strategy, Smith was now on his own; Galarza had resigned in a wrangle with Meany that resulted in the revocation of NAWU's charter. As a result, Meany could release AWOC dues he had previously impounded, money that could now be used to defray organizing costs. Thus strengthened, and expecting the imminent end of the *bracero* program, Smith initiated a strike wave more extensive than anything California agriculture had seen since the early 1930s. Smith's organizers targeted the workers who gathered each morning at Central Valley "shape-up" points, where they could be hired by labor contractors who would board them onto buses for transport to the fields. This was one of few settings where an organizer could speak with them as a group, as Smith had done outside auto plant gates, a tactic with which he was familiar. As it happened, however, the workers at the shape-up points were mostly the Anglo ladder crews and fruit tramps who returned each year for the tree fruit harvests. They were a dustbowl remnant in an increasingly Mexican workforce. This greatly limited AWOC's potential reach.

Smith's approach was as follows: before calling a strike, he would contact the grower or appropriate association, such as the Cherry Association or Canning Peach Association, demand a $1.25 per hour minimum wage, and, since most of the work was piece rate, ask the grower or association to bargain. When the employers refused, organizers would converge on the shape-up points, pass out leaflets, and urge workers to strike to raise wages. Sometimes AWOC would "salt" supporters among the crew, who would then organize walkouts from the fields or orchards.[65]

When a crew walked out, AWOC notified the California Department of Employment, which sent out investigators. If they certified that workers had left their jobs in a labor dispute, the department was legislatively barred from referring replacements.[66] More important, federal law (PL 78) provided that the U.S. Department of Labor could not permit *braceros* at the site of a labor dispute that "seriously affects the operations in which they are engaged."[67] Although the language of this law was subject to interpretation by various agencies and was the object of litigation, AWOC nevertheless succeeded in using this handle to get *braceros* removed from over half the sites in which they had been working before a walkout. AWOC also got them barred as replacement workers at those sites.[68] AWOC organizers spread strikes from Stockton cherries in May, to Fresno peaches in June, to Yuba City pears in July, to Tracy tomatoes in August, to Lodi grapes in October, and to Strathmore olives in November[69]—99 strikes in that first year, of which 92 were certified and in which more than 5,000 workers took part.[70] But they did not demand union recognition; when a grower raised wages, the organizers would just move on.

Taken by surprise, many growers did raise wages. And that earned AWOC a reputation among farm workers. The strikes also showed that farm workers were willing to strike, especially Anglos and Filipinos already organized enough to take advantage of union support. Consequently, they put pressure on the *bracero* program. Yet these strikes did not produce contracts or a stable membership. They were subject to the same limitations as earlier strikes led by the IWW, the CAIWU, and the NFLU. Gains were made where short-term shortages gave workers the labor market power to raise wages, but AWOC did not find a way to turn this short-term labor market power into long-term change. Once a crop was harvested or lost, AWOC's power was gone. Moreover, workers were targeted based less on their characteristics as workers than on the kinds of workplaces that organizers deemed favorable for organizing; as a result, little was done to organize the resident Mexican families that formed the growing core of the farm workforce. In June 1960, AWOC claimed it had signed up 4,000 members. After a union audit, Meany adjusted the figure to 3,000.[71] It was not a lot.

Return to the Imperial Valley

That winter, Clive Knowles of the UPWA asked Smith to collaborate in a drive among lettuce workers in the Imperial Valley.[72] Because Smith had focused on the workplace rather than the community, he had no other winter organizing plan. He therefore put his staff at the disposal of Knowles, who assumed field command.[73] A group of lettuce workers, or *lechugeros*, led by Francisco "El Machete" Olivares, a farm worker veteran of the Imperial Valley melon strike a decade earlier, came to the UPWA after growers had announced a change in the pay system for the winter harvest that would begin in December.[74] At the peak, some 10,000 workers—7,500 *braceros* and 2,500 domestics—harvested 40,000 acres of lettuce.[75] The year before, the *braceros* were paid 80 cents per hour, and the domestic workers earned a piece were of 25 cents per box, which allowed them to make up to $3 an hour. This year, however, in response to UPWA complaints that *braceros* were discriminated against, the Imperial Valley Growers Association announced that everyone would be paid 90 cents per hour. Over 800 workers turned out to a meeting called by the UPWA to demand restoration of the piece rate and an hourly minimum rate of $1.25.

Although the Imperial Valley had become an organizer's grave-yard—for CAIWU in 1934 and the NFLU in 1951—Knowles was impressed by the fact that AWOC had been getting *braceros* removed from the fields all summer. He thought, too, that the incoming Kennedy administration would be even more likely to enforce the ban against using *braceros* for strike breaking. Knowles' plan was to continue the wage strikes and *bracero* removal that Smith had been doing all summer. However, the scale he envisioned was larger. Because *braceros* far outnumbered domestic workers in the lettuce fields, his strategy relied far less on worker support than on the union's ability to use its political power to move the federal government to radically constrict the labor market.

The lettuce season got under way in December. The organizers waited to make their move, however, until the Department of Labor was about to change hands with Kennedy's inauguration. On January 5, 500 workers voted at an AWOC-UPWA meeting to strike on January 16 if their demands were not met. Their demands included $1.25 an hour, union recognition, sanitary facilities, rest periods, transportation, seniority, and a hiring hall. The first grower targeted for a strike was Bruce Church, Inc., a major Salinas, Yuma Valley, and Imperial Valley lettuce shipper. On January 13, the state certified that 83 of Church's 98 domestic workers had struck. On January 16, the U.S. Department of Labor ordered all 600 of the Church *braceros* out. Despite the fact that other growers loaned Church crews and offered to buy his crop, it appeared that the AWOC stratagem could work. At a mass meeting later that day, the union announced plans to expand the strike; within the next 10 days, as the new administration took office, it struck 13 more companies. Of 696 domestic workers, 367 went on strike, placing access to 2,052 *braceros* at risk. By January 27, nine growers had lost their *bracero* certifications, and *braceros* were withdrawn from the fields of two more at the request of the Mexican government.

The Imperial Valley growers fought back. They convinced a Superior Court judge to ban picketing at the Church ranch. The first arrests came on February 3, when 250 strikers blocked the entrance of a labor camp that housed 500 *braceros*. The pickets disobeyed an order to disperse by Sheriff Bud Hughes, who was backed by a posse of over 100 highway patrol officers, sheriff's deputies, and other armed citizens. Hughes then picked out 13 leaders and arrested them for unlawful assembly. These included Knowles, 5 AWOC organizers, and 2 UPWA organizers.[76]

The growers also made surprising headway with the new administration. A Department of Labor order to remove 1,700 *braceros* from the fields of the 15 growers struck up to that point was immediately suspended by President John F. Kennedy's new labor secretary, Arthur Goldberg, who had been just two weeks on the job. Rather than removal, Goldberg called for an emergency meeting of the parties to "resolve the dispute."[77] The next week, this took place, although the growers' representatives refused to talk to the union people. Undersecretary Willard Wirtz instead met with each side separately.[78]

The outcome was a surprise. Goldberg ordered the removal of *braceros* from the growers' struck fields, but not from the fields of struck growers. In other words, *braceros* had to be removed from the particular field at which a strike had been certified but could be moved to other fields of the same company. Since lettuce shippers harvest multiple fields in overlapping sequence, they could keep their *braceros*. In the worst case, they could sell the crop in a struck field to another grower, who would be free to harvest it since he had not been struck there.[79] Commenting on this reversal of Secretary Mitchell's far more activist policy, the *Imperial Valley News* declared: "Growers are now said to feel that Secretary Goldberg is more sympathetic to their cause than was his predecessor James Mitchell."[80]

Frustrated, AWOC and UPWA organizers tried to get Mexico to exercise its right under the Migrant Labor Agreement to remove its nationals from strike zones to protect their health and safety. Strikers ran through the Corona *bracero* camp swinging broomsticks and attacking the camp manager, a labor contractor, and several *braceros*.[81] Although the raid—plus a federal court order limiting what the U.S. Labor Department could do—got the Mexican government involved, it also gave local law enforcement a license to act. Later that night, Sheriff Hughes raided the El Centro Labor Temple, breaking down the door and arresting 5 organizers, including Knowles again. Arrests continued over the next few days, eventually reaching 38. The charges included assault with a deadly weapon, felonious assault, trespassing, kidnapping, riot, and aggravated assault. Bail for all defendants came to $258,875, an amount far beyond what the unions could raise.

By mid-February, with 70 percent of the harvest complete—and 3,000 acres of lettuce plowed under, because of what the growers called "poor market conditions in the East"—the Mexican government demanded the withdrawal of its citizens from the employ of struck growers. It filed protests with the U.S. Departments of Labor and State and halted recruitment of further *braceros*. The Labor Department was under the gun, and on February 24, it finally withdrew authorization for the employment of *braceros* in any field affected by a strike. On March 5, Goldberg withdrew authorization for *braceros* not just from struck fields, but from all growers struck to that point. He said, "We must maintain friendly relations with this great power to the south.... [T]his is the dominant consideration in this situation." Had such an order come early in February, it might have brought victory to the union. But by early March, the strike was substantially over, with most of the leaders in jail or out on bail. On March 17, Smith and Knowles called it off.[82]

a little too late : strike over w/o victory

The strike had inflicted economic losses on the growers, but it had not stopped the lettuce harvest. It resulted in negative publicity for the union, led to the arrest of over 50 strikers and union officials, and run up fines and legal bills approaching $50,000, which the AFL-CIO had to pay. Perhaps most important to George Meany, it embarrassed the new Democratic administration. (Knowles claims he heard afterward that Kennedy had said to Goldberg, "Get rid of that thing, get it out of our hair, we don't have time for it.")[83] At a February Executive Council meeting, Meany suggested that it might be time to close AWOC down. The council voted to leave it up to him.[84] Fathers McCullough and McDonald, who had joined the picket lines, reaped a similar reward. They were transferred from their parishes in San Jose and Stockton because the bishop of San Diego protested their role in the Imperial Valley.[85]

For the lettuce strike to succeed, it would have needed the steady support of the Department of Labor—which, if it were to act, would have required steady pressure from the AFL-CIO. Other than Meany, though, no one in the AWOC leadership had any control over this. Besides, Meany had other fish to fry.

In the wake of the failed lettuce strike, Meany, instead of trying to improve upon AWOC's strategy, cut off the organization's funding. The absence of decision makers with a strong personal commitment to devising a winning strategy for organizing farm workers, compounded by the absence of organizational incentives or venues for creative thinking left AWOC without the strategic capacity to make the next move.

AWOC does not have means to succeed

Nonetheless, AWOC's experience spurred others to try different approaches. On the one hand, as modest as its success had been, it created an opportunity for the Teamsters to revive their old "responsible union" strategy. On the other hand, the limitations under which

AWOC labored inspired others, in particular Cesar Chavez, to commit to finding a way to do what AWOC could not.

The Teamsters

AWOC's efforts in the Imperial Valley did convince one lettuce shipper, Bud Antle, Inc., to sign a contract covering its field workers. But not with AWOC. The contract was with Local 890 of the Western Conference of Teamsters (WCT). The first contract to emerge from the 1960s wave of organizing went to the Teamsters, not because their leaders had figured out a new way to organize farm workers, but because they had recognized an opportunity for their familiar strategy of organizing employers.

By this time, the Teamsters were no longer affiliated with the rest of the national labor movement. The AFL-CIO had expelled them on grounds of corruption in 1957. An investigation by a U.S. Senate select committee[86] led to the retirement of Teamster president Dave Beck, his imprisonment for embezzlement, and two criminal indictments against his vice president, James R. Hoffa.[87] When Hoffa was nonetheless elected to succeed Beck, the AFL-CIO suspended the affiliation. The suspension, however, only freed the Teamsters to compete more aggressively with other unions. And having grown dramatically over the decade—by 1960, the Teamsters had a national membership of 1.48 million, an annual income of more than $7 million, and a staff of more than 10,000 paid representatives in the United States and Canada[88]—the Teamsters had the resources for a fight.[89]

Bud Antle provided them with an opportunity. Like other major lettuce shippers in the Imperial and Salinas valleys, Antle was a major user of *braceros*. A former dustbowl migrant himself, Antle was a maverick within the industry and no stranger to labor conflicts. He held contracts with the Teamsters and the UPWA for packinghouses, coolers, and truck drivers, but he was also among the first to figure out how to turn union work into non-union work by moving vegetable packing from the sheds to the fields. In the early 1950s, he had replaced lettuce packing in unionized sheds with packing in the fields by *braceros*.

But in 1960, Antle faced bankruptcy, because the year before he had to settle a $12 million complaint for trying to corner the lettuce market in violation of a state marketing order. He was also embroiled in a conflict with the UPWA over an attempt to set up a non-union carrot-packing operation.[90] During the Imperial Valley lettuce strike, he offered to sign a contract with the UPWA covering lettuce and celery field packers. The local union representative was interested, but regional UPWA officials were collaborating with AWOC, and they refused. When the two unions then struck 18 Imperial Valley lettuce shippers, Antle was among them. At the strike's end in February 1961, and again in March, Antle offered the UPWA a contract covering the lettuce and celery packers, a proposal the union rejected each time.[91]

So in April, as the Salinas Valley lettuce harvest began, Antle was worried that AWOC would resume its lettuce strike. And when the UPWA sought the removal of 1,000 *braceros* in support of a Salinas strawberry strike it had organized, Antle made his move.[92] On May 4, he signed a contract covering lettuce and celery packers—not with any of the unions he thought might strike him, but with Bud Kenyon, president of Teamsters Local 890.

Although it was a multiyear agreement, the Teamsters' contract with Antle was of little, if any, use to the workers it supposedly covered. It dealt only with wages, left control entirely in the employer's hands, and excluded *braceros*. Since Antle's lettuce and celery crews were *braceros*, the contract actually covered only a few machine operators. By insulating Antle from claims of a domestic labor dispute, however, the contract secured his supply of *braceros*. It also committed the Teamsters to help Antle get *braceros* if needed, making them the only union in America to support the program.[93]

Three days after signing the contract, Antle resigned from the Salinas Valley Grower-Shipper Association before it could expel him. Association spokespeople said they already had expelled him, appalled that he would break ranks on a labor matter. The growers also raised wages to forestall further labor problems,[94] which hardly endeared Antle to them. But Antle had acquired new friends. Two years later, in May 1963, he would receive a $1 million loan from the Teamsters' Central States Pension Fund.[95]

The Teamsters' official rationale for signing a field contract was similar to the rationale offered by UPWA for its alliance with AWOC: jobs were moving from sheds into fields due to the discrepancy between field and shed wage rates, and the union was just following jobs which were already in its purview. The Teamsters, however, were not proposing an alliance with a field workers' union to bring field wages up (so that it would not matter where the work was done). They were not proposing to organize field workers at all. The Teamsters' strategy was simply to make sure that no one else did—and, thus, that no other group of workers in the industry's interconnected chain of production could impinge upon the *help the growers*

Teamsters' own freedom of maneuver or to compete with them for the employer's dollar. This is what the Teamsters meant by "securing their jurisdiction."

The strategic emphasis on securing jurisdiction emerged from the difficult struggle to organize the chaotic trucking industry. Because truck transport was integrated into almost all aspects of the economy, the union could not limit its jurisdiction either to a specific category of workers or to a single industry. And it could secure its jurisdiction ① and prevent other unions from intruding on it only by organizing—or keeping others from organizing—an ever-wider scope of economic activity.

A second way in which the Teamsters learned to secure their jurisdiction was to take advantage of opportunities created by other unions' ② efforts to organize. Since Teamster leaders saw it as the union's job to keep employers in business—and not to pursue social goals contrary to the interests of employers—the Teamsters union offered an attractive alternative for employers hoping to avoid dealing with a more radical labor organization. The Teamsters called it "responsible unionism." Often, they would sign contracts to get in the door with an employer by focusing only on wages and leaving issues of control entirely in the hands of the employer.[96] This was how the Teamsters had established their key position in agriculture—in fights with the CIO in the 1930s and 1940s.

To the top Teamster leaders, this defensive strategy also seemed more appropriate to agriculture than did an offensive one, because they believed that organizing field workers was a hopeless undertaking. As labor scholar Don Garnel reports, Einar Mohn, the new president of the Teamsters' Western Conference,

> had studied this backwards and forwards, and he said, "You know, this is almost going to be a losing proposition. In the first place there's a high turnover of people. It's not like a trucking company that continues to use drivers over the years. Down there it's like every year you've got different workers coming in and working there, so even if you organize the group the prior year, they are not going to be around the next year."[97]

Because Mohn had been appointed to his new job by Hoffa in return for supporting Hoffa's election, his primary focus at the time of the Antle contract was on securing his base in the Western Conference. Supporting a local initiative by Bud Kenyon, who was a close friend of one of Mohn's more powerful division chiefs, was a convenient way to do that—and a way to do something about organizing, without having to do too much.

On top of this Mohn was also the Beck protégé who had led the 1946 campaign to drive the CIO from California's canneries. Protecting jurisdiction by top-down organizing—that is, convincing employers rather than workers to sign up with him—was a strategy with which he was very comfortable. Mohn, who was 55 in 1961, had been educated as a bacteriologist. After organizing the dairy in which he worked, he was recruited by Beck to become his "smart guy." Beck brought him to Washington to be his executive assistant in 1952, and from there Mohn rose as a strategist, negotiator, and administrator. He became a polished executive, active in Democratic politics,[98] did not curse or drink heavily and was known as a straight arrow, a Teamster leader without the mob connections for which other Teamster leaders were known.[99] He was, in other words, the kind of man with whom employers could happily sit down to learn what the Teamsters really wanted.

Accountability within the Teamsters operated through a large, complex, and highly politicized bureaucracy. Although local union leaders and the International's officers in Washington, DC, were elected, accountability to the rank and file was extremely limited. The International's president had the authority to take over locals and keep appointing loyal officials until they had enough of a base to get elected. And voting for the International's officers occurred only at conventions at five-year intervals. The real power in the Teamsters lay with the union's staff—at the local and international levels and in the WCT, an intermediate level of union bureaucracy that itself had 13 divisions to coordinate organizing, bargaining, and legislative work.[100]

Although authority within the staff appeared to be top-down, it was actually more complicated. Leaders of local unions constituted the WCT governing body, but the International's president appointed the WCT chair, who also held other elective positions within the union. The president of a local union could also serve as a general organizer appointed by the International's president and a division director appointed by the WCT chair—with each position bringing its own salary. In this political structure, power was a product of continual negotiation, and accountability was governed by the fluctuating relationships within the union bureaucracy. It is illustrative that the decision to sign with Antle was made not by a single leader, but by Local 890 president Bud Kenyon, Cannery Division director Peter Andrade, and Western Conference of Teamsters president Einar Mohn.

However, in 1961, the priorities of most WCT and national Teamster leaders lay somewhere other than in organizing field workers. Mohn was focused on the Western Conference—which Hoffa had recently appointed him to head and where his control was unstable, dependent as it was on maneuvering among local and regional leaders—as well as on efforts by Hoffa himself to establish his own base on the West Coast in order to take control of the bargaining and pension fund administration that the WCT had previously handled.

The local Teamster leaders were more concerned with what seemed to be a threat to an employer whose business they wanted to protect. Bud Kenyon, a former barber, had moved steadily through the ranks to become the leader of Local 890. In 1961, he was 50 years old and well connected with white workers and employers in the produce industry.[101] His friend, predecessor, and now boss, Pete Andrade, had organized sheds and drivers in the past and was similarly connected in the vegetable industry.[102] But they too had limited interest in or knowledge of field workers.

Indeed, Mohn, as he later declared, was "not sure how effective a union can be when it is composed of Mexican-Americans and Mexican nationals with temporary visas."[103] For white local Teamster leaders, which most of them were, an influx of Mexican field workers into their locals would only be a cause for concern, especially when it came to getting reelected.

The Bud Antle contract was no organizing breakthrough, and it revealed little about the Teamsters' capacity to devise effective strategy in a changing environment. Much could already be discerned, however, about the strategic capacity that the Teamsters would bring to the challenge of union organizing when they did later tackle it. Their leaders lacked both the proactive motivation to organize farm workers and good information about the farm worker world. And they were not connected to networks that could have brought such perspectives to them.

Moreover, the Teamsters deliberated about strategy in a fashion—not unlike that of AWOC—which excluded broader input. The style is perhaps best articulated in this description by Ralph James of how Hoffa ran his local in earlier years:

> Hoffa ran his local in much the same way a competent old-time sheriff kept law and order with his half a dozen deputies. The job is done well, but not by formal rules. The sheriff's mind is a storehouse of knowledge about the power centers in his town; he knows when to use them and how to steer around them if necessary. These are not secrets to be shared

with even the most trusted lieutenant. He does not call his entourage in for "policy discussions"; the deputies are not asked their opinions on appropriate action. Instead, their chief thinks things through as best he can and then acts with determination—albeit sometimes crudely. His lieutenants are given precise orders, and, when the need is great, they are all assigned overlapping tasks. Often they do not comprehend why they are performing certain functions; wasted time and effort may be common place, but they know it is important that they do precisely what they are told. They depend upon their chief for status and reward, and he relies upon them for information and action.[104]

Local unions and executive boards held monthly meetings, the Western Conference of Teamsters and its councils and divisions met regularly, and a national convention met every two years. Although these deliberative bodies could be venues for developing strategy, they were usually settings in which union officials ratified privately negotiated maneuvers. They were also limited to the professionals, for as Beck had once explained, "Unions are big business. Why should truck drivers and bottle washers be allowed to make big decisions affecting union policy? Would any corporation allow it?"[105] *Path to failure*

When organizing resources were needed, it was usually the International that provided them.[106] Although it cost little to get the Antle contract signed, that would not always be the case. Indeed, outlays for organizing could be considerable, because a large professional staff ran the Teamsters, and the role of volunteer activists was very limited. Moreover, the Teamsters' staff was compensated on an entirely different scale than AWOC's. In 1960, Teamster organizers were paid $20,000 a year, compared to AWOC's $4,000.[107] Since these resources ultimately came from existing members (and existing budgets), not from prospective members, money spent on organizing could become a political issue. On the other hand, a local union had a lot to gain if, as was the case with the Antle contract, additional dues could be generated without new overhead.

If the Antle contract was neither a breakthrough nor evidence of a successful strategic capacity of the Teamsters, it was evidence that the Imperial Valley strike had done real damage—and that the Teamsters posed a challenge to any other union trying to take advantage of it. Given the circumstance, it is surprising that AWOC planned no follow-up. A few AFL-CIO spokespeople decried the Teamster incursion, but even though Mohn said the contract meant that the Teamsters were in the farm worker organizing business to stay,[108] neither AWOC nor anyone else in the AFL-CIO made an organized response. On the other hand, neither did the Teamsters. In spite of the fact that they had the field to themselves for the next year and a half, they made no further moves to organize farm workers until 1966, in the wake of UFW successes. The Teamsters' quiescence for five years—until they were sought out again by an employer faced with a new threat—is one more indication of how little commitment they had to farm worker organizing.

AWOC IN HIATUS

In June 1961, acting on George Meany's recommendation, the AFL-CIO Executive Council voted to cut off further funding for AWOC and transfer its members to other unions. Union auditors had discovered that AWOC's membership numbers had been inflated. According to Meany, the numbers, the legal fees and fines, the jurisdictional issues, and what he argued was a lack of return on $500,000 invested convinced him that it was time to cut his losses. Still, the Antle contract was evidence of the impact of the Imperial Valley strike. It was the AWOC strike wave that Senator Williams' committee, in its 1961 report on migratory labor, cited as "serious unrest in our agricultural economy," requiring action.[109] AWOC had inspired hope among farm workers, inflicted losses on growers, and put the heat on the Kennedy administration. And it is possible, although the evidence is only circumstantial, that Meany's moves were part of a deal cut with the Kennedy administration, promising to curb AWOC in return for an orderly phasing out of the *bracero* program.

Smith, who remained AWOC's director, announced that he would stay in the fields until his funds were exhausted and then organize farm workers for any union that would hire him.[110] But while another 47 strikes were recorded in California in 1961, only a small proportion got certified because no union was in the fields with enough resources to get it done.[111] The 1961 season was thus the first in two years in which the deployment of *braceros* was unimpeded. Ironically, it would prove to be AWOC's most strategically creative period.

In Washington, the struggle over the *bracero* program continued. Over the objections of *bracero* supporters, who proposed a four-year continuation of the existing program, the administration proposed measures which would increase the secretary of labor's authority to intervene in the *bracero* program to improve wages and working conditions for domestic farm workers. After lengthy hearings, Congress voted to extend the program for two more years, until December 1963, but with new conditions. Amendments increased the labor secretary's power to establish minimum wages, required that domestic workers be offered the same wages and conditions as *braceros* before *braceros* could be hired, and banned the use of *braceros* for year-round work or on machinery.[112] And although President Kennedy signed the extension, he declared that he did it only in deference to diplomatic relations with Mexico. The president directed Secretary Goldberg to make full use of his new authority to protect domestic workers.[113]

braces cont.

Meanwhile in California, AWOC was left to do what it could with what remained of its resources. To support himself and his research director, Henry Anderson, Smith drew on dues money he had squirreled away. Anderson assumed the leadership of a team of AWOC volunteers: former organizers, farm workers, and a community of UC students living in a Stockton "harvest house." They began to implement an organizing strategy closer to that of McCullough than anything AWOC had done up to that point. It was based on mobilizing volunteer support among farm workers, farm worker advocacy groups, and within the labor movement itself.[114] The volunteers targeted resident Mexican families, organized them as area councils in Stockton, Modesto, Porterville, and elsewhere, and focused on addressing community concerns such as housing and health care.

Their six-month-long organizing drive culminated with a three-day conference of more than 200 farm workers and supporters in Strathmore—the California olive capital—in December 1961. The purpose was to "compare ideas about things that had worked, and things that hadn't worked, and things that might work in the future" and hear "inspirational speakers."[115] The keynote speaker, the famed socialist Norman Thomas, had attended a similar California farm labor conference 25 years before. Attendees also heard from Father McCullough, Galarza, and Chavez.[116]

One paradoxical result of the conference was a decision to send a delegation to the AFL-CIO convention in Miami the following week to appeal for the restoration of AWOC's funding.[117] Observers report a moving appeal to the convention by AWOC organizer Maria Moreno. Adding to Moreno's voice were Eleanor Roosevelt and Walter Reuther. In response, Meany restored the funds, but he deferred any resumption of organizing for more than a year.[118] This delay is all the more remarkable because the Kennedy administration by then had renegotiated the Migrant Labor Agreement with Mexico. The administration won agreement to a six-month limit on any *bracero*'s stay in the

United States, increased occupational insurance benefits, and a guarantee that wages would not be set below a benchmark which the secretary of labor determined would avoid an adverse effect on domestic workers. The new agreement also spelled out a detailed procedure to govern the removal of *braceros* in the event of strikes and lockouts. As a specific response to AWOC's strike wave during the previous year, *braceros* would be removed wherever the secretary of labor determined that 50 percent of an employer's domestic workers were on strike.[119] In March 1962, Secretary Goldberg instituted the nation's first statewide adverse-effect rates, ranging from 60 cents an hour in Arkansas to $1 an hour in California.[120] Compared with 1961, when 315,846 *braceros* were imported, the number for 1962 would be cut to 194,978, of which 116,000 worked in California.[121]

to support strikes

Instead of taking advantage of this opportunity, however, Meany appointed a new AWOC organizing director, C. Al Green, whose first priority was to help reelect California governor Pat Brown in November. Green fired Anderson, closed down the area councils, and returned to AWOC's old way of doing business. (He kept Smith on staff as an assistant until Smith retired a year later.) With the winding down of the *bracero* program, the opportunity was there, but with the exception of a brief foray into the asparagus fields in April, AWOC did no new organizing for another full year.[122]

didn't take advantage

THE FARM WORKERS ASSOCIATION (FWA)

In April 1962, convinced that the AFL-CIO would never stick with the task of organizing farm workers, Cesar Chavez and his collaborators launched the FWA. Within a year, they devised a strategy to build a base of support among Mexican farm worker families. And although their initial approach was not that different from that of McCullough or Anderson, the story that FWA leaders began to tell—about the nature of the challenge, why they were called upon to deal with it, and why they had hope of succeeding—was. This story was not only new; it was rooted in their own experience as Mexican immigrants and in their depth of commitment and clarity of understanding, all of which set the FWA leadership apart. Most important, however, the FWA leaders structured their work in such a way as to develop the capacity to keep adapting their strategy until they found a way to deal with the limited labor market power, the marginal political influence, and the racial isolation that had bedeviled almost every previous organizing

fed of Ag workers

why different

attempt. Unlike most of the AWOC and Teamster organizers, they did not think they had the answers; they knew they would have to learn how to get the answers to accomplish the goal they had set for themselves.

The story of the launching of the FWA properly begins in 1958, with the UPWA's decision to fund a special CSO project led by Cesar Chavez. This project was intended to support the organizing of citrus packinghouse workers in Oxnard.[123] The initiative got under way with house meetings, a voter registration drive for the November 1958 election, citizenship classes, and the establishment of a social services center. However, it was clear from its first general meeting—attended by 600 people—what the big issue in Oxnard was jobs. The *braceros* had them all.

Drawing on his experience in issue campaigns conducted over the previous five years, Chavez devised a direct-action strategy in consultation with Fred Ross. He mobilized workers to document the fact that California's Farm Placement Service had been referring them to jobs that did not exist—and to dramatize the situation with marches and pickets. In January 1959, just as Democratic governor Edmond G. Brown took office, workers picketed the head of the Farm Placement Service when he appeared at an installation of local Farm Bureau officers. With the support of Democrats whom the CSO helped to elect, such as State Controller Alan Cranston, Chavez also focused a spotlight on the director of the California Department of Employment, which oversaw Farm Placement. When the federal Bureau of Employment Security investigated, Chavez presented the evidence to support his charges. In April 1959, the 100–200 people participating in daily marches began to conduct "work-ins" on ranches that refused to hire them. Meanwhile, the marches grew larger and culminated in the burning of job referral cards, which made for television coverage embarrassing to growers and politicians alike. In May, when President Eisenhower's labor secretary, James Mitchell, came to visit, workers picketed him, demanding jobs.[124]

In the end, the southern California director of the Farm Placement Service, William Cunningham, was fired for taking bribes from growers. His boss, Ed Hayes, was forced out because of his ties to growers. And the Brown administration confirmed that—as Fred Ross later put it—the "service had been placing Mexicans illegally in preference to domestic workers, who were deliberately horned off by people … whose duty it is to assure them of their rights."[125] The growers began to hire more local people, arranging to pick them up at the CSO office, turning it into a de facto hiring hall.

In one year in Oxnard, Chavez recruited 950 members, who each made an initial dues payment of $3.50; enrolled 650 in citizenship classes; organized a credit union; operated an ongoing rummage sale, which cleared $200 per month; maintained a service center; registered 300 new voters; and instigated a statewide investigation of the Farm Placement Service.[126]

Yet, when he tried to build on these successes by organizing the workers into a union, neither the UPWA, which was committed to AWOC, nor the CSO agreed. So in August 1959, at the peak of his success but lacking funds to continue, Chavez abandoned the project to return to the CSO, where he became executive director.[127]

Besides expanding CSO educational and service center programs, Chavez took advantage of the fact that 1960 was a presidential election year and conducted a major voter registration drive, much of it funded by the AFL-CIO. Since California voters were registered by deputy registrars, few of whom were Mexican American, the CSO recruited, trained, and qualified some 500 new registrars. These registrars put in some 120,000 hours of work to register 137,096 new voters, mostly Mexican-American Democrats. Although CSO had the community base, it was the financial support of the AFL-CIO that made it possible to hire the 11 full-time and 9 part-time workers to coordinate this effort.[128] The registration drive turned into get-out-the-vote campaigns to elect Mexican Americans to local office. Consequently, Mexican Americans began to emerge as a constituency to be wooed by statewide and national candidates—as in the Viva Kennedy drive of October 1960, in which Chavez and others from the CSO were active.

Building upon its success in the November 1960 elections, the CSO then launched a major legislative initiative to secure the extension of old-age pensions for noncitizens. The fate of these noncitizens—the immigrant generation of the 1920s and 1930s, parents of many CSO leaders—had become a major issue among Mexican Americans. Thus, when Dolores Huerta, at this point the CSO's legislative director, found an able mentor and collaborator in San Francisco assemblyman Phil Burton, the initiative succeeded.[129]

In the face of these successes, Chavez wanted to continue the work of building a farm workers union, which he had begun in Oxnard. The fact that the *bracero* program had been extended yet again gave him little confidence that waiting for the program to end was good strategy. On the contrary, his own experience in Oxnard in 1959 and the AWOC strike wave of 1960 both suggested that mobilizing farm workers themselves to take direct action could hasten the end of the program.[130] When the

AFL-CIO withdrew its support for AWOC in June 1961, Chavez saw it as evidence that the labor movement could not be trusted to do the job.[131] On the other hand, the effectiveness and commitment of AWOC's volunteers—after funding was halted—was apparent at their December 1961 Strathmore conference, which Chavez, Ross, and Huerta attended.

The civil rights movement had also innovated a whole set of new tactics for making racial justice claims. In the spring of 1960, SNCC's sit-ins captured the nation's attention, and in 1961, the Congress of Racial Equality (CORE) launched its first freedom rides. Both tactics used local direct action to mobilize outside pressure on local authorities. The potential of religious alliances was evident not only in the role of the churches in the civil rights movement, but in the organizing interest of the CMM, for which Ross and Chavez had been providing training for years. In 1961, Chris Hartmire became the Migrant Ministry's new director and committed himself to the cause. As he later said, his training with Ross and Chavez had engendered "a belief in what CSO was doing. And a desire to stay connected. I went to almost every board meeting and convention of CSO from then on."[132]

In early 1962, Chavez decided it was the time—or at least his time—to begin organizing farm workers. The CSO's 35 chapters and organizing committees could provide a base on which to build.[133] So in consultation with Ross, Huerta, and others, he submitted a farm worker organizing proposal to the CSO annual convention in Calexico on March 16. Although the board approved the proposal, the CSO's urban leaders argued that the organization should cooperate with existing unions, not try to replace them, and the convention voted down the Chavez proposal.[134]

As a result, Chavez resigned to do the job himself. He moved his family from Los Angeles to Delano, a town of 12,000, where he and his wife had family who would support them. Located at the southern end of the San Joaquin Valley, Delano was also at the heart of the table grape industry, an industry that provided longer-term employment than most crops. Delano growers used few *braceros*, relying instead on resident Mexican families, migrants from Texas, and Filipino field-packing crews. It was a good place to begin organizing if the target was the resident Mexican farm worker families who were a growing part of the workforce.[135]

Although Chavez had savings of only $1,200, he rejected offers of outside funding, relying on his family, colleagues, and networks built through his work with the CSO to support his effort.[136] Katherine Peake, a supporter of CSO, offered him $50,000 but, concerned with becoming dependent on "outside" support, he turned it down.[137] He also turned down a $21,000-per-year job to direct the Peace Corps in a four-country region of South America.[138] His core team consisted of his wife, Helen, and their eight children; his cousin Manuel, a former used car salesman; and his brother Richard, a Delano carpenter. Ross, Huerta, and Gilbert Padilla continued their paid work on CSO projects, but also served as volunteer organizers with Chavez.[139] Julio Hernandez, Antonio Orendain, Rodrigo Terronez, and other farm worker officers of CSO chapters became key volunteer organizers as well.

Every one of them was a Mexican American or a Mexican immigrant who had grown up or now lived in California's agricultural valleys. Many knew what Renato Rosaldo called the "borderland" experience of growing up Mexican American in the 1940s.[140] All were family people, with children. Manuel Chavez, who had been raised with Cesar like a brother, sold produce and used cars. He was 37 years old and had been in and out of prison for several years when Chavez recruited him in 1962. Padilla had been in the U.S. Army in Japan and was working as a cleaner in Los Baños when Chavez first recruited him for the CSO six years earlier. He was now, at 35, an organizer for the CSO. Julio Hernandez, 41, and his wife, Josefina, had been labor contractors in Corcoran, where they joined the CSO. The backgrounds of these first FWA organizers were thus varied; all had in common, however, a personal stake in the outcome of this project.

Chavez also invited Chris Hartmire, the new Migrant Ministry director, to be a full participant in creating the new group. In June, the Reverend Jim Drake, another graduate of Union Theological Seminary, came to work for Hartmire and was assigned to Chavez for training. He served as Chavez's driver for much of the summer, and he too became deeply involved in the FWA. Both Hartmire and Drake were in their 20s and from white, middle-class backgrounds— Drake had grown up in California's Coachella Valley, where his family settled after leaving Oklahoma and where his father was a teacher and minister—but they shared a vocation to improve the lives of farm workers.[141] And their inclusion in the FWA's strategic conversations expanded the organization's perspective.

The organizers began by conducting a census of farm workers in each of their communities, asking them how much they thought they should be earning and identifying those who showed some interest in organizing.[142] Chavez traveled from place to place to conduct the census, while the other organizers gathered the information in the communities in which they were working.[143] They followed with a house-meeting drive to develop a constituency for the new organization, recruit the leadership it would take to build it, and develop programs around which it could take shape.[144] House-meeting hosts were either CSO members with whom Chavez had worked during the previous 10 years or new contacts turned up through the census campaign— but most were members of resident Mexican farm worker families.[145] Although Delano was the home base, it was clear from the beginning that the association was to be statewide in scope. Indeed, its leaders may already have been thinking of expanding into a national organization, as the CSO had.

The six-month house-meeting drive began in April and culminated in a "founding convention" in the banquet hall of a Mexican restaurant in Fresno on September 30, 1962.[146] The convention was modeled on CSO proceedings and included an invocation, pledge of allegiance, adoption of Robert's Rules of Order, and taking of minutes. It was chaired by Chavez and conducted in Spanish. Three guests addressed the meeting: Father Ed Cown of Del Rey, Hartmire of the Migrant Ministry, and Jose Corea, the national president of the CSO. Chavez reported that 25,000 people had registered in the census.[147] The 200 farm worker delegates voted to organize farm workers, lobby for a farm worker minimum wage of $1.50 per hour, establish dues of $3.50 per month, and adopt a red, white, and black "farm worker eagle" flag and the motto "Viva la Causa." Dues would be used to develop death benefits, a credit union, a farm worker cooperative, and social service assistance for members. The new organization named itself the Asociación de Trabajadores Campesinos, the Farm Workers Association. The word *asociación*—not union—was selected to avoid discouraging workers who had had negative experiences in earlier unionization attempts and to avoid provoking any premature reaction from the growers. *Campesino* was descriptive of the Mexican peasantry, whose movement since the Mexican Revolution was evocative of land, dignity, and resistance.

Contexts

The meeting elected 11 temporary officers and charged them with drafting a constitution. These included a president, a secretary-treasurer, a general director, and 8 vice presidents, each responsible for a county. Chavez did not stand for election as president, choosing instead to serve as general director. J. L. Martinez of Sanger was elected president and Antonio Orendain, secretary-treasurer. The delegates also appointed Huerta as their legislative advocate, and they decided to pay General Director Chavez a salary of $60 per week plus $15 for gasoline.

FIGURE 3.2. Dolores Huerta registers delegates to the FWA founding convention, Fresno, 1962. *Source:* Walter P. Reuther Library, Wayne State University Archives

Three months later, the FWA reconvened for its constitutional convention at Our Lady of Guadalupe Church Hall in Delano,[148] adopted its new constitution, and elected permanent officers. Cesar Chavez was elected to the newly merged office of president and general director. Manuel Chavez was elected secretary-treasurer. Ten vice presidents were elected, including Rodrigo Terronez, Gilbert Padilla, Julio Hernandez, and Dolores Huerta. In addition, Frank Ortiz, Manuel Ayala, Julio Hernandez, Tomas Becerra, and Antonio Orendain were elected *vocales* (trustees).[149] Although the constitution provided that only farm workers could be elected to the board, Padilla and Huerta were exempted from this requirement at Chavez's request.

By this time, the FWA had also established a small benefit which would be paid upon the death of anyone in a member family: $1,000 for a head of family, $500 for a spouse, and $500 for each child from 6 months to 19 years. Each person in the family also had his or her own union card.

The preamble of the constitution, drawn from Pope Leo XIII's *Rerum Novarum*, read:

Rich men and masters should remember this—that to exercise pressure for the sake of gain upon the indigent and destitute, and to make one's profit out of the need of another, is condemned by all laws, human and divine. To defraud anyone of wages that are his due is a crime which cries to the avenging anger of heaven.

Objectives specified included uniting all farm workers; winning recognition; engaging in collective bargaining; engaging in cultural, civic, legislative, fraternal, economic, educational, charitable, welfare, and social activities; and guarding members' democratic rights and responsibilities.[150]

Chavez's salary was also raised to $75 per week, *cuando había fondos* (when/if there was money), and a credit card was provided for gasoline.[151] In an important deviation from the approach they had learned in the CSO, the FWA leaders modified Alinsky's model, in which full-time, hired organizers are supposed to act as offstage trainers and coaches but are limited to carrying out the will of elected volunteer leaders.[152] Chavez had been unhappy with that arrangement in the CSO. He was convinced that the organizers who were building an organization, especially a union, should have the authority to do the job as well as the accountability for doing it.[153] Having a full-time, elected general director was also closer to the union tradition in both Mexico and the United States. As Huerta later explained, "Cesar had studied the structure of the CSO...and he tried to correct his mistakes in the NFWA: mainly he wanted the people who did the work to make the decisions."[154]

The attention that FWA leaders devoted to getting the structure of their organization "right" reveals their deep commitment to organizing itself as a means of economic, political, and cultural empowerment and their mindfulness that they were doing something quite new. It was not only a matter of getting the growers to pay more money. They had to create an organizational mechanism that could achieve this and more. As Chavez later said, "A union is not simply getting enough workers to stage a strike. A union is building a group with a spirit and an existence all its own....a union must be built around the idea that people must do things by themselves, in order to help themselves."[155]

Thus, the FWA arrived at a strategy in early 1963: organize a self-sustaining farm worker organization rooted in farm worker families resident in local communities, and strengthen them through the provision of mutual benefits. Eventually, this organizational solidarity would be put to work in the labor market to get contracts from employers,[156] but FWA leaders assumed it would take at least five years to build enough strength to confront the growers.[157] The critical error that other farm worker organizers had made, they said, was trying to strike and organize at the same time.[158]

From the very beginning, the FWA leaders approached their strategic challenge differently from their rivals, especially in terms of learning. The AWOC leaders, despite the fact that the farm worker organizing environment was radically different from anything they knew, tried to organize as they always had. The same was true of the Teamsters' leaders. FWA leaders, however, knew they had to *learn* how to organize a union—not least because they had never done it before. As Chavez said:

> When we came to Delano, we said, "We're going to organize farm workers. We don't know how, but we have some ideas. We don't have anything planned because even life itself can't be planned, and we're dealing with a lot of lives, we're dealing with human beings."...You can't say that if you take steps one, two and three, then everything follows. That would be predicting human nature. No one can do that.[159]

Thus, they drew models and tactics from everything they knew: from Alinsky, from unions, from Catholic retreat training, from CSO. They borrowed the FWA death benefit from Mexican burial societies and fraternal lodges. They drew on cultural and religious traditions to begin telling the story of their new organization in flag, motto, name, and song.

Because FWA strategy was developed by a large and diverse team— very rare for such a small organization—it could draw on an unusual combination of identities, social networks, and organizing experiences, which extended from the farm worker community into the worlds of community organizers, Mexican-American activists, religious groups, and liberals throughout California. These networks combined strong ties to the farm worker community and the religious community with weak ties to many other groups that would play important roles in the organizing. Their combination of personal, vocational, and professional commitment infused the effort with a strong motivation to develop strategy that would make it work.

These characteristics of the FWA leadership distinguished it from AWOC and the Teamsters. The FWA was able to make more of its diversity than either AWOC or the Teamsters could have (had they had it) because the FWA strategized in an ongoing conversation anchored in regular board meetings, frequent inclusive strategy sessions, and annual conventions.[160] The commitment to this deliberative approach was based less on democratic theory than on the fact that the leaders knew they had to learn how to accomplish the mission they had undertaken, and they knew they would have to help each other figure it out as they went along.

In terms of resource flows, the FWA was more dependent on its constituency than were the other two groups. The FWA's financial resources were based on membership dues of $3.50 per month per family, collected in cash by local representatives. Dues entitled family members to the small death benefit, social services, and, eventually, access to a credit union and a newspaper. Chavez's personal savings and individual contributions from supporters supplemented these resources, but never outweighed them. The FWA's human resources at this point included one intermittently paid staff member. In addition, the Migrant Ministry paid Padilla part time and offered the services of Drake and Hartmire as they were available.[161] However, most of the organizing was done on a volunteer basis by board members, representatives, and other activists, requiring extraordinary levels of motivation. These human resources flowed upward from the base, just as the FWA's financial resources did.

Chavez, of course, played a key role. Critical to his leadership in this period was his ability to identify, recruit, and develop other leaders, while holding his team together so that its diversity could become a source of strength and not of division or paralysis. Chavez, who modeled the depth of personal commitment required to fulfill this mission, was a virtuoso in the craft of organizing: gifted in building relationships, possessed of a rich strategic imagination, but firmly anchored in the practical reality of what does and does not work. He set a high standard for the organization. Yet during the years of this account, the FWA never became a one-man show, nor did Chavez want it to become one.

characristics of a leader

Accountability in the FWA was thus based on the leaders' responsiveness to farm worker members and to those doing the day-to-day work of the organization: each other. FWA leaders earned their legitimacy based on election by the constituency they were organizing and commitment to doing the work of organizing that constituency. On a day-to-day basis, they were accountable to Chavez as general director and to each other in board meetings. The group had other allies as well, but it never found itself so dependent on any one of them that an ally's priorities could supplant its own.

CONCLUSION

In summary, then, AWOC, the Teamsters, and the FWA each took advantage of the new opportunities for farm worker organizing that emerged in the late 1950s and early 1960s. However, they responded with different strategies that resulted from their differences in strategic capacity. At this point in the narrative, there is not yet enough evidence to distinguish the effectiveness of one leadership team or strategy from another. Nonetheless, the relationship of strategic capacity to strategy is already plain. The strategies of AWOC and the Teamsters projected the experiences, networks, and repertoires of the leaders who chose them in the absence of accountability structures, resource flows, or deliberative processes that could have led them to think differently. FWA strategy was also a projection of the experiences, networks, and repertoires of the leaders who devised it; as a result, it was not only more varied, but was also better matched to the farm worker organizing environment and to the broader support community. Just as important for the future, the FWA's launching already demonstrated the accountability mechanisms, resource requirements, and deliberative processes that would enable it to turn these assets into far greater resourcefulness than the other two organizations.

As we will see in the next chapter, as events continued to unfold during 1963 and 1964, these differences in strategic capacity influenced the different ways in which the three organizations responded to the end of the *bracero* program and the peak of the civil rights movement—and situated them very differently for the beginning of the Delano grape strike.

FOUR

A Storm Gathers

Two Responses (1963–1965)

This is a trade union dispute, not a civil rights movement or a religious crusade.

—C. Al Green, AWOC director

How have the Negroes won their battles? When everyone expects them
to run...they kneel and pray. When they appear beaten, they turn their defeat
into victory. They use only what they have, their bodies and their courage....We farm
workers have the same weapons—our bodies and our courage....The day we farm workers
apply this lesson with the same courage they have shown in Alabama and Mississippi—
on that day, the misery of the farm worker will come to an end.

—El Malcriado, no. 14, July 9, 1965

Between 1963 and 1965, the imminent demise of the *bracero* program and the gathering momentum of the civil rights movement created new organizing opportunities and new resources for farm worker organizers. As the farm labor market grew unsettled, the arena of contention shifted from Washington to California and from legislative committees to the fields. Both the AFL-CIO's AWOC and the FWA found they had to respond to these new conditions. In early 1965, both groups were drawn reluctantly into strikes. The

2 groups drawn into strike...
statrigic capacity differing.

difference was that the FWA leaders had the strategic capacity to learn from this experience in ways that the AWOC leadership did not. The FWA leaders actually enhanced their strategic capacity by expanding and diversifying their team. This development set the stage for the radically different ways the two groups would conduct the Delano grape strike beginning in September 1965.[1]

NEW OPPORTUNITIES, NEW RESOURCES: LABOR MARKET CRISIS AND CIVIL RIGHTS (1963–1964)

In 1963, state and national political currents were running against the *bracero* program. In the 1962 elections, Democrats retained control of Congress, and California governor Edmund G. Brown won a second term by defeating former Vice President Richard Nixon. When congressional hearings on the *bracero* program began in March 1963, the AFL-CIO, the National Council of Churches, and the U.S. Catholic Conference opposed any continuation of the program. The Kennedy administration proposed a final one-year extension, but only if the growers agreed to offer domestic workers conditions which the Labor Department determined were comparable to those offered to *braceros*: workers' compensation insurance, housing, and transportation. The growers reacted by demanding that Congress curb the authority of Kennedy's labor secretary. And all sides rejected a House Agricultural Committee proposal to continue the existing program with *no* new conditions. So on March 29, 1963, the House voted 174–158 to simply let the program die at the end of the year.

The reaction was immediate. Predicting economic disaster, the growers began mobilizing at state, national, and international levels. The Mexican government sent an ambassadorial letter, pleading that the program continue, and Senator William Fulbright, Congress's most respected voice on foreign policy, argued that the Mexican request must be heeded. Thus, when the Senate voted on the issue in August, it granted a one-year extension of the *bracero* program. In an amendment offered by Senator Eugene McCarthy, however, the Senate also required that growers offer domestic workers "comparable conditions." On December 4, 1963, the full Congress approved this measure with the understanding it would be the *bracero* program's last extension, an understanding to which Senator Allen Ellender, chair of the Senate Agriculture Committee and "godfather" of the program, reluctantly agreed.[2]

bracero system shut down

But the growers did not give up. Blocked at the federal level, they shifted the arena of conflict to California, where they made *braceros* a 1964 election issue. In January 1964, the California Council of Growers launched its campaign by warning consumers to expect higher prices as a result of a "terrific loss in crops"[3] once the *bracero* program was ended. In February, the *San Francisco Examiner* declared: "A great labor crisis has slowly begun to build on the rich California farm lands. It is dangerous. It is fascinating."[4] To deal with the loss of *braceros*, some growers proposed importing an increased number of temporary resident aliens, or "green carders," under the emergency provisions of Public Law 414, the basic U.S. immigration statute since 1952.[5] Others wanted the federal government to undertake a massive interstate recruitment drive to find domestic workers to fill the jobs.[6] Still others hoped to revive the *bracero* program itself once a disastrous year revealed the truth of their labor shortage claims. Whatever their approach, the fact that the growers expected the government to continue taking responsibility for providing farm labor kept this a prominent public issue.

Growers' claims of an imminent labor crisis were matched by equally strong claims by farm worker advocates that if growers improved working conditions, they would attract enough domestic workers. To some extent, state officials responded to this argument. In January 1964, in order to call attention to the need for improved farm worker housing, the California State Senate Committee on Labor and Welfare held public hearings in San Bernardino, Visalia, and Sacramento.[7] In February, the legislature adopted a new public assistance program that, for the first time, offered support to families with an unemployed father in the home—a boon for seasonally employed farm worker families. (The bill was passed despite grower objections that this "welfare subsidy" would only push wages higher and encourage strikes by reducing farm workers' dependency on low-wage work.)[8] In March, Governor Brown became involved in an investigation of Tulare County farm worker conditions, when he held joint hearings with the U.S. Department of Labor at which over 50 organizations testified.[9]

Brown also solicited two reports: one on farm labor demand from the grower-oriented Giannini Foundation of Agricultural Economics at UC Berkeley and another on farm labor supply from the labor-oriented Industrial Relations Department at UCLA. Not surprisingly, the Berkeley report found that more workers would be needed, and the UCLA report found that plenty of workers would be available if wages were raised.[10]

By November 1964, the issue was considered so urgent that President Lyndon Johnson, within a week after his election, met with Governor Brown and Mexican president Gustavo Díaz Ordaz. At this meeting, Brown proposed a compromise; when the *bracero* program was over, the U.S. Labor Department would allow growers to bring in a large number of emergency green-carders under the usual rules, which required growers to pay them a wage determined by the labor secretary to be high enough to have no adverse effect on domestic employment. This source of foreign workers, Brown proposed, would be phased out over the following five years by steadily increasing the wage that growers had to pay until it reached 125 percent of the adverse-effect wage set by the labor secretary, at the time $1.25 per hour. Brown's proposal satisfied neither the supporters nor the opponents of the *bracero* program, and a tide of opposition sank it. Taking a cue from Brown's proposal—but without a phase-in period—Labor Secretary Wirtz decided to act, raising the adverse-effect wage immediately. As of April 1, 1965, any grower applying for emergency help under PL 414 would have to pay a minimum wage of $1.40 per hour.[11]

Anticipation of the end of the *bracero* program had already begun to destabilize the California labor market. A newly restricted farm labor supply, coupled with Wirtz's decision, not only created pressure on employers to raise wages but also created the opportunity for workers to use this new source of leverage to organize.

Just as the end of the *bracero* program created new organizing opportunities, the civil rights revolution created new resources for organizers with eyes to see them. In April 1963, the Southern Christian Leadership Conference launched its Birmingham campaign, and television viewers across the country watched nightly as black children confronted police dogs, fire hoses, and angry mobs. On June 11, President Kennedy used federal troops to integrate the University of Alabama. The next day, June 12, Mississippi NAACP leader Medgar Evers was assassinated. One week later, the president introduced the Civil Rights Act. The movement also spread north as CORE and other groups organized rent strikes in Harlem and sit-ins on San Francisco's auto row.

As claims made in the name of racial justice became harder to ignore, so did claims in the name of economic justice. Americans began to rediscover poverty in their own country, as it was being documented by advocates such as Michael Harrington, whose *Other America* was a call to arms.[12] In June 1963, President Kennedy directed his Council on Economic Security to come up with a plan to fight poverty. And on August 28, 250,000 people marched on Washington to hear Dr. Martin Luther King, Jr., preach his dream of freedom *and* jobs. For much of 1964, in the wake of President Kennedy's assassination, new and challenging questions of racial and economic justice stayed at the top of the national agenda. In July 1964, after declaring a War on Poverty to achieve the Great Society, President Johnson signed the Civil Rights Act, and in August, he signed the Economic Opportunity Act.

The central role of young people in the civil rights movement in the South inspired students across the country to become active in similar campaigns, national in scope but carried out in local organizing projects. Students for a Democratic Society (SDS) launched its Economic Research and Action Project in an attempt to bring civil rights organizing tactics to white working-class communities in Newark, Chicago, Cleveland, and Philadelphia.[13] For their part, California students interested in civil rights began to focus on local farm workers. Over 60 students attended the first National Student Association conference on farm labor held at Redlands, California, in November 1963, where they heard representatives of farm worker organizations and discussed summer projects.[14]

As the focal point of the farm labor controversy shifted from the national to the state and local levels, state and local advocacy networks also began to mobilize in ways that emulated the civil rights movement. In 1962, former UPWA organizer and Imperial Valley strike leader Clive Knowles, Santa Barbara philanthropist Katherine Peak, and Jewish Labor Committee leader Max Mont organized the Emergency Committee to Aid Farm Workers in southern California.[15] In 1963, former AWOC research director Henry Anderson formed the Citizens for Farm Labor (CFL) in the San Francisco Bay Area. The CFL led public education campaigns, testified at legislative hearings, and published *Farm Labor*, a monthly journal reporting on farm worker organizing and advocacy.[16] The CFL's executive committee included several experienced labor activists: Anderson; Father Thomas McCullough, who had started the Agricultural Workers Association in Stockton; Berkeley graduate student Wendy Goepel; ILGWU (International Ladies' Garment Workers' Union) labor activist Ann Draper; and two attorneys. Its 39-member advisory board included a diverse array of figures: 5 clergymen, including Chris Hartmire of the California Migrant Ministry; Congressmen Phillip Burton, Albert Song, and Henry Gonzales; six professors, including Seymour Martin Lipset and Peter Odegard; three lawyers; four Mexican-American community leaders, including Herman Gallegos and Cesar Chavez; Fred Ross and Norman Thomas.[17]

The CFL and the Emergency Committee were different from past farm worker advocacy groups. One reason was that they operated at the local and state level. Another reason was that they supported organizing as well as policy reform.

The California Migrant Ministry (CMM) also became more active as debate over the *bracero* program stirred state and local denominational controversies. Tensions brewed between rural congregants responsive to the growers' economic concerns and urban congregants responsive to the workers' social justice claims. In the face of this challenge, Chris Hartmire and others had to become even more-articulate advocates of the farm worker cause. They won an important victory when the CMM's governing body, the California Church Council, adopted its "Goals for the Migrant Ministry," which linked urban middle-class churchgoers to the farm worker community.[18] By 1965, Hartmire was raising an annual budget of $180,000 from the National Council of Churches, diverse denominational sources, and grants from the Rosenberg Foundation. He utilized these funds to support himself, Jim Drake, a small staff, and a variety of farm worker programs.[19]

The emergence of all of these groups was a new and potentially important resource available to farm worker organizers.

AWOC INITIATIVES: ORGANIZING LABOR CONTRACTORS

AWOC stepped up its activities and changed its strategy, but this was more in response to new leadership than to new conditions. In early 1962, the AFL-CIO appointed a new AWOC director, C. Al Green, a 60-year-old white Plasterers Union official with a building trades background that was far closer to Meany's than his AWOC predecessor Norman Smith's had been.[20] Green devoted his first year at AWOC to campaigning for Governor Brown's reelection and replacing most of Smith's people.[21] When he finally did turn his attention to farm workers in the spring of 1963, he followed a typical building trades approach—trying to organize labor contractors, the middlemen who supplied crews of workers to employers—not the laborers themselves. Green's staff staged early morning pickets at contractor pick-up points, disrupting farm labor recruiting until the contractors agreed to sign up their workers for AWOC and to deduct AWOC dues from the workers' pay. Green called his staffers "business representatives," not organizers. It was a building trades term descriptive of their approach.[22]

However, contractors in the constrained, highly skilled construction labor market played a very different role from farm labor contractors. The latter, for the most part, had no leverage to demand higher pay for their workers and instead competed with each other by reducing labor costs to employers. In turn, they made their own profits by reducing income to workers.[23] Nonetheless, following the building trades model, Green required no specified wage rate from the contractors.[24] Even though he had grown up in the Anglo cannery town of Modesto,[25] Green had no links to farm workers. Moreover, he seemed unaware that his approach was highly unpopular with Mexican farm workers, who had endured a corrupt labor contractor system for many years.

As a result, from the beginning of 1963 to the end of 1964, AWOC's 22 paid business representatives signed contracts with 136 labor contractors. In this way, they recruited a membership of 4,500 workers paying monthly dues of $2—when they worked. It was just what George Meany wanted.[26] But there remained hundreds more contractors whom AWOC could not sign up. Consequently, AWOC's approach failed to establish union control over jobs, raise wages, or create an organized base among workers, who soon learned that AWOC contracts meant paying dues for nothing in return.[27] AWOC seemed to many of them to be "hiring the coyote to guard the chickens."[28]

One positive result of Green's focus on contractors, however, was his support for Filipino AWOC organizers, such as Larry Itliong and Ben Gines,[29] many of whom were the "bosses" of skilled and stable Filipino crews. Since the 1920s, Filipino crew bosses—unlike other farm labor contractors—had been able to negotiate with the growers on behalf of their crews. These Filipino leaders were pleased to affiliate with AWOC and thus with the "legitimate" labor movement,[30] and Filipinos were AWOC's one organized support base among farm workers. As a result, Itliong acquired considerable influence with Green.[31]

FWA INITIATIVES: BUILDING A MEMBERSHIP

In contrast with AWOC's attempt to create a dues base by signing up farm labor contractors, the FWA decided to build its dues base by organizing Mexican farm worker families with a community-based social services program. It was very challenging.

Following the mobilization for its January 1963 constitutional convention, the FWA's dues-paying membership declined, dropping to some 12 families by July, most of them related to FWA officers. Rather than abandon the effort, however, FWA leaders tried to come up with new ways to make it work.[32] Recalling his thinking at the time, Chavez said later:

> It is the seasonal farm workers who have been in the U.S. for some time, but who have not been able to find a full year's employment, who are most likely to be interested in joining the association and in seeing an eventual union of farm workers.... agricultural workers who are FWA members [are] local families who depend on seasonal farm work. Most of them live, year-round, in the southern San Joaquin Valley. Almost all are family men. They are a stable group to work with, and they are capable members of an ongoing organization.[33]

Based on knowledge of their constituency, FWA leaders believed that an organizing strategy based on social services and death benefits could work, but it would take time and persistence. It was their accountability to their farm worker constituency—and dependence on them for organizing resources—that motivated the organizers to find ways to address the needs of that constituency. As Chavez later explained:

> A union must have members who pay dues regularly.... Because they pay so much, they feel they are the important part of the organization; that they have a right to be served. They don't hesitate to write, to call, to ask for things—and to reaffirm their position in the association.... the idea that the members are, alone, paying the salary of a man who is responsible to them is very important.[34]

Personal service work had been a part of the FWA organizers' experience in CSO, where attempts to institutionalize it in the form of service centers had proved to be difficult to sustain financially.[35] Nonetheless, the FWA pursued the same goal—and for the same reasons. Due to their economic, political, and cultural vulnerability, farm workers were subject to abuse by a wide range of individuals and institutions with which they interacted. For example, employers and labor contractors failed to report deductions, pay promised rates, attend to job injuries, etc. County welfare departments, the Department of Motor Vehicles, the Immigration and Naturalization Service, finance companies, and law enforcement were equally problematic. As a result, a predatory business developed to assist farm workers with these problems for a fee, a business in which labor contractors were often involved as well. These notaries, translators, and "fillers-out" of forms often charged hefty fees for shoddy service. They were known as "coyotes."[36]

The FWA service program provided an alternative to the coyotes, but not without its own bite. As organizers, not social workers, those who provided services—Chavez, Orendain, Huerta, Padilla, and others—were interested not only in solving individual problems, but also in building an organization capable of institutional change. They thus limited services to members of the association who had paid their dues in full. In addition, they often turned cases of individual abuse into campaigns targeting specific labor contractors or welfare officials, linking these problems to a need for institutional reform—just as Chavez had done with the *bracero* program in Oxnard in 1959.[37] Although this kind of service had been a mainstay of immigrant organizations in the United States since the nineteenth century—the stuff of fraternal associations, unions, churches, and political machines—AWOC leaders, focused as they were on jobs rather than on workers, failed to see it as an organizing strategy.

The FWA also developed a family death benefit, one similar to those offered by the burial societies popular with immigrant workers at the turn of the century and by the Mexican lodges of the 1920s. Chavez persuaded the California Life Insurance, a small company interested in a rural trade, to sell the FWA a group insurance plan—which was paid for with $2 of the $3.50 dues paid each month by each family.[38] Families also turned to the FWA for help in negotiating with funeral homes inclined to take advantage of them in times of need.[39]

Each of these initiatives brought in new members, but their dues payments were irregular at best. The FWA finally turned the corner on membership recruitment and maintenance when it launched the Farm Workers Credit Union in January 1964 at the organization's second constitutional convention.[40] In the CSO, Chavez and the others had learned how to organize credit unions.[41] For the start-up capital, Chavez persuaded his brother Richard to mortgage his Delano home for $3,700.[42] With this, the new credit union was able to make small loans to members who otherwise depended for credit on employers, labor contractors, finance companies, and loan sharks. With the purchase of a $5 share, FWA members could join the credit union.[43] Many kept their dues up to date for that purpose.

Together, these programs helped organizers to anchor FWA membership in tangible benefits, forged relational bonds among organizers and members, and created a shared experience of what could be accomplished together. The leaders could thus describe the FWA as an organization accountable to its farm worker members and meeting their needs through collective action. The fact that the organization was

Mexican-led also provided evidence of what "we" could do in a world dominated by powerful institutions which, for the most part, were Anglo.[44]

As they developed these programs, the FWA leaders continued to adapt the form of their organization. Based on Chavez's belief that those who do the work should be authorized to make the decisions, they reduced the size of their board from 12 people with varying levels of engagement to the 5 core people who were actively leading the organizing effort. Instead of 10 regional vice presidents on the board, they decided on 3 general vice presidents, each concerned with the entire operation. Padilla, Huerta, and Hernandez were elected to these positions at the next convention. This smaller board of directors was more functional than the old one had been. And in place of regional vice presidents, the new board selected local leaders, or *representantes*, on the basis of their commitment to building the organization's membership. These local leaders were given the authority and responsibility for organizing in their communities.[45]

The core leaders then strengthened their collaboration by multiplying the venues in which they worked together on specific tasks. The credit union board, for example, made up of Chavez, Huerta, Hernandez, Roger Terronez, and Felix Zapata, met regularly and had its own set of tasks to accomplish. Its loan committee, made up of board and nonboard members, met monthly to review loan applications. As the size of the organization began to grow, these regular occasions for deliberation among FWA leaders encouraged the development of collaborative work routines and provided venues for bringing new people into real decision-making roles.[46]

About the same time that it was struggling to get its programs off the ground, the FWA suffered a setback. Cesar Chavez's cousin Manuel Chavez, who had been elected secretary-treasurer at the January 1963 convention, was arrested at the end of that year for forging checks. Manuel Chavez was convicted and went to prison for 18 months. Although Cesar had great respect for his cousin's street smarts, the two men's lives had developed along different paths. Manuel had been in and out of prison for state and federal offenses from 1952 to 1962.[47] Cesar had hoped to reform him by getting him involved in organizing, but after the check-forging incident, he was compelled to let him go.[48] The board temporarily appointed Antonio Orendain, a CSO leader, to fill the post, a position to which he was elected at the next convention. The scandal could have been devastating to this fragile new organization had its leaders and their constituency not shared the trust, relationships, and history to get through these events with no further repercussions.

Chavez organized close to full time, even though the organization did not yet have sufficient funds to support him. Others found a variety of ways to do the work. Padilla, for example, worked full time for CSO, setting up service centers in Santa Maria, Madera, and elsewhere, while organizing for the FWA as well.[49] Jim Drake, hired by the CMM to develop a Goshen community center, also organized members for the FWA.[50] Not until August 1964 did the FWA finally have enough members to begin paying Chavez $50 per week and to allow Huerta to move to Delano and join him full time at the same salary.[51]

Pragmatically experimental about how to get the organizing done, the FWA collaborated with the CMM to organize the Farm Workers Organization (FWO), located 30 miles northeast of Delano in the Tulare County town of Porterville. Because Tulare County had the lowest per capita income in the state, despite an abundant agriculture, it had become a focus of attention for farm worker advocates. The American Friends Service Committee had been working there since 1954, and in early 1964 the Teamsters and ILWU announced their intention to set up offices there as well.[52] FWA leaders too wanted to establish a base in Tulare, but they did not have the money to hire more organizers. But the CMM did.

The same year, with funding from the Rosenberg Foundation, the United Church of Christ Northern California Conference, the Board of Homeland Ministries, and the Porterville Congregational Church, the CMM joined the Kings-Tulare Migrant Ministry to launch the Tulare County Community Development Project. The project, in turn, began organizing the FWO. They hired several staffpeople: the Reverend Jim Drake to lead the effort; the Reverend David Havens, another CMM recruit, to assist; and FWA leader Gilbert Padilla to organize. Modeling the FWO on the FWA, the trio began a house-meeting drive, held a founding convention, established dues of $2 per month, opened a service center, and set up a gas-, oil-, and tire-buying cooperative. Yet the new organization was not a carbon copy of the original. Adhering more closely to the Alinsky model than the FWA, the organizers structured the FWO so that volunteer farm worker leaders were elected officers, while the staff—Drake, Havens, and Padilla—worked for them. The oil and gas co-op was also their own initiative and became a model that the FWA attempted to follow later in Delano.[53]

Continuing to look for new ways to reach farm workers, Chavez convinced former Catholic Worker and CFL activist Bill Esher to move to Delano late in 1964. Esher would edit *El Malcriado*, a farm worker newspaper. Chavez and others conceived the paper in the tradition of *La Cotorra*, a popular Mexican magazine of political satire.[54]

The name they chose meant "upstart," "problem child," or "one who doesn't know his place." Covers of the first issues featured cartoons archetypical characters: Don Sotaco, the farm worker; Don Coyote, the labor contractor; and El Patroncito, the grower—all drawn by Mexican-American cartoonist Andy Zermeno. Initially published only in Spanish, *El Malcriado* was sold in the small grocery stores that dotted the *barrios* of farm worker towns such as Richgrove, Parlier, Earlimart, and Delano. In addition to hortatory articles on farm worker rights (written by Chavez, for the most part) and items of general interest, the paper publicized the FWA's latest successes. One story about an Anglo labor contractor whom the FWA targeted made a strong impression on future farm worker leader Eliseo Medina:

> I used to go to People's Cafe and I saw a copy of *El Malcriado*, telling about the...contractor...who got nailed by the labor commissioner. You have to remember...nobody ever challenged the growers and the labor contractors were like the princes of the church....then all of a sudden, here's this report that this contractor—a white guy, no less—it wasn't just any old contractor, but a white guy who got nailed. All of a sudden it was sort of like Mexicans could do stuff and they could win. And I said, "Wow!" Prior to that, remember, when I came to this country, they made me swear that we would behave ourselves and...not break any laws....And...they're not only rocking the boat—they're winning![55]

Within a year, *El Malcriado*'s circulation would reach 3,000: 2,000 in Spanish and 1,000 in an English edition.[56]

By late 1964, the FWA had achieved enough stability to open a headquarters in Delano located at 102 Albany Street in a former grocery store on the edge of town, across from a vineyard. Interestingly, the former store had also served as an evangelical church for a time. With the FWA's name and black eagle logo proudly posted outside, the office consisted of a large waiting room with countertop service by FWA volunteers and staff. In addition, there was a set of inner offices, including one for the credit union and another for Chavez; the latter featured a bright red desk crafted by his brother Richard, a carpenter.[57]

On Sunday, January 24, 1965, when FWA leaders gathered in Delano for their third constitutional convention, membership was growing. The FWA had $1,700 in the bank, while its credit union had assets of $25,000.[58] It opened a headquarters, published the first issue of a newspaper, and boasted members in farm worker towns from one end of California to the other: Calexico, Brawley, San Ysidro, Oxnard, Lamont, Arvin, Bakersfield, Wasco, Delano, Earlimart, McFarland,

Huron, Corcoran, Exeter, Porterville, Lindsay, Selma, Fresno, Gilroy, San Jose, Stockton, Lodi, Acampo, Healdsburg, and Eureka.[59]

The organization also changed its name from the FWA to the NFWA, the National Farm Workers Association, La Asociación Nacional de Trabajadores Campesinos. Members who migrated from the Rio Grande Valley, Texas, wanted to know if they could belong to the same organization when they returned home. Changing the name was a way to reassure them—and, at the same time, to stake a claim beyond the borders of California.[60]

By blending narrative elements drawn from Mexican cultural traditions, Catholic social teaching, and the civil rights movement, FWA leaders began to tell a story about their association that went well beyond an account of a community organization or union. They described themselves as a "farm worker movement." In the first issue of *El Malcriado*, an article entitled "Nuestro Solido Movimiento" (Our United Movement) put it this way:

> El movimiento de la Asociación de Trabajadores Campesinos es organismo que tiene sus socios los cuales son las familias. La unidad de vida viene al movimiento de la cooperación del trabajador. La Asociación de Trabajadores Campesinos es una empresa colectiva, que por medios colectivos, trata de proporcionar los medios económicos que el pueblo campesino en California necesita para asegurar su vida: social, moral, y económica para el y su familia. Pero al mismo tiempo trata de devolver al hombre esa independencia y libertad que le aseguran la conciencia de su dignidad y de su solidaridad....Esta unidad supone sacrificios, pero estos son necesario por la vida....El que conoce los principios no es igual al que los ama. Viva la Causa![61]

> [The movement of the Farm Workers Association is composed of member families. Our unity rests on the cooperation of working people. Ours is a collective enterprise that strives to secure the economic resources that California farm workers need to secure the social, moral, and economic well-being of themselves and their families. We also strive to restore to each person the autonomy and freedom each of us requires to live in the knowledge of our own dignity, in solidarity with others. Achieving unity will require sacrifice, but sacrifice is a condition of life. To know these principles is not the same thing as to love them. Viva la Causa!][62]

Within a year, the NFWA would transform itself into La Causa, a farm worker movement in deed as well as word.

By early 1965, the differences between the NFWA and AWOC had become stark. The NFWA strategy grew from an understanding of the farm worker world, while AWOC's strategy projected Green's understanding of labor organizing upon that world. For leadership, the NFWA created a network of farm worker representatives; AWOC drew upon a pool of labor contractors. The NFWA continued to expand the role of volunteer leaders and developed multiple new deliberative venues; AWOC's work was conducted by paid organizers under Green's direction. Clearly, the experience of those who devised NFWA strategy was much closer to that of their constituents. Despite this greater expertise, however, the NFWA leadership remained far more open to fresh approaches. They knew they had to learn how to do something they hadn't done before: organize a union. Their diversity of experience made them mindful of the many ways they could proceed.

THE "REVOLUTION" BEGINS: 1965

California was in the midst of what the *Los Angeles Times* called a "revolution in agriculture."[63] For the first time in 23 years—since 1942—growers would have to harvest their crops without *braceros*. Moreover, despite their efforts, very few PL 414 green-card workers had been authorized to take their place. Some Stockton tomato growers were threatening to close down.[64] Other growers were investigating U.S. trust territories, such as Guam, as sources of cheap labor free of restrictions.[65] The Philippine ambassador reported that growers had tried to "place an order" with him for 2,000 workers.[66] And in March, Governor Brown joined in, echoing growers' claims that they would need 10,000 foreign workers for the lettuce and asparagus harvests.[67]

As the crops began to mature in April, Agriculture Secretary Wirtz appointed a California Farm Labor Panel of three academics to determine if there was a labor shortage and thus a need to admit emergency green-carders.[68] Although the panel rejected requests from northern California growers for 6,700 foreign workers, it did recommend importing 1,500 Mexicans for the tomato and asparagus harvests and permitting the use of 1,000 Japanese and Filipino nationals already in the United States.[69] Wirtz agreed.

Trying to navigate a line between doubting insistent grower demands and trying to meet them, Wirtz authorized 1,000 more foreign workers for the Salinas lettuce harvest, but Salinas ended up with more workers than jobs.[70] Wirtz also mobilized intrastate, initiating an "A Team" program to recruit high school athletes to work in California's fields. The few who responded were ready to leave almost as soon as they arrived, in some cases signing up with AWOC and going on strike.[71] At a Los Angeles town hall meeting in June, Wirtz reported that only 1,964 foreign workers were at work in California, compared with 36,300 on the same date in the previous year.[72] In July, the director of the California Department of Employment, Albert Tieberg, called for 16,500 foreign workers to harvest the tomato crop, a request the Wirtz panel approved in August.[73]

The continuing chaos and controversy stimulated ongoing public interest in the farm labor issue. The California Democratic Council "applauded the end of the *bracero* program," while the California Republican Assembly called for its "reenactment."[74] State legislators introduced more than 18 farm labor bills that called for everything from unemployment insurance to a "little Wagner act" to protect labor union organizing among farm workers.[75] Although the growers' hold on the state senate killed all but the most innocuous legislation, contemporaneous federal court rulings on reapportionment indicated that the days of a grower-dominated senate might be numbered. As one rural paper put it:

> Supreme Court decisions threaten to nullify the checks and balances which have over the years worked so well in the California legislature.... if both the senate and the assembly are apportioned on a population basis, vast rural segments of our state will lose representation and influence.[76]

From the workers' point of view, things looked more promising than they had in many years. Wages had risen from under $1 per hour in 1963 to $1.25 per hour in early 1965; given the adverse-effect level that Labor Secretary Wirtz had set, they were likely to rise to $1.40 per hour wherever growers needed green-carders—or other growers had to compete with them for laborers. At the same time that Dr. King was leading civil rights supporters in a march from Selma to Montgomery, Alabama, Wirtz conducted a "march" of his own through California. From March 24 to 30, he took the press on a well-publicized tour of agricultural centers to investigate the "labor crisis" firsthand.[77] The farm labor story, as *Farm Labor* reported, was "carried on the front pages of the daily press for a week."[78] In Stockton, the *San Francisco Examiner* reported, Wirtz observed "workers sitting in the dirt of the field, eating their sandwiches out of a bag [while] the growers [were] enjoying a big barbecue at the ranch house."[79] In Salinas, he found that two out of three fields he visited had no toilets.[80] In Indio, he led reporters on a tour of one-room shacks without gas that housed seven workers for $25 each per month.[81] When the tour was over, the *California Farmer* commented, "Wirtz landed in Sacramento and marched to the sea burning most vestiges of hope for *braceros* behind him.... Agriculture put on one of the most shocking displays of poor public relations... ever seen."[82]

The growers, Wirtz concluded, had "cried wolf" about labor shortages again and again. In reality, the government response was quite adequate to the growers' real needs. "The most significant fact," he declared, "is that all crops are being harvested despite all this talk."[83] Moreover, growers had plainly done nothing to create the conditions for farm work that were necessary to attract employees. Protestations by growers that no one understood their "peculiar" problems were sounding more and more like the protestations of southern white segregationists that no one understood their "peculiar problem."[84]

Student leaders organized a statewide conference on farm worker poverty and formed a Student Committee for Agricultural Labor (SCAL) at UC Berkeley and one at Stanford.[85] By June 1965, nine student groups inspired by the 1964 Mississippi Summer Project, which had brought several hundred northern students south to organize black voters, launched their own summer projects in the San Joaquin Valley.[86] UC Berkeley SCAL members worked in the fields and assisted local farm worker organizers.[87] UCLA tutors served in a Kern County labor camp near Arvin. The Student Medical Conference Migrant Program of USC and the Los Angeles College School of Nursing were active in five counties. The Sacramento State College Agriculture Committee took part in community organizing programs in eight counties. The Berkeley YWCA led a summer tutorial project near Yuba City. The American Friends Service Committee hosted a tutorial project in the Linell labor camp in Tulare County. The Garces High School Catholic Student Project, led by LeRoy Chatfield, ran tutorial projects in Kern County. And the CMM hosted summer volunteer programs in five counties.[88]

ORGANIZING INITIATIVES: AWOC AND THE NFWA

AWOC and the NFWA confronted similar opportunities and challenges but engaged with them in very different ways. Responding to the panic among growers, the U.S. Department of Labor invited unions to help recruit replacements. AWOC accepted. The NFWA declined. Although both AWOC and the NFWA acquiesced when workers demanded strikes to take advantage of new circumstances, the two organizations conducted their strikes quite differently. The NFWA seized on the new sources of public support created by the civil rights movement and poverty programs, while AWOC shunned them. While AWOC remained true to its established strategy, NFWA leaders began to reverse themselves on the questions of strikes and outside funds, adapting to new realities.

The point is that the disparate choices made by the leaders of the two groups reflected not only differences in the strategies with which they began but, more important, their disparate capacities to adapt strategies to new circumstances. The NFWA's strategic capacity continued to grow as it forged links with new people who would bring new connections, experiences, and tactics into its dynamic work.

Recruiting Replacement Workers

The first new challenge facing AWOC and NFWA leaders was how to respond to the Labor Department effort to recruit domestic workers by turning to organizations with farm worker constituencies to supply them. As a natural outgrowth of its building trades strategy, AWOC saw this as an opportunity to get its foot in the door by becoming a supplier of workers. In a letter to the president of the Stockton Asparagus Association, Green complained that AWOC contractors had room for 5,000 workers in their camps, which growers were refusing to utilize.[89] In a follow-up to Wirtz, he asked why AWOC had not been contacted when it could supply workers.[90] He claimed that AWOC could recruit domestic workers, and taking a page from the Teamsters, he even offered to help growers to secure foreign workers if they couldn't get enough from the union.[91] Apparently, no grower needed workers badly enough to turn to AWOC to recruit them.

Leaders of the region's most prominent Mexican-American organizations were also interested in recruiting workers for the growers. By contrast, the NFWA chose a different course. It focused not on recruiting workers, but on organizing them to make claims on their recruiters.

The NFWA challenged the mainstream Mexican-American groups on this issue, a move that would have been far more difficult for an Anglo-led group. Governor Brown appointed a former AWOC organizer and Mexican-American Political Association (MAPA) activist, Hector Abeytia, to his staff and charged him with the task of gaining the cooperation of Mexican-American organizations in recruiting farm labor, a task to which 39 state employees were assigned and for which 4 special consultants to the U.S. Department of Labor were hired. The consultants were former MAPA president Bert Corona, current MAPA president Ed Quevedo, and representatives of the CSO and GI Forum.[92] Abeytia convened a meeting in Delano to get Chavez's support. But Chavez demurred, arguing that Abeytia and the consultants were hurting workers by making it easier for the growers to avoid raising wages enough to recruit them.[93] Soon after, the NFWA picketed outside the MAPA convention in Fresno, which finally persuaded MAPA to stop recruiting.[94]

Although the government recruitment program paid the salaries of a few activists for a time, it failed to produce the workers that growers said they needed. For most workers, the problem had never been knowing where to find jobs but, rather, improving the wages and working conditions at those jobs. Because the NFWA leadership, unlike AWOC, had strong ties to the Mexican-American community, it could challenge the traditional leaders to support a more aggressive political agenda. And in the years ahead, this would have real consequence for battles with Governor Brown.

A Spring of Strikes

Responding to workers who hoped to make use of their newfound labor market strength, AWOC and the NFWA both led wage strikes in the spring of 1965. These were AWOC's first strikes since 1961 and were initiated not by Green but by Itliong, Gines, and other Filipino leaders, who presented Green with a fait accompli. With the end of the *bracero* program, the Filipino crew leaders saw an opportunity for greater leverage in their specialized labor markets: asparagus, table grapes, and vegetables. In March 1965, during the labor shortage scare in asparagus, Itliong led a strike of Filipino crews in the Stockton area to raise wages.[95] The struck growers applied to the state for help in recruiting 2,900 workers, but California Department of Employment director Tieberg rejected the request because of the strike.[96] As a result, asparagus workers won a wage increase, though not union recognition or a contract. Sensing an opportunity, Green sent out his first appeal to California unions for money to support AWOC's organizing activities. The California Federation of Labor consequently announced the beginning of an "all-out drive" to organize farm workers.[97]

Itliong followed up on his Stockton success by moving on to organize Filipino crew leaders 400 miles to the south in the Coachella Valley desert, site of the season's first grape harvest. Coachella table grape shippers faced high growing costs because of expensive water, poor soil conditions, and low yields. But because their table grapes were the first of the season, they could earn very high prices.[98] In addition, grapes, unlike other fruits, stop maturing once they are picked. Due to the fact that grapes have to be cut at precisely the right moment,[99] an early harvest strike in Coachella was more threatening than an ordinary harvest strike. As leaders of skilled field packing crews, the Filipino crew bosses demanded that growers raise wages from $1.25 an hour plus 25 cents a box to the $1.40 per hour that Wirtz had specified should be paid to foreign workers.[100] Coachella growers had not used *braceros*, relying instead on skilled Filipino field packing crews and Mexican migrants. The demand for a raise to $1.40 per hour was based more on the legitimacy afforded by the labor secretary than on any interest of Coachella growers in obtaining foreign workers.

AWOC singled out Coachella's largest grape grower for a work stoppage during the grape thinning season at the end of May. The 1,000-acre David Freedman Company shipped one-seventh of the table grape production of the entire valley. Freedman's president, Lionel Steinberg, was an unusual grower. A liberal, Stevenson Democrat who now lived in Beverly Hills, he was a former chair of the Fresno County Democratic Central Committee and past president of the California Young Democrats. He had been denied appointment as Kennedy's secretary of agriculture because of a labor dispute with the UPWA, which sought union recognitions in his citrus packing shed.[101] By contrast, AWOC did not demand recognition, so in a few days, Steinberg raised the hourly wage to $1.40. The other Coachella growers followed suit.[102] AWOC immediately followed up with a tomato strike in the Imperial Valley, which raised hourly wages there to $1.40 as well.[103] AWOC was on a roll.

By May, the NFWA too was leading a strike, despite the fact that its leaders had thought they would not be ready for a successful strike for another two years.[104] Skilled rose grafters near McFarland, five miles south of Delano, had been promised $9 per 1,000 plants grafted but were being paid only $6.50–$7.00. Epifanio Camacho, an immigrant worker with a "troublemaker" reputation, had heard of the NFWA and asked Chavez for his help.[105] Although only 4 workers showed up at the first meeting called by Camacho and Chavez, eventually 67 of the 85 workers employed by Mt. Arbor, the largest nursery in the area, signed cards to authorize the NFWA to represent them. Their grafting skills made them hard to replace.

Challenged by worker demands and also by AWOC's success in raising wages elsewhere, the NFWA decided to take a chance on a strike. Chavez assigned himself, Huerta, Padilla, and Drake (who took a "vacation" from the Migrant Ministry) to provide support.[106] At a Sunday meeting on May 2, the day before the strike, workers pledged on a cross not to break the strike. Hoping to avoid violence, they decided to stay home rather than set up picket lines. To avoid taking chances, however, Huerta, Drake, and other organizers visited the workers' homes the next morning before dawn, checking on any who had their lights on, a sign they could be preparing for work. The first day, everyone remained at home, and Huerta tried to arrange a meeting with the nursery manager. But he threw her out of his office, denouncing her as a Communist. Turning then to Hartmire for a task he would perform many times in the future, Chavez asked him to use his office as a clergyman to contact the Mt. Arbor headquarters in Shenandoah, Iowa, to arrange a bargaining session.[107] The company rejected this approach as well. By then, a few migrant workers from the town of Tangancicuaro in Michoacán, Mexico, went back to work. NFWA leaders decided to send a letter to the mayor of the town, asking him to post a list of *esquiroles* (strike breakers) on the town bulletin board, and the mayor complied. This novel tactic was used again in later strikes and paid off, but the Mt. Arbor strike did not last long enough for the Tangancicuaro bulletin board to have any effect. Mt. Arbor hired labor contractors to break the strike. Because skilled grafters were hard to find, however, the contractors couldn't fill the nursery's needs. At the end of the fourth day of the strike, Mt. Arbor raised wages to $1.40 per hour, and the workers voted to go back to work. The area's other nurseries followed suit, yet no union contract was signed.[108]

The NFWA leaders interpreted the strike as a success, but they were also acutely aware of how difficult it had been to sustain, how resistant the employer had been, and how remote a goal union recognition could be. They learned that to be successful in the long run, they would have to devise tactics to stop strike breaking by labor contractors, identify individual strike-breaking workers, and find ways to influence them. Like AWOC, the NFWA leaders had not figured out how to leverage short-term labor market pressure into a long-term contract. Unlike AWOC, though, the NFWA leaders knew they didn't know.

While AWOC mobilized wage strikes in the Coachella and Imperial valleys that spring, the NFWA launched a new kind of strike that grew out of its community-based membership. Emulating the civil rights movement: a rent strike. Among its Tulare County members, the NFWA counted a few of the 170 farm worker families who lived in the Woodville and Linnell farm labor camps 30 miles northeast of Delano. The federal Farm Security Administration (FSA) had built the camps in 1938 as temporary housing for migrant workers. The 16-by-20-foot tin or wood shelters one electric and gas outlet; cold water faucets located at a garbage stand outside every fourth cabin; and toilets and showers in communal buildings that also housed laundry tubs and clothes lines. In the 1940s, the FSA turned the camps over to the Tulare County Housing Authority, which rented them for $18–$38 per month per cabin, four persons to a cabin. By 1965, the housing authority had accumulated an $80,000 surplus from these rentals. But when the county health department found 51 health and safety violations, instead of drawing on the surplus to build new units, the authority decided to raise the rent by 40 percent to finance the construction.[109] NFWA members who lived in the camps turned to Drake and Padilla for help. They, in turn, consulted with San Francisco civil rights lawyer James Herndon and learned that renters could legally withhold rent payments from their landlord. As a result, they put the money in an escrow fund until substandard housing was brought up to code.[110]

With the help of student summer volunteers from SCAL,[111] they started a rent strike on May 22, picketing the Tulare County Housing Authority. Continuing through June and July, the strike peaked in a six-mile march of 300 strikers to the county seat in Visalia on July 16. The march, one of the first events in which the NFWA's black eagle flag was seen flapping in the breeze, was described by *Fresno Bee* reporter Ron Taylor as more evocative of rural Alabama than rural California.[112] In fact, Hartmire, who proposed the march, had marched in Selma, Alabama, just three months before.[113] NFWA organizers also contacted the Los Angeles branch of CORE, one of the country's most active civil rights groups, which sent organizers Bob Solodow and Bob Fisher to help with the nonviolent protest.[114] March participants included not just farm workers and SCAL members, but also members of CORE, SNCC, Citizens for Farm Labor, and the Welfare Rights Organization of Oakland.[115]

As tactical and relational ties to the civil rights movement developed, the NFWA continued to reinterpret its story. In the July 9 *El Malcriado*, an editorial entitled "Igual Que Los Negritos" (Just Like the Negroes) said:

> Como han ganado sus batallas los negros? Se han unido frente a los perros, mangueras de los bomberos, policías brutales y aguijones eléctricos para arrear ganado. Cuando los amenazan ellos cantan su canción de lucha, "Nosotros Venceremos." Cuando todo el mundo espera que ellos corran, a lo contrario se hincan y rezan. Cuando se miran batidos ellos hacen de la derrota la victoria. Ellos usan lo único que tienen, sus cuerpos y su valor y con esto siguen venciendo.
>
> Nosotros los campesinos tenemos las mismas armas—nuestros cuerpos y nuestro valor. Pero apenas empezamos a usarles estas armas. En McFarland los campesinos siguieron el camino ya anadeo por los negros. Aquí demostramos el poder de la unidad y esto nos gano un poco del dinero que el patrón nos ha estado robando.
>
> En la huelga de las rentas el campesino devuelta enseña lo que ha aprendido del movimiento negro. Hemos aprendido que cuando nos unimos, podemos hacer al gobierno que acuda nuestro llamado y enmiende su modo imperioso contra la gente pobre. La comisión de viviendas del condado de Tulare, tiene miedo al poder de la gente organizada.
>
> Cada día mas y mas gente trabajadora están comprobando su valor como lo hacen los negros en su movimiento. El día que nosotros los campesinos apliquemos esta lección con el mismo valor que se ha demostrado en Alabama y Mississippi en este día el tristeza del campesino terminara.[116]

[How did the Negroes win their battles? They united to face dogs, fire hoses, brutal police and cattle prods. When threatened, they sing a song of struggle, "We Shall Overcome." When everyone expects them to run, they kneel and pray. When they appear beaten, they turn defeat into victory. They use only what they have, their bodies and their courage, and with these they continue to win.

We farm workers have the same weapons—our bodies and our courage. But we have barely begun to use them. In McFarland the farm workers followed in the path of the Negroes. Through the power of unity, we won a little of the money the bosses have been stealing from us.

In the rent strike, we again showed what we have learned from the black movement. We learned that when we unite, we can make the government respond, changing the arbitrary ways it acts toward the poor. The Tulare County Housing Authority fears the power of organized people.

Every day more and more working people prove their courage as the Negroes are doing in their movement. The day we farm workers apply this lesson with the same courage the Negroes have shown in Alabama and Mississippi; on that day the misery of the farm worker will come to an end.][117]

Although AWOC's Coachella Valley grape strike was big news in the farm worker world, the NFWA's rent strike evoked images of the South, welcomed volunteers, and attracted enough interest to be featured in movement publications that reached far beyond California.[118]

In August, the NFWA won its rent strike when the Tulare County Superior Court ruled that no rent increase was justified. The Tulare County Board of Supervisors ordered the housing authority to repair or replace the units within six months.[119] The rent strike also transformed the largest concentration of farm worker families in Tulare County into a bastion of NFWA support. As Chavez later described it:

> Short of getting into an agricultural strike, the rent strike, which lasted through the summer, was one of the best ways of educating farm workers that there was a union concerned with their economic interests. It was one of the first demonstrations where the black eagle flew.[120]

Moreover, the links forged with students and civil rights organizers during the rent strike brought new people into the NFWA orbit, people whose networks added to the NFWA's growing set of connections to diverse sources of urban support. In August, when the Voting Rights Act became federal law and, a week later, a riot broke out in the Watts ghetto in Los Angeles, the issue of racial justice—and questions of violence and nonviolence—came to be seen in a newly urgent context, especially in California.[121]

At the same time, NFWA leaders began to grapple with a more challenging public support question: the new War on Poverty. At issue was how the newly established Office of Economic Opportunity (OEO) would allocate millions of dollars earmarked to assist the rural poor. Governor Brown requested $3.4 million in antipoverty funds for a "Migrant Master Plan" to fund migrant centers, housing units, facilities for education, job counseling, sanitation, health care, and day care.[122] Although AWOC did not see the OEO as relevant to its labor market concerns, the NFWA, with its focus on the community, saw it as a very serious topic. Chavez, Padilla, and Hernandez attended an antipoverty conference in Arizona, while Huerta had testified in Washington about farm worker conditions when Congress was designing the OEO program.[123] Wendy Goepel, a Berkeley student who had volunteered with the NFWA for the previous year, also knew how to write grant proposals.[124]

On the one hand, NFWA leaders preserved their autonomy and constituency accountability by avoiding outside funds—from unions, philanthropists, and even churches. It was in this spirit that the CMM decided that it would not apply for, accept money from, or serve on OEO-sponsoring committees. In a formal resolution, the Migrant Ministry argued that "accepting OEO money would prostitute the concept of redressing the power balance between workers and growers. The OEO by its very nature lacked the freedom to support militant community organizing."[125]

On the other hand, the NFWA leaders thought it prudent to protect their organizing turf—the community—especially once experience taught them that community-based organizing could help to win strikes. If the NFWA did not get control of the OEO funds, others would, and those others might not share the NFWA's organizing agenda. The American Friends Service Committee, for example, used federal funds to set up a farm worker training program. The CSO applied for funds to put its service centers on firm ground. New groups were appearing simply because there were funds to be had.[126] If someone were going to get the money, the NFWA leaders reasoned, better they use it to build a union than let it fall into the hands of others, who might use it to make unionization harder.[127] With the rent strike in full swing, the NFWA applied for an OEO grant of $500,000 to hire 20 service workers who would organize a wide range of social services, cooperatives, and educational projects.[128]

Grape Strike Warm-Up

By July, on the eve of the Delano grape harvest, both unions were on strike again, this time without much success. AWOC tried to reprise its Coachella success in Arvin, the season's second major table grape region, some 50 miles south of Delano. Unfortunately, the strike failed because the Arvin growers were under less economic pressure than their Coachella colleagues and had easier access to alternative San Joaquin Valley labor sources. After El Rancho Farms in Arvin had 24 strikers arrested for parading without a permit, the Filipino crews went back to work with no wage increase.[129]

At the same time, inspired by the rent strike and angered by a variety of grievances, workers at the J. D. Martin ranch between Delano and Porterville asked the NFWA for support. Some 70 members of the Tulare rent strike families were hired to pull leaves, a horticultural practice necessary to allow maturing grapes access to the sun. To increase production, the grower had instructed the foreman to fire the slowest worker at the end of each day, so the workers raced through the fields.[130] There were no toilets. In Padilla's words, "every time a woman would go take a piss, the supervisor would follow [her] and watch [her] piss."[131] The workers turned to the NFWA for help; once again ready to try their luck, Drake, Padilla, Huerta, Chavez, and others agreed. When they showed up in the fields on July 29, holding aloft big signs saying *huelga* (strike), the workers walked out.[132] Uncertain what to do with the strikers—there seemed little point in having them picket vineyards in which no one was working—the organizers unwisely let them drift away. With no active way to participate in the strike, the strikers became vulnerable to pressures to return to work.[133] The organizers were also unable to figure out any way to go after the labor contractors, who soon began breaking the strike. After about a month of harassment, Martin raised wages and the NFWA called it off.[134] Although the result was an increase in wages, the benefits were realized mainly by strike breakers. The strikers were not organized and there was no contract. It was another lesson about the need to engage workers in their own struggle, whether on the job or on strike, and about the critical difference between a wage increase and a union contract.

CONCLUSION

By the summer of 1965, AWOC claimed 4,500 members, while the NFWA could claim no more than 1,200 families, of which no more than 200 paid dues. But it was the NFWA that had prepared itself for the future. It began to define itself not only as a union but also as a farm worker civil rights movement, a far more effective approach. And it began looking to forms of public support that lay beyond local labor markets, a critical move which AWOC did not make.

These strategic differences initially grew out of differences in the life experiences of the two sets of leaders. Chavez and his collaborators understood the farm worker world better than Green did, and they cared more about it. Strategic capacity is a matter not only of information and motivation, but also of capacity to learn. NFWA leaders continually examined their successes and their failures to learn how strikes worked, while AWOC leaders did not.

The NFWA's learning was enhanced by the diversity of its leadership team, which grew as new farm worker leaders and volunteers, such as Esher and Goepel, were added to it. Moreover, because both the core leadership and volunteers participated in the day-to-day, tactical decision making involved in each strike, the newcomers learned how to function as part of a leadership team, while the top leaders learned firsthand about the on-the-ground realities about which they had to strategize. The NFWA's top leadership used its regular board meetings, credit union meetings, and strategy sessions as venues for learning. The whole organization was infused with a spirit of experimentation as described in one of Chavez's favorite "organizing manuals," Gandhi's *Autobiography: The Story of My Experiments with Truth*.[135]

AWOC, on the other hand, suffered from a split between its leaders and its most dynamic organizers: Itliong, Gines, and the other Filipinos. Although excluded from formal strategy making, the Filipino organizers had more knowledge of their constituency and a greater commitment to it than did Green, Livingston, or Meany. Yet AWOC lacked the deliberative venues within which Green and the other strategists could learn from the organizers, farm workers, or anyone else. There was not even much conversation between Green himself and the AFL-CIO leadership in Washington, DC. Because of this, AWOC's whole was less than the sum of its parts, and its strategy remained unchanged. While the NFWA leadership took their strikes as a learning opportunity, the leaders of AWOC considered them diversion from the real work of developing alliances with labor contractors.

The NFWA's capacity for continuous learning, its motivation to learn, and its access to an array of ever-changing but relevant information set it apart. This capacity made it possible for the NFWA to achieve its breakthrough victory in the next strike it undertook, the Delano grape strike. AWOC, on the other hand, would end up with almost nothing to show for the more than $1 million it spent over the past five years—except for having started the Delano strike, which the NFWA then won.

FIVE

The Great Delano Grape Strike (1965–1966)

There is a tide in the affairs of men,
Which, taken at the flood, leads on to fortune;
Omitted, all the voyage of their life
Is bound in shallows and in miseries.
On such a full sea are we now afloat;
And we must take the current when it serves,
Or lose our ventures.

—William Shakespeare, *Julius Caesar*, IV, iii, 217

GROWING GRAPES IN DELANO

The heart of the California table grape industry, the 37,000 acres of vineyards in the Delano district of Kern and Tulare counties produced 67 percent of the entire fresh grape crop, 10,533 car lots of the 15,733 shipped in 1965. In addition to a natural shipping season that was the longest in the state, growers could ship out of cold storage facilities well into February and March. A particularly important part of the state's total grape production, the 500,000 tons harvested for the table—13 percent of the crop—accounted for 20 percent of the earnings of $31 million in 1965.[1]

Control of the Delano table grape industry was in the hands of 38 firms. Only 2 were based outside the Delano area: the DiGiorgio Fruit Corporation and Schenley Industries. The remaining 36 growers were a tightly knit and remarkably homogeneous group. Most were first- or second-generation Croatian Americans whose families had immigrated to California in the 1920s. Four of the growers were Italian Americans, whose families had also immigrated to the Delano area.[2] As the author John Gregory Dunne wrote of the Croatian Americans:

> [They tend] to stick together and have little social intercourse with the non-Slav growers. Nor do they wander far from their vineyards; there is neither a Slav lawyer nor a Slav doctor in Delano. Around here all we ever talk about is grapes. [Jack] Pandol and his two brothers both married Zaninoviches. The social life of the growers revolved around the Elks Club and the Slav Hall, not around a country club. Only Slavs and people married to Slavs can be members of the Slav Club.[3]

Prohibition, which was a disaster for other California vintners, created an opportunity for these immigrants to market fresh grapes to major cities, where other immigrants could purchase them to produce homemade wine. The Delano growers thrived. And although the 1930s were very hard on them—the repeal of Prohibition sharply reduced the home wine market and the Depression limited the emergence of a consumer market for fresh fruit[4]—by the 1950s, better times had returned.

Table grape production requires a reliable labor force since grapes that are sold fresh in retail stores must be selected for appearance and packed to hold up during the journey to distant cities. Achieving this quality requires horticultural work for much of the year, beginning with pruning and tying in the winter, followed by girdling, thinning, tipping, and leaf pulling in the spring and early summer. Grapes must be harvested at precisely the right moment to meet sugar standards because, unlike tree fruit, they stop ripening once picked. Skilled crews pack them in the fields into shipping lugs, which are trucked to coolers for shipment by truck or train or to be held in cold storage. Table grapes are thus costlier to produce than grapes grown for other uses. Wine grapes, for example, destined for the crusher, require only pruning before they are harvested into large tanks, an operation in which quantity matters more than quality. In 1965, labor accounted for a tiny proportion of the cost of producing wine grapes, but it accounted for one-third of the cost of growing table grapes.[5]

There was a certain benefit in this for table grape workers, who had far greater continuity of employment than most farm workers. Employment of table grape workers in Delano typically peaked not just at harvest, but at three times in the course of a year. In 1961, for example, 3,000 workers were employed in January and February, 3,000 in May and June, and a harvest peak of 4,200 in July, August, and September. Unlike the more industrialized agribusiness sectors, such as citrus, lettuce, or tomatoes, most table grape growers never used *braceros*. Regular employees could secure as much as nine months of continuous employment, and even seasonal grape workers were mostly local residents, who could average 119 days of work a year.[6] A small number worked year-round.

The table grape growers' dependence on these workers gave them a powerful incentive to try to control them and to resist unionization. Control was facilitated by the creation of ethnic employment niches, similar to the ethnic distinctions that defined most aspects of the Delano community. A small cadre of year-round white workers— tractor drivers, irrigators, and maintenance employees living in company housing—enjoyed the most secure employment. Skilled Filipino packing crews, the core of the table grape workforce, who were hired through crew bosses for eight or nine months out of the year and provided with camps in which to live, were relatively secure as well. The next—and far larger—tier of workers were Mexican and Mexican-American families living in Delano, McFarland, Earlimart, and Richgrove.[7] They worked in the fields, typically for five to seven months a year, though with far more turnover and less individual job security than the Filipinos had. Finally, a tier primarily consisting of Mexican green-card immigrants and Mexican-American migrants from Texas would be hired at peak periods for brief stints. All together, about 70 percent of the Delano table grape workforce was Mexican.

In the usual way of agricultural cycles, good times lead to overplanting. So it was in 1965, when new vines, which take seven years to reach full maturity, started to dampen the market with excess supply.[8] By and large, however, the Delano growers were doing well. They did not engage in the sophisticated marketing of the Sunkist or Sun Maid co-ops, but their family-owned corporate farms were huge—typically with 2,000 to 3,000 acres of vineyards,[9] and ranging up to the 12,000 acres of table grapes owned by the Giumarra Fruit Corporation.

[handwritten margin note: anti-union growers]

They were quite satisfied with things as they were. In fact, in 1963, two years before the Delano strike, they had rejected a proposal to create a "marketing order" that would have created a mechanism for taxing themselves to pay for collective advertising and a more aggressive marketing strategy.[10]

The two outsider companies did not have much impact on this comfortable order. The outsiders shared few economic interests with the local grower community, played only a minor role in it, and were, in turn, viewed with some suspicion. DiGiorgio had a long history in the grape industry, and in defeating attempts to unionize it, but over the years the company's interests had shifted. In 1947, the firm broke the NFLU strike. In 1961, it won $150,000 in damages from AWOC after the union showed a film about the strike. By 1965, however, the family business was managed from a San Francisco office and led by a graduate of eastern prep schools. DiGiorgio's 4,400-acre Delano ranch, Sierra Vista, was only one of four major ranch properties owned by the company and operated by its hired managers. Furthermore, farming in general accounted for only 10 percent of its sales of $2.3 million. The bulk of its business was in food processing and wholesaling.[11]

As one of the country's four major liquor distributors, Schenley Industries was even more of an outsider because its business was not agriculture at all.[12] It secured a base in the postwar wine market by buying wineries and the vineyards that came with them. In 1941, Schenley bought the Cresta Blanca winery in Delano with its 4,700 acres of wine grapes and, in 1942, the Roma winery in Fresno.[13] Lewis Rosenstiel, Schenley's chair and CEO, had little in common with the other Delano growers. The son of a Jewish businessman from Cincinnati, he built up a firm with closely held assets of $506 million and sales in 1965 of $461 million, nearly three times the value of the entire California grape crop.[14] His company held union contracts in wineries, distilleries, warehousing, and transport operations and took pride in a pro-union labor relations policy. Schenley was recognized for its fair employment practices as the first major U.S. corporation to hire an African-American vice president.[15] Unlike DiGiorgio, in 1952 Schenley settled an NFLU strike in its California vineyards by providing a wage increase, establishing grievance procedures, and rehiring locked-out workers.[16] Although Schenley had a long record of philanthropy and community involvement, the community in which Rosenstiel had a stake was not Delano.[17]

CALLING A STRIKE: VIVA LA HUELGA!

On September 8, 1965, 800 Filipino workers organized by AWOC struck 10 Delano grape growers, demanding a wage of $1.40 an hour plus 25 cents per box. Two weeks later, on September 20, at least as many Mexican workers, organized by the NFWA, struck an additional 10 growers.[18] By the time the rains brought the table grape harvest to an end in November, 32 growers had been struck, over 5,000 workers had indicated support for one of the two unions, and a movement began to emerge, intended to achieve the revolution in agriculture that the *Los Angeles Times* had predicted.

The strike began at the initiative of AWOC organizers Larry Itliong and Ben Gines and a group of Filipino crew leaders intent on building on their previous success in the Coachella Valley. AWOC director Al Green's attention was focused elsewhere. He was negotiating with Teamster organizer Jim Smith to launch a joint drive among citrus and packinghouse workers later in the year, but he agreed to support the Filipinos in the meantime—mainly to avoid alienating them. If there were to be a grape strike, Green expected it to be quickly won or lost, as in Coachella and Arvin, depending on whether the Filipino grape workers who walked out actually stayed out.[19]

Two weeks before the strike, on August 23, Itliong sent registered letters to the Delano growers, requesting a meeting to discuss wages and working conditions. All but two were returned unopened.[20] Two days before the strike, Itliong chaired a meeting of AWOC members at the Filipino Community Hall to consider options. The next evening, September 7, they voted to strike. Because many were reluctant to picket employers for which they had worked for many years, they decided to sit-in at the camps in which they lived, simply refusing to go to work the next day. AWOC would provide meals for strikers at the Filipino Community Hall, housing if needed, and a $35 per month strike benefit.[21] AWOC organizers would remain on salary and expenses as before. On Friday, September 10, the *Fresno Bee* ran the headline "Strike Idles 1000 Workers in Kern Fields,"[22] and the growers began to evict strikers from their homes in the camps.

The leaders of the NFWA were entirely unprepared for the strike that broke out in their midst and struggled to respond strategically. "Cesar had a plan all along," Jim Drake later said, "but it was a plan for organizing the NFWA, not a strike. Within 48 hours the events of the [AWOC] strike blew that plan clear to hell." As Padilla remembers it:

Cesar called and said, "You better come. The world's coming to an end." The first day, September 8th, I drove to Delano, and Bill Esher [the editor of *El Malcriado*] and I went to the office and we went to Filipino Hall to a meeting of the Filipino leaders. There were a couple of hundred people. Then Green came. We went back and reported to Cesar, who said to find Larry and offer to help. We weren't sure what to do. We offered to help with leaflets and stuff.[23]

Conscious of the limited effectiveness of their own past efforts at Mt. Arbor and J. D. Martin, NFWA leaders were dubious of their capacity to sustain a major strike; neither could they ignore a strike that had hit a nerve with 2,500 Mexican workers, many of whom were NFWA members who wanted a wage increase as well.[24] As Eliseo Medina, who was 18 years old at the time, later recalled:

> We all knew what had happened in Coachella, how the Filipinos struck. It was in the papers, on the radio. They got $1.40, and the strike was coming north. There was lots of tension. You could feel it in the air. Something was going to happen, but you didn't know what.[25]

Some in the NFWA thought AWOC called the strike just to put the NFWA on the spot.[26] But if the NFWA were to break the AWOC strike, how, they asked themselves, could that prepare them to build an organization one day strong enough to conduct strikes of its own?

Chavez urgently called together his leadership team—Padilla, Huerta, Drake, and others—to discuss their options. They decided to put out a leaflet calling on NFWA members to support the strike of the Filipinos.[27] On the Friday that the growers began their evictions, the NFWA began distributing its leaflet.

Over the next few days, sensing an opportunity and willing to take some risks, the NFWA not only offered to help the Filipino strikers, but also decided to test support among Mexican workers for a strike of their own. They mobilized a public strike vote to be held on Thursday, September 16—Mexican Independence Day—in the hall of Our Lady of Guadalupe Church, the religious center of the Delano Mexican community. As it had done before, the NFWA called on its cultural traditions both to encourage attendance and to inspire courage and commitment. The NFWA leaders decided that they would risk leading a strike if the turnout were substantial and if the workers agreed to three conditions. These conditions that indicate that the NFWA had already begun to redefine its strategy and to interpret its effort as something more than just a labor dispute:[28]

Statigy for being successful! (handwritten)

1. The NFWA had no strike fund, so there would be no financial support for strikers or salaries for the leaders—who would have to share in the economic sacrifices of their members. It would have been *one for all* (handwritten) difficult for AWOC to ask this degree of sacrifice of its members or *b/c* (handwritten) its organizers. However, the NFWA had built up considerable trust *part of* (handwritten) among farm workers. Its volunteer organizers were highly motivated. *movement* (handwritten) Its leaders had developed the confidence that they could survive by relying on each other and on volunteer resources.[29] They all agreed to strike without funds. A choice made out of necessity soon became a source of solidarity as shared sacrifices ratcheted up the shared commitment of organizers and members.

2. The strike would be nonviolent. This was new to the farm worker community and to agricultural strikes in general. Chavez had long been interested in Gandhi; reframing the Delano strike as a Gandhi-like nonviolent struggle helped the NFWA to garner support from church groups.[30] It also echoed the civil rights movement. At least since the NFWA's rent strike in June and July, it was clear that identification with the civil rights movement could help to mobilize public support.[31]

3. The NFWA's strike would be for union recognition, not just for the wage increase that AWOC sought. The NFWA's wage demands for table grapes were the same as AWOC's: an increase from $1.20 per hour plus 10 cents per box to $1.40 per hour plus 25 cents per box. Since NFWA members also worked in wine grapes, which were harvested and packed differently, they had additional demands of $1.40 per hour plus $12 per gondola for the first picking, $16 per gondola for the second picking, and $22 per gondola for the third.[32] The fact that the NFWA framed the strike in terms of recognition would remind unions and other urban supporters, particularly the churches, that farm workers remained unprotected by the National Labor Relations Act, had to strike for recognition, and therefore deserved their support.

The meeting, as Medina later remembered it, was dramatic:

Then they call a meeting for Our Lady of Guadalupe on September 16. Everybody's full of revolutionary fervor. So I go to the meeting. Even though I didn't like church much. It's packed. I'd never met Cesar Chavez. I didn't know what the hell he looked like. Padilla...introduces him and he's a little pipsqueak. That's Cesar Chavez? He wasn't a great speaker, but he started talking and made a lot of sense. We deserved to be paid a fair wage. Because we're poor we shouldn't be taken advantage of. We had rights too in this country. We deserve more. The strike

Simple enough for everyone to understand (handwritten)

wouldn't be easy. The more he said how tough it would be the more people wanted to do it. By [the] time the meeting ended...that was it for me.[33]

The 1,000 enthusiastic Mexican farm workers present voted overwhelmingly to accept the three conditions and to go on strike.[34] At a follow-up meeting on Sunday, September 19, at the American Legion Hall, NFWA representatives from throughout the area completed plans for beginning the strike—*la huelga*—the next morning.[35]

This was the beginning of the Delano grape strike, which unfolded as a minor labor dispute for AWOC but as the first step in the birth of a farm workers movement for the NFWA. In the weeks ahead, the difference between the two became increasingly clear. As the strike issue of *El Malcriado* (now published in English as well as Spanish) editorialized:

What is a movement? It is when there are enough people with one idea so that their actions are together like the huge wave of water, which nothing can stop. It is when a group of people begins to care enough so that they are willing to make sacrifices. The movement of the Negro began in the hot summer of Alabama ten years ago when a Negro woman refused to be pushed to the back of the bus. Thus began a gigantic wave of protest throughout the South. The Negro is willing to fight for what is his, an equal place under the sun. Sometime in the future they will say that in the hot summer of California in 1965 the movement of the farm workers began. It began with a small series of strikes. It started so slowly that at first it was only one man, then five, then one hundred. This is how a movement begins. This is why the Farm Workers Association is a movement more than a union.[36]

AWOC's Green, on the other hand, insisted, "This is a trade union dispute, not a civil rights movement or a religious crusade."[37]

BUILDING A MOVEMENT: VIVA LA CAUSA!

As the strike unfolded over the next few days, NFWA leaders had to keep figuring out, with new urgency and limited resources, how to proceed and what to do next. It was an ongoing task that drew deeply on their strategic capacity. Their tactical choices, in turn, began to reshape the contours of the organization and its leadership in ways that expanded that strategic capacity still further. The AWOC leaders, with their limited strategic capacity, showed little flexibility and did little that innovating. Moreover, because of their abundant material resources, they could afford to remain isolated from their own strike leaders and potential allies, cutting off their best chance for increasing their strategic capacity.

The two groups' approaches to collaboration followed this same pattern. The NFWA reached out, but AWOC rejected its proposals. As Chavez described it:

> Sunday we met with Al Green...and I proposed that we have a joint strike committee, a joint finance committee—they had all the money, we didn't have any—and a joint picket line. We said we would recognize him as the leader of the strike.... But he turned us down. He said, "I'm just an organizing committee. I'm not authorized to make those kinds of deals." "Well, can you call Washington?" I asked. "No I don't want to call Washington....It's not necessary." So I asked if we could issue a joint press statement. "No, I don't think that's wise." There was nothing more to say.[38]

Hartmire later remembered:

> [Chavez called me] to come up to Delano because he wanted to work out a cooperative relationship with AWOC, and he wanted me to mediate it. I met with Cesar and Al Green. I realized I was there to witness and, if necessary, to speak out about what I had witnessed.[39]

Chavez had experience dealing with a wide range of organizations, including labor unions, which gave him insight into the politics of the situation. He had the courage to attempt a collaboration that he knew would be problematic and the foresight to see that he might need a witness as to who offered to cooperate with whom. Green, on the other hand, saw nothing to gain from broadening the strike leadership and rejected collaboration outright. Because of who their leaders were and how they operated, this rejection ultimately left the NFWA free to develop new tactics, while leaving AWOC cut off from new ideas.

Attending to the differences in the NFWA's and AWOC's responses, we can see strategic capacity in action. While AWOC maintained traditional stationary picket lines, the NFWA leaders devised a new approach: roving picket lines. While AWOC organizers drew salaries and dispensed strike benefits from an AFL-CIO-supplied strike fund, NFWA leaders created a support network, making the most of the varied support it could provide. While AWOC told the story of the strike

AWOC = wealthy but that proves to be detrimental

haters finna hate

FIGURE 5.1. AWOC and NFWA strikers on the picket line, Delano, 1965. *Source:* John A. Kouns

to itself, its members, and the public as just another labor dispute, the NFWA told a story of the birth of a new movement, rooted in specific ethnic, religious, and political traditions, and reached out to incorporate the legacy of the civil rights struggle. While AWOC conducted regular business meetings, the NFWA created weekly Friday night meetings, which were solidarity celebrations combining theater, song, special guests, and interpretations of the week's events. While AWOC limited its strike activity to picketing, the NFWA turned to the tactics of civil disobedience, including voluntary arrests. Although every one of the tactical choices made by NFWA reflected the strategic capacity of the leaders making it, it also increased that capacity by deepening the organizers' motivation and broadening their access to new sources of information.

Learning to Picket

After its sit-in tactic failed—because the growers had evicted strikers from their camps during the first few days of the strike—AWOC took the traditional union approach to picketing, assigning its strikers to stationary picket lines at their employers' cold storage facilities. AWOC leaders assumed that, if they could keep the skilled Filipino workers out of the vineyards, the growers would eventually see that replacement workers couldn't do the job as well and would then agree to the Filipinos' demands. This was how AWOC's past strikes were won. So AWOC's picket lines were not meant to keep strike breakers from working in the vineyards, but to keep the strikers busy so they wouldn't return to work themselves. As a result, AWOC leaders felt no need to change their tactics when the picketing had little impact on the growers' operations. Green talked about the Teamsters and unionized railroad workers honoring AWOC's picket lines at the storage facilities and thus disrupting the growers' shipping. In practice, however, the Teamsters would drive their trucks up to a picket line and turn them over to supervisors, who would take them in, load them up, and bring them back out.[40] By sticking with traditional picket lines, AWOC was thus confining itself to a tactic of very limited impact.

The NFWA had no picketing tradition; it was something to be learned. The first lesson came on Monday, September 20, the first morning that the NFWA joined the strike, when only 200 of its activists reported at 3:30 a.m. The NFWA leaders realized that, for their strike to be effective, grower production *would* have to be disrupted. This would require the participation of many more workers from many more farms than 200 people could picket AWOC-style. The improvised result was the roving picket line tactic. Strikers set out in car caravans, arrived at grape fields waving flags and banners, called the workers out of the fields, and then moved on to the next location. But how to know which fields the workers would be in? The NFWA leaders quickly devised a method. They assigned a key organizer to each farm worker town in the area—Padilla to Earlimart, Huerta to Richgrove, Drake to McFarland, Chavez to Delano—who would meet each morning with strikers from the area and send out scouts to identify the locations where growers were preparing for work or where workers had been spotted. These tactics eventually got most of the local grape workers and even many of the replacement workers, whom growers recruited from as far away as Texas, to walk out. Because many of them then left the area to find work elsewhere, the job of convincing the next contingent of replacement workers to strike continued to fall on a small core of activists. They continued to come up with new, invented-on-the-spot tactics to do so. Are the people in the fields working far from the road? Let's try using loudspeakers to reach them. Are employers bringing out their own loudspeakers to shout us down? Let's get there before they do. Someone came up with the idea of pressuring the labor contractors to take their workers elsewhere. Someone else created the idea of picketing in front of the contractors' homes. Yet another person came up with the idea of picketers saying masses in front of the contractors' homes. With these inventive ways of picketing, it turned out that a relatively small core of NFWA activists could sustain a strike longer, at more farms, and for less money than anyone expected.[41] What is more, the regular participants in the roving picket line turned into the core of a full-time cadre, many of whom would become organizers.[42] Thus, the NFWA's capacity to creatively adapt to unforeseen challenges enabled it to deepen its capacity further by developing more leaders, who then learned to devise strategies and tactics in their own right.

New tactics ↓
New leaders ↓
new ideas / diversity

Creating a Strike Fund

On Sunday, the strikers celebrated the first week of their combined strike with a joint AWOC-NFWA march welcoming Bay Area labor union members, who had come to Delano after a six-hour car caravan. Although the march was a joint effort, only AWOC could count on the regular support of the AFL-CIO.[43] NFWA leaders had to look to their own networks to find resources elsewhere.

Hartmire, for instance, built on his experience in southern civil rights protests and recruited clergy delegations, like those that had gone to Mississippi, to come to Delano. The delegations could see conditions firsthand, then return home to raise food and money.[44] The first such delegation arrived in the second week of the NFWA strike. Hartmire recalled:

Cesar and Jim Drake and I brainstormed that delegation together. I was trying to get people to come and bring food, the beginning of the weekly caravan-to-Delano campaign. [That first delegation] included Episcopal bishop Walters of Stockton, Reverend Robert McAfee Brown, and others. There were 10 or 12....I had to identify people who would be willing and who would also have connections. It was a fact-finding delegation....And the growers...ran a disc [plow] right next to Bishop Walters and just made him filthy with dirt. The growers say, "There's not a strike." And this innocent, sweet old guy says, "Well, I don't know. I saw the picket line and then I saw people come out of the fields to join the picket line. It certainly looked like a strike to me." But he wasn't as innocent as he appeared. He was a spry old labor guy from way back. [The delegation] held a press conference calling for negotiations, covered by the local press. The report was circulated to the constituency. There was no effort to get general press, but to educate the church constituency.... The churches contributed mainly food and bodies, not money.[45]

Civil rights groups such as the Bay Area Friends of SNCC, student organizations such as SCAL, and others also began to send delegations. In contrast, AWOC leaders, with sufficient resources of their own, rejected offers of outside support, except those that came through what they considered to be legitimate labor channels. While this decision did AWOC leaders no harm financially, it isolated them from a public that was becoming increasingly interested in the strike.[46] This closed off yet another way that AWOC could have grown its strategic capacity—a fact of which NFWA was taking full advantage.

The extent to which the NFWA was adapting not just its tactics but also its strategy to new conditions became clear in another funding decision. On October 6, the NFWA was awarded almost $270,000 of the OEO grant for which it had applied the previous June, when its strategy for building a union was to start by offering social services and community problem solving. OEO officials, oblivious of the fact that the NFWA was now leading a grape strike, finished processing the application and announced the award. This called forth a firestorm of protest from Delano growers and their allies, including the San Joaquin Valley's Democratic representative, Harlan Hagen, the city council of Delano, and the California Council of Growers.[47] Five days later, on October 11, the OEO announced that the grant would be held up, pending investigation.[48] The political reality was that the NFWA had to abandon either the grant or the strike. In his biography of Chavez, Ron Taylor quotes Thomas Karter, who was chief of the OEO Migrant Division at the time and who flew to Delano to meet Chavez:

> During our discussion...it became clear to Chavez that he could not operate a poverty program and organize a strike at the same time. He decided that the strike and the concepts of collective bargaining and union recognition were more important than the $267,000 grant and calmly informed me that he would not accept the OEO grant until the strike was successful.[49]

Had there been no grape strike, it is quite possible that the NFWA would have followed the path of other community groups, such as the Del Rey–based Center for Community Development, which received a $250,000 grant about the same time and was later transformed into a social services agency.[50] But when the NFWA decided to strike, it changed its strategy to match its actions.

Ethnic identity, rooted in the experience of Mexican immigrants in the United States, had been central to the NFWA's organizing strategy since its founding. As the Delano strike unfolded, rich Mexican cultural narratives and Roman Catholic religious traditions provided what economist Albert Hirschman has called "moral resources," resources that actually grow with use. Strikers and organizers drew upon these resources to sustain their commitment to La Causa.[51] Masses celebrated by "*huelga* priests" became part of the weekly striker routine, affirming the value of the shared sacrifice that the strike required.[52] Ethnic traditions of mutual support among extended families provided the model for the mutuality at the core of the striker community.[53] Mexican historical narratives of revolutionary struggle came alive as slogans began to appear on walls and fences that read: *Viva Juárez, Viva Zapata, Viva Chavez!*[54] The Teatro Campesino, a theater troupe organized by Luis Valdez—a 23-year-old college student from a Delano farm worker family who had been involved in SNCC, visited Cuba, and worked with the famous San Francisco Mime Troupe before joining the grape strikers—told the story of the strike in songs, *actos*, and comic presentations, combining elements of Mexican folk theater, commedia dell'arte, Bertolt Brecht, and the San Francisco Mime Troupe. The Teatro Campesino exposed the relations among growers, contractors, and workers for what they were, bringing humor, pride, and celebration to the whole enterprise.[55] Eventually, it became a model for urban Chicano theater throughout the Southwest.[56]

By the second week of the strike, the NFWA had established a weekend routine of Friday night meetings and Saturday delegations that wove these strands together. The Friday night meetings, usually led by Chavez, were two-hour celebrations at which each new chapter in the story of the strike was told in reports, the words of supporters, skits, and songs. About 200 strikers, their families, and NFWA volunteers typically packed "Negrito Hall," a small building owned by an African-American women's association in the town of Delano. Delegations of religious, student, labor, and community activists who had come to join the picket line the next day would present gifts of food and money at the Friday night meetings—and leave inspired to do more. The Friday night meetings were not a venue for strategic or tactical deliberation; those types of discussions occurred in regular meetings among picket captains, organizers, and NFWA leaders. Nonetheless, the telling of the unfolding story of the strike was as important as the devising of strategy, because it sustained the commitment of the strike participants. As Medina later put it:

I loved the Friday night meetings. They were like revivals. There was *keeps morality up* all this great fun, and reports and speeches. A strong sense of solidarity. We're all in it together. Hearing people come from San Francisco, L.A., [and] places that I never even knew existed. It was all very new....People would come, and ministers and priests....And then they announced all these famous politicians and unions. Shit! Wow! It was like I was drinking fine wine.[57]

The NFWA's ethnic approach enabled it to reach out to farm workers who knew little about the specific economic goals of the strike, but who understood it as an effort by "Mexican people" to help themselves.[58] It also meant that the strike could draw economic, political, and moral support from Mexicans and Mexican Americans in cities and towns throughout the state. As Alberto Rojas, an Oxnard community activist who later became an NFWA organizer, later recalled:

In 1965, we heard the strikers needed food so we start[ed] taking food collections. There was lots of talk, radio, newspapers; I remembered my father and grandfather [talking about it]. I didn't even think of it in terms of a union. I thought more of our people's right to be able to be respected....We're human beings too....We, the Mexican people, it was like the people are asking for help. I took food. Went to the picket line. The cops came. It was a taste of fear and [a] feeling we accomplished something. We felt good.[59]

Of course, AWOC also held daily strike meetings. But they were dull affairs focused on administrative questions, the distribution of strike benefits, and picket line attendance.[60] And although ethnic identity did contribute to the solidarity of AWOC's Filipino base, it was not embraced by the organization led by Anglos Smith and Green, neither of whom understood its value.

The NFWA's interpretation of ethnic identity went beyond creating strong bonds of solidarity among workers; it also was a way to reach out to a far broader public. In 1965, the systematic discrimination to which Mexicans had been subjected in the Southwest was a story not well known by the rest of the country, but one about which NFWA leaders could speak from their own experiences. Public support for the civil rights movement suggested that the rest of the country might be ready to hear it. It was a story that helped to explain the dire circumstances in which farm workers lived and, at the same time, distinguished the NFWA as more than just another union and the farm worker struggle as more than just another strike. It was the story that would turn this movement into what author Peter Mathiessen in the *New Yorker* called the next chapter in the "new American revolution."[61]

Furthermore, La Causa rooted its claims in Catholic social teachings, which not only afforded workers access to what Catholic moral philosopher Charles Taylor calls "moral sources" of solidarity, commitment, and hopefulness.[62] It also attracted a new generation of laity and clergy at a time when church leaders in Rome were concluding Pope John XXIII's Second Vatican Council (Vatican II), a dramatic reinvigoration of the Catholic social justice tradition. Chavez had also learned in the 1950s that affiliation with the church could insulate an organization like the NFWA from the red baiting that had been so effective in scuttling farm union organizing efforts in the past.

Vatican II and the civil rights movement offered farm worker organizers a great opportunity, but only the NFWA leaders seized it. Their vision limited by their narrow lenses, the AWOC leaders didn't even recognize it and probably couldn't have acted on it even if they had. Ironically, the NFWA's seemingly insular ethnic approach ultimately garnered it an expanding circle of diverse and increasingly committed adherents.

expansion & diversity

Practicing Civil Disobedience

Among the gravest challenges the NFWA faced was the potential for violence on the picket lines. The very first week of the joint strike—with tensions rising among scabs, strikers, and supervisors—the growers hired armed security guards and secured injunctions intended to limit pickets. Committed to nonviolence, Chavez called on the CORE and SNCC organizers with whom the NFWA had formed relationships during the Tulare rent strike. He asked them to send people to Delano to train the NFWA strikers in the methods of nonviolent protest, including dealing with the police, maintaining discipline, devising creative alternatives, and resisting grower provocations. Chavez recalled: "We needed somebody who could talk to the cops—or who had the confidence to talk to the cops. The Mexicans couldn't handle it at first. They had to be trained into the job."[63]

The training in nonviolence introduced the NFWA strikers and leaders to new skills, as well as to new ways of thinking about tactics. Since nonviolent protest is not about passivity, but about coming up with alternative ways of winning one's battles, the training provided a further foundation for creative thinking. At the same time, it brought urban civil rights activists more actively into the farm workers' cause. Many of the picket captains in the early days of the

NFWA strike were volunteers from CORE and SNCC, such as Bob Solodow, Bob Fisher, and Rodney Freedland.[64] Access to such people, their knowledge, and their constituencies helped the NFWA to adjust tactics. Once again, the new tactics expanded the strategic capacity of the NFWA leadership.

By the fourth week of the strike, the growers had become successful at recruiting strike breakers. Strikers from the two unions may have raised growers' costs and reduced the quality of their product, but they were not able to stop the harvest. Workers no sooner left the fields than others would take their places. Despite this dynamic, AWOC continued to maintain its stationary picket lines, waiting for the growers to feel the need for skilled workers, or for the season to end—and, thus, for the strike to be over one way or the other. In the face of this, NFWA stepped up its efforts to reach the strike breakers in the fields. When growers complained that this was interfering with the work of the harvest, Kern County sheriff LeRoy Gallyen decided to stop it.[65] On Saturday, October 16, his office announced that picketers who called out to workers in the vineyards over loudspeakers were disturbing the peace and would be arrested.

Faced with such situations in the past, AWOC looked at the law and the costs and withdrew from the fray. NFWA leaders were more motivated to keep at it. Inspired by an openness to experimentation, the civil rights experience among NFWA organizers, and Chavez's admiration for Gandhi, they proposed a new way to respond to the sheriff—a way new, at least, to the world of farm workers. Using what Chavez, quoting Gandhi, called "moral jujitsu," they turned the aggressive action that local law enforcement intended to cripple the picketing into opportunities for civil disobedience that would generate wider public support for the strike.

Once again, leaders and picketers developed the specific tactics on the spot, by trial and error. After a rushed Saturday evening strategy session, NFWA leaders decided to test the sheriff's ruling. On Sunday, October 17, the Reverend David Havens read Jack London's "Definition of a Strikebreaker" over a loudspeaker to strike breakers in the vineyards and was arrested. The rousing scene inspired the NFWA leaders to try the same thing on a larger scale. They came up with the idea of staging mass arrests; they would alert reporters and time the mass arrests to coincide with Chavez's first Bay Area speaking tour, scheduled for that week. Two days later, on Tuesday morning, the NFWA advised reporters that mass arrests were imminent. After the camera crews arrived on the scene, 44 strikers and their supporters—including Helen Chavez, 8 other women, and 11 members of the clergy—lined up beside a vineyard at the edge of the road, shouted "Huelga!" They were promptly arrested and taken to jail.[66] Hartmire recalls:

> I was supposed to be the outside contact, but the sheriff grabbed me, and threw me in the car, right while I was talking with Harry Bernstein from the *L.A. Times*. [Bernstein] was totally offended that this guy interrupted the conversation. The sheriff was just used to having the power and doing what comes naturally. Harry's story was the one that was picked up [by the national press]...and I learned quickly that calling from Delano was like calling from Selma, from the front lines.[67]

Speaking to several thousand students at a UC Berkeley rally that day, Chavez interrupted his remarks to read from a note that he had just been handed, informing him of the arrests. He asked the students to contribute their "lunch money" to the strikers. The arrests not only linked Delano with sites of similar civil disobedience in the South, but Chavez's talks at Berkeley, San Francisco State, Stanford, San Jose State, Mills College, and elsewhere netted $6,700.[68] For student volunteers, "going to Delano" became the California version of "going to Mississippi."[69]

In the following weeks, arrests and injunctions proliferated, generating new strength, public sympathy, and an array of new problems, including the need for lawyers familiar with civil disobedience. Victor Van Bourg, a well-known San Francisco labor lawyer who represented AWOC, was not such a lawyer. Via connections to Citizens for Farm Labor, however, they found Alex Hoffman, a Bay Area lawyer who had been active in civil rights work and in the free speech movement at UC Berkeley. He agreed to move to Delano, where he served as the NFWA's attorney until the spring of 1967—over one and a half years. The first lawyer to join the NFWA's leadership circle, he brought a new perspective and a set of connections that further enhanced the union's strategic capacity.

THE GROWERS FIGHT BACK

[handwritten margin note: growers goliath?]

The Delano growers were a relatively insular community whose limited strategic capacity left them vulnerable to the Goliath problem. They could not see how the NFWA's resourcefulness could possibly trump their access to the resources that had served them well in the past. They formed the South Central Farmers Committee to coordinate their response to the strike. Free of the economic constraints that had forced the Coachella growers to react to the strikers and believing that the Delano work stoppage would soon end, as the stoppage in Arvin had, the growers offered no wage increase, no negotiations, and no compelling public defense of their position. Indeed, at first, the growers ignored the public dimension of the strike entirely. As grower Bruno Dispoto said, "We had a crop to harvest. Telling our story was secondary. And anyway, people just weren't buying the good-guy growers story."[70]

The growers cajoled strikers who were feeling economic pressure to return to work. They recruited replacements, initially from Bakersfield and eventually from as far away as Texas. They hired armed guards to patrol their fields and turned to local law enforcement to inhibit the picketing. Like AWOC, however, they failed to see the public as a party to the strike, were ill prepared to deal with the press, had no interest in explaining their position to church delegations, and generally reacted with anger toward outsiders who seemed suddenly to be taking an interest in their business without knowing anything about it.[71] As Ron Taylor, a *Fresno Bee* reporter at the time, later recalled:

> After the grape strike had started, Robert MacAfee Brown and a whole bunch of other preachers from all over the country had come in and were going to meet with the growers.... The growers stiffed them for lunch. They didn't show up.... That was a typical reaction of the local growers, and then they brought [Joseph] Brosmer [from the Agricultural Labor Bureau in to help them].[72] ... When the grape strike started...I got approval from the paper to do a three-part series. One was on the strike itself. One was on Chavez and the Filipinos, and one was going to be on the South Central Farmers. I wanted to balance the thing. But when I asked to meet with the farmers, Brosmer wouldn't let Martin [Zaninovich, the Delano grower who headed the South Central Farmers Committee] or anybody else talk to me.... Brosmer sat there and gave me their line of bullshit. I wrote the stories [and he was furious with them]. He asked to see Dick Skinner, the managing editor, and he wanted to get me fired, and Skinner said, "I want you to prove everything you're saying [that Taylor got it wrong]." Of course he couldn't. So they dismissed him and told him to go to hell. He was not much of a public relations man![73]

In the story that the growers eventually did try to tell the public, they made three arguments: there is no problem, there is no strike, and the uproar is all the work of outsiders (i.e., Communists, civil rights groups, and churches). On October 2, for example, the *California Farmer* reported: "the labor dispute instigated in the Delano area by the AWOC is almost totally ineffective....the actual number of workers involved was almost impossible to pinpoint accurately but...most place the number as somewhere between 400 and 800."[74] Or, as the California Council of Growers put it in a newsletter on November 1:

[W]orkers are averaging $1.60/hour, [some] over $2.00 hour, plus free housing, and utilities...[which is why] the emphasis shifted from a straight labor dispute to a civil rights demonstration....[And now] the civil rights forces have taken over...although they continue to use Chavez and his FWA as a front....[T]he presence of these ministers and civil rights people has no purpose except publicity.[75]

On November 9, the *San Francisco Examiner* quoted Brosmer:

Poverty? The last survey I looked at showed them making $1.95/hour. Why would they want a $1.40/hour guarantee? They don't need it and they don't want a union contract either. It's just an idea of that Chavez and a couple of other union leaders trying to feather their own nests....These pickers don't want a union. They've got real fine relationships with the employers. Really personal. A union would destroy them.[76]

The Delano growers were not stupid men. Jack Pandol, for instance, shrewdly observed to John Gregory Dunne that "all Chavez is trying to do is replace my power structure with his."[77] Although insular, there were individuals among them who did recognize the legitimacy of striker demands, if not their desire for a union. But for one of them to break ranks to negotiate would have been, in Dunne's words, "a breach of community faith, an act that would forever tarnish his credentials among his neighbors."[78] This gave the NFWA a real strategic advantage. As Taylor put it, "Martin and his friends...have large operations and they are sophisticated people in many ways; there are some nice guys, some bad guys. But they dealt only...in Delano."[79] Although they made an effort to galvanize Delano's white community by forming Citizens for Facts from Delano,[80] and they sponsored an organization of Mexican-American and Filipino labor contractors known as the Kern-Tulare Independent Farm Workers,[81] their appeals to an outside audience for the most part misfired.

Claims that were conventional wisdom within the world of the Delano growers, when articulated in the San Francisco and Los Angeles press, bore an eerie resemblance to claims the public had heard for the previous 10 years out of the mouths of defenders of the southern status quo. Delano talk of Filipino and Mexican "boys" sounded like Alabama talk of black "boys."[82] The exercise of authority that was seen as legitimate within Delano seemed distinctly illegitimate elsewhere. As the attorney for one of the largest Delano growers told Dunne:

> The growers have put on a miserable performance. They had a case and didn't present it. They were sullen and stolid and the only thing they could think of was calling everyone a Communist. They're so paternalistic. They don't understand why people want to be responsible for their own condition. All this stuff they give about "We know our men and they're happy." It doesn't ring true.[83]

The close ties at the heart of this industry—which were key to its control over the labor market, the marketing of its product, and power within the local community—made it much harder for the industry to see itself as others saw it. The growers' very cohesion obscured what others could see was taking shape in their midst. Not unlike Goliath, the growers thought they stood on familiar turf, facing a small warrior without a sword. As the turf began to shift, however, they found they were facing a shepherd, not a warrior, who could turn stones into a weapon more powerful than a sword.

TARGETING SCHENLEY: VIVA EL BOICOTEO!

As the strike wore into November and it became clear that rain would end the harvest before the strike would be resolved, the organizers had to decide whether to continue the strike and, if so, how. After the rains, there would be no more work in table grapes until the pruning and tying in January. Although the local Mexican workers who were the NFWA's base of support usually did much of this winter work, the pruning and tying could be done by a smaller number of workers over a longer period of time. Growers continued to ship grapes from their cold storage facilities throughout the winter, however, which suggested that interference with shipping could exert economic pressure on growers and thus sustain the strike. The last farm strike that extended beyond the end of the harvest, however, was the NFLU's failed DiGiorgio campaign 15 years before—not an auspicious precedent.

Given these realities, AWOC leaders, especially Green, were inclined to write off the Delano strike and refocused their attention on organizing the citrus industry with the Teamsters.[84] The NFWA also tried to keep options to the strike open by extending its organizing to Bakersfield and by deferring rather than outright rejecting the OEO grant. The grape strike was nonetheless generating real momentum for the NFWA with its Friday night meetings, weekly caravans, steady stream of visitors, and growing core of volunteers. Despite their uncertainty, the NFWA leaders decided to take advantage of the momentum. Their strategy, however, became clear only as they began to redefine the arena of the conflict.

This is how it happened. Because Green's promises that the Teamsters would help stop grape shipments had turned out to be empty, some of the younger Filipino strikers began working with the NFWA to follow truckloads of grape shipments to Los Angeles and San Francisco, hoping to interfere with the unloading. On November 17, four NFWA pickets posted themselves at Pier 50 on the San Francisco docks, with hopes, but no actual plan, for winning support from the rank-and-file longshoremen loading Delano grapes for shipment to the Far East. As Padilla tells the story:

> We went there as the grapes were being loaded onto ships to Japan... and I'm standing out there with a little cardboard, with a picket [sign], "Don't eat grapes." then some of the longshoremen asked, "Is this a labor dispute?" And I [was nervous and didn't know whether we were legally allowed to use the term, so I] said, "No, no, no labor dispute." So they would walk in. Jimmy Herman came over and asked me, "What the hell you doing?" And I told him we were striking. He knew about the strike but wanted to know, "what are you asking for?" And I was telling him, and then he says, "Come with me." He took me to his office; he was president of the clerks [a Longshoremen's Union local]. He took me to his office and he got on his hands and knees, Jimmy Herman, and he made picket signs. And he told me, "You go back there and don't tell nobody about who gave you this. But you just stand there. [You] don't [have to] say a goddamned thing." The sign said, "Farm Workers on Strike." And everybody walked out of that fucking place, man! That's the first time I felt like I was 10 feet tall, man! Everybody walked out. So then they asked what's happening and we were telling them, and Jesus Christ, man, I never seen anything like it. There were trucks all the way up to the bridge, man! So they stopped and Jimmy says, "You're gonna get an injunction as soon as the people find out what's happening. In the meantime you got to stop them. You go ahead and do it. They ain't gonna do nothing to you.

Can't do a thing to you, but they're gonna go after…Harry Bridges [the Longshoremen's Union president, who] will have no choice but to ask you to leave, because if they get an injunction, they'll get fined. So you do it until that happens."[85]

Because 1,250 cases of grapes from the Pagliarulo farm in Delano had been loaded on board the *President Wilson*, the longshoremen stopped work. The ship, which had been scheduled to leave with 400 passengers for the Far East, stayed tied up in port until the grapes were removed, whereupon the longshoremen agreed to go back to work.[86] At the end of November, a similar action on the Oakland docks got 2,500 cases of DiGiorgio grapes removed.[87] This was a powerful tonic to the strikers, but lawsuits against the Longshoremen's Union and the NFWA—by Pagliarulo for damages of $59,000 and by DiGiorgio for $38,000—led to a December 15 court injunction against further picketing of the docks.[88] This was the point to which the NFLU had gotten in 1949, when it was enjoined from picketing DiGiorgio produce at Safeway. Unlike the NFLU, however, the NFWA did not respond to the injunction by dropping its boycott. Instead, the NFWA leaders were determined to find a way to continue it. The question they asked was: "How?"

Their answer—a consumer boycott—originated in the work of SNCC volunteers who had learned how to research the northern connections of segregated southern institutions and whom Chavez asked to research the growers. While the holdings of most growers were agricultural, the researchers discovered that Schenley not only produced Roma wine but also marketed well-known whiskey brands, such as Cutty Sark.[89] As early as October 12, SNCC and CFL had organized a picket line—made up of some 50 volunteers from student, civil rights, Mexican-American, and church groups—at Schenley's San Francisco headquarters.[90] Schenley's easy-to-recognize list of consumer products came quickly to mind when picketing grapes at produce terminals and docks was stopped. Legally, workers could not refuse to handle the products of Delano growers; there was nothing illegal about consumers refusing to buy them, however. Although shoppers could not distinguish one grape from another, they could distinguish Schenley's liquor brands from those of its competitors. As the NFWA leaders talked about it, they came up with the idea of picketing Schenley products at the stores in which they were sold. Launching a consumer boycott of Schenley would also be a way to put to work student volunteers, who were still coming to Delano to support the strike even though there was now little to do there. The students could return to the cities and organize Schenley boycotts. Chavez named Jim Drake of the CMM and Mike Miller of San Francisco SNCC to coordinate the plan.[91]

The NFWA leadership took advantage of the approaching Christmas season and the 100th day of the strike to launch the boycott. They also saw the holiday season as an opportunity to reinvigorate the religious and labor support, both moral and financial, that would be needed to sustain the strikers in Delano through the winter. With the support of CMM, SNCC, CORE, and SDS networks, the NFWA dispatched a corps of student volunteers and strikers to major cities across the United States to organize picket lines at liquor outlets in communities likely to be responsive.[92] Drawing tactics more from a civil rights than a labor repertoire and uncertain of its liability under the secondary boycott laws, the NFWA instructed organizers to ask consumers to shun only Schenley products, not the stores at which they were being sold.[93] Because the NFWA could not afford to send them funds, boycott organizers had to fundraise to meet their operating costs, including subsistence for themselves, in every city to which they were assigned. Although the AFL-CIO did not support the Schenley boycott, boycotters secured room, board, an office, and a telephone from sympathetic union locals in many cities.

The NFWA launched the boycott on the weekend of December 12—the feast day of our Lady of Guadalupe, a major saint's day for Mexican Catholics—at a Fresno conference of some 60 people. The conference was convened by SNCC and the NFWA to mobilize urban support for rural organizing.[94] For the entire week, the NFWA orchestrated a cascade of events to recapture public attention. To kick things off, the NFWA called for a "nationwide informational picket of Roma wines" from December 18 through December 31.[95] On Monday, December 13, a delegation of 10 national church leaders organized by Hartmire arrived to meet the strikers, observe the conditions, and witness the picketing firsthand. The next day, the four Roman Catholic, one Jewish, and six Protestant leaders issued a statement in Delano that bolstered the strikers and offered renewed justification for their urban support:

> The suffering of farm workers and their children cries to heaven and demands the attention of persons of conscience. Farm workers are worthy. Their labor is important to the agricultural industry. It is both natural and just that they should participate in the decision-making process about wages, working conditions, and automation.... [T]his basic right is being denied to farm workers in this valley.[96]

While the clergy visited Delano, NFWA supporters in the Bay Area were working the AFL-CIO national convention in San Francisco. Although many of the delegates that year were focused on supporting President Lyndon Johnson's policy in Vietnam, the convention also acted on Resolution No. 221, introduced by Reuther, which called on affiliates to help with "moral" and "financial" support for AWOC members on strike.[97] The challenge for the NFWA was to get some of that support directed to itself. With help from Reuther's youthful California regional director, Paul Schrade, and from CFL activist Ann Draper, the NFWA succeeded. Persuaded to join the celebration of the 100th day of the strike in Delano, Reuther invited Meany to join him. But Meany had no interest.[98] On December 16, Reuther arrived in Delano, leading an entourage whose members included: the UAW; the AFL-CIO's Industrial Union Department, a bastion of Reuther support; and some 60 or 70 members of the national press corps, whom Reuther bused to Delano.[99]

As the first national figure to visit Delano, Reuther brought the grape strike to national attention.[100] After leading a march through town in defiance of a city ordinance banning marches, meeting with an awestruck mayor and city council, and meeting the few growers who would see him, he was welcomed by an enthusiastic joint rally of AWOC and NFWA members packed into the Filipino Community Hall. The NFWA organizers focused on turning out their people so that the cheering when Chavez was introduced would leave little question as to the identity of the real leader of the strike. In his talk, Chavez showed that he had done his homework, comparing Reuther's support for striking farm workers in Delano with John L. Lewis's support for the sit-down strikers in Flint, a key moment in the birth of Reuther's UAW.[101] When Reuther himself spoke, it was clear that the NFWA had made its point. He concluded his remarks by pledging support for the strike of $5,000 a month for the duration: $2,500 from the AFL-CIO's IUD and $2,500 from the UAW. Despite the fact that Resolution No. 221 had mentioned only the AFL-CIO's AWOC, the money was to be split 50-50 between AWOC and the independent NFWA. Reuther even added a one-time Christmas bonus of $5,000.[102] As Ron Taylor later wrote:

> Rows of TV cameras recorded the event, dozens of reporters from the big dailies in NY, Chicago, Detroit, SF, and LA filed their stories. *Time* and *Newsweek* took notice of the happenings. The first media event involving a national figure was a success for everyone but the disgruntled farmers.[103]

This was the first substantial support from organized labor that the NFWA had received and the first regular support upon which it could count over the long haul. With it, the NFWA leaders saw how the conflict between Meany and Reuther, which was responsible for launching AWOC in the first place, could also create opportunities for an independent union. Later that night, as some NFWA leaders gathered at Richard Chavez's house to toast the moment, Chavez expressed his ambivalence over accepting the outside funding. "Tonight," he said, "we lost our independence."[104] But, in fact, the NFWA had learned a valuable lesson: how to retain its autonomy by managing the political dynamics among powerful organizations that would have liked to control it.

AWOC was invited to join in the boycott but declined for legal, political, and strategic reasons. Legally, its leaders were concerned that the National Labor Relations Act's ban on secondary boycotts might apply. Politically, they wanted to avoid problems with the distillery workers and other unions that represented Schenley employees.[105] Strategically, Green wanted to put aside the grape strike in the interest of collaboration with the Teamsters to organize citrus workers in Strathmore.

FIGURE 5.2. Walter Reuther visits Delano, pledges support, December 1965. *Left to right*: Larry Itliong, Reuther, Cesar Chavez. *Source:* © 1978 George Ballis/Take Stock

As it turned out, Green's tin ear would hamper the citrus effort as well. Although he and Jim Smith of the Teamsters had been planning it since August, they picked December 14 to stage their kickoff rally in Strathmore—the day after the AFL-CIO voted to support the grape strike and when all eyes were focused on Reuther and Delano. The citrus drive, Teamsters Joint Council 38 president George Mock said at the rally, "is part of a long-range plan to organize workers in every commodity that is packed and shipped in California.... [W]hether it takes one year or ten years, we intend to keep going."[106] Nonetheless, Green's vision of a pathway to the future remained narrow. "The citrus effort," he said, "is an honest-to-God trade union fight, not a civil rights demonstration.... I am relying on union support. The NFWA is administered by ministers. We will continue in our own union way."[107] Although AWOC and the Teamsters had opened joint offices throughout eastern Tulare and Kern counties during the winter and early spring of 1966, Reuther's visit to Delano scotched any AFL-CIO plans to abandon the grape strike, at least for the time being.

By focusing national attention on the Delano grape strike, Reuther's visit also drew attention to the boycott being launched across the country in support of the strike. On December 22, the *San Francisco Chronicle* reported that local liquor stores had begun removing Schenley products in response to NFWA pickets.[108] In Los Angeles, entertainer Steve Allen joined a pre-Christmas Schenley picket line.[109] In Harlem, a march organized by CORE cleared Schenley products from the shelves of 49 liquor stores in one day.[110] As the attention of those interested in farm labor problems turned to the grape strike, the struggle over the *bracero* program faded into memory. So in January, few were surprised when Wirtz declared that no foreign workers would be needed in California in 1966.[111]

Only the growers seemed to miss the point. On December 24, Martin Zaninovich issued a statement that the boycott was "perverting the spirit of Christmas."[112] Vineyard owner Bruno Dispoto summed up the reaction of Delano growers to the boycott, the interfaith delegation, Reuther's visit, and all the publicity:

Our workers have rejected them for what they are, perpetrators of hate and deceit in order to victimize innocent Filipinos and Mexican-American groups. They work in an area where the finest labor and management relations have existed for many years.... The latest action of the NFWA, with the assistance of SNCC and CORE...is the wildest kind of vengeance by an irresponsible group. We firmly believe the general public, when the facts are known, will voice their opinion against such deplorable acts as boycotting. We are sincerely looking forward to the riddance of these outside agitators and rabble rousers and college kooks and a few migrant ministers and priests.[113]

MARCH TO SACRAMENTO: VIVA LA VICTORIA!

The NFWA had kicked off the boycott before Christmas, but as the dreary Delano winter wore on into January and February with no word from Schenley, the leadership focused on how to use the winter lull to strengthen the union's position. The strikers lost some ground when growers had little difficulty finding enough workers to do their winter field work, in part because they had raised wages to undercut the union. But because the next labor market test would not come until the spring preharvest, the leadership focused on strengthening the boycott, devising tactics to discourage local workers from returning to work in the spring, and strengthening the union's base outside of Delano to discourage migrant workers from coming to the strike zone at all.

One way to intensify the pressure on Schenley was to launch secondary boycotts of retailers selling Schenley products.[114] Unlike the secondary boycott attempted by the NFLU in 1947 and the more recent picketing of the docks, this secondary boycott would be directed at consumers, not employees, asking customers to shop elsewhere. A union whose members were covered by the NLRA could not legally have called for such an action. As Judge Meredith Wingrove had ruled in the case arising from the NFWA's dockside picketing, however, the act's exclusion of agricultural workers left the NFWA free of this constraint.[115]

The NFWA also committed more leadership to the boycott by sending some of its more effective organizers out to the key markets: Jack Ybarra to San Francisco, Gilbert Padilla to Los Angeles, Tony Orendain to Chicago, Eddie Frankel to Detroit, Ida Cousino to Cleveland, and Sal Gonzales to Boston.

To focus the work of volunteer committees, assign them clear goals, and evaluate their effectiveness, the NFWA launched a campaign to get a half million consumers to fill out a three-part pledge card. One part would go to Schenley, a second part to the NFWA, and a third part, listing Schenley products, would be kept by the supporter.[116] By the end of February, boycott coordinator Drake claimed to be in contact with committees in over 100 cities in 30 states.[117]

expansion

Within the farm worker world, the NFWA took advantage of the financial and human resources generated by the strike to open offices in Earlimart, McFarland, and Bakersfield.[118] It also persuaded the California Center for Community Development (CCCD), an OEO spin-off funded in part by Reuther's Citizens Crusade, to open offices in regions where its staff could do volunteer work for the NFWA, as the CSO and the Migrant Ministry had done in the past. Chavez's cousin Manuel had returned to the NFWA after his release from prison at the beginning of the strike and became a CCCD organizer in Morgan Hill, in one of California's coastal valleys. From this base, he organized NFWA committees in the Salinas Valley, where the NFWA had previously done little organizing. In February, he led 300 workers in a march on the Monterey County Welfare Department to protest a requirement that welfare recipients perform work for 25 cents an hour.[119] Chavez also assigned a newer member of the leadership team, LeRoy Chatfield, to Los Angeles and San Francisco to raise funds for consumer cooperatives modeled on the farm workers' credit unions, an approach he hoped to rely upon if the strike failed.[120]

Chatfield, who later became the first director of the National Farm Workers Service Center, was 31 in 1965. Raised in Colusa County, where his Roman Catholic family were rice growers, he joined the Christian brothers at 15, graduated from St. Mary's College in 1956, served as a teacher at Garces High School in Bakersfield, and spent four years at San Francisco's Sacred Heart Seminary before returning to Garces High School as vice principal. He met Chavez through Catholic social action networks, such as the Catholic Worker. In October 1965, after Chavez invited him to help with the grape strike, he asked to be released from his vows if that would be required to work with the strikers. A year later, he married Bonnie Burns, a San Francisco teacher who volunteered for a summer farm worker project that he ran. They later had five children.[121]

It was during this winter lull, early in February, that the NFWA leadership made a most important strategic decision. When faced with critical choices, Chavez gathered the key people at a supporter's home near Santa Barbara to spend three days figuring out what to do. Besides Chavez, the strategy team included Huerta, Drake, the Teatro Campesino's Valdez, farm workers Robert Bustos and Tony Mendez, and several other strikers and volunteers who had become active in the strike, including me.[122] One of the best ways to give a sense of the creative process—and the interactions of the people and ideas central to it—is to quote from my notes:

As proposals flew around the room, someone suggested we follow the example of the New Mexico miners who had traveled to New York to set up a mining camp in front of the company headquarters on Wall Street. Farm workers could travel to Schenley headquarters in New York, set up a labor camp out front, and maintain a vigil until Schenley signed. Someone else then suggested they go by bus so rallies could be held all across the country, local boycott committees organized, and publicity generated, building momentum for the arrival in New York. Then why not march instead of going by bus, someone else asked, as Dr. King had the previous year. But it's too far from Delano to New York, someone countered. On the other hand, the Schenley headquarters in San Francisco might not be too far—about 280 miles which an army veteran present calculated could be done at the rate of 15 miles a day or in about 20 days.

But what if Schenley doesn't respond, Chavez asked. Why not march to Sacramento instead and put the heat on Governor Brown to intervene and get negotiations started. He's up for re-election, wants the votes of our supporters, so perhaps we can have more impact if we use him as "leverage." Yes, someone else said, and on the way to Sacramento, the march could pass through most of the farm worker towns. Taking a page from Mao's "long march," we could organize local committees and get pledges not to break the strike signed. Yes, and we could also get them to feed us and house us. And just as Zapata wrote his "Plan de Ayala," Luis Valdez suggested, we can write a "Plan de Delano," read it in each town, ask local farm workers to sign it, and to carry it to the next town. Then, Chavez asked, why should it be a "march" at all? It will be Lent soon, a time for reflection, for penance, for asking forgiveness. Perhaps ours should be a pilgrimage, a *peregrinación*, which could arrive at Sacramento on Easter Sunday.[123]

Although the march would not arrive at Governor Brown's door until April 10, the NFWA had tried for some time to persuade him to mediate. In January, Ronald Reagan had announced his candidacy for governor with a call for a return to the *bracero* program. He held Brown responsible not only for farm labor shortages, but for the "civil disorder in Berkeley and Watts."[124] NFWA leaders reasoned that Brown's election year vulnerability created an opportunity for them to pressure him to get talks going with the growers. Most immediately, they learned that a California "fair trade" law protected the pricing practices of the liquor industry, and they thought that making a political issue of it during this period might encourage Schenley to deal with them.[125]

Chavez, Huerta, and others had a history with Brown going back to the CSO and the Viva Kennedy campaign. Although he was an ally of sorts, his approach had not been to support unionization. Rather, he assigned $3.5 million in federal funds (the bulk of the $5.2 million allocated by the Office of Economic Opportunity for California migrant and seasonal farm worker projects) to a "migrant master plan," setting up 10 migrant service centers around the state.[126] This was the tack that California governors took ever since Hiram Johnson responded to farm labor strife by creating the California Immigration and Housing Commission in 1912. It was an approach that seemed to satisfy urban liberals interested in the poor without antagonizing powerful agribusiness interests. In fact, shifting the cost of farm worker housing and services to the public provided a kind of subsidy to growers, while at the same time redefining farm labor conditions as a "social problem" rather than a "labor problem." A dramatic expansion of the poverty program could also be counted on to mute farm worker advocates by hiring them as social services providers, securely on the state payroll, a danger the CMM noted at the time.

It was clear that convincing Brown to use his influence to urge growers to the bargaining table was going to take some doing, so when an opportunity to challenge him to act arose sooner, the NFWA seized upon it. Huerta noted that, on February 20, Brown was to appear at the California Democratic Council (CDC) convention in Bakersfield, just 30 miles from Delano. The CDC, the liberal political association that had rebuilt the California Democratic Party during the 1950s, found itself increasingly at odds with officials it had helped to elect, such as California's powerful assembly speaker, Jesse Unruh, as well as the governor himself.[127] At this convention, Brown and others were hoping to unseat the incumbent CDC president, Simon Casady, for criticizing President Johnson's Vietnam policy. If Vietnam divided the delegates, however, they were united in support of the farm workers and had donated more than $5,500 in response to an impassioned appeal by novice San Francisco assemblyman Willie Brown (no relation to the governor).[128] The NFWA decided to try to take advantage of the delegates' support.

When the governor arrived at the meeting, NFWA pickets appeared at the entrances to the building with signs calling on him to mediate the strike. To avoid the picketers, Governor Brown used an underground entryway. Yet the CDC delegates themselves echoed the NFWA's demand for action in a unanimous resolution that called for legislation

FIGURE 5.3. Sen. Robert Kennedy visits Delano, pledges support, and is welcomed by Cesar Chavez, March 1966. *Source:* © 1978 George Ballis/Take Stock

to establish collective bargaining rights in agriculture, support of the Schenley boycott, and intervention by the governor.

Brown was not moved. The next day, on February 21, he said:

> I will probably go to Delano. I sympathize with the problem. But for me to use the weight of my office to ask for negotiations would be to intercede on one side of the dispute. Economic forces must determine the outcome. We have collective bargaining laws to take care of the differences between workers and employers.[129]

Although it was unclear which collective bargaining laws Brown meant, it was clear he was not yet ready to act.

In Washington, however, Senator Harrison Williams, the New Jersey Democrat who headed the Subcommittee on Farm Labor, responded to Reuther's request to hold hearings in California on S. 1866, a bill that would extend the National Labor Relations Act to cover farm workers. The hearings were to convene on March 14 in Sacramento, March 15 in Visalia, and March 16 in Delano.[130] For the NFWA, they presented another timely opportunity to refocus national attention on the grape strike, line up new support, and show farm workers that they had allies who could call the local growers to public account. To achieve these goals, the NFWA wanted the newest member of the committee, Senator Robert Kennedy, to attend. With Reuther's encouragement, he did.[131] The weaving together of diverse networks of people and ideas that characterized the planning of the *perigrinación* thus also characterized the preparations for its kickoff.

The NFWA targeted the week of March 14–20 to mobilize the kickoff of the march. The timing of the hearings provided Father James Vizzard of the Catholic Rural Life Conference with a deadline around which to organize support for a joint statement by California's seven Roman Catholic bishops, urging the inclusion of farm workers under the NLRA.[132] The hearings also created a venue in which growers could be called to public account. Zaninovich of the South Central Farmers Committee, for example, testified: "There is no strike among the Delano farm workers'. The so-called strike is pure myth, manufactured out of nothing by outside agitators who are more interested in creating trouble in the United States than in the welfare of farm workers."[133]

There were also surprises. A new organization, the Kern-Tulare Independent Farm Workers, asked to testify. Claiming to be the "authentic" voice of farm workers, it corroborated the growers' claims. The ploy backfired when questioning by Senator Kennedy revealed that leaders of the new organization were labor contractors employed by the growers and that its members included growers themselves.[134] The capstone event for many, however, was when Kennedy suggested that Kern County sheriff LeRoy Gallyen "read the Constitution of the United States" and think again before arresting strikers whom he thought "might" violate the law before they had done so.[135]

On March 16, the NFWA took advantage of the national media, who were in town to cover the hearings, to announce the start of its 280-mile, 28-day march to Sacramento the very next morning.[136] The timing—and the reaction of the local authorities—could not have been better. When the helmeted and club-wielding Delano police formed a line to block the march's departure on the ground that it was a "parade without a permit," the photographs, newspaper stories, and television images that flashed around the country evoked images of a similar police line in Selma, Alabama, the year before.[137] Only this was California. Eventually, Governor Brown intervened by prevailing on the mayor to allow him to assign the California Highway Patrol to escort the marchers to the city limits. The march was on its way.[138]

FIGURE 5.4. March to Sacramento, March 1966. *Source:* Jon Lewis

As shown in map 5.1, the route of the march winded through the farm worker towns dotting the agricultural heartland of California. The march was led by a farm worker carrying a banner of Our Lady of Guadalupe, the patron saint of Mexico, portraits of *campesino* leader Emiliano Zapata, and banners proclaiming *peregrinación, penitencia, revolución* (pilgrimage, penance, revolution). Strikers also carried signs calling on supporters to boycott Schenley.[139] Of the 67 strikers selected to march the distance, the oldest, William King, was 63, and the youngest, Augustine Hernandez, was 17. Their average age was 31. 18 were women.[140] Although Green again declined to participate, declaring that AWOC was in "a trade union dispute, not a civil rights movement or a religious crusade,"[141] some AWOC members did—including Manuel Vasquez, a Mexican AWOC member, whom the NFWA members sagely elected march captain.[142]

During the first week, a farm worker advance team devised routines for mobilizing local farm worker committees to welcome the marchers, feed them, house them, organize a rally each evening and a mass the next morning. At each rally, Luis Valdez proclaimed the "Plan de Delano" calling for the "liberation of the poor farm worker," modeled on Mexican revolutionary Emiliano Zapata's "Plan de Ayala." Each

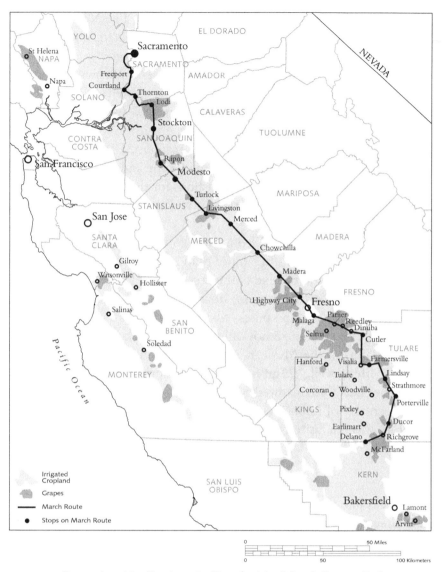

MAP 5.1. Peregrinación, Penitencia, Revolución: March Route, Delano to Sacramento, March 17–April 10, 1966. *Source:* Raven Maps

night, local farm workers would add their signatures to it. At the end of the mass the next morning, the farm worker who had carried Our Lady of Guadalupe from the previous town would place her in the hands of the farm worker from this town who would carry her to the next.

Meanwhile, in San Francisco and Los Angeles, organizers mobilized supplies, support delegations, and facilitated the picketing of Schenley.[143] San Francisco's Roman Catholic bishop authorized Catholics to join the *perigrinación*, as did the Episcopal bishop. The Northern California Board of Rabbis came to share Passover matzo, the "bread of affliction," with the marchers, in the Jewish tradition.[144]

One week into the march, on March 23, Governor Brown announced that he would "probably" meet with the "dedicated strikers."[145] On March 26, he said he would "pay his respects." Chavez responded, "We are not interested in respect from the governor, we are interested in action."[146] The Delano growers also responded at the end of the first week. In a speech to the California Grape and Treefruit League, Zaninovich attacked the California bishops for their statement, threatening the church's tax-exempt status if it continued to be involved in "politics."[147]

As the march progressed from town to town up the valley, public interest grew, especially after more than 1,000 people welcomed the marchers to Fresno at the end of the first week.[148] Daily bulletins began to appear in the Bay Area press, stories about who the strikers were, why they would walk 300 miles, what the strike was all about.[149] The march came to symbolize not only the farm workers' call for justice, but the claims of the Mexican-American community for a new voice in public life as well.[150] And for the second spring in a row, California newspaper headlines featured a farm labor story. In 1965, the story had been Secretary of Labor Wirtz's "march" through California. In 1966, the story was the farm workers' own march.

AWOC's Demise

Two weeks into the march, as it proceeded from Fresno to Stockton, the new director of organizing for the AFL-CIO, William Kircher, arrived to take a look. Kircher was a protégé of John Livingston, whom he succeeded in the position, and thus was an opponent of Reuther and a rival of Paul Schrade.[151] Meany was furious with Reuther, his nemesis. Who, Meany told Kircher, "[Reuther] was there [in Delano] for one day and got six years of publicity."[152] When Meany instructed Kircher that his first job as organizing director was to make "the AWOC problem go away,"[153] he must have thought he had found a man well suited for the task at hand.

And so he had, although the task at hand was not quite the one Meany had in mind. Kircher was a man whose life experiences had led him to see unionism more as a vocation than a job, especially in a situation like that of the farm workers, which spoke to his Roman Catholic faith and his liberal politics. Kircher had grown up in Athens, Ohio, one of 11 children in a German-Irish Roman Catholic family.

Inspired early on by radical newspaperman Heywood Braun, Kircher graduated from Ohio University in 1936 with a degree in journalism and found work with a California newspaper. He returned home for family reasons, became a salesman, married, and had two children. After he was rejected for military enlistment in 1940 due to a physical disability, he went to work in a General Electric defense plant, where he became a charter member of UAW Local 617. From there, he rose to become the UAW's regional education director, and after being defeated by the Reuther slate in a run for regional director, he was recruited to a West Coast organizing position under Livingston. In 1951, he followed Livingston to Washington, DC, and served as his assistant on the Wage Stabilization Board. In 1953, he followed Livingston to Detroit, serving as his assistant in the union's General Motors Department. In 1955, when Livingston became AFL-CIO organizing director, Kircher was again invited to assist but declined to move his family. He instead became the AFL-CIO's assistant regional director in Cincinnati and became active in reform Democratic politics, civil rights work, and fighting off Teamster raids. In 1964, he moved to Washington to once again be Livingston's assistant and in 1965, became his successor.

Kircher was, thus, a kind of borderlander himself—occupying a space between the bread-and-butter unionism of the AFL and the social reform unionism of the CIO. Although he was Livingston's protégé, Kircher had a feisty love-hate relationship with him, quite dissimilar to the relationship he later would have with Meany.[154] This background, along with the diversity of his organizing experience in different regions and industries, taught him how to pay attention—and to learn.[155] Moreover, to solve "the AWOC problem," he was given a degree of autonomy his predecessor had not enjoyed. At 51, Kircher was determined to make a mark in his new leadership role,[156] and he was uniquely equipped to do so.

Kircher was introduced to the farm labor scene at the Senate hearings in Delano. As he later recalled, "It was obvious Cesar had taken over the strike and that he had a lot of charisma and ability to work. But I didn't get a chance to really see him in action until those Senate hearings Pete Williams held in California."[157] Kircher was especially impressed with how Chavez handled the red baiting by Congressman Hagen. He joined the march:

I got some old clothes, and I figured the best goddam way to find out what was going on was to avoid the experts and live with the people, so

I walked with them, and I talked with them.... I happen to be a practicing Catholic and I go to Mass on a daily basis if I can, and here we were, going to Mass every morning, meeting every night, and Cesar began to talk [to me] more.... The whole thing had a strong, cultural religious thing, yet it was organizing people.... Chavez knew...that to approach the organization of these people like an organizer going into an auto plant some place, was ridiculous.... while Chavez directed their attention to their economic needs, he pulled them together through...the cultural religious form.[158]

As Kircher took part in the march, he got to know Chavez and the NFWA leaders. As he experienced the limitations of Green's leadership of AWOC, he became convinced that AWOC's future lay in persuading Chavez to affiliate. "My first judgment," Kircher said, "was that AWOC was crazy" for ignoring the movement in its midst and courting the Teamsters instead. "But as I got talking to Green, it was obvious the problem was jealousy. The whole identity of the cause had gone over to Chavez and the NFWA."[159] As for Green's alliance with the Teamsters, an organization Kircher had fought in Ohio and Pennsylvania, Kircher summed up the results as "the Teamsters had organized 8 or 9 citrus packinghouses and had won NLRA elections, but AWOC seemed to receive no benefits."[160]

The NFWA leaders, however, remained skeptical of affiliation with the AFL-CIO, which they feared would compromise their autonomy. Chavez said, "I just knew that a big organization was not going to let a little organization get it into trouble. They had too many things at stake if we started raising hell with strikes and boycotts."[161] Kircher invited Dolores Huerta to go to Mass with him. She suspected he just wanted to "check her out" to see if she was a Communist.[162] Both Schrade, Reuther's man, and Kircher, Meany's man, had become frequent visitors to the march. But Reuther had recognized the NFWA's independence, while Meany was responsible for six years of AWOC. Although this made Schrade a more attractive suitor, it was the rivalry itself that most benefited the NFWA, giving it greater leverage to negotiate its position than might otherwise have been the case.

For Kircher, the situation came to a head as the march approached Modesto, Green's home base, when a local paper reported that the local AFL-CIO would boycott the march when it arrived. Chavez gave Kircher the clipping, asking him how he could invite the NFWA into the AFL-CIO when this was the AFL-CIO's position. Kircher later recalled:

Here I am, director of organizing for the whole goddamn federation, reading in the Turlock paper that the AFL-CIO is boycotting the goddamn march. Not only that, but AFL-CIO leaders are charging the NFWA is not really a union…that kind of crap. This was Green, it was his line…so we drove to Stockton.[163]

The next morning, Kircher summoned Green to a meeting, reminded him who was in charge, and told him that since Modesto was Green's home base, Kircher would judge Green's influence in the labor movement by how large a reception he organized for the farm workers there. When the march arrived, late that afternoon, the reception committee at the side of the road was joined by an unlikely array of Anglo Modesto union officials holding signs: "Glaziers Union Local 79: Viva la Causa!" and "Asbestos Workers Local 1215: Viva la Huelga!" It was a gesture, but a pretty empty one. Kircher said that he would not embarrass Green by firing him; rather he ordered him to fade into the background. Kircher shut down the citrus organizing and focused AWOC on the Delano strike. He transferred AWOC's funds and headquarters from Stockton to Delano, where Larry Itliong was put in direct control over his end of the grape strike.[164] Kircher's intent to affiliate the NFWA—and let AWOC go—could not have been clearer.

Breakthrough

On the afternoon of April 3, as the marchers rested in St. Mary's Square in Stockton, Chavez received a call at the local CSO office across the street from someone claiming to be a lawyer for Schenley. Thinking it a prank, Chavez refused the call. When he finally took it, the caller turned out to be Sidney Korchak, a Los Angeles labor negotiator. He was calling to arrange a meeting to discuss recognizing the union and negotiating a contract—the next day!

Schenley was worried that the spotlight of the increasingly visible march would focus on the company when it reached Sacramento. This threat was underscored by a San Francisco Teamsters local that had temporarily refused to load Schenley's products the week before. Furthermore, Los Angeles Bartenders Union leader Hermann "Blackie" Levitt began circulating a letter threatening a bartenders boycott.[165] As Schenley vice president James Woolsey later testified before the California Senate Subcommittee on Agriculture:

These reprisals and the publicity presented a threat of serious damage to our business on a nationwide scale. Our sales department felt that even more damaging than any decline in our sales was the adverse publicity that accompanied the boycott and the NFWA organizing activities.... These were key factors in our later decision to recognize NFWA.[166]

Lewis Rosenstiel, 75, the Schenley CEO, contacted Korshak, an old Chicago associate, to fix the problem. Korshak, 58, the son of a Jewish Chicago businessman, had received his law degree in 1930, defended figures associated with the Chicago mob, and moved in the late 1940s to California, where he won a reputation as a "fixer" with labor, the liquor industry, and the movies.[167] Korshak invited Levitt, also from Chicago and a friendly adversary, to join in the discussion. Rosenstiel proposed selling the Delano property, but Korchak sensed an opportunity to turn the problem into good publicity for Schenley and suggested recognizing the union instead. Rosensteil had a long history of good relationships with unions and no stake whatever in the Delano grower community. So he agreed.[168]

Chavez met with the strikers, asked permission to leave the march, and recruited Hartmire to drive him to Los Angeles, seven hours to the south. The next morning, Chavez, Hartmire, and a few others made their way to Korshak's Beverly Hills mansion to find Korshak, Levitt, Teamster representatives, and Kircher waiting for them. Schenley was prepared to recognize a union, Korchak said, but was skeptical of the NFWA and wanted the AFL-CIO—or the Teamsters—to co-sign any agreement.[169]

Politically, it was an intricate dance. Who would co-sign? Korchak invited the Teamsters to the meeting because they had contracts with Schenley and had conducted the Bay Area work stoppage. He knew they needed to be on board with any agreement.[170] He also knew that the Teamsters had decided to try to woo Chavez to join them, so they would not want to antagonize him. And more than the Teamsters wanted to sign with Schenley themselves, they wanted to make sure that Schenley did *not* sign with the AFL-CIO.[171] Kircher, meanwhile, would have liked Schenley to sign with AWOC and certainly did not want any agreement signed with the Teamsters, but he too did not want to antagonize Chavez. He had to recognize that it was the NFWA, not AWOC, which the state of California had certified as the union striking Schenley. Also, it was the NFWA that controlled the boycott and whose goal it was to retain its autonomy without losing Schenley. Korshak broke the impasse when he suggested a recognition agreement between the NFWA and Schenley, witnessed but not co-signed by Kircher on behalf of the AFL-CIO. It was a solution to which all three unions could agree, and they did.[172] Although a full contract remained to be negotiated, the agreement provided an immediate 35 cents per hour wage increase to a new minimum of $1.75, a union hiring hall to eliminate labor contractors, and a check-off for the NFWA credit union.[173]

The dynamics of this meeting would play out again and again in the course of the farm worker struggle, as the NFWA learned to preserve its autonomy by balancing its rivals against each other. It could exercise this autonomy, however, only because it had built its own base among farm workers and developed its own allies within the Mexican-American community, churches, civil rights groups, liberal Democrats, and students, as well as the labor movement itself. It was one such alliance that had produced perhaps the most unlikely, yet significant, presence at Korchak's house: Chris Hartmire, who came as a witness to the proceedings. His presence put constraints on what the labor people would say and do, and it kept one of the NFWA's most important constituencies on board. (It also gave Hartmire great credibility with his own religious network.) It would have been easy for the NFWA to become a pawn in a larger game between the Teamsters and the AFL-CIO or between Meany and Reuther. That it did not turn out this way shows not only the vigilance with which the NFWA protected its autonomy, but also the "canniness" Chavez had learned. As he liked to say, with Schenley, he "killed two birds with one stone, and kept the stone."[174]

On the morning of April 6, Chavez reached the marchers over a mobile phone, which had been installed in a Volkswagen "press van," as they passed through the Tokay vineyards on the outskirts of Lodi. As they gathered beside the road to hear the report, the press secretary on loan from SNCC, Terry Cannon, climbed on top of the van. Shouting over a bullhorn, he announced that the NFWA had just signed a recognition agreement with Schenley Industries. The new minimum would be $1.75 per hour, and labor contractors were to be eliminated. Negotiations would begin within 30 days for a complete contract covering 500 Delano grape workers. Although Cannon's remarks had to be translated into Spanish, the cheering began while he was still speaking English. But even as the marchers cheered their victory, they began turning over their "Boycott Schenley" signs to write "Boycott S&W" and "Boycott Treesweet"—products of the powerful DiGiorgio Corporation. It would be their next target.[175]

The reaction of the California Council of Growers was predictable:

> While the NFWA and its religious cohorts were righteously preaching democratic processes and marching on Sacramento, the leaders were closeted elsewhere, working out a deal that denies workers any voice in the

FIGURE 5.5. Marchers arrive at Sacramento, April 1966. *Source:* Jon Lewis

proceedings.... Schenley Industries, whose farm operations are incidental to their basic whiskey-making business, is not representative of California agriculture, where growers steadfastly refuse to sell out their employees and force them into a union which does not represent them.[176]

The next day, Thursday, April 7, DiGiorgio announced that it too would recognize a union, although only after a secret ballot election among its agricultural workers determined which union they wanted, if any: the NFWA, AWOC, or the Kern-Tulare Independent Farm Workers.[177] On Good Friday, as the march wound along a narrow levee road above the Sacramento River, pausing every so often to observe a station of the cross, Chavez responded. The NFWA would participate in elections, but only if NLRB rules protected workers from unfair labor practices. Until terms were agreed upon the union would suspend neither its strike nor its boycott. Kircher expressed AFL-CIO support for the NFWA position, explaining that AWOC declined to participate in the election in recognition of the NFWA's claim to represent DiGiorgio's workers.[178] The DiGiorgio boycott would be launched as planned.

On Easter Sunday, April 10, 10,000 supporters gathered to welcome the marchers to Sacramento, joining the 51 *originales* who had completed the entire march. Speakers at the rally included a panoply of religious, labor, political, and Mexican-American leaders—but not Governor Brown. He had decided to "spend the day with his family" at Frank Sinatra's house in Palm Springs. Addressing the crowd at the capitol, Huerta called on Brown to convene a special session of the legislature to deal with collective bargaining rights for farm workers. She threatened a general strike if he failed to act.[179] Along with all the excitement over Schenley, the NFWA also announced a DiGiorgio boycott until fair terms were set for an election. The fact that Governor Brown failed to meet with the marchers attracted little press coverage. The Mexican-American community, however, took it as a direct affront—and that gave the NFWA new bargaining chips with the governor, which would soon become even more valuable.

HOW DID IT HAPPEN?

Leaders of both the NFWA and AWOC made tactical choices about how to deal with a grape strike that neither had planned, but they drew upon different strategic capacities. AWOC organizers, operating within a strategic frame focused on local labor markets, targeted the hardcore of the table grape industry, counting on their members' skill and solidarity to provide sufficient leverage to get wages raised. AWOC's top leadership, however, had made no commitment to this choice and put more faith in developing an alliance with the Teamsters that they believed would give them the power to get contracts with employers. When the grape strike unfolded as it did—with the participation of an NFWA that fast became a social movement organization with broad urban support—the AWOC leaders lacked the motivation, knowledge, or learning practices to adapt their strategy to such unforeseen circumstances. Only when the AFL-CIO national leadership, as a consequence of internal political rivalries, replaced Livingston with Kircher as the director of organizing did AWOC's strategy begin to change.

Initially, the NFWA targeted growers based on where its constituency happened to work. A more specific target emerged, however, as the experimental process of probing, pushing, and trying a little of this and a little of that continued. A Delano outsider, Schenley,

FIGURE 5.6. Ten thousand welcome marchers to Sacramento, April 1966.
Source: © 1978 George Ballis/Take Stock

was more vulnerable than the core employers on which AWOC was concentrating. NFWA leaders only made this discovery, however, as they searched for alternatives to AWOC's approach. In response to each challenge—for instance, how to sustain pressure on employers after the end of the harvest—they kept coming up with innovative tactics for generating funds, sustaining the commitment of strikers and volunteers, getting their message to the public, launching the Schenley boycott, and marching to Sacramento, choices that culminated in the breakthrough recognition agreement. As the NFWA kept looking for the loose thread with which it could unravel the cloth, they found the one that led to Schenley. As Chavez often said, "It's not so important that you make the right decision. What is important is that you do all you can to make the decision, you make the right decision."[180]

It was also due to its strategic capacity that the NFWA reframed itself as a movement. The leadership was open to learning from its links to civil rights organizations and the narrative they articulated. Not only in rhetoric, but also in action, the NFWA came to interpret itself as an oppressed minority struggling for its freedom, rather than as just another union. This narrative, as old as Exodus and as current as the march from Selma to Montgomery, helped the NFWA to build a critically important bridge to the urban public at a time when "labor solidarity" had lost the moral force it had in the 1930s. The NFWA situated itself within a moral framework that coupled racial justice claims with economic justice claims in a new way.

The credibility to author this reinterpretation resided in the identities of NFWA leaders, forged in their experience as Mexicans in the United States and, in other cases, as organizers and clergy. Most important, however, was that the new narrative was grounded in a new "relational context," as sociologist Margaret Sommers calls it. This context was created as a result of choices the NFWA leaders made about how to sustain a strike community in the face of severe financial constraints.[181] People who committed themselves to the strike full time without pay—leaders, volunteers, and farm workers—became the critical core of what social scientists call the "zealots," the "unconditional cooperators," or the "critical community" at the heart of any social movement.[182] To retain the support of the strikers, the NFWA leaders believed they had to share their sacrifice—living on strike benefits of $1 per week (later, $5 per week) and on donated food obtained from the "strike store."[183] The decision to make this personal commitment, which Chavez called the spirit of "servanthood," brought the NFWA officers to Delano. Once there, it deepened their commitment to winning the strike. It also gave union leaders the moral authority to attract similar levels of commitment from others.[184]

Because the cost per person was so low (food, a bed, $1 per week), the NFWA could add full-time volunteers relatively easily. So it began to accept the students and religious activists who came to Delano to join the strike on the same terms.[185] By enabling large numbers of people to volunteer, the NFWA developed a new talent pool from which it could draw the leadership to meet the myriad new responsibilities that soon emerged. Expansion of this cadre—for which the roving picket line had served as a core—enabled the NFWA to field unusually large numbers of full-time troops for strike, boycott, and political activities.

In a setting as open as the NFWA, new people altered, expanded, and enriched the original team in ways that enhanced its strategic capacity. They served as picket captains, strike organizers, and boycott organizers. Some later rose to top leadership roles. Volunteers included young farm worker leaders such as Eliseo Medina, an 18-year-old Mexican immigrant when he joined the strike. Medina was trained as an organizer, elected to the credit union board, became the Chicago boycott director, and, later, a vice president of the union. Marcos Muñoz, a 20-year-old Mexican immigrant from Bakersfield, could neither read nor write English or Spanish. Nonetheless, this very talented organizer ultimately became the Boston boycott director. Maria Saludado, 22, and her sisters, Petra and Antonia, grew up in a farm worker family, worked in the fields as children, and became boycott organizers in Philadelphia, New York, Chicago, and elsewhere.[186] Students involved in the civil rights movement, such as Bob Solodow, Bob Fisher, and Luis Valdez, came to Delano as volunteers and served in a variety of roles. Jessica Govea, an 18-year-old Chicana from Bakersfield whose family had been active in the CSO, dropped out of college, went to work in the union's service program, became an organizer, designed the union's medical program, and was eventually elected to its national Executive Board. After growing up in Bakersfield, attending Harvard for three years, and serving with SNCC for two years, I too came to Delano, at age 22. Eventually, I became the director of organizing and was elected to the national Executive Board.[187]

A third font of volunteers was the religious community. It yielded people such as Bill Esher, LeRoy Chatfield, and Kathy Lynch, a volunteer inspired by the civil rights movement and Vatican II.[188] Others, such as the Reverend Gene Boutilier and Phil Farnam, were recruited as migrant ministers.

Finally, dedicated lawyers with a passion for public service and a commitment to social change, such as Alex Hoffman and Jerry Cohen, came to serve as full-time and part-time resources for the union.[189]

The result was the emergence of what I call a "charismatic community" based on "vows of voluntary poverty" and sharing a "religious" commitment—in this case, to winning the strike.[190] Religiously oriented NFWA leaders, especially Chavez, searching for tactics to sustain this level of commitment, engaged this community in telling a new story about itself. This new narrative incorporated diverse cultural and religious traditions and created shared symbols: the ritual of daily picket lines, the celebratory interpretations at Friday night meetings, and, of course, the march to Sacramento. The depth of commitment of the individuals who chose this collective enterprise—to each other, to their goals, and to their own values—inspired a new understanding of who they were, what they could do, and where they were going. The striker community became a crucible of cultural change in which all was in flux as old identities melted down and merged into new individual and collective identities.[191] Farm workers were transformed into *Chavistas*, supporters into *voluntarios*, the grape strike into *La Huelga*, the NFWA into *La Causa*, and Cesar Chavez into a legendary farm worker leader. This cultural dynamic infused the NFWA with significance for farm workers, Mexican Americans, students, religious activists, and liberals far beyond its political reach as a community organization or its economic influence as an ethnic labor association. As a contemporary observer wrote:

> During October, the Delano Grape Strike grew into a movement. Ministers and college students joined the picket lines. Union members in Los Angles, Oakland, San Francisco, Fresno, and Washington donated money. Civil rights, Mexican-American, union, liberal and church groups throughout the state gathered food, clothing and money. Strike leaders visited campuses to raise money.[192]

The combination of deep motivation and open deliberation was at the heart of the NFWA's strategic capacity—especially its ability to make rapid, informed, and creative decisions to take advantage of fleeting opportunities. As Taylor observed:

> Whenever a major issue arose, Chavez called Huerta, Padilla, Antonio Orendain, and Julio Hernandez into consultation. These were the NFWA executive board members, and their policy meetings often lasted far into the night, as they argued, talked, fought, and talked some more.[193]

Meetings also usually included Drake, Hartmire, and others, as the leadership circle grew to include them.

The more successful the NFWA became in enacting a farm worker movement, the more leverage it gained with AWOC and the growers. This occurred in the form of the rhetorical transformation from a labor dispute into a movement for the liberation of the farm worker. The relational context among leaders, strikers, and supporters was radically reconfigured as the strike acquired new meaning for many in and out of Delano. Finally, the arena of struggle was redefined as one in which urban supporters could play a role like that of northern supporters of the civil rights movement. This organizational transformation, in turn, deepened the motivation of its leaders, increased their access to information, and enhanced their learning practices so they acquired an even greater capacity to devise strategies that would take them where they wanted to go.

CONCLUSION

In 1966, Henry Anderson, the director of Citizens for Farm Labor, wrote:

> When the books and doctoral dissertations are written on this movement in years to come, they may well single out this period, the early spring of 1966, as pivotal: the point at which, after many a false start, the tide really did turn and begin to roll back.[194]

He was right. The NFWA found ways to turn short-term power into structural change—change in the very context in which the farm labor struggle would unfold—that had eluded every previous effort to organize farm workers. And in that new context, the NFWA crossed thresholds never crossed before. It learned to translate urban support into the economic power needed to require agricultural employers to recognize a union—without relying on the tools that unions had used in the 1930s, which were now illegal. The world of agribusiness turned out to be less than monolithic as divisions emerged between the local grower-shippers and national corporations with equity in their brand names. Learning to leverage these divisions was critical to the development of effective strategy. For almost the first time, farm workers began to believe that unionization was possible, especially when they experienced the reality of the Schenley contract. It not only raised wages from $1.25 per hour to $1.75 per hour—a 40 percent increase—but eliminated the hated labor contractor system and promised job security and a medical plan. Medina recalls:

> We all knew about it. They just won a contract. They were paying a hell of a lot more than anybody else. I didn't know what a contract was, but I knew there was a union and they were paying a bunch of money. It was the first time that I really saw that we could really win.[195]

Success, however, brought a powerful counterattack from the growers, this time in collaboration with the Teamsters. It is to this story that we now turn.

SIX

Meeting the Counterattack

DiGiorgio, the Teamsters, and UFWOC (1966)

The decision was made to test Chavez's resolve and learn more about his true intentions.... So I was sent to contest him in DiGiorgio.

—William Grami, director of organizing, Western Conference of Teamsters

Those bastards. We shook the tree and now they're trying to pick the fruit.... if they get away with it this time, we'll never get them off our back.

—Cesar Chavez, director, United Farm Workers Organizing Committee, AFL-CIO

EVEN AS THE breakthrough with Schenley yielded a host of new opportunities for the NFWA, it called forth a powerful counterattack from the other Delano growers, which threatened the union's very survival. The attack challenged the NFWA leaders to quickly master a whole new level of strategic complexity; they needed to consolidate their past gains, even while carrying the fight forward. At the same time, they were competing with another union and battling growers on a far greater scale. The NFWA proved to be up to the task because it had developed the strategic capacity to respond quickly and creatively, expanding the size, scope, and diversity of its operations to enhance its strategic capacity still further. As a result, the NFWA improbably won the first union representation election held among farm workers and delivered the first setback to the alliance between the Teamsters union and California agribusiness, an alliance that was originally forged in the 1930s. This is how it happened.

LEARNING TO MANEUVER: THE TEAMSTERS INTERVENE AT DIGIORGIO

The day after Schenley recognized the NFWA, Robert DiGiorgio, president of the DiGiorgio Fruit Corporation, broke ranks with the remaining Delano grape growers. He called on the California State Conciliation Service to conduct secret ballot elections on his farms to determine whether or not his workers wanted a union. He offered AWOC, the NFWA, and the Kern-Tulare Independent Farm Workers—or any other union wishing to appear on the ballot—the opportunity to electioneer on company premises during nonwork hours. But there were two conditions. The NFWA had to call off its strike and boycott of DiGiorgio products, and it had to agree that if it won the election, contract negotiations would be subject to binding arbitration.[1]

The next day was Good Friday, April 8. As the *perigrinación* wound its way along a narrow levee road above the Sacramento River, pausing every so often to observe a station of the cross, Chavez, in consultation with leaders who had joined him on the march and others who could be reached by phone at the rest stops, formulated a response. It was not easy. By proposing elections, DiGiorgio confronted the NFWA with a strategic dilemma. The church leaders, liberals, and others whose support the union needed for a boycott expected the NFWA to agree to elections. But because the outcomes of union representation elections are influenced by a host of technical matters, the NFWA could afford to call off the boycott (its only real muscle) only after election terms were established that gave it a reasonable chance of winning. Losing an election, even an unfairly conducted election, could cripple the new union by undermining its overall claim to represent farm workers.[2]

Two complicated key issues confronted the NFWA: first, who could participate in the election, and second, who could guarantee its fairness? Would the eligible voter list include workers who had struck DiGiorgio's 4,800-acre Sierra Vista ranch in Delano, many of whom had left the area? How about the strike breakers hired to replace them? Would it include migrants who had worked for only two days or only year-round employees? And what about the workers at other DiGiorgio properties: 4,500 acres of table grapes at Borrego Springs, 9,000 acres of diversified crops at Arvin, and 1,500 acres of tree fruit at Marysville and Yuba City? Was the NFWA expected to give up a boycott of the DiGiorgio Corporation in return for elections to be held only at the Delano property?

The fairness issue was equally tricky. Because of the control that employers exercise over workers' livelihoods, the National Labor Relations Act barred them from using this power to commit "unfair labor practices," such as threatening to discharge workers for supporting a union. In recognition of the immense power of intimidation arising from an employer and union working together, the law also banned employers from campaigning on behalf of any one union and against its competitors. Because farm workers had been excluded from the federal labor law, what protections would they enjoy, who would enforce them, and what kind of sanctions would apply in case of violations? In the particular case of Mexican immigrants, who would encourage them to trust a secret ballot election when their experience in Mexico was that voting ratifies power, only very rarely contesting it successfully?

In the end, the NFWA did agree to participate in elections, but only if the NLRB's rules were put in place to protect DiGiorgio workers from unfair labor practices. Until such terms were agreed upon, the union would suspend neither its strike nor its boycott. And in no case would the NFWA participate in an election in which the employer-dominated Kern-Tulare Independent Farm Workers was on the ballot. On behalf of the AFL-CIO, Kircher expressed support for the NFWA's position and declared, furthermore, that AWOC recognized the NFWA's claim to represent DiGiorgio workers. Therefore, AWOC declined to compete in the election itself.[3]

AWOC Robert DiGiorgio was a formidable opponent. He was the first grower to seize the public relations initiative since the strike began. He had assumed leadership of the corporation in 1962, at age 55, upon the retirement of his uncle Joseph, its founder. It was clear, however, that he belonged to a different world. Robert grew up in New York City and attended Lawrenceville Academy, Yale, and Fordham Law School. Upon entering the family business in 1937, he developed far more interest in marketing than in farming, and unlike other Delano growers, he lived in San Francisco where he networked with the California business elite. He served on the boards of the Bank of America, Carter Hawley Hale, Pacific Telephone, Union Oil, and Newhall Land and Farming Company. His public service activities included being a trustee of the University of Southern California and of the United Nations Association. He was a member of California's most elite clubs: Commonwealth Club, San Francisco Gold Club, Pacific Union Club, Bohemian Club, Metropolitan Club, and Yale Club.[4] DiGiorgio was enough of an outsider to recognize that the arena of conflict reached well beyond Delano and required a more sophisticated response than the Delano growers had made in the past. Yet he was also enough of an insider to want to avoid recognizing the NFWA if he could.

The NFWA needed substantial leverage to negotiate these complex election questions successfully, but due to its earlier successes, it had more on its plate than the DiGiorgio boycott. Because spring work had begun, the NFWA were compelled to resume picketing to maintain

FIGURE 6.1. DiGiorgio boycott ad, *El Malcriado*, May 1966. *Source:* Andy Zermeno

credibility with the workers and the public and to retain state certification of its strike. At the same time, it had to negotiate its first collective bargaining agreement—the Schenley contract—which would establish new norms for the industry. And, finally, it had to negotiate terms of affiliation with the AFL-CIO.

To meet these challenges, Chavez delegated responsibility among an expanded circle of collaborators. In addition to dealing with the press, Chavez took responsibility for negotiating the AFL-CIO affiliation in collaboration with Kircher, consulting with Schrade and Reuther, and keeping NFWA board members included in key decisions.[5] He also engaged Kircher—along with Fred Ross, Dolores Huerta, Gilbert Padilla, Julio Hernandez, Jim Drake, and Alex Hoffman—to negotiate election rules with DiGiorgio. Huerta took responsibility for negotiations with Schenley and working with a newly elected negotiating committee of Schenley workers—counseled by the Longshoremen's Union leaders, whose organization held farm labor contracts in Hawaii. Responsibility for organizing at DiGiorgio was delegated to Ross, whom Chavez persuaded to come to work full time with the NFWA to train a new generation of organizers recruited from among the strikers and volunteers.[6] Drake became Chavez's administrative assistant. Other Migrant Ministry staff were assigned to the boycott. Chris Hartmire continued to mobilize religious support, often serving as a witness to the negotiations. Although Kircher was a new and uncertain member of the team, the years of experience the others had working together, their commitment to one another, their knowledge of each other, and the deliberative facility they developed over time allowed the NFWA to expand its scope of operations and gain access to new sources of information, thus enhancing its ability to learn from experience.

The NFWA resumed picketing at DiGiorgio on Thursday, April 14, 1966, just four days after the *perigrinación* arrived in Sacramento. The tactical objective, however, was not to persuade workers to walk out. Rather, it was to communicate with those housed in camps owned and operated by DiGiorgio, to which the NFWA had no legal access. If there were an election, the NFWA would need their support.[7]

A few days later, during a three-day strategy session at a retreat near San Jose, NFWA leaders confirmed their decision to proceed with the boycott. They decided to target S&W Fine Foods and Treesweet Juices, DiGiorgio's most well known, identifiable, and widely marketed products. They mapped out initial steps and assigned staff. CMM staffer and acting boycott director Phil Farnum dispatched ace volunteer organizers Bob Solodow, Bob Fischer, Ida Cousino, and Eddie Frankel to launch boycotts in New York, Boston, Philadelphia, Cleveland, and Detroit. Although most farm worker organizers were assigned to organize at DiGiorgio, others were deployed to the boycott efforts in San Francisco, San Jose, Los Angeles, and other California cities.[8]

NFWA leaders found that they could win significant support from labor for this boycott because Kircher was wooing them to affiliate with the AFL-CIO. On May 6, despite the potential for complaints from other unions that held contracts with DiGiorgio's nonagricultural enterprises, Kircher convinced the AFL-CIO Executive Council to endorse the boycott, opening the door to similar endorsements by state labor federations, local labor councils, and national unions.[9] Later that month, at the UAW convention in Los Angeles, Reuther led 3,000 U.S. and Canadian delegates in an enthusiastic welcome to a delegation of strikers led by Chavez. The UAW members committed to organizing boycotts when they returned home.[10] For most labor leaders, this meant providing office space, food, and other support to NFWA organizers deployed to their cities and to the local labor activists eager to take part.

Building on tactics learned during the Schenley boycott, the NFWA initiated this boycott by announcing to supporters and to the press that it would distribute 2 million leaflets to consumers urging a boycott of the targeted DiGiorgio products, conduct a three-part pledge-card campaign similar to the one used against Schenley, and target the major chain stores that retailed DiGiorgio products. By mid-May, retailers in Los Angeles, San Francisco, San Jose, and Fresno were removing S&W products from their shelves.[11] A counterboycott of cooperating retailers, organized by the Farm Bureau, only increased the visibility of the NFWA boycott by generating further controversy in grocery store parking lots.[12]

As picketing and boycotting went forward and both the NFWA and DiGiorgio maneuvered to secure more favorable facts on the ground, the talks between them stalled. A first meeting was hosted by the State Conciliation Service on April 20, but Chavez broke it off when he learned that a DiGiorgio security guard had just assaulted striker Manuel Rosas and volunteer Ida Cousino on the picket line. The NFWA filed a $640,000 damage suit.[13] Subsequent meetings with DiGiorgio representatives in April and May yielded few results.

Meanwhile, Robert DiGiorgio was not shy about using his influence with his employees. His foremen began pressuring them to oppose the NFWA. As long as the union was barred from DiGiorgio fields and camps, the foremen could continue to do so without serious challenge. In addition, the company sent letters from DiGiorgio himself to all employees. In one, he wrote:

> We have been trying to arrange an election through officials of the State of California to allow you to tell us if you want to be represented by one of three unions now active in the area, AWOC, NFWA, or the Tulare-Kern IFWU, or if you want no union, as it has been in the past. So far only the Kern Tulare Independent Farm Workers Union has agreed to an election....the NFWA has...refused to have an election...because it knows it does not represent you.[14]

The NFWA organizers faced a tough challenge.

The Teamster Surprise

On Friday, May 13, when NFWA organizers made house calls, they discovered that the terms of the challenge had suddenly changed. That evening, workers began to ask them about the green "Teamsters Farmworkers Union" authorization cards that their foremen had told them to sign.

In the preceding weeks, the NFWA had begun a campaign to get DiGiorgio workers to sign cards that authorized the NFWA to represent them. With these authorization cards, organizers created a list of supporters among the current workforce. They began to develop a network of leaders among them who could be trained to challenge the bosses, and they could prove that they represented the workers. At first, they didn't think the Teamsters meant to interfere with their campaign. The NFWA organizers thought the Teamsters must be organizing DiGiorgio's packinghouse workers, just as they had organized in the packinghouses while AWOC organized in the fields, back when AWOC and NFWA were conducting their joint drive in the citrus industry.[15] After all, it was less than a month since Teamsters Joint Council 38 president George Mock declared his support for the NFWA in Sacramento. In addition, Teamsters Joint Council 42 had just endorsed the boycott in Los Angeles.[16]

An impromptu Saturday morning meeting between Huerta and Jim Smith, the Teamsters Joint Council 38 organizer who had worked with AWOC in the citrus drive, revealed that the Teamster cards were the first step in a campaign to offer DiGiorgio a "responsible union alternative."[17] So early Monday morning, NFWA organizers posted themselves at entrances to the fields and passed out leaflets urging workers not to sign Teamster cards. Shortly afterward, in a move that would have been illegal employer interference under the NLRA, ranch supervisor Richard Meyer issued a leaflet urging workers to sign with the Teamsters.

The company turned to the Teamsters when it realized that the Kern-Tulare Independent Farm Workers had no credibility and that AWOC posed no alternative to the NFWA, now that the latter had AFL-CIO backing. DiGiorgio's alliance with the Teamsters had a history. DiGiorgio held Teamster contracts in its canneries, warehouses, and trucking operations ever since the company and the union collaborated in a campaign against the labor radicals of the 1930s and 1940s. As another grower commented, however, the alliance's present purpose was strictly anti-NFWA. "If the only way we can get that son of [a] bitch [Chavez] is by falling in bed with Hoffa," he said, "then we'll fall in bed with Hoffa."[18] A Teamster official put it this way:

> It was like the town was being shot up for 8 months by a gunslinger and was just waiting for someone to come along and save it. They knew that we were gunslingers too, but they put a badge on us anyway, hoping that when we'd meet up with Chavez, we'd bump each other off.[19]

Teamster leaders claimed to have signed the Antle contract in 1961 to "protect their jurisdiction" from AWOC, but by 1966 they plainly had an additional reason for wanting to curb the NFWA: racial politics. Einar Mohn, president of the Western Conference of Teamsters, cited job flight from unionized sheds to nonunion fields as the reason for signing up Antle field workers. Yet the Teamsters had no contracts in the grapes, and grapes had almost nothing to do with canneries. What stifling the NFWA *could* do, however, was to squelch the aspirations of its Mexican-American members, thus securing the political positions of the Anglo Teamster leaders.

Anglo Teamster leaders in California knew they were sitting on an ethnic time bomb, as its membership became increasingly Mexican American. Urban Mexican-American Teamster locals, such as Los Angeles Local 208, made up of transport workers, were already supporting the NFWA. Moreover, Mexican and Mexican-American women, many of whom worked in the fields part of the year, formed a growing proportion of the Teamsters cannery workers. Because they were seasonal workers, they rarely attended union meetings, ratified contracts, or voted for union officials in elections usually conducted during the off-season. As a result, the Teamsters' cannery contracts could get away with distinguishing between full-time workers, who tended to be white men earning reasonable wages and benefits, and seasonal workers, who tended to be Mexican women earning only slightly more than field workers did. The NFWA, with its demands not only for economic justice, but for racial justice and self-determination as well, was thus a political threat to the entire set-up.[20] By 1966, the success of the civil rights movement combined with the emergence of the first generation of Mexican-American political leaders to give racial politics new potency.

As at Antle, then, Teamster strategists took opportunistic advantage of DiGiorgio's search for an alternative to the NFWA. As in the past, their tactics relied more on organizing employers than workers. In short, they counted on the DiGiorgio foremen with the power to hire and fire to use their authority to intimidate workers under their supervision into signing up with the Teamsters. As I recounted in chapter 2, the Teamster officials leading this intervention had learned the strategy in campaigns against the ILWU, UCAPAWA, and the FTA in the 1930s and 1940s. The move against the NFWA at DiGiorgio was initiated by Sacramento Joint Council 38 president Mock and his organizer Jim Smith, the same duo who had partnered with AWOC's Al Green in the aborted campaign to organize in the citrus industry the previous year. They, in turn, had the support of a formidable coalition, including: Peter Andrade, the director of the Teamsters' cannery division; Einar Mohn, the director of the WCT; and to some degree, Jimmy Hoffa, the president of the International.[21]

Driving the campaign was the new WCT organizing director, William Grami,[22] an aggressive organizer who once described himself as a "strategic quarterback" and a "warrior" who enjoyed hunting and could "outfox" and "outfight" his opponents.[23] Grami was a Roman Catholic, a second-generation Italian American, married with two children, and at 40, eager to make his mark. The son of an immigrant police officer, he quarterbacked his high school football team, served with the U.S. European invasion forces in World War II, and attended Santa Clara College. He returned from a second tour of duty as a ranger in the Korean War. In 1953, he was hired by Richard King, chief of the Watsonville Teamster local, to be a Teamster "business agent," representing cannery and produce workers. Reassigned to Santa Rosa in 1954, he became the local president there and led a successful strike of apple processors. Close to Bruce Mohn, Einar's son, he became the organizing director of the Western Conference of Teamsters in 1964. He hoped one day to rise from this position to lead the union. A Democrat who said he believed in the "common man,"[24] Grami nonetheless had no personal or vocational interest in farm workers and no ties to any of the urban support constituencies that had become so important in the conflict. He did have a strong interest in success.

Other Teamster leaders had varied personal stakes in the DiGiorgio effort. Andrade, the head of the cannery division since the late 1950s, had the most to lose from an NFWA success, both jurisdictionally and politically. His now largely Mexican-American membership had grown increasingly dissatisfied with Teamster representation—for both ethnic and economic reasons. Mohn was skeptical, but he had his own reason to support the DiGiorgio effort as long as it did not become too costly.[25] At their June 1966 convention, the Teamsters would elect a new general vice president to take over if Hoffa went to jail, and Mohn was in the running. Success in organizing farm workers could be a feather in his cap.

For his part, Hoffa was fighting to stay out of jail and had little interest in farm workers.[26] He had no reason to oppose Mohn, Andrade, and Grami, whose support he needed for more pressing concerns like securing a national freight agreement. Thus, although he subsidized the Teamsters' DiGiorgio organizing effort, there is some evidence that he would have preferred to try affiliating the NFWA.[27] As Al Brundage, who was Mohn's general counsel at the time, told me years later in an interview:

> Hoffa was not an anti-Chavez guy. He would not have minded if Chavez organized the farm workers....His interest was in...this national freight agreement. And while he didn't stand up and oppose—at general Executive Board meetings, Grami and Pete [Andrade] would make reports, Einar would go along, but Jimmy was not gung ho to do anything to Cesar. Nor was it his interest to raid other unions. He wanted to get back into the AFL....While Hoffa was there we were talking about cooperation with the Farm Workers. Until [Frank] Fitzsimmons became president, Grami was pressing "let's raid Cesar" on the theory he would take the canneries. That was a lot of baloney....Grami was looking for all kinds of ways that he could further his own career.... Pete...with some enthusiasm was going along. Einar was sort of dragging his feet but was being dragged.[28]

At the time, however, what Hoffa and Mohn told *Fresno Bee* reporter Ron Taylor was that the Teamster move was logical because the Teamsters were already representing workers in the canneries, packing sheds, and cold storage plants that processed the fresh fruits and vegetables. They said the Teamsters were merely protecting their jurisdictional flank by organizing field labor.[29]

In any case, a coalition formed of Teamster leaders who saw the NFWA threat to the growers as an opportunity for their union—and for their own careers within the union. Except for the 40-year-old Grami, all were white men over 50 who had risen to their positions based more on their skills as negotiators or political operatives than as organizers. Although they had ties to Teamster locals in rural areas and in cities, they had no ties to farm workers nor to any of the farm workers' urban supporters outside the labor movement. Their homogeneity constrained their strategic capacity for a fight with the NFWA, despite their command of enough resources to sustain a fight for a very long time.

The Fight over Elections

As the number of actors multiplied and the need to sustain the momentum of the campaign grew more urgent in the face of a rapidly advancing season, the fight over the terms of the DiGiorgio election grew more intense.

Bolstered by his new allies, Robert DiGiorgio became far more aggressive in organizing his workers to oppose the NFWA. On May 16, a crew leader sympathetic to the NFWA, Ophelia Diaz, was fired for refusing to sign up her crew for the Teamsters, urging them instead to support the NFWA. She also refused to testify on behalf of the security guard whom she had witnessed assault Rosas and Cousino on the picket line on April 20. A DiGiorgio employee for 24 years and a crew leader for 17, she was told that her "work had deteriorated" in the three weeks just prior to her discharge. The next week, her husband, Henry, a foreman at another struck ranch, was also fired.[30] The same day, DiGiorgio bused 200 workers to Delano from Borrego Springs, so the company would not have to hire local workers, who would be accessible to the NFWA in town. The Borrego Springs workers could be housed in company camps where the NFWA could not reach them. And on May 20, DiGiorgio got an injunction restricting NFWA pickets to the main entrance to the ranch. By denying them the opportunity to picket along public roads, the court order effectively closed off the only way that the NFWA could communicate with a major portion of DiGiorgio's workers: addressing them over loudspeakers from the side of the road.[31]

Since NFWA organizers had no access to the camps, how would they now communicate with the workers whose support they needed to meet the Teamsters' challenge? The NFWA's answer shows how its leaders learned to strategize their way out of tight spots—by attending to new ideas from people who knew what was going on, namely the workers themselves. As Chavez later recalled the events:

After several days of particularly futile picketing, people were...impatient and discouraged. As I just couldn't come up with any solution, I called a meeting at the American Legion Hall in Delano. The meeting soon got around to the idea that we were losing because we were not using violence, that the only solution was to use violence. We spent most of the day discussing that. Then, although we had taken a vote at the beginning of the strike to be nonviolent, we took another vote.

Before the meeting ended I had run out of ideas of things to do, but I knew that in them, the people, there were answers, and I needed their help to find those answers. A couple of hours later, three ladies said they wanted to see me.... the first thing that came to my mind was that the ladies wanted money for some personal need. I asked them to come into my little office.

First, they wanted to make sure that I wouldn't be offended by what they wanted to tell me. Then they wanted to assure me that they were not trying to tell me how to run the strike. After we got over those hurdles, they said, "we don't understand this business of the court order. Does that mean that if we go picket and break the injunctions, we'll go to jail?"

"Well, it means that you go to jail, and that we will be fined," I said.

"What would happen if we met across the street from the DiGiorgio gates, not to picket, not to demonstrate, but to have a prayer, maybe a mass?" they asked. "Do you think the judge would have us arrested?"

By the time they got the last word out, my mind just flashed on all the possibilities....I got Richard and had him take my old station wagon and build a little chapel on it. It was like a shrine with a picture of Our Lady of Guadalupe, some candles, and some flowers....We parked it across from the DiGiorgio gate where we started a vigil that lasted at least two months. People were there day and night.

The next morning we distributed a leaflet...inviting people to a prayer meeting at the DiGiorgio ranch and made the same announcement on the Spanish radio. People came by the hundreds. We brought loudspeakers and tried to get the people in the camp to come to the mass, but I don't think more than 10 came out. Most of them were out at the fence looking and seeing a tremendous number of people.

taking ideas from everyone

They were very impressed. There was also so much confusion; our guys found themselves talking to our members inside the camp for the first time in about three weeks.

The next day…when the trucks brought the people from the fields to eat at the company mess hall, about eight women decided to come to where we had the vigil instead of going to the mess hall. The supervisors got the trucks in the way to keep them from coming, but the women went way out through the vines and wouldn't be stopped. They knelt down and prayed and then went back.

That was the beginning. The same evening about 50 women came. The next evening, half the camp was out, and from then on, every single day, they were out there. Every day we had a mass, held a meeting, sang spirituals, and got them to sign authorization cards. It was a beautiful demonstration of the power of nonviolence.[32]

But this creative breakthrough had occurred only at the Sierra Vista ranch in Delano. To avoid being outflanked by the Teamsters, the NFWA also had to reach the workers at DiGiorgio's other properties. So it assigned organizers to each of them. Fred Ross held overall responsibility and led the Delano campaign. Manuel Chavez led a team in Borrego Springs. Gilbert Padilla a team in Marysville, while I was responsible for the Arvin team.[33]

FIGURE 6.2. Strikers maintain vigil, DiGiorgio labor camp, May 1966.
Source: Paul Fusco/Magnum Photos

Although organizing DiGiorgio workers remained the primary focus of NFWA's effort, it strengthened its position by mobilizing its supporters as well. Most notably, it secured letters of protest from Roman Catholic church leaders, in particular Chicago archbishop John Cody, urging the Teamsters to withdraw from Delano. The surprised Teamster leaders, many of whom were Roman Catholic, initially responded to pressure from this unexpected quarter. According to Grami:

> The pressure on the Teamsters became fantastic, particularly that of the Catholic Church. They had missed the civil rights movement and they weren't going to miss this new Chicano movement and jumped in, to get their place on the placard. It was that pressure on Mohn that he became particularly concerned about and thought we should withdraw.[34]

Mohn called two meetings with the NFWA almost immediately—one on May 21 and another on May 31[35]—but they got nowhere. The May 21 meeting included many key players: Andrade, Mock, Smith, and Wendell Kiser of Joint Council 38; Jack Goldberger, who was Hoffa's representative; and longshoremen leaders Harry Bridges and Lou Goldblatt. Chavez afterward claimed that the Teamsters agreed at this meeting to stay out of the DiGiorgio fray, but Mohn came out of the meeting with a different impression. He said the only agreement was that the parties would "stay in touch." The Teamsters' plans, he said, were "indefinite." "The NFWA," he said, "gets a lot of publicity, but little is known of its real goals, whether it will shape up into a trade union or a civil rights movement."[36]

Three days later, Hoffa announced that he was committing $5,000 a month to organizing farm workers and that he had the longshoremen's support in this. (Although the Longshoremen's Union had supported the NFWA in the past, its bargaining interests were deeply intertwined with those of the Teamsters.) Mohn's May 31 meeting with the NFWA broke up after 10 minutes.[37]

The situation grew even more confusing on June 7, when Mohn suddenly announced that the Teamsters were withdrawing from DiGiorgio after all and were doing it solely to please the Catholic clergy. He made the pledge in letters to California's seven Roman Catholic bishops and to Archbishop Cody.[38] Meanwhile, Smith, on the same day and with the apparent backing of Mock, demanded exclusive recognition of the Teamsters as representatives of the farm workers at DiGiorgio's

Borrego Springs ranch.[39] Hoffa appeared to resolve the confusion by supporting Mohn. Hoffa affirmed that the Teamsters were withdrawing from DiGiorgio. He also said, however, "We are going to continue our campaign to organize farm workers."[40]

With the Teamsters seemingly out of the picture, the NFWA and DiGiorgio resumed talks on Tuesday, June 14, and prospects for agreement looked promising. DiGiorgio abandoned its preconditions, ~~teamster gone~~ while the NFWA agreed to submit an election proposal to a vote of its membership in Delano on Sunday.[41]

But all was not as it seemed. Behind a conciliatory front, the NFWA's opponents were still maneuvering for a more favorable position. The California Council of Growers denounced the "church pressure" that prevented workers at DiGiorgio from "making a free choice,"[42] and DiGiorgio foremen collected the signatures of some 400 workers on a petition asking the Teamsters to return.[43] Now, a week after Mohn and Hoffa promised a Teamster withdrawal, Mohn presented those signatures to Bishop Aloysius Willinger of the Fresno Diocese, in which Delano was located. The bishop had been an NFWA critic since the strike began the year before. On June 16, Bishop Willinger took public issue with his brother bishops, declaring that DiGiorgio workers were entitled to "free elections" and that the Teamsters should have the right to appear on any ballot along with the NFWA. The next day, the Fresno County Farm Bureau, the California Council of Growers, and the DiGiorgio Corporation echoed Willinger's call.[44] The day after that, Mohn announced that Hoffa would decide what to do on Monday, June 20, in a meeting at the Teamsters convention in Miami.[45]

Despite a flurry of concern generated by Willinger's statement and Mohn's announcement, on Sunday NFWA members voted to proceed with elections and authorized Chavez to negotiate guidelines with DiGiorgio when their meetings resumed the next day. At the end of this meeting, all seemed well, although two questions remained unresolved: which unions would appear on the ballot, and whether strikers would be eligible to vote. Since Chavez and Kircher needed to be in Los Angeles on Tuesday to sign the Schenley contract, the parties agreed that they would use the time to "consult with their principals" and resume talks on Wednesday. On Tuesday, however, when Kircher checked with DiGiorgio's attorney about the time and place, he was told there would be no meeting.[46]

Instead, on Wednesday, June 22, without prior agreement from the NFWA or AWOC, DiGiorgio announced it would hold elections at Delano and Borrego Springs in just three days, on Friday, June 24.

Voting would take place from 6:00 a.m. to 5:00 p.m. at the Sierra Vista ranch and from 7:00 a.m. to noon at Borrego Springs. The elections would be supervised by the accounting firm of Touche, Ross, Bailey and Smart. Monsignor Roger Mahoney, Willinger's chancellor, and the Reverend R. B. Moore, a Delano African-American clergyman long opposed to the NFWA, would be observers. Strikers would not be eligible to vote.[47]

Big percent of FWA

Chavez and Kircher denounced these elections as "phony," yet the Teamsters accepted them because, Mohn said, they would give "the workers a means of expressing their views."[48] Apparently, the outcome of the Mohn and Hoffa meeting in Miami was that the Teamsters would decide whether to return to DiGiorgio *after* the workers voted—or after DiGiorgio demonstrated it could deliver them.

Why did DiGiorgio and the Teamsters think they could get away with this sleight of hand? Most probably, they didn't understand what they were up against. Although DiGiorgio and the Teamsters were well connected to elite business and political networks, the only direct knowledge they had of the workers was from the reports of the foremen. Although they used their local connections to successfully bring Bishop Willinger into the picture, they had no ties to the church members, students, liberals, and Mexican-Americans who were the NFWA's outside supporters. (The Teamsters did have links to organized labor, but these were of little use, because the AFL-CIO was actively backing the NFWA.) DiGiorgio and the Teamsters also possessed few allies in the working press, no counterpart to Ron Taylor of the *Fresno Bee*, Harry Bernstein of the *Los Angeles Times*, and Dick Meister of the *San Francisco Chronicle*, for whom the NFWA had become David doing battle with two Goliaths.[49]

why failed

teamster & growers

The NFWA Responds

The NFWA leaders judged their chances of winning the phony election as slim. First, had very limited access to the DiGiorgio workers housed in the camps. Second strikers were not eligible to vote. Third, no unfair-labor-practice mechanism existed. In an impromptu meeting on Wednesday night, they decided that they could not legitimate such an election by participating. Neither could they ignore it, though, for if any election went forward, no matter how unfair, the results could be used to undermine their claim to represent the workers and to legitimate a quickly drawn contract between DiGiorgio and the Teamsters. Such a contract would be difficult to dislodge. How, then, should they proceed? Caught between two unacceptable alternatives, the NFWA

Making the best (handwritten)

leaders devised a dual strategy to organize DiGiorgio workers to boycott any election and, simultaneously, to discredit the election with the public. Success depended on mobilizing the two constituencies with which DiGiorgio and the Teamsters had the least contact: the workers and the public.[50]

When they learned that DiGiorgio had called a press conference for the next day, Thursday, June 23, at the San Francisco Press Club, Kircher and Huerta flew up from Los Angeles to crash it. As soon as DiGiorgio announced the election, Kircher interrupted, charging that DiGiorgio was a liar and creating a confrontation that was televised that evening. Meanwhile, AWOC and the NFWA filed a motion in Superior Court to prevent DiGiorgio from using their names on the ballot, a motion granted the next day. Both moves put the election under a public cloud.[51]

Simultaneously, the NFWA assigned Ross to Delano and Chavez himself to Borrego Springs with the task of organizing a boycott of the election among DiGiorgio workers. Learning that the workers were to be bused by their foremen, crew by crew, to the voting site, the organizers worked through inside contacts to encourage them to stay on the bus. They reasoned that it would be easier for workers intimidated by their employer to cooperate in collective inaction than to vote individually against the supervisor's wishes. The NFWA organizers also passed out four different leaflets the day before the election, urging a boycott and countering the company's leaflet in which it urged its workers to vote for the Teamsters.

Since the road was visible from the election site, the NFWA also mobilized supporters from the surrounding farm worker towns to picket on the road. As the buses began to arrive at the polling place, the workers on board could see some 400 other farm workers who had *public support* (handwritten) turned out to encourage them to stay on the bus, as well as the Catholic priests who had come to lead the picketers in prayer.[52]

At the end of the day, of the 732 workers eligible to vote, only 385 had voted. Of the 385 who voted, 281 voted for the Teamsters, 60 for *relatively successful* (handwritten) no union, 17 wrote in AWOC or the NFWA, and 41 cast blank ballots. All sides claimed victory. Asserting that the election proved that his workers wanted the Teamsters, DiGiorgio invited them to negotiate a contract. Asserting that the election was rigged and that it also proved that most workers did not want the Teamsters, Chavez announced that the NFWA would intensify its boycott, possibly extending it to include the Bank of America, with which the DiGiorgio Corporation shared five corporate directors.[53]

The NFWA quickly rallied its allies. Religious leaders, the Mexican-American community, the AFL-CIO, and the Democratic Party called on Governor Pat Brown to investigate claims that the election had been rigged.[54] In the June 7 Democratic primary, Brown narrowly won renomination over Los Angeles's conservative mayor, Sam Yorty, and in November he would face Republican Ronald Reagan. Brown was already vulnerable to Reagan's claims that in the last year alone, he had mishandled the free speech movement at UC Berkeley and the Watts riots in the black ghetto of Los Angeles. The governor did not need new problems with an angry Mexican-American constituency.

Fortuitously, many of the Mexican-American political leaders most offended by Brown's failure to receive the march in Sacramento were attending the Mexican-American Political Association (MAPA) convention in Fresno on Saturday, June 25. At this convention, MAPA would make its candidate endorsements. After an urgent presentation by Huerta, the convention conditioned its endorsement of Brown on his investigating the DiGiorgio election.[55] After calls arrived from U.S. senators Harrison Williams and Edward Kennedy, the AFL-CIO, and various religious leaders, Brown agreed to a meeting the next day, Sunday.[56] In this meeting with Chavez from the NFWA, Hartmire from the Migrant Ministry, Kircher from the AFL-CIO, Corona and Quevedo from MAPA, and California State Controller Alan Cranston, Brown agreed to intervene if it could be shown that the election had been unfair. On Tuesday, he called on the American Arbitration Association to recommend a professional to investigate the election and to propose a fair resolution of the charge that its results did not reflect the wishes of the workers.[57]

Although just one week passed since DiGiorgio had announced its plans for an election, the NFWA's ties with workers in Delano, Mexican-American political leaders, the churches, liberal Democrats, and the AFL-CIO enabled it to respond strategically on multiple fronts simultaneously.

Brown's agreement to intervene was a victory, but since nothing was settled, both sides escalated to gain more leverage. On Monday, June 27, NFWA organizers sent to contact workers at DiGiorgio's Borrego Springs ranch took advantage of their local grievances to pull them out on strike. On Tuesday, when Chavez, Hartmire, and Father Vincent Salandini, a Roman Catholic priest from San Diego, accompanied 10 of them back into the camp to retrieve their belongings, DiGiorgio had all of them arrested on charges of trespassing. They were stripped, shackled, transported, and jailed in San Diego, 150 miles away.[58]

On Wednesday, AWOC and the NFWA filed a suit in San Francisco charging DiGiorgio with intimidating its workers, ordering them to vote, telling them how to vote, and otherwise infringing on the rights of workers under state collective bargaining laws, which did not entirely exclude farm workers.[59]

The NFWA escalated the boycott as well. On Saturday, June 25, the day after the phony election, 80 students were dispatched to expand the boycott. They just completed a summer project training sponsored by SNCC, the National Student Association, the National Student Christian Federation, the Young Christian Students, and the Students for a Democratic Society (SDS).[60] Boycotters already in place reported "cleaning" (getting DiGiorgio products removed from) 400 stores in Cleveland and 500 in New York. The California Council of Churches endorsed the boycott, and the San Francisco Board of Supervisors declared that July 10 would be Huelga Day.[61]

The NFWA also gained ground on the election front. On June 30, the American Arbitration Association appointed Professor Ronald Houghton, a respected labor arbitrator and professor at Wayne State University, to mediate the election dispute. Brown asked the parties to agree to accept Houghton's recommendations. When the NFWA and AWOC agreed immediately, Senators Williams and Kennedy jointly urged DiGiorgio and the Teamsters to do the same. Outflanked, the Teamsters and DiGiorgio finally acceded.[62]

So on Tuesday, July 12, after two weeks of intense investigation based on more than 200 interviews of representatives of the unions, DiGiorgio management, DiGiorgio workers, Catholic and Protestant clergy, private citizens, and state officials, Houghton's team issued its report. It found that the elections were indeed invalid and recommended that new elections be held on August 30. Houghton proposed several terms. Field workers and packinghouse workers would vote in separate units. Both strikers and strike breakers would be eligible to vote; specifically, those eligible would be all workers on the Delano payroll as of September 19, 1965, the day before the strike began, or between September 20, 1965, and August 15, 1966, 15 days prior to the election. If the workers voted for a union, the parties would have 45 days after the election results were certified to negotiate a contract. Unresolved issues would be submitted to binding arbitration by Houghton and Sam Kagel, a legendary San Francisco waterfront arbitrator who had also arbitrated Teamster contracts until 1958, when

Hoffa replaced him. The arbitrators' award—their decision as to the terms of the contract, including wages and benefits—would be retroactive to the date the election results were certified. The loser would be barred from organizing for one year. The American Arbitration Association would establish the election procedures and supervise the election. And if all sides accepted these terms, all strike and boycott activity would stop.[63]

Because they had no other alternative, the Teamsters and DiGiorgio accepted immediately. The NFWA, however, had to submit the proposal to a vote of the strikers the next day. Chavez had to explain why it was a good idea to give up boycotting and picketing in return for an election, rather than recognition of the union as had been demanded. He was also concerned that the question of elections at DiGiorgio's other properties in Arvin, Marysville, and Yuba City were left pending. Nonetheless, the strikers voted to accept. Chavez assigned Ross to negotiate the rules of access and eligibility with the arbitrators, Teamsters, and DiGiorgio. The agreed-upon eligible voter list included 2,000 workers, of whom only 700 were currently employed by DiGiorgio.[64] Although the NFWA did not win on every point, the effort to get the phony election undone and to put fairer election procedures into place succeeded.

On July 16, the NFWA declared its DiGiorgio boycott at an end. During the previous 14 weeks, 53 full-time people organized boycotts in 12 major cities. These organizers could now be redeployed to the election campaign.[65] The NFWA had put itself back in the game, but it was a game its leaders now had to figure out how to win.

CONFRONTATION AT DIGIORGIO: A CONTRAST IN STRATEGIC CAPACITY

The NFWA's continued credibility with the public would now depend upon demonstrating the union's credibility with the workers. Conversely, the opportunity to demonstrate credibility with the workers was the result of having enough credibility with the public to make the boycott a real threat to DiGiorgio. Indeed, losing an election conducted with the safeguards that the union had demanded—and won—would be a disaster. It was life or death for the new union. As Chavez later said, "I knew that if we lost this one, we would lose the union, because the public wouldn't have supported us after that."[66]

Union leaders had to balance their vital organizational interest in winning the election—which required keeping striker activists working on the campaign—against the individual interests of strikers who wanted to go to work at Schenley to enjoy the benefits for which they sacrificed. It was an acute dilemma for the union because it ran the hiring hall where Schenley now obtained its workers. In some cases, striker families sent one member to work at Schenley while others served in the DiGiorgio campaign.[67] In other cases, it worked as Eliseo Medina, who would later become a union board member, described it:

> So we tried to form a crew to go to work there [at Schenley]. Because I knew Dolores [Huerta] and others, I thought I was in good. So she says fine, [you can work at Schenley,] but we have this little campaign for the next 30 days. It was July and the harvest wouldn't start until August. We have this little election. So she introduced me to Cesar. And they assigned me to a tall white guy named Fred Ross. It was the Sierra Vista election with the Teamsters.[68]

In contrast, the Teamsters, whose approach depended on mobilizing growers more than the workers or the public, thought they were in a win-win position. Grami explained: "If we win [the election], we'll organize faster. If Chavez wins, he becomes that much more potent, and the growers are already afraid of him, scared of the lengths to which he'll go. So they'll come to us that much quicker."[69]

After the quick and phony first DiGiorgio election, this campaign unfolded as a six-week morality play; "right" faced "might," and most observers thought that "might" would win. As *Fresno Bee* reporter Ron Taylor later recalled: "The media was swarming around. We were pretty much on the outside trying to find out what was on the inside. It was theater. But the idea that you guys [the NFWA] could take on DiGiorgio—and the Teamsters—and win just defied history."[70]

By comparing the campaigns of the NFWA and the Teamsters, we can observe differences in the strategic capacity of the two organizations even as they faced asymmetric strategic challenges. As "incumbents" supported by the employer, the Teamsters needed only to convince workers that their best course was to avoid risking the unknown. As the Mexican *dicho* (folk saying) counsels, "Mejor malo por conocido que bueno por conocer (loosely, better the devil you know than the angel you don't)." On the other side, the NFWA, as the challengers, needed to convince workers that their best course was actually to take risks. How the two unions structured these opposite-pointing campaigns—in terms of accountability, deliberative processes, and the resources upon which they relied—once again reflected the identities, experiences, and networks of their leaders. Not surprisingly, the resulting strategies were very different. More surprising is the dramatic difference in the effectiveness of the strategy each union devised.

LEADERSHIP: IDENTITIES, EXPERIENCES, NETWORKS

Grami led the Teamsters' campaign with a cadre of 6 to 10 professional Teamster organizers and business agents loaned by locals from as far away as El Paso.[71] They earned salaries of $20,000 or more from their home offices,[72] which was also where their political allegiances and connections lay. As professionals, each expected to be given an assignment and left pretty much on his own to fulfill it, as did Grami himself. In Teamster fashion, responsibilities, perks, and power relations in general were also matters of continual negotiation up and down the hierarchy. For the most part, these politics, rather than any particular commitment to farm workers, are what drove these men.

Grami and his organizers—and Mohn and Andrade, the superiors with whom he consulted and negotiated his own authority[73]—drew on a repertoire of familiar tactics they had learned in strikes, negotiations, and NLRB elections. In the DiGiorgio election, they used all of them: collaborating with the employer; relying on company forepersons, who after all had eight or more hours a day with their workers, to influence their votes; making a show of Teamster power; showering potential voters with small trinkets (cans of fruit, key chains, toys); and red baiting their competitors, a tactic Mohn had learned well in the cannery campaigns of the 1930s and 1940s. The Teamster organizers thought they knew all there was to know about how to win the DiGiorgio election. There was nothing to learn.

The NFWA organizing team, by contrast, was made up of young farm workers and volunteers with strong vocational and personal commitments to the cause, but very little experience. Fred Ross, with his 30 years of organizing experience, led them and consulted regularly with Chavez, Kircher, and Huerta. Still, the most seasoned veterans on Ross's team, those who became his coordinators, were hardly more than beginners. For example, there was Anglo volunteer Ida Cousino, just returned from the Cleveland boycott, and farm workers Roberto Bustos and Pete Cardenas, who began learning to organize on the march to Sacramento. Eliseo Medina, the young man who had hoped for a job at Schenley, had no experience at all but was drafted as a coordinator because he seemed sharp and promising. The full team eventually grew to 25 farm workers, 5 Anglo volunteers, and 2 former DiGiorgio forepersons, Joe Serda and Ophelia Diaz. It also eventually included 12 professional AFL-CIO organizers, who were loaned by Kircher late in the campaign.[74] Except for these 12, all were highly motivated volunteers who had never worked on a union representation election. For that matter, neither had Ross or Chavez. They knew they had a lot to learn. And for this, Ross and Chavez drew on the experience they did have.

As community organizers, Ross and Chavez were experienced in developing leaders within a community and training them to rally their neighbors to a common effort. In their electoral work, they learned to organize precinct-by-precinct voter-registration and get-out-the-vote campaigns; success depended on knowing how to count votes. Kircher offered advice based on his union experience, but

FIGURE 6.3. Fred Ross and Cesar Chavez, Delano, August 1966. *Source:* Jon Lewis

FIGURE 6.4. Organizers' meeting, Delano, August 1966. *Source:* Jon Lewis

given the AFL-CIO record, the NFWA skeptics drew on that experience selectively. What their experience taught them was that they needed to identify, recruit, and develop leaders among the 700 currently employed DiGiorgio workers eligible to vote. Therefore, they had to train organizers to develop those leaders. And they had to do it all in six weeks.

New plan

For Ross, organizing was a vocation that demanded a disciplined mastery of the craft. In that light, training skilled organizers on a large scale, in a short time, under conditions that required rapid response was a daunting challenge. Moreover, they faced adversaries intent on counterorganizing by exercising authority over the workers at least eight hours a day. It was a whole different ballgame from the community organizing context in which he had trained Chavez, Huerta, and Padilla. But based on his experience in learning from experience, the demands of the moment, and the only resources the NFWA had in abundance—the time, motivation, and life experience of the organizers and the DiGiorgio workers themselves—Ross designed a campaign that relied far less on the Alinsky style of the hotshot solo performer than on an organizing team, shaped by training, learning, and development. It resembled nothing so much as a school for organizers.

STRUCTURE: ACCOUNTABILITY, RESOURCES, DELIBERATION

Ross's system was anchored in several critical elements: meetings three times a day for planning, training, and evaluation; the scrupulous accounting of lists of names, signatures, and commitments; and a strict accountability of organizers to coordinators, coordinators to Ross, and Ross to Chavez. This disciplined structure, however, was built around the core of a deliberative framework for daily analysis, evaluation, and innovation. Organizers discussed themes, reviewed leaflets, tallied numbers, analyzed problems, and reconsidered approaches. This approach allowed trainees to acquire the basic tools of the craft, while at the same time taking part in a learning process through which they could understand, evaluate, and respond to their experiences and thus engage their creativity. As the organizing team grew to include farm workers, students, clergy, and AFL-CIO organizers, this structure created a venue within which a diversity of views could enhance the NFWA's strategic capacity, rather than tearing it apart—as could quite easily have occurred.[75]

Grami's job did not require training new organizers, much less developing farm worker leaders. Most of the Teamsters' organizing was done by DiGiorgio forepersons, who hired, supervised, and disciplined workers and who got them to sign Teamster cards and otherwise support the Teamsters. They explained that if they wanted to keep their jobs, this was the right thing to do. Teamster organizers compared notes informally with forepersons as needed, and the organizers met as a group once a day to exchange news and coordinate activities. Relying on the estimates of supervisors and organizers, they didn't think that monitoring the thinking of individual voters was required. The notion of analyzing events together and changing their practices based on the discussion would have been entirely foreign to these independent operators. They saw no need for a different kind of meeting, nor any need to establish a deliberative process for considering the campaign's strategic choices. Those decisions were handed down from above, and they were driven by the internal Teamster political interests of the key players—Hoffa, Mohn, Andrade, and Grami[76]—rather than the strategic requirements of the situation.

The result was unambiguous. On the one hand, the NFWA structured its campaign in terms of accountability and deliberation, which encouraged tactical innovation and adaptive strategy. On the other hand, the Teamsters structured their campaign to discourage all those things.

The organizer's day began with an early morning distribution of "El Mosquito Zumbador (the buzzing, or stinging, mosquito)," the NFWA's leaflet of the day, to DiGiorgio workers. It featured cartoon attacks on DiGiorgio and the Teamsters, comparisons of Schenley pay stubs with Antle pay stubs, and so forth.[77] Following the leaflet distribution, organizers gathered at 8:00 a.m. for the first meeting of the day. They met at the "pink house," a two-bedroom, stucco bungalow behind a converted cleaning establishment, which had become their headquarters. They compared notes, discussed tactics, and accepted assignments for noon.

The election rules allowed organizers access to DiGiorgio camps for an hour at noon and an hour after work. The noon visits especially became a main venue of the campaign as Teamster and NFWA organizers converged on the camps. Both violated a rule that limited the number of organizers present to 7 each at lunch and 5 each in the evening. The NFWA often had as many as 20 or 25 organizers scattered among the six camps, which were known by everyone as the Black, Mexican, Filipino, Anglo, Puerto Rican, and Women's camps. The focal point, however, was the so-called bullring at the Mexican Camp, where all the men ate lunch. At the bullring, the star performer for the Teamsters was Oxnard organizer Art Cheverria, who kept up a barrage of taunts and enticements for the entire hour, over loudspeakers mounted on his Teamster van. Teatro Campesino director Luis Valdez, also gifted with a bullhorn, would counter. The Teamsters called the NFWA Communists. The NFWA responded by distributing free copies of Robert Kennedy's exposé of Teamster corruption, *The Enemy Within*.[78]

After the noon visits, the NFWA organizers returned to the pink house to debrief, eat, and rest. At around 5:00 p.m., they gathered for the afternoon meeting to plan the evening's house calls. Ross worked the voter eligibility list like a precinct list, with a three-by-five card for each person on the list. Every one on the list had to be tracked down, talked to, and then coded as to how likely it was that he or she would support the NFWA. One of the team's coordinators would meet with each organizer each afternoon to update their cards, monitor the progress of the campaign, evaluate changes in sentiment, and provide coaching.[79]

Each evening, one group of organizers went to the camps and another went to visit local workers in their homes. Medina recalls:

Fred had a system. He drilled us before we went in, sent us out with index cards, kept us up all fucking night making reports. It was exciting, it was great! It was new. Here's a whole group of people. And it was very disciplined. It left nothing to chance. I was part of Carranza's team, going out making house calls outside the camp. Four of us started to be real close friends, we were the "stars" who would go out and do the work—Bustos, Carranza, Cardenas, and I. And Ruth Trujillo and Alice Tapia.[80]

Ross never let up. When the 12 AFL-CIO organizers arrived to work on DiGiorgio's Anglo and black employees, he later told me, "We duplicated their work because we felt some were too casual. We didn't leave anything to chance."[81]

Grami's operation looked very different. Although the Teamsters opened an office on Main Street in Delano and staffed it with four or five organizers, the campaign was run out of a two-room suite at the Stardust Motel, Delano's finest. Author John Gregory Dunne, caught up in the morality play, described the Teamster organizing team this way:

> Outside the office was a row of cars, all new models, including a Cadillac and a Thunderbird, plastered with blue and silver posters that said simply "Teamsters." A half dozen Teamster organizers lounged around outside, drinking beer and comparing golf scores. Some had changed into swimming trunks and were trying to get the others to take a dip in the Stardust pool before lunch. Sitting inside the office was a painted and lacquered blond secretary reading a copy of *The Enemy Within*.[82]

Organizing People

Under the election rules, the Teamsters and the NFWA both had access to the list of eligible voters. But they organized these workers in very different ways. In fact, each saw vulnerability in what the other thought was its strength. The Teamster organizers and the company forepersons told workers that a vote for the Teamsters was what the company wanted and would bring the greatest benefits. The Teamsters thought that their large new cars, their expensive leather boots and jackets, their physical toughness, and the power of their union would impress the DiGiorgio workers with both the promise and the threat that the Teamsters union wielded.[83] The NFWA, they warned, was made up of Communists, radicals, and undesirables who wanted to cause trouble, when a worker's first concern ought to be earning money to support his or her family.

The NFWA organizers, for their part, emphasized that Mexicans, Puerto Ricans, Filipinos, and blacks all had to stand up for their rights. They presented Teamster power as a liability. They reminded the DiGiorgio employees of abuses they had suffered at the hands of employers and asked how they could entrust their fate to an Anglo union in bed with the employer. They emphasized that the NFWA was *their* union, not that of the Anglo bosses and Teamsters. Farm worker organizers were not professionals like the Teamsters, but former farm workers or students who dressed modestly at best, wore no fancy rings, and, for the most part, drove old cars.[84] About those Teamster organizers who were themselves Mexican Americans, Medina recalls, "I thought they were with the company, sell-out Mexicans. Any Mexican worth his salt needed to be on the side of the [NFWA]."[85]

The NFWA campaign was not only about ethnicity, however. Organizers argued that their new Schenley contract was better than the Teamsters' Bud Antle contract and most Teamster cannery contracts. The Schenley contract specified a minimum wage of $1.75, a 40 percent increase over the prestrike rate of $1.25. It replaced labor contractors with a union hiring hall. Lastly, it provided a medical plan, grievance procedure, and seniority system. The Antle contract offered none of that, and its hourly minimum was $1.23.[86] The NFWA also provided social services, a credit union, and a death benefit, and it had announced plans to build a medical clinic in Delano.

Nonetheless, signing an NFWA card and signing a Teamster card—and there were many farm workers who did both—meant two very different things. Especially for the Mexicans, but also for other people of color, signing an NFWA card meant taking a risk, expressing solidarity with one's fellows, making a claim, and asserting an ethnic identity. Signing a Teamster card meant protecting one's job, doing what the boss wanted, and, in the eyes of many, denying one's ethnic identity. Signing an NFWA card expressed anger or hopefulness; signing a Teamster card expressed fear or resignation. And it was not at all clear which emotions would prevail in the voting booth.

THE CAMPAIGN UNFOLDS

The first week of campaigning, July 18–24, was so aggressive that Houghton decided to appoint a full-time representative to mediate claims of election-rule violations. On Monday, DiGiorgio violated unfair-labor-practice rules by laying off 190 of its workers, including

20 "submarines" whom the NFWA had infiltrated into the workforce.[87] On Tuesday, at the request of the growers, the California Senate Agriculture Committee held hearings in Delano, the thrust of which was to red bait the NFWA. Those summoned to testify included Mickey Lima, head of the California Communist Party, and Saul Alinsky, reputed to be the radical behind it all.[88] And, in a scare tactic barred from NLRB elections as an unfair labor practice, Robert DiGiorgio testified that he intended to sell Sierra Vista.[89]

During the second week of the campaign, on July 28, the NFWA and AWOC announced their merger at a San Francisco press conference.[90] The timing was intended to reassure workers who were skeptical that the NFWA was not a "real" union. The announcement, along with approval of the formal merger two weeks later, yielded a flurry of publicity about the AFL-CIO's support for the NFWA.[91] The Teamsters denounced the merger but to some extent profited from it. A division surfaced within AWOC, as leaders committed to the old-style union approach resigned, some of them going over to the Teamsters. Ben Gines, for example, a former assistant director of AWOC, resigned over differences with Itliong, claiming that he wanted to be part of a union, not a civil rights movement.[92]

During the week of August 1, the third week of the campaign, Ross began to play his tactical hole card—the so-called dragnet. In his many years of organizing get-out-the-vote campaigns, Ross learned that the key to winning an election was having a list of who your supporters actually are and, one by one, getting them to the polls on election day. After carefully reviewing the eligibility list of 2,000, he determined that almost 1,000 workers were gone from the local area, and many of them had signed cards with the NFWA. If they could be found and persuaded to return to Delano to vote, they would be likely supporters. Kicking off the effort with a mailing to the entire list, including 500 addresses in Texas and Mexico, Ross then dispatched a team of organizers to find these workers and bring them back to Delano. The organizers were to appeal to these former DiGiorgio employees on grounds of ethnic solidarity, worker solidarity, and the promise of economic improvement, which the Schenley contract made real. Ross's team tracked down eligible voters as far away as Juarez, Mexico. Both unions targeted current DiGiorgio employees, but only the NFWA, drawing on its more diverse organizing experience, thought to launch a long-distance get-out-the-vote campaign.[93] The week culminated with an NFWA-AWOC unity fiesta, attended by some 2,500 people, at which contributions totaling $5,000 were received from labor delegations from throughout the state.[94]

At the end of the fourth week of the campaign, DiGiorgio once again urged his workers to vote for the Teamsters. In a letter questioning the "good faith" of the NFWA, he urged those who preferred the status quo ante not to waste their vote by voting "no union." If they did that, rather than vote for the Teamsters, he said, the NFWA could win the election. "We think the Teamsters are the best bet, but it's your choice," he wrote.[95]

Asked to comment on DiGiorgio's endorsement, Grami said, "We could imagine they liked the businesslike approach of the Teamsters as compared to the revolutionary, vicious, irresponsible approach of the NFWA."[96] Sounding like AWOC's Al Green, Grami denounced Chavez:

> [The NFWA organizing campaign is] the greatest fraud ever perpetrated on the American public.... The Teamsters believe the farm worker is entitled to be represented by a *legitimate* union and not to be used as [a] revolutionary tool for the New Left to build a power base for political action. Our representatives are adhering strictly to *accepted trade union techniques* and pointing out to the workers how *a legitimate and long established organization* like the Teamsters can assist them. We are not dragging in a lot of unrelated issues or people who have no direct connection with the labor movement.[97]

Accepted trade union techniques included inviting DiGiorgio workers to "food, fun, and fellowship" on Sunday, August 21, 10 days before the election. The Teamsters, now calling themselves "Union de Agricultura," sponsored a fiesta at which Teamster organizers and hundreds of DiGiorgio workers heard Mohn promise:

> We will win this election and appoint a committee from amongst the workers who know your needs. These workers will tell the union what they want, and Teamster bargaining strength will be used to negotiate for them. All colors, races, and creeds have full and equal membership in the Teamsters.[98]

ENDGAME

As the election neared, the NFWA rallied its allies on all fronts. The tension grew when several Teamster representatives assaulted NFWA organizers Eliseo Medina and Robert Edmunds during lunch hour on DiGiorgio property. Consequently, Kircher got the Seafarers Union to send in a few "representatives" of its own to keep an eye on the Teamsters.[99] The following day, Chavez flew to Chicago to attend the AFL-CIO Executive Council meeting at which the merger of the NFWA and AWOC was formally approved. A few days later, at the NFWA's preelection fiesta, a telegram from Governor Brown was read, congratulating the AFL-CIO and NFWA on their merger, as were telegrams from 42 AFL-CIO unions and from Senator Robert Kennedy.[100]

By election day, August 30, 1966, it was clear that the NFWA had succeeded in making the DiGiorgio election a top news story. But how would the story end? Harry Bernstein, the labor reporter for the *Los Angeles Times*, did not think the NFWA could win the vote. Jimmy the Greek was giving Las Vegas odds of 3–1 against the NFWA. Television networks predicted that the new union could not make it. Even Chavez's mentor, Saul Alinsky, predicted that the Teamsters were too strong to beat.[101]

Starting at 5:00 a.m., cars driven by NFWA supporters were dispatched to pick up workers who were not working and take them to the polls.[102] The voting began at 6:00 a.m. and continued until 8:00 p.m. Red, white, and blue curtains covered the polling booths. Dunne describes the scene:

> I drove to the Teamsters headquarters. The office was empty except for a secretary filing her nails with an emery board. The NFWA headquarters, however, was alive with activity. Scores of cars clogged the street outside the office and dozens of workers milled around on the sun-parched lawn. The NFWA had told all workers not in the fields to report to the office before going out to Sierra Vista so that the union could get a line on the number of votes it had. Each voter was checked off on a list and assigned to a car to take him [*sic*] out to the polling place.[103]

Medina later remembered:

> Election Day, we had a system. Cards, appointments, people coming in, priests, and nuns. A beehive of activity. I remember watching on the news the Teamster office, nobody in the office, and [the Teamster spokesman] says, "It's in the bag." It was a very strong message about how you don't take anything for granted, and you work up to the last minute.[104]

When the polls closed, the locked ballot boxes were loaded into California Highway Patrol cars, along with observers from the NFWA, the Teamsters, and DiGiorgio, and transported to San Francisco, where the votes would be counted under state supervision. The next day, hundreds of strikers and supporters gathered at Filipino Hall to learn the outcome of the election as soon as it was known. As Medina described the scene:

> Cesar announced the shed vote first. Then he announced the field vote. It took a minute to sink in, and then, instantaneously, there was this huge jumping up and down. It was the sweetest....I never even thought I wanted to do anything but what I was doing at this time.[105]

Of 2,000 workers eligible to vote, 1,343 had cast ballots in the 15 hours of voting. Of those who cast ballots, 300 were challenged. The vote among packinghouse workers was 97 Teamsters, 45 NFWA, and 12 no union. The vote among field workers was 331 Teamsters, 530 NFWA, and 7 no union.[106] According to the American Arbitration Association, 513 of these votes were cast by workers not currently employed at Sierra Vista, most of which went to the NFWA. As Dunne wrote, "Chavez's out of town policy had paid off."[107] Delano merchants closed their stores in a "day of mourning." The victory rally at AWOC's Filipino Hall, however, was tumultuous.

Assessing the Teamsters, Ross's take was:

> Well, they made the mistake that powerful groups usually make. They underestimated the strength of the opposition. They thought with the powerful organization of the Teamsters and the fact [that DiGiorgio] would be able to throw their weight around, that they would beat us.... They believed the migrants had scattered like the sands of the desert, that we'd never be able to round them up.... They underestimated our willingness to work and to win.[108]

CONCLUSION

The NFWA crafted moves in response to the opportunity created by DiGiorgio's election proposal. When the Teamsters intervened, the NFWA figured out how to outmaneuver them among workers, churches, Mexican Americans, liberals, the AFL-CIO, and the governor. By figuring out how to make the DiGiorgio election rules negotiable, the NFWA put itself back in the game, a game it won outright by adapting the electoral tactic of a get-out-the-vote campaign.

Given the Teamsters' roots in the agribusiness industry, they were a far more serious threat to the NFWA than AWOC had been. As it turned out, the Teamster strategy suffered from constraints similar to those of AWOC. Their leaders lacked diversity in terms of age, race, gender, and background. Their motivations were occupational, not personal or vocational. Their networks and tactical repertoire were limited, and their organizational structure did not encourage innovation or learning. Similarly, the resources upon which they relied to fund organizing were internal funds, primarily those of the International—so they had no need to respond to any constituency other than an internal one.[109] They could continue to pursue a dysfunctional strategy, and no one to whom they had to listen could call them on it. They reacted quickly to a familiar opportunity to offer DiGiorgio a responsible union alternative, just as they had at Bud Antle in 1961. But this time, they found themselves in unfamiliar circumstances and repeatedly beset by surprises—from the pressure that came at them from the Roman Catholic church to the involvement of California's governor.

The NFWA, in contrast, began with a more diverse and motivated leadership team and expanded it, thus gaining access to more salient information, diverse networks, and tactical experience. As a result, for example, Ross's understanding of training and Kircher's knowledge of union elections enriched the NFWA's organizing repertoire, already eclectically based in community, electoral, and issue organizing. At the same time, it multiplied the deliberative venues within which it could coordinate the use of those resources, thus developing the strategic capacity to deal with an increasingly complex situation. In the NFWA, *delegation* often meant taking responsibility not only for doing a job, but also for mobilizing one's constituency to get the job done. For example, Hartmire was responsible for mobilizing religious leaders, while Kircher mobilized the AFL-CIO. Only such a diverse, yet coordinated, leadership team could have managed so many fronts at once. The union's reliance on resources drawn from such varying sources, especially the volunteer time of workers and urban supporters, required that it remain attuned to what the volunteers would support. This, in turn, contributed further to the development of effective strategies.

Because it had to train organizers to deal with the Teamster threat, the NFWA developed a whole second tier of leadership, who were learning how to strategize within limited domains and would later allow the union to "get to scale." The DiGiorgio campaign provided these novices with the opportunity to acquire basic organizing skills and the use of an organizational structure that supported creativity based on mindful reflection on experience. Antonia Saludado, who was 20 years old when her family joined the grape strike, was one of them. Her memory of what amounted to six weeks in leadership school suggests the flavor of the experience:

I said, "Ahh. My God. Look what we did." And I started crying. I said, "Did we do this? Did we really do this?" I told myself, "Look at what we did." I count myself as one of the leaders, I should say. A small leader but I would say a leader of the people.[110]

This way of conducting an organizing drive—and at the same time creating strategic capacity—was Ross's particular contribution. It could be more or less replicated in each boycott city and on other organizing drives. Indeed, it was almost immediately needed again.

The Teamsters could have won the DiGiorgio fight. If the NFWA had accepted the terms on which DiGiorgio first proposed an election, the Teamsters could have won it. If the NFWA had not scuttled the Teamster-DiGiorgio alliance by drawing in the governor, a difficult-to-dislodge contract with the Teamsters could have been signed. And had the NFWA not organized a dragnet to mobilize strikers, the Teamsters could have won the second election, too. That they did not win was the NFWA's great victory. Yet it was also what drove the Teamsters to take up the cudgels again. As we shall see in the next chapter, they decided to expand the fight, and the NFWA needed to expand once more in response.

SEVEN

Launching a New Union
(1966–1967)

*No se vende el piel, hasta que se muere el oso. [Don't sell the bear skin
until the bear's dead.]*

—*Mexican Dicho*

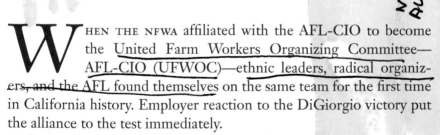

WHEN THE NFWA affiliated with the AFL-CIO to become
the United Farm Workers Organizing Committee—
AFL-CIO (UFWOC)—ethnic leaders, radical organiz-
ers, and the AFL found themselves on the same team for the first time
in California history. Employer reaction to the DiGiorgio victory put
the alliance to the test immediately.

One consequence of the victory was that it inspired wine grape
workers at Perelli-Minetti vineyards near Delano to join the strike.
The Teamsters intervened by providing strike breakers, claiming to
represent them, and signing a contract behind the UFWOC picket
lines. Recognizing that they would become a Teamster "hunting dog,"
driving one ranch after another into the Teamsters' sights if they didn't
fight back, UFWOC launched a boycott of the company's wines despite
the fact that the existence of a Teamster contract could inhibit labor
support. In turn, the Teamsters launched a "Teamsters Farm Workers Union" to challenge UFWOC among the field workers of other

major vintners throughout California: Christian Brothers, Almaden, and Gallo.

This conflict could have ended in any number of ways that would have crippled the new union but instead, by May 1967, it became clear to Perelli-Minetti and the other growers that a Teamster contract could not protect them from a UFWOC boycott. The Teamsters realized that without employer cooperation they could offer UFWOC little competition in the fields. All sides went to mediation, UFWOC suspended the boycott, the Teamsters withdrew from the fight, and Perelli-Minetti transferred the contract to UFWOC. Contracts with five more major vintners quickly followed a jurisdictional agreement with the Teamsters, clearing the way for UFWOC's table grape boycott: would unionize the entire industry within three years, bring 70,000 farm workers into the new union, and, despite many more ups and downs, lay a foundation for seven more years of successful organizing.

How did affiliation with the AFL-CIO, despite the traditional labor movement's history of failure in the fields, enhance the NFWA's strategic capacity? Why couldn't the Teamsters devise a more effective strategy after their "responsible union" approach failed? When the Teamsters tried to learn from UFWOC by mimicking its tactics, why didn't it work? And how could the new union expand the scope and scale of its operations to be able to consolidate its success, fend off new challenges, and launch new initiatives? The answers can be found again, although at a whole new level, in the capacity to generate effective strategy over...and over...and over.

BIRTHING A UNION: UNITED FARM WORKERS ORGANIZING COMMITTEE, AFL-CIO

Although Chavez had come to terms with the need for affiliation with the AFL-CIO, not everyone active in the NFWA looked forward to it. Opposition came from AWOC organizers who did not expect to be part of the new leadership, NFWA members suspicious of Filipino leaders, and volunteers who feared the NFWA would turn into an outpost of Meany's bureaucratic—and Cold War—unionism. On the other hand, after maneuvering to secure a portion of Reuther's funds in December, Chavez came to see it as a matter of negotiating the right terms.[1] Furthermore, the aggressive intervention of the Teamsters encouraged the NFWA to find ways to counterbalance the Teamsters' urban labor base.

Despite its fragility, the NFWA enjoyed considerable bargaining leverage because it had greater success in organizing farm workers than anyone else ever had, and it now led a farm worker movement. The fact that this resource was now of interest to Meany, Reuther, and the Teamsters—in addition to its original base of the churches, liberals, students, and Mexican Americans—gave the NFWA the power to negotiate affiliation on terms that preserved its autonomy.

A deliberative process that began in May not only educated NFWA leaders about the AFL-CIO, but the fact that NFWA members and supporters needed persuasion actually gave the NFWA more leverage to negotiate desirable terms with the Federation.[2] Skepticism of the AFL-CIO, particularly among the clergy and volunteers who played such an important part in the NFWA, gave Chavez more bargaining chips:[3]

> I said wonderful—but I expected we would have many problems, a lot of education to be done. The education went on for months and months. I would call Bill in Washington and tell him, "We're having another meeting!"[4]

Kircher further explained:

> We had open meetings, two big meetings, giving a complete explanation of the merger. We also had meetings of the leadership. I'll bet that the top leadership of the UFW, at the point the merger took place, knew more about union structure and autonomy and constitutional relationships than 75% of the leadership of the labor movement below the national level today.[5]

The extensive meetings, debates, and discussions—and the pressure of preserving unity during the DiGiorgio campaign—overcame all objections. The NFWA board, strikers, and membership voted to affiliate.[6]

Structurally, UFWOC looked different from any prior organizing committee, especially in terms of accountability. Unlike AWOC, UFWOC had its own constitution, a virtual copy of the original NFWA constitution, including a preamble by Pope Leo XIII. It provided:

> [S]upreme governing authority of the United Farm Workers Organizing Committee shall reside in the members in convention assembled through representative[s] of their own choosing.... In the original interim period between conventions, this governing authority shall reside in the National Executive Board.[7]

FIGURE 7.1. National AFL-CIO director Bill Kircher presents UFWOC charter to Cesar Chavez and Larry Itliong, Delano, August 1966. *Source:* Jon Lewis

Vesting governing authority in a membership—and its elected leadership—established a source of accountability quite different from that codified in the "Rules and Regulations of AWOC." In AWOC's case, Meany was in charge and appointed a "Chairman and Director" to head a committee of seven other AFL-CIO officials, who oversaw an operating committee. The members of the operating committee were in turn also to "be appointed or approved by the President of the AFL-CIO."[8]

UFWOC, however, was to be governed by an Executive Board: Chavez as director; Itliong as assistant director; Orendain as secretary-treasurer; and Padilla, Huerta, Phillip Vera Cruz, and Andy Imutan as vice presidents. Itliong was the AWOC organizer who had led the grape strike. Vera Cruz had been active in the Delano area since the 1950s. Imutan, a new immigrant from the Philippines, had emerged as a leader during the course of the strike. Similar to a wartime unity cabinet, this ethnic and organizational amalgam of leaders was to be provisional, pending a constitutional convention to be held when the union had won enough contracts to become self-supporting, or at least after the strike was over.[9]

A union membership that now included NFWA members, AWOC members, and new members working under contract at Schenley required new forms of governance as well. The Schenley workers elected a ranch committee, which was responsible for administering its own affairs, a whole new source of leadership and accountability for UFWOC.

The reorganization of the NFWA increased its strategic capacity by strengthening its deliberative processes. Because the Executive Board now included Filipino workers, it became even more heterogeneous. *diversity* Although this created strains, especially because so much media attention focused on Chavez, it also created benefits. Furthermore, the election of ranch committees, the selection of crew stewards, and the creation of negotiating committees multiplied the sites of deliberation within the new union.

The NFWA also negotiated financial arrangements with the AFL-CIO that gave it stability without dependency. Merging operations eliminated the salaries of AWOC's 22 paid organizers, allowing the $10,000 per month the AFL-CIO had committed to AWOC to go further. Nonetheless, the NFWA's current expenses ran at $25,000 per month, gasoline alone costing $4,000 per month and the telephone another $1,600 per month.[10] The NFWA thus had to continue to generate funds from other sources, including dues contributed by farm workers now covered under contracts, as well as contributions from churches, individual unions, liberals, students, and others. The fact that the AFL-CIO did not cover all the costs allowed the new union greater autonomy.

The most significant hedge against dependency on the AFL-CIO, however, was the fact that the NFWA cadre worked for subsistence, subsidizing the entire effort with its own labor and supplemented by rural and urban volunteers. No one could buy human resources of this quality at any price.

Having taken great care to prepare for the merger within the NFWA, Chavez acted decisively once the deal was done. Within 72 hours of becoming the director, he drove to the AWOC headquarters in Stockton, terminated its contracts with labor contractors, and met with its organizers. They were invited to join UFWOC—not at the $125 per week they had been earning, however, but on the strike benefits received by the NFWA staff. All of them quit, except for Itliong.[11] Ben Gines and Marcello Thomsi went to work for the Teamsters. Chavez explained:

> The job can't be done unless there is a commitment. If we're going to lead people and ask them to starve and to really sacrifice, we've got to do it first, do it more than anybody else, because it isn't the orders, it

isn't the pronouncements, it's the deeds that count. I wanted them to suffer with the strikers. I demanded full commitment.[12]

While opportunities created by the Schenley victory had challenged the NFWA to learn to manage a new level of complexity, the DiGiorgio victory created challenges of yet another order of magnitude. Again, learning to meet these challenges not only stretched the strategic capacity of the new union, it enhanced it in four ways:

1. Huerta was responsible for contract administration at Schenley, including the election and training of a ranch committee and setting up a hiring hall. She now began preparing a negotiating committee for talks with DiGiorgio and for UFWOC's first arbitration, which would begin in January.[13] Bargaining committee and ranch committee members became a new source of leadership for the union.

2. Because of its California success, UFWOC leaders, especially Chavez, were called upon to play a national role with farm workers, the emerging Chicano movement, and labor. Two days after the DiGiorgio election, for example, Chavez accompanied Reuther to Mexico City to support his effort to develop an auto council there.[14] He returned via Texas, where he joined a 500-mile march from the Rio Grande Valley to the state capital at Austin. The march had grown out of a strike of *meloneros* (melon pickers), sparked by volunteer organizer Gene Nelson. By the end of May, it had acquired a meaning for the Texas Mexican-American community similar to that of the grape strike for the Mexican-American community of California. Eventually, Chavez would send Orendain, Padilla, Drake, and others to lead the Rio Grande Valley campaign.[15] Chavez was also in demand elsewhere as farm worker organizing efforts broke out in Washington, Wisconsin, Ohio, Michigan, and Florida, led typically by young Mexican Americans like Jesus Salas in Wisconsin and Lupe Gamboa in Washington.[16]

3. Although Governor Brown would lose to Ronald Reagan in the 1966 election, UFWOC's endorsement became a resource with which the union could bargain in political circles, especially when coupled with access to its organizers. UFWOC's labor allies had pressed it to endorse Brown, a move they believed would help to persuade disaffected liberal and Mexican-American voters to vote for him. Despite internal dissent, on September 29, 300 workers representing the UFWOC membership voted to support Brown. A committee of Huerta, Imutan, Hernandez, and Veracruz then met with Brown to get his commitment to call a special session of the legislature to consider collective bargaining legislation for farm workers if he won.[17]

4. Chatfield, whose Los Angeles work culminated in December with a Joan Baez concert at Santa Monica Civic Auditorium that raised $20,000, moved to Delano to open the National Farm Workers Service Center, Inc. (NFWSC). The NFWSC was a newly incorporated 501(c)3, established with the support of AFL-CIO Industrial Union Department director Jack Conway, a long-time Reuther collaborator.[18] Through the tax-exempt NFWSC, UFWOC could gain access to funds for social services, cooperative development, and training that were not available to it as a union.

Once again, the new union had to face new threats generated by its success. This time, the test came just two weeks after its victory over DiGiorgio.

FIGHTING TO SECURE THE FIELD: THE PERELLI-MINETTI STRIKE AND BOYCOTT (1966–1967)

Just as Mohn and Grami had predicted, the UFWOC victory at DiGiorgio created new opportunities for the Teamsters that allowed them to seize the initiative and take the campaign in a new direction. On September 16, Mexican Independence Day and the second anniversary of the Delano strike vote, the Teamsters signed a contract with Perelli-Minetti & Sons, a Delano vintner that UFWOC members had struck the week before. Because Perelli-Minetti was a relatively small vintner, employing a peak of no more than 50 field workers, UFWOC leaders had to decide whether to target it with a major campaign, despite the Teamster contract, or to focus on larger employers without Teamster contracts. UFWOC decided that it had to fight.

On Friday, September 9, a week after the DiGiorgio election, 48 workers struck Perelli-Minetti vineyards, a 2,280-acre wine grape ranch south of Delano. They demanded an increase in the piece rate of $6 per ton and union recognition. Because it grew no table grapes, Perelli-Minetti had not been struck the year before, and this strike was not planned. Chavez explained, "We wanted to have a place where we could recycle pickets. We had a lot of our people there and one day they just decided to strike, so we had to take care of the strike."[19]

In response to a request from UFWOC, owners Fred, William, and Jean Perelli-Minetti met with UFWOC representatives Huerta, Hoffman, and myself the next day. The union proposed ending the strike in return for recognition based on a card check election, a proposal to which the Perelli-Minetti owners said they would respond on the following Tuesday. In the interim, the California Department of Employment certified the labor dispute.[20]

On Monday, Tuesday, and Wednesday mornings, while awaiting a response from their employer, Perelli-Minetti workers picketed the ranch entrances. On Thursday, three busloads of new workers arrived, led by Marcello Thomsi, a Filipino labor contractor and former AWOC organizer, and escorted by the Teamsters. On Friday, September 16, Perelli-Minetti announced that it had signed a union contract with the Teamsters, based on "proof" that the Teamsters represented its new employees.[21]

For Teamster leaders, Perelli-Minetti provided a target of opportunity, especially after the embarrassing defeat at DiGiorgio threatened political support within their own union. As Grami explained: "Without the pressure Chavez was applying, the Teamsters would have found it much more difficult to move in many of the industries.... In grapes, the Teamsters had minimal power."[22] Although the Teamsters had come to Delano only because of DiGiorgio, they anticipated an ongoing struggle with the UFW and made allies of former AWOC organizers and labor contractors disgruntled with the merger.[23] They offered to provide Perelli-Minetti with a workforce, a contract that left the employer in control, and an apparently powerful ally in dealing with UFWOC. With wage rates well below those of Schenley, the three-and-a-half-year contract retained labor contractors, offered no job security in the form of seniority, permitted the employer to reorganize work at will, and provided no on-the-job grievance procedures. For UFWOC, Perelli-Minetti was yet another sneak attack by the Teamsters that undermined its efforts by offering growers a way out.[24]

As UFWOC leaders gathered for a three-day strategy session at St. Anthony's Seminary in Santa Barbara, they reflected on their recent experiences with Schenley and DiGiorgio, which was enhanced by "research" retrieved from Perelli-Minetti's office trash, which the Mexican *Chavista* janitor delivered to UFWOC headquarters nightly.[25] Antonio Perelli-Minetti, a contemporary of Joseph DiGiorgio, was of a cohort of Italian immigrants who got their start at Italian Swiss Colony and went on to become vintners. Many, like Ernest and Julio Gallo, held union contracts covering their winery workers since the 1930s, although Perelli-Minetti did not. He bought wine grape vineyards, built his own winery, and entered into supply arrangements with wholesalers and distributors around the United States. Reorganized as

26 family corporations in 1956 with a net worth of $5.5 million, the company farmed 2,800 acres of wine grapes near Delano. They processed 11,000 tons of its own wine grapes and 40,000 tons of the grapes of other growers annually. A manufacturer of bulk wine, vermouth, and brandy, Perelli-Minetti marketed its products under different brand names: Tribuno Vermouth; Ambassador and Eleven Cellars wine, which were distributed by the California Wine Association, a cooperative it owned with three other vintners; and six brandy labels, including Aristocrat and Victor Hugo. The company remained firmly under family control. One son, Fred, was the plant manager. William, a former mayor of Delano, was the field manager.[26] Mrs. Fred Perelli-Minetti was president of Citizens for Facts from Delano, a grower-supported organization formed early in the grape strike.[27]

Despite the complexity of this operation, the multiple entities involved, and the fact that Perelli-Minetti associates had some union

FIGURE 7.2. The Teamsters and Perelli-Minetti "in bed together," *El Malcriado*, January 1977. *Source:* Andy Zermeno

contracts, UFWOC leaders decided that they had to respond to keep the Teamsters from remaining a viable option for employers under pressure.[28] And because the Teamsters were organized in the cities, had ties to the liquor industry, and collaborated with many AFL-CIO unions, UFWOC also had to learn how to explain why a Teamster contract was not "legitimate." On Tuesday, September 20, UFWOC announced a boycott of Perelli-Minetti.

GROWING STRATEGIC CAPACITY: MANAGING MULTIPLE CAMPAIGNS

Although the boycott was announced on September 20, the strategic challenge of bringing coherence to multiple strands of tactical activity delayed the launch for another six weeks. Loose ends at DiGiorgio and the opportunity to get the union's first table grape contract intervened.

Although the DiGiorgio election had included properties at Delano and Borrego Springs, the disposition of the Arvin ranch and northern California orchards remained pending. Talks continued among DiGiorgio, the Teamsters, and UFWOC over election procedures, but nothing was resolved. Although the orchard season was ending, work at Arvin would continue for some time. So on September 26, Ross set up shop in UFWOC's first field office in Lamont, a farm worker town a few miles southeast of Bakersfield, where Hank Hasiwar had held his first meeting of DiGiorgio workers in 1947.[29] Although the Arvin ranch hired a peak of 1,200 workers in grapes, peaches, plums, and potatoes, only 700 were at work in late September. These included 150 Anglos, many of whom were year-round workers who lived in company-owned bungalows; 300 Mexicans, most of whom lived in company-owned temporary housing; about 100 Puerto Ricans from Lamont; and about 100 African Americans from Bakersfield.

Although seasoned by their Delano success, the 25 UFWOC organizers faced a new challenge; they had to win the majority support of workers who were *currently employed*—and therefore subject to employer pressure. Furthermore, among these workers, Mexicans were a minority. The organizing had begun in June, however, and because there had been no strike, the union leadership among the workers had not been replaced with strike breakers. The organizers were confident that they could win an election if one were held, but they had to find a way to press DiGiorgio to agree before the season ended.[30]

Chavez delegated the responsibility to Ross and his team.[31] Ross targeted Governor Brown because he had played a key role in arranging the first election, had a relationship with Robert DiGiorgio, and faced a difficult election less than two months away. Working with an organizing committee of 30 farm workers, organizers gathered the signatures of 384 workers on a petition that a delegation hand delivered to the governor at his home in Los Angeles, 100 miles to the south. The governor urged them to make their demands directly to DiGiorgio. So Ross drew on a story that Alinsky often told of how John L. Lewis encouraged workers to organize by declaring that "the President wants you to join the union."[32] Organizers drafted letters from Brown to members of the full committee and put Brown's advice that they demand their right to vote on a union in writing. After Brown signed them, organizers mailed them special delivery from post offices in Arvin, Lamont, and Bakersfield. Just after the letters arrived, organizers darted from home to home, inviting committee members to an emergency meeting to decide how to respond to the governor. After two hours of late-night deliberations, they decided to "follow the governor's advice." They would leave before dawn the next day, drive the 300 miles to DiGiorgio's headquarters in San Francisco, and insist that DiGiorgio agree to an election.[33]

At noon the next day, Monday, October 24, a delegation of 20 DiGiorgio workers were welcomed by 200 supporters and the Teatro Campesino, which was performing on a flatbed truck parked in front of DiGiorgio's Montgomery Street headquarters in the heart of the San Francisco financial district. Taking the elevator to the top floor, they requested a meeting with Robert DiGiorgio. Told that he was at lunch, they said they would wait. Told he was not coming back, they said they would stay. Told he would meet with them the next day, they came back. But when no agreement on an election was reached, in part because DiGiorgio said he needed agreement from the Teamsters, they decided to remain in his office. As the sit-in wore on, four Bay Area labor leaders joined them, including the presidents of the San Francisco and Oakland Labor Councils. That night, television news showed images of farm workers and labor leaders being carried out of DiGiorgio's offices into waiting paddy wagons. Released on bond, the group returned to resume the sit-in the next morning. Upon their return, they found that, rather than escalate, DiGiorgio would agree to an election in 10 days, on November 4. It would follow the same rules as the Delano ranch election. In other words, it would be supervised by the State Conciliation Service, and anyone employed between October 18 and October 26 would be eligible to vote. Robert DiGiorgio also signed a letter to his supervisors guaranteeing that no disciplinary action would be taken against any worker who had missed work to take part in the sit-in.[34]

The next day, Mohn announced that the Teamsters would not participate in this election, but they "would continue to organize farm labor."[35] Although 5 of Grami's 25 full-time organizers had been assigned to the Arvin ranch, their Delano experience had taught them to avoid elections. Some claim that Brown's last-minute appointment of Mohn to the University of California's Board of Regents may also have influenced what the governor called Mohn's "act of labor statesmanship."[36] Regardless, on November 4, 556 workers voted: 285 voted for UFWOC, 199 for no union, and 72 cast challenged ballots.[37] UFWOC won its second election victory and established its first base outside Delano—and had done so at the very ranch that Mitchell, Hasiwar, Galarza, and the NFLU had struck unsuccessfully 19 years before.

Meanwhile, on September 28, UFWOC found itself with another new strike on its hands, a further reaction to the Delano victories. Two hundred table grape workers struck the Goldberg, Mossesian, and Hourigan ranch in Delano. Goldberg and his partners owned no land but purchased crops on the vine that they picked, packed, and sold. Because they had not been operating the year before at the time of the grape strike, many of their workers were UFWOC members. And since the crop they purchased grew on vines owned by Schenley, these workers thought that they should be covered under the Schenley contract. Immediately, 80 percent of the workers signed up with UFWOC, the union demanded recognition, the employers refused, and the strike began. With limited resources, isolated from other Delano growers who viewed the trio as "Jewish, Irish, and Armenian bandits," Goldberg and his associates lost the remainder of their late summer Thompson grape crop.[38] The strike became a union cause when picketer Manuel Rivera was hit by a truck driven by a Goldberg partner at his packing shed and suffered permanent injuries.[39]

In exchange for workers returning to harvest the fall Emperor crop, Goldberg agreed to a November 15 election supervised by the State Conciliation Service. Anyone employed between May 15 and October 28 was eligible. Farm worker organizers Robert Bustos and Pete Cardenas led the campaign. Of 377 ballots cast, 285 voted for UFWOC and 38 for no union.[40] Although UFWOC heralded the election as a major breakthrough that led to a signed contract, unlike the Schenley situation, the development had little strategic value.[41] Goldberg was too much of an outsider. The next year, the other Delano growers simply didn't sell him any grapes. On the other hand, by revealing the difficulty of breaking into the table grape industry by nibbling around its edges, the lessons learned from this strike influenced the UFWOC leaders in another important way. As it turned out, the experience become valuable the following year, when they decided to target the largest table grape grower in the industry: Giumarra Vineyards Corporation.

LAUNCHING THE BOYCOTT:
OLD LESSONS AND NEW

UFWOC finally launched the Perelli-Minetti boycott as the holiday season began in November. Ross set up operations in San Francisco, while Gene Boutilier, a migrant minister, set up in Los Angeles.[42] During the prior two boycotts, UFWOC leaders learned how to form, target, and dispatch organizing teams to focus on key retail outlets for particular brands. Although Perelli-Minetti sales were concentrated in San Francisco, Los Angeles, New York, and Chicago, the union targeted the California cities first to build momentum quickly.

Because UFWOC had affiliated with the AFL-CIO, it kicked off the boycott with an official labor endorsement, countering the Teamsters' claims that only their contract was legitimate. The Bartenders Union, which played a key role at Schenley, and the Retail Clerks Union, which represented southern California supermarket employees, officially notified liquor outlets of the boycott. Organizers learned from their experiences in the DiGiorgio boycott about the value of casting a wide net; as a result, they distributed 100,000 leaflets and signed up 20,000 supporters on pledge cards. Although the union made little initial effort outside California, the Union of American Hebrew Congregations and the Central Conference of American Rabbis called on Manischewitz Kosher Winery, a major purchaser of Perelli-Minetti wine, to use its "good offices" to get them to bargain with UFWOC. Ecumenically, a pre-Christmas picket line of Santa Clauses in front of Macy's launched the public campaign in New York.[43]

As both a major market for Perelli-Minetti and a major source of farm worker support, UFWOC designated San Francisco to be the primary target city. Ross's team of full-time organizers eventually grew to a small army of 35. Medina explains:

We would visit liquor stores and ask them to take out Tribuno Vermouth and Ambassador Brandy. Then we'd picket until they took it down. Every other weekend I'd come home and report to Friday night meetings. Of course, I greatly exaggerated.[44]

Boycott organizers responsible for devising strategies in their own cities learned by trial and error how to target their efforts more effectively and how to improve their tactics, in much the same way that leaders of the union had drawn on their strategic capacity to learn. The farm worker organizers, who led nine of these campaigns, and the student volunteers, who led three, had all been trained in Ross's "organizing school," the DiGiorgio campaign.[45]

At first, they focused on liquor stores located in Mexican and African-American communities, where picket lines were most effective. As they learned more about sales patterns, they shifted their focus to chains. They found that they could hold chain stores in sympathetic neighborhoods hostage in order to obtain an agreement from the entire chain to respect the boycott. Although Perelli-Minetti labels were not as well known as those of Schenley, organizers learned that once a product lost shelf space, the damage to sales could be long lasting. The boycott became a more potent threat than they had anticipated.

On January 9, Thrifty Drug Stores, a major California chain, removed Perelli-Minetti products from its shelves. On February 27, 85 Purity Stores joined them.[46] By the end of February, 450 stores in the Bay Area and 600 in Los Angeles had given similar commitments.[47] And on March 4, UFWOC launched a statewide campaign in 12 California cities against Mayfair Stores, the supermarket chain that was the major Perelli-Minetti retailer.[48]

The Teamsters Try a Counterboycott: Why Motivation Matters

The Teamsters' counteroffensive had surprisingly little effect, despite Mohn's pledge to provide "full financial and manpower assistance" to the effort.[49] The Perelli-Minetti contract specified that if the company's products were subject to boycott, the Teamsters were obligated to "do everything within their power to counter such pressure." So by January, Grami and Andrade were trying to mobilize local union officials to conduct a "coordinated program of boycotts and picketing" to "expose" the "unjust persecution of Perelli-Minetti" and to encourage retailers to buy its products.[50]

Yet the Teamsters had little ability to mobilize volunteers, and their full-time paid local union officials had more pressing concerns. As

Grami tried to solicit support for his effort, for example, Los Angeles Joint Council 42 was picketing local retailers with which it had its own disputes, efforts that it hoped would win public support. They could only lose in a fight with farm worker supporters. Teamster locals with Mexican-American membership were also sympathetic to UFWOC. For example, one Latino leader, Jerry Veracruse, coordinated Teamster consumer boycott activities in southern California, a role he fulfilled energetically with respect to Teamster targets. When it came to UFWOC, however, he had little commitment to organizing counterpickets.[51] AFL-CIO unions with which Teamster locals had relationships also raised their voices on behalf of UFWOC. The *East Bay Labor Journal* reported that the Teamsters were "escorting strikebreakers through UFW picket lines" and editorialized against "Teamster Sabotage."[52]

"Framing" the Teamsters: Who Authors the Story?

With limited active support within their own local unions, Teamster leaders faced an even more formidable task in trying to counter UFWOC support among religious leaders, students, liberals, Mexican Americans, and others who had taken an active part in its campaigns. To be sure, UFWOC organizers had to explain the complexity of a boycott of a retail chain that sold vermouth made from wine made from grapes, some of which were picked by workers under a Teamster contract. But just as at DiGiorgio, the Teamster intervention played into UFWOC's claims on behalf of racial justice and self-determination.

For urban supporters, UFWOC framed the grape strike as a struggle of an oppressed minority fighting for its freedom. For these same supporters, the Teamsters were a powerful and corrupt white union conspiring with powerful white growers to deny the rights of powerless Mexican farm workers. This moral conflict was far easier to grasp than the intricacies of jurisdictional disputes, secondary boycotts, and marketing arrangements. The farm worker struggle enacted a narrative in which growers, Teamsters, and local law enforcement were on one side, and farm workers, churches, and their supporters were on the other.

Resonant with the public's understanding of the civil rights movement more than of labor disputes, this narrative had established itself in the course of the previous year. Once in place, it proved very difficult for growers or the Teamsters to counter since most of what they did reinforced it. In language reminiscent of terms used by Green, Grami declared: "The NFWA is not a labor union, as the Teamsters know a labor union.... the Teamsters do not want support from beat-niks, out-of-town agitators, or do-gooders."[53] They got none.

It is important to note that the UFWOC boycott did not rely solely on symbolic framing. Organizers recruited supporters one by one from churches, unions, and student groups. With these supporters, they organized the boycott store by store. People stationed in front of the stores told their story to shoppers every day and turned them away. Thus, UFWOC's boycott activity reenacted its framing of the struggle on a daily basis. The Teamsters' activities also reenacted UFWOC's framing of the struggle. On February 20, for example, UFWOC organizer John Shroyer was beaten in front of a San Francisco Purity Store by three "research workers" for Teamsters Local 85. They were later convicted of assault.[54]

Reclaiming the Secondary Boycott: Seeing with Outsider's Eyes

Because of its outsider perspective, UFWOC discovered how to reclaim the secondary boycott during the Perelli-Minetti episode. As recounted earlier, the AFL-CIO had assumed the secondary boycott was no longer a viable tactic, since it crippled the NFLU 19 years earlier. When the UFWOC picketing of Mayfair began to have an effect, Mayfair sought an injunction to ban it, declaring it was the victim of an "illegal" secondary boycott. UFWOC had burned out its first attorney, Alex Hoffman. Victor Van Bourg, on the other hand, a prominent San Francisco labor lawyer who represented AWOC, came with the merger. Treating the farm worker conflict as business as usual, Van Bourg had stipulated in court that UFWOC would not promote a secondary boycott.[55] The victory at DiGiorgio's Arvin ranch brought with it a small peanut-shelling plant that fell within the NLRA definition of a commercial shed because DiGiorgio did not grow the peanuts it processed. Since the 15 peanut-shelling workers were covered by the NLRA and were UFWOC members, Van Bourg concluded that UFWOC was covered by the NLRA and could not secondary boycott.

Dissatisfied with this approach, however, and believing "there was more to it than that," Chavez, Drake, and Chatfield recruited Jerry Cohen, a young lawyer who worked at the McFarland office of California Rural Legal Assistance, who was unhappy with the fact that the legal assistance program was barred from supporting the union.[56] In his first year of legal practice, Cohen had no background in labor law to recommend him, but he had an interest in constitutional law. With a history of student organizing at Amherst and involvement with the free speech movement, civil rights movement, and antiwar activities at Berkeley, he had a "love for the fight." Cohen explains:

> At that point, I said, "I don't know anything." And he [Chavez] said, "That's fine, we don't know anything either....We'll just learn this together....But you can't do it from over there. They have conditions in their grant; they have pressures from politicians; just forget it." So in March I came to work for the union.[57]

On Cohen's first weekend with the union, Chavez took him to Van Bourg's office to reclaim the legal files, where he noticed the secondary boycott stipulations. He recalls: "You look at the law new, and it's the first thing that jumps out at you: it's unfair and there's a simple way to deal with it."[58] Not seeing how 15 peanut-shelling workers could bar the entire union from secondary boycotts, he devised a scheme with Chavez and Kircher to place them in a separate, directly affiliated AFL-CIO local, removing them from UFWOC and thus leaving it free to boycott. This maneuver protected UFWOC's use of the secondary boycott, critical not only to the Perelli-Minetti boycott but for the far more extensive table grape boycott that would follow. This illustrates the limited strategic capacity of AFL-CIO lawyers, who saw what they expected to see. By contrast, the fresh eyes of the UFWOC leaders, who had used the law creatively during 10 years of administrative hearings, saw new opportunities. Their young civil rights–oriented lawyer looked at the situation freshly as well. Chavez told Cohen, "That was a fabulous thing you told me. That's going to change our power....Don't worry that you don't know. You knew something that Van Bourg didn't know."[59]

The Teamsters Organize Farm Workers: Why Tactics Are Not Enough

While the Teamsters tried to counter the UFWOC boycott in the cities, they also tried to mimic UFWOC tactics in the fields by launching a "farm workers union" of their own. Grami reported that, by September 16, the Teamsters were spending $15,000 a month to pay 25 full-time organizers in Arvin, Marysville, Salinas, and southern California—a level of financial support roughly comparable to that of the AFL-CIO.[60] A month later, Mohn chartered Teamster Local 964, a new local that would be known as the United Farm Workers Union, led by Oscar Gonzales.[61] Recognizing that ethnicity had something to do with their difficulty in winning worker support at DiGiorgio and public support in their fight with the boycott—and dissatisfied with the performance of their own professional organizers—Grami and Mohn tried to emulate the AFL-CIO by finding an independent Mexican association to affiliate. Gonzales was their answer.

Gonzales, 37, a Mexican-American auto worker, had become active in one of the organizations formed to recruit domestic workers to replace *braceros* in 1964: the Community Recruitment of Personnel, or CROP, led by Les Grube of San Jose.[62] An activist at Sacred Heart Roman Catholic Church in San Jose, he also linked up with a farm worker group in nearby Gilroy, which was organized by Father Ronald Burke.[63] By networking with other community activists funded by the OEO to run farm worker service centers, he formed the United Farm Workers Union based in the coastal valleys in which the NFWA did little organizing: San Jose, Watsonville, Salinas, Hollister, Gilroy, and Santa Clara.[64] Gonzales's chief lieutenant, Alberto Rojas, a farm worker activist from Oxnard, helped to organize a service center there funded by the Emergency Committee to Aid Farm Workers in the early 1960s. A fundraiser for the center, Peter Lauries, introduced him to Gonzales, and in November 1965, Gonzales, Rojas, and others formalized their network as the Alianza de Campesinos.[65] Rojas recalls:

> Peter [Lauries] invited him [Gonzales] down to talk to us in the program. We went to see him and he had what was called the United Farm Workers Union. He said he was okay with Cesar, but "we have a union, this is our union" in San Jose....He was a Chicano, married, a couple of kids, had a white guy working with him, had an office and a secretary.[66]

Although most Mexican-American activists supported UFWOC, some, like Gonzales, thought it unfair that Chavez should "get all the money from the AFL-CIO" while "we get nothing."[67] Rojas recalls:

> Late in 1965 or early 1966, Oscar called to tell me the AFL-CIO was giving Chavez $10,000 a month. We went to meet with Cesar with Jim Drake, Gilbert Padilla, and Dolores [Huerta], at the Coffee Cup. Oscar said he thought he could organize farm workers in his area, but he wanted some of the financial help that Cesar was getting. Cesar said it's being spent here, the battle is here. Oscar got into an argument—we have workers, but we don't have any money. So Cesar said if you want to join the movement, come and join here in Delano. Oscar said we weren't going to do that. Cesar said, okay, we'll be friends and work with each other. This was after Schenley, after the march. Then we didn't have much contact with Cesar. Later we met again and Oscar

wanted me on board. He said I knew people in Calexico, Oxnard, etc. Together with his people in Gilroy, Watsonville, San Jose. So I joined Oscar's board [as] one of the vice presidents. There were about eight on the board from Gilroy, San Jose, Watsonville.[68]

From August 23 to September 23, 1966, while the NFWA was occupied with the DiGiorgio campaign, Gonzales led 200 workers in a tomato strike at Aguilar Farms near San Jose.[69] Describing himself as a "third force" in the farm labor movement, he claimed a membership of 1,500 in Santa Clara and San Benito counties.[70] This brought him to Grami's attention, and in October, Grami offered him $10,000 per month to organize farm workers as part of the Teamsters. Rojas recalls:

> Oscar [Gonzales] called me and said the Teamsters want to talk to us, to go to Delano to organize. I was hesitant, but we went to meet with them in Burlingame. It was after the DiGiorgio election. It was with Bill Grami, and Einar Mohn came in briefly.... Grami said that we could do a better job than some of their people actually working with the workers: "We don't have that kind of contact with the people. But we don't know if you can do it either." They had a boycott going in L.A. and wanted us to produce people for their program and said they'd pay for buses, food, etc., if we could get people to go to L.A. from Oxnard. I think they were testing us. Then they offered us $10,000 a month, but wanted us to go to Delano.... I didn't want to go to Delano. I wanted to organize in the oranges, but they wouldn't do that—maybe the strawberries. Oscar was very eager, he had had some tomato strikes, didn't have much money.... Oscar said the people they hired to work in Delano were making them look bad. "We were the legitimacy."... Oscar said we had to survive and we can get these guys to pay some of the costs—and we can get the truckers to help. The Teamsters said it would be no problem.[71]

Learning from their loss at DiGiorgio, Grami and Mohn realized the importance of the UFWOC connection with the workers, but saw it as a question of ethnic legitimacy rather than of leadership.[72] Strategy remained their exclusive domain and resources still came entirely from within the union, where their accountability rested as well. The fact that the Teamsters never admitted Gonzales to their leadership circle limited his group to serving as an instrument of Teamster strategy. Similar to AWOC's employment of Mexican-American and Filipino organizers, to whom it gave no authority either, hiring people of the right color added little strategic value.

Another blow to the effectiveness of the Gonzales effort was his organization's failure to honor the expectations of farm worker activists who signed on believing that Teamster organizing drives would soon be launched in their own communities among workers employed in citrus, strawberries, and other crops. They further expected any strikes to be buttressed by Teamster support for their picket lines. But that would have required the Teamsters to abandon the responsible union strategy for which Gonzales provided the cover—a fact that became clear when Rojas organized a strike of 400 workers at Goldman's Egg City in Oxnard and called on the Teamsters for help. The help did not come, the strike was lost, and the workers returned to work without contracts or improvements.[73]

The "gift" of Teamster resources may actually have inhibited the development of strategic capacity within the Gonzales group. His team did have roots in the farm worker world, although their motivations were more personal and occupational than vocational. Moreover, their organizing experience was limited. Their networks outside of the farm worker world were confined to OEO contacts with no interest in controversy. Accountability was to an eight-person board that Gonzales selected, and Gonzales was accountable to Grami. Since they paid relatively high salaries, relying little on volunteers, they depended on Teamster funding. UFWOC, on the other hand, generated funds from many places and used them to support many more people. Gonzales's 28 organizers earned as much as $1,500 per month, while the full-time UFWOC volunteers—117 families and 75 single people—subsisted on strike benefits of $20 per month plus housing, food, and gas, equal perhaps to another $200 per month.[74]

The association of Gonzales with the Teamsters thus enhanced the strategic capacity of neither group because strategy remained firmly in the hands of the Teamster leaders, affirmed by their control over resources and accountability. UFWOC, on the other hand, enhanced its strategic capacity by incorporating former AWOC leaders into its leadership team and by winning access to new resources on terms that enhanced its autonomy.

NEGOTIATING A WAY OUT: IT'S HARDER TO CLEAN UP A MESS THAN TO MAKE ONE

Even before the Perelli-Minetti boycott took hold, Hoffa began to explore ways to resolve the conflict.[75] On January 13, at Hoffa's request, Korshak convened a meeting of Teamster officials and UFWOC leaders to discuss a way out.[76] On January 21, Chavez sent registered letters to Mohn and Perelli-Minetti proposing compulsory arbitration to resolve the dispute. Mohn was "not available for comment," and Grami dismissed the idea. But Hoffa asked Harold Gibbons, his former executive assistant, a Teamster vice president, and the union's "official" liberal, to work out a deal with Kircher.[77] On January 25, Gibbons met with Kircher and, on the same day, reported the basis for an agreement to Hoffa. On one hand, UFWOC would organize farm workers, packing sheds on farms, and trucks on farms. The Teamsters, on the other hand, would organize over-the-road trucks, processing off farms, and canneries. He also reported that a follow-up meeting would be held with Chavez and the WCT leadership.

At the follow-up meeting in February at the Beverly Rodeo Hotel, as reported by John Gregory Dunne:

> Chavez and the Teamsters worked out an agreement on almost every facet of farm labor organization.... The Teamsters were ready to sell Perelli-Minetti out that night. They got in easy; they could have got out easy. Sidney Korshak was there and he could have tied up all the loose ends.[78]

But reaching agreement took much more maneuvering because Perelli-Minetti would not release the Teamsters from their contract, and a change in Teamster politics persuaded Mohn to take another shot at UFWOC. On March 7, Hoffa ran out his string of attempts to avoid prison, and he was remanded to Lewisburg Federal Penitentiary to serve a 13-year sentence for jury tampering. He resigned as the International's president and turned over the reins to his hand-picked caretaker, Frank Fitzsimmons. Fitzsimmons' focus on national freight negotiations and a steel haulers strike, however, created a hiatus in leadership at the top.[79] Mohn, who hoped to be named to the vice presidency vacated by Fitzsimmons, saw it to be in his interest to cooperate with Grami and his allies, who wanted to take more aggressive action against UFWOC.[80] Thus, at the end of March, San Francisco Teamster Joint Council 7 directed its 42 locals to deny help to any AFL-CIO union that "supports UFWOC's efforts to discredit the Perelli-Minetti contract." It also authorized a letter to liquor dealers from Grami, which claimed that the "Perelli-Minetti contract is superior to Schenley, considered in total."[81]

In response, UFWOC escalated the boycott and dispatched 20 organizers to launch full-time boycotts in New York, Chicago, and Milwaukee, the top brandy market in the United States.[82] In New York, Distillery Workers Local 1222 helped UFWOC to obtain agreement from the Tribuno Vermouth distributor to honor the boycott.[83] Chavez recalled:

> We found out where he was selling his bulk vermouth and we began to boycott the bulk buyer labels. We told them, "we are boycotting your whole line, even though only one label is scab."...Perelli-Minetti's vermouth was very popular in New York and this bulk buyer was handling it, so he called Perelli-Minetti and told him no more....There was one section...devoted to kosher wines....We got the Jewish groups behind us and we put the squeeze on.[84]

In Los Angeles, boycotters organized "sip-ins" in the Brookside wine-tasting rooms.[85] In San Francisco, all but 200 of 1,700 members of the Glass Bottle Blowers Union employed by Owens Illinois Glass Company, manufacturers of Perelli-Minetti bottles, honored a UFWOC picket line.[86] In May, Perelli-Minetti sued *El Malcriado*, UFWOC, and the AFL-CIO for $6 million in damages.[87]

The organization of this boycott, like earlier boycotts, required thousands of hours of calls, meetings, and picket lines undertaken by a growing cadre of leaders, whose experience with the boycott, in turn, expanded the union's strategic capacity. Reflecting on his experience as the Chicago boycott director, Medina explains:

> Nobody from Delano was telling me how to do this. I talked to lots of people and asked them what they thought, as I figured out what to do....I learned...about civil disobedience. We would have rallies, fancy fundraisers, and then fundraisers in the Latino community. We did all kinds of sit-ins in the stores, pray-ins, etc. You always felt encouraged to think creatively about new strategies. I was encouraged by what I saw. Like the fasts Cesar was doing. Reading about sit-ins in the South. By then I'm aware of the civil rights movement. We borrowed, we improvised, and in some cases we took it a step further. I learned to talk to everybody you can. Go out and talk, talk, talk, and then people will help you. I hit the unions for money. The students for support. The churches, moral validation. There was lots of encouragement to try new things. We didn't know there were limits. We were young. We didn't know any better. But from that first day, I learned that you could do things that you never thought you could do, from when they took out Jimmy Hrones. We started having boycott conferences; we were learning from each other. It wasn't like a real tight agenda. Ideas would feed off each other....There was no one silver bullet; you needed to try different things. The most important thing

was persistence. You just stick, stick, etc. And you have to build a structure to support all that.[88]

Although he received little day-to-day direction from Delano, Medina's three years of on-the-job training had prepared him for his new leadership responsibilities. Ross, Chavez, Padilla, Huerta, and others had mentored him in a series of campaigns in which he learned new tools and creative ways of using these tools and acquired the motivation to try. Because the demand for leadership in the growing movement always exceeded the supply, he and others were given greater and greater responsibility for leadership: 35 former farm workers would become boycott directors during the grape boycott.

In a spring offensive, Grami ratcheted up his operation by hiring 28 organizers to face off with UFWOC organizers led by Manuel Chavez.[89] The Perelli-Minetti boycott had given Christian Brothers, Almaden, and Gallo enough concern that they considered acceding to UFWOC demands for union recognition. Christian Brothers, wholly owned by the religious order of the same name, nominally recognized UFWOC just after the Schenley agreement. The company delayed, however, as long as UFWOC's attention was elsewhere. It now agreed, however, to a card check election for its Napa vineyards on March 12—which UFWOC won.[90] The Teamsters tried to sign up enough workers to intervene, but could not. In April, UFWOC demanded recognition from Almaden and Gallo. National Distillers Corporation, a Schenley competitor, acquired Almaden, a vintner that hired a peak workforce of 700 at ranches near Hollister, Livermore, and Los Gatos. The company agreed to a card check election on May 12. The Teamsters also tried to sign up the Almaden workers but in the absence of much response, declined to take part.[91] Gallo, which hired a peak workforce of 600 on its 6,000-acre ranch near Modesto, responded to the UFWOC demand for recognition by affirming:

> [The company] has collective bargaining agreements with several labor unions, and does not oppose unionization of its agricultural employees if those employees so desire. We feel the question of representation should be decided by our farm employees in a fair and democratic manner, in an election supervised by the state, so that our farm employees may have a free choice.... we are asking the State Conciliation Service to arrange such an election.[92]

When the Teamsters established picket lines at Gallo to demand that the company recognize their union without an election, the workers ignored them, as did Gallo.[93] The Teamsters also picketed Franzia because it had agreed to an election with UFWOC.[94] These tactics served them poorly, however, because the Teamster strategy was based on employer—not worker—support. By the end of April, the Teamster operation had clearly foundered and Perelli-Minetti began to realize that a Teamster contract could not protect it from the boycott. Both parties had reasons to look for a way out.

An interfaith committee of northern California religious leaders now followed up on a January proposal for mediation to which Perelli-Minetti had never responded.[95] Led by Rabbi Joseph B. Glaser, chair of the Social Action Commission of the Board of Rabbis of Northern California, the committee included the Reverend Eugene J. Boyle, chair of the Commission on Social Justice of the Roman Catholic Archdiocese of San Francisco, and the Reverend Richard Byfield, chair of the Department of Christian Social Relations of the Episcopal Diocese of California.[96]

The committee assumed the daunting task of coordinating the interests of all three parties: the Teamsters, UFWOC, and Perelli-Minetti. Perelli-Minetti had to agree not only to release the Teamsters from their contract, but also to sign a new contract with UFWOC, which would set them apart as the first local grower to break ranks. Schenley and DiGiorgio were outsiders. The Teamsters had to agree not only to release Perelli-Minetti, but also to entirely abandon their organizing ambitions among farm workers. Unless both conditions were met, UFWOC had every incentive to show that the Teamsters could not protect their partners by sustaining the boycott on Perelli-Minetti.

On Friday, April 28, Rabbi Glaser convened a meeting of the Teamsters, Perelli-Minetti, and UFWOC at his offices in San Francisco.[97] Key players from all parties were present: Chavez, Huerta, and Drake from UFWOC; Grami from the Teamsters; William, Fred, and Mario Perelli-Minetti; and Glaser's committee, which now included Methodist bishop Donald Trippett, Episcopal bishop Kilmer Meyers, and Dr. J. David Illingworth of the United Presbyterian church. UFWOC and the Teamsters agreed to negotiate a jurisdictional agreement, after Chavez reviewed the prospect with his membership. Glaser proposed that UFWOC end the boycott if Perelli-Minetti would agree to be bound by the terms of such an agreement when reached.[98]

On May 26, UFWOC and the Teamsters were finally close to an agreement along essentially the same lines as those in Gibbons' memo to Hoffa six months before. The Teamsters could organize workers in food processing, trucking, and the like, and UFWOC could organize field workers. Therefore, only a small category of mechanized work remained unresolved—and the problem of what to do with Gonzales's "Teamsters farm workers union."[99] Earlier that month, sensing that the Teamsters were cooling off, Gonzales had gotten into a heated debate with Grami, called him a "son of a bitch," and pulled a knife. Rojas remembers:

> There were maybe 27 or 28 people full time in Gilroy, Oxnard, Calexico, San Diego, Santa Maria, but mostly up north. We started signing up lots of workers, but things were cooling off with the Teamsters.... Oscar got very upset, claiming Jimmy Hoffa had told him they would stick with us, and he pulled a knife out of his briefcase on Grami. Grami was very cool. His eyes were on Oscar every second and his guys were ready too.[100]

At the end of May, Grami got back to them:

> We get a call two weeks later and Oscar says to come to a meeting where Chavez is going to be. The Teamsters are talking to him. I think they want out. We meet at a convent in Menlo Park. There's Grami, and Cesar, some other Teamsters and some priest, Father Gene Boyle. They say they want peace in the labor movement. Oscar asks what's happening. Grami says we'll support you guys and your salaries, but we want to settle. The Teamsters want out, we're going to live in harmony with the UFW, we're going to organize other segments of agriculture and they're going to organize farm workers. But we'd like you guys to join with us. Cesar said he had to talk to the workers. He says you would have to move to Delano. So we went back, thought about it, talked to our families, and I was willing to move. Then we went to Delano and met with Dolores and Jim and said we wanted Oscar on the board. But Oscar said he wanted me on the board too. But Oscar really didn't want to come. I was the only one to go.[101]

Chavez reports on the same meeting from his perspective:

> We met with the Teamsters alone and demanded that they end all their farm labor organizing activities. So they just cut Oscar Gonzales' neck off. I've never seen anything like it. Bill Grami called him in from an anteroom and said cold-bloodedly, "we don't need you any more." Just like that. "As of now, no more money. We want you to hand the farm workers the key so they can go to your office and get some of the stuff that they need."[102]

By the end of May, then, a settlement between UFWOC and the Teamsters was at hand. Relying on the assurance of Glaser's committee that Perelli-Minetti had committed to negotiate the transfer of its Teamster contract, UFWOC suspended the boycott. On June 7, negotiations began, but Perelli-Minetti seemed determined to avoid becoming the first local Delano grower to capitulate to UFWOC.[103] There was little progress. In a series of angry exchanges with Perelli-Minetti's lawyer, Glaser threatened his committee's full support for a renewed boycott.[104] When talks broke down on July 8, UFWOC announced resumption of the boycott.[105] On July 12, the two unions announced their jurisdictional agreement, along with the news that Gallo had agreed to recognition procedures.[106] Talks resumed again on Friday, July 14, and agreement was reached with a signing scheduled for Delano on Tuesday. Although UFWOC was able to modify the wage rates in the Perelli-Minetti contract, it was compelled to take the rest of it largely as is, which was a source of internal dissatisfaction. When Fred Perelli-Minetti, offended at having to sign with UFWOC, refused to speak to Chavez directly and insisted on communicating only through his lawyer, Chavez decided that fasting for the three intervening days was "a good way to give thanks."[107] When glitches developed, Chavez continued his fast for a week, until the agreement was signed at a July 21 press conference in the Delano VFW Hall.[108]

UFWOC achieved dual objectives: (1) causing the Teamsters to withdraw not only from Perelli-Minetti, but also from the fields, and (2) winning a contract after showing that the Teamsters could not deliver on the responsible union option. Had retaining the Perelli-Minetti contract been of great enough priority for the Teamsters to take legal, contractual, and financial risks to crush UFWOC, they might have done it. However, only Grami was ambitious enough to try, and he was not in charge. Of course, there is no guarantee that had they risked more, they would have won. From 1973 to 1977, they would commit far more to such an effort, yet would fail again nonetheless.

UFWOC won its first contract with a local grower, a company whose family owners had very strong ties to the rest of the Delano grape industry, but who was vulnerable because of their marketed wine products. Perelli-Minetti's resistance, however, was indicative of what lay ahead. In the July 25, 1967, *Los Angeles Times*, O. W. Fillerup, spokesperson for the California Council of Growers, denounced church leaders who had joined in a "cartel which appears designed to literally bludgeon California farmers until they respond to the whims of the powerful bosses of organized labor."[109]

CLEARING THE FIELD: RETURN
TO THE TABLE GRAPES

When a resolution of the Perelli-Minetti dispute seemed to be at hand, the UFWOC leadership began an extensive internal debate about how to proceed. The context for this debate, however, was one in which the union had grown the strategic capacity to operate on multiple fronts at once, including building its own infrastructure. In March, it dedicated "the 40 acres," a property two miles outside Delano that would become its new headquarters.[110] The nonprofit NFWSC bought it to house a cooperative gas station, administrative offices, and a medical clinic. In April, the DiGiorgio contract brought over 1,000 new members into the union, many of whom shared in a back pay award of almost $100,000.[111] And on May 10, the Schenley workers voted to extend their contract for another year. So for the first time, UFWOC began to realize substantial income from dues, enhancing its autonomy. Out of a total 1967 income of $520,990, union dues accounted for $82,424. With the AFL-CIO subsidy of $10,000 per month, however, UFWOC still had to raise $27,000 per month, over half its budget.[112]

With the Teamsters out of the picture, UFWOC could take the initiative for the first time since calling the Schenley boycott a year and a half earlier. On the one hand, as was evident from the vintner agreements, the boycott threat was real enough that wine companies would agree to recognition. Unfortunately, workers employed directly by the wineries were only a fraction of the workers hired by the growers from which they bought most of their grapes. Kircher argued that UFWOC should build on this base and wrap up the California wine industry.[113] On the other hand, UFWOC leaders were attuned to the fact that the table grape workers had launched the strike. Moreover, table grapes provided the bulk of the employment in grapes, especially for resident farm worker families. Lastly, the union had won no operative table grape contracts. Since Delano table grape growers had refused to sell grapes to Goldberg, that contract was a wash. Although DiGiorgio harvested wine grapes, plums, and other fruit, it had gotten out of the table grape business. The Arvin contract, however, brought 1,200 workers into the union, most of whom lived in Arvin, Lamont, and Bakersfield. Many of these individuals had ties to workers employed by the largest table grape grower in the state, the Giumarra Vineyards Corporation. Giumarra was the acknowledged leader of the table grape industry.

To break the resistance of the table grape industry, UFWOC leaders considered targeting Giumarra. The company enjoyed annual sales of $12 million on its 12,170 acres, but only the small Delano portion of its 6,340 acres of table grapes had been struck in 1965.[114] Targeting Giumarra offered UFWOC a way to expand the strike and place La Causa once again in the public eye. If the strike failed, at the very least the union could recruit a new cadre of strikers with whom it could staff a boycott of Giumarra grapes. Of course, no one knew how to conduct a boycott of grapes without labels visible to consumers; then again, no one had known how to boycott Perelli-Minetti either.

After lengthy deliberations in meetings of strikers, expanded strategy sessions, and board meetings—intended as much to convince Kircher as to make a good choice—UFWOC decided to target Giumarra. On June 5, Ross set up shop in Lamont with a team of 35 organizers, Manuel Chavez took charge of Delano. The Giumarra campaign got under way.[115] When Giumarra refused to recognize the union, the workers struck on August 3. After injunctions were issued to shut down the picket lines, on September 14 the union called a boycott. The union organized an operation to track table grapes with the Giumarra label to particular chain stores. When the other table grape growers loaned Giumarra their labels in an effort to frustrate this tactic, UFWOC responded with a boycott of all table grapes, which was far easier for consumers to support. Three years later, it brought the entire table grape industry under contract.

Although Ronald Reagan had become the governor of California in January 1967 and had appointed advocates of the *bracero* program to high positions, these changes no longer had the same impact on farm worker organizing. Since the *bracero* program had ended in 1965, the struggle moved into a new domain beyond legislative chambers. It moved into the fields and the cities, where farm worker organizations could marshal considerable power. Not until a second, greater counterattack in the 1970s did UFWOC have to return to legislative chambers in order to survive.

RISE AND FALL: RETURN OF THE TEAMSTERS (1970–1977)

The 1970 Salinas Valley Lettuce Strike

UFWOC's historic victory over the grape industry in 1970 elicited a renewed Teamsters-growers alliance, but on a grander scale. In 1966, after the Schenley victory, it had taken the NFWA a year and a half to turn the threat around. This time, it took seven years during which the UFW had to "fight for its life."[116]

In late July 1970, on the same day that the Delano grape growers settled with the union, the Salinas Valley vegetable growers announced that they had signed 200 contracts with the Teamsters. The law did not require workers' consent, and none had been given. As word of the emerging victory in the grapes had spread, vegetable workers in coastal valleys grew increasingly vocal in their demand for a union. The Salinas Valley Grower-Shipper Association seized the initiative by inviting the Teamsters—with which its members had trucking contracts—to sign contracts covering their field workers. While Hoffa was in jail, Mohn ran the WCT and Grami ran the organizing. Frank Fitzsimmons, the acting International president, went along to gain internal political support to permanently replace Hoffa. The Teamsters offered growers a "responsible" alternative of granting lettuce workers, who had been earning a piece rate of 32 cents a box for five years, an increase of just 0.5 cents per box per year for the next five years.[117] In a major test of its strategic capacity, especially the depth of the leadership it had developed, the UFWOC responded to the Teamsters and created the organizational infrastructure needed to bring 70,000 new members into the union, administer contracts, and deliver benefits. And it had to do so in the unwelcome political context in which Reagan was governor of California and Richard Nixon was president of the United States.

On August 24, 1970, after mediation by the U.S. Catholic Bishops Committee broke down, UFWOC led 7,000 Salinas and Santa Maria Valley vegetable workers out in the largest farm labor strike in California history.[118] A strike fund was provided by the California Province of Franciscans in the form of an emergency loan of $250,000.

Strikers demanded that the employers rescind Teamster contracts signed without their consent and recognize their "own" union. In just one week, the strike and boycott persuaded the largest lettuce grower, Interharvest, to do just that—and grant an immediate 30 percent wage increase! Interharvest belonged to United Brands, the old United Fruit Company and distributor of Chiquita bananas, which had been purchased by New York investors who planned to market lettuce under the same brand.[119] A company already fighting off public criticism of labor abuses in Central America, it had little interest in becoming the target of a UFWOC boycott as well.[120] As with Schenley and Steinberg, the outsiders among the growers signed first. A Purex subsidiary followed a week later. And one week after that, Pic N Pac, a subsidiary of Boston's S. S. Pierce that employed 2,000 strawberry workers, followed suit.

But on September 16, Mexican Independence Day, Monterey County Superior Court judge Anthony Brazil ordered the strikers back to work because they were engaged in an illegal "jurisdictional" strike.[121] UFWOC declared a lettuce boycott and began to replace grape strikers who were returning home from the boycott cities with vegetable strikers.[122]

Victory brings new challenges and new opportunities, which can themselves become challenges. As UFWOC focused on launching its lettuce boycott, farm workers across the country began to call on the union to expand into Oregon, Washington, Idaho, Kansas, Wisconsin, Ohio, Arizona, New Mexico, Colorado, Texas, and Florida.[123] Simultaneously, growers and their legislative allies in those states and in California introduced legislation to ban boycotts, outlaw strikes at harvest time, and adopt other measures to inhibit farm workers' unionization.[124] Although UFWOC resisted these attempts with tactics ranging from a 1-day boycott of Oregon lumber to a 24-day fast by Chavez in Arizona, the counterattacks consumed valuable resources, energy, and leadership.[125]

Creating the organizational capacity to incorporate 70,000 members required training hundreds of farm workers to serve as stewards, ranch committee members, organizers, and representatives. Contracts had to be administered, hiring halls managed, old benefit programs expanded, and new ones established. UFWOC had to deliver on promised medical clinics, a retirement community for elderly Filipinos, and social service centers. This required a staff of some 300 in 25 field offices in California, Arizona, and Florida, in 35 boycott cities across the United States, and at the new headquarters in the Tehachapi Mountains near Bakersfield, Nuestra Senora Reina de La Paz (Our Lady, Queen of Peace).

The move from Delano to La Paz, the site of a former public tuberculosis sanatorium, enabled the UFWOC leadership to create a full-time volunteer community, retreat center, and administrative headquarters removed from the daily claims of members in Delano. La Paz grew eventually to a community of over 250. Although it offered financial and managerial benefits, critics argued that its isolation encouraged a loss of accountability to farm worker constituents.[126]

UFWOC generated the economic resources to support its expansion in three ways:

1. The union's full-time staff contributed a major labor subsidy by continuing to serve as volunteers. As in the strike, they earned a weekly stipend of $5, housing, a food allowance, food stamps, and a car, if needed in their work. As shown in table A.3, a summary of data reported in UFWOC LM-2 reports to the Department of Labor, despite this subsistence scale, the cost of staffing more than doubled from $204,000 in 1969 to $490,000 in 1971.

2. UFWOC contracts began to produce substantial dues income. Revenue from dues jumped from $239,000 in 1969 to $1.11 million in 1971, when it accounted for 60 percent of the union's income. Dues of $3.50 per month were deducted automatically from each member's pay and sent to the union.

3. UFWOC's fundraising program ran the gamut from "street hustling" to suburban bake sales, to major institutional contributions from unions, churches, and others. In 1971, it raised $462,000, almost $60,000 more than the $403,000 raised at the peak of the grape boycott in 1969. UFWOC also expanded the 501(c)3 entities it had formed to be able to use tax-exempt funds for social services, clinics, and the like: the Martin Luther King Fund, National Farm Worker Health Group, and National Farm Workers Service Center (NFWSC).[127] It also began its own political action committee, the Citizen Participation Day fund, which was financed by a day's pay from each worker under contract each year.

By early 1972, with UFWOC assets approaching $1 million and dues income nearing $2 million, the AFL-CIO judged UFWOC to be no longer an organizing committee and chartered it as the United Farm Workers of America, AFL-CIO (UFW), the first national farm workers union.[128] As a national union, the UFW had to revise its 1963 constitution, elect a new national Executive Board, and hold a constitutional convention, which was planned for Labor Day 1973. The structure to be decided would significantly impact the union's future strategic capacity. Against this backdrop, events intervened to make it a very different kind of convention than anyone expected.

Back to the Boycott: The 1973 Grape Strike

During the summer and fall of 1972, as the presidential campaign of Senator George McGovern against Richard Nixon heated up, the UFW, the Teamsters, and the growers had their eyes on the 200 grape contracts due to expire early in 1973. Although Senator Edward

Kennedy began his keynote speech to the 1972 Democratic National Convention by addressing his "fellow lettuce boycotters," negotiations with the vegetable industry had produced few results.[129] Growers and Teamsters, united in their support of Nixon, formed a further alliance to stop the UFW, an alliance brokered by Nixon advisor Charles Colson.[130] In December, Mohn announced that the Teamsters were resuming the fight.[131] In January 1973, Teamster president Fitzsimmons proclaimed the new alliance at the National Farm Bureau Federation convention in Los Angeles.

In April, when the Coachella Valley grape contracts expired, most of the growers renewed them—but with the Teamsters.[132] The law did not require workers' consent, so they struck in protest when they found out they had the support of a $1.6 million emergency strike fund created by the AFL-CIO.[133] The Teamsters recruited strike breakers, sent in "guards" to protect them, and the 1973 grape strike got under way.[134]

As the harvest moved north, UFWOC's three-year-old victory unraveled as one grower after another signed with the Teamsters. By August, when the UFW called off the strike, two strikers were murdered, while picketers endured 44 shootings, 400 beatings, and 3,000 arrests. For example, a Kern County deputy sheriff clubbed Nagi Daifullah, a 24-year-old Yemeni immigrant, to death. Juan De La Cruz, 65, was also shot by a strike breaker while picketing.[135] When it was all over, UFWOC was left with 10 contracts, 6,000 members, a shattered dues income, and a fight for its life. Three years after what many thought had been the definitive breakthrough in farm labor organizing, the UFW found itself back on the boycott; this time it was grapes, lettuce, and Gallo wine.

Thus, in September, when 343 delegates met in their first constitutional convention, it was as a government-in-exile.[136] They elected a new national Executive Board, but delegates had little interest in questions of internal union organization, representation, and accountability—including the fact that the constitution made no provision for local unions, districts, or any intermediate level of representation. Political units were limited to the five-person ranch committees elected annually by fellow employees and a nine-person national Executive Board, which would be elected at a national convention every four years. The only link of local to national was via the staff, who were accountable to the board. The composition of the board did indicate a continued commitment to diverse leadership: Chavez, Huerta, and Padilla of the old NFWA; Filipino leaders Pete Velasco and Phillip Veracruz of AWOC; Richard Chavez and three of the younger organizers active since the grape strike, Eliseo Medina, Mack Lyons, and me. Although the

FIGURE 7.3. United Farm Workers, national executive board, September 1973, Fresno. *Left to right:* Dolores Huerta, Mack Lyons, Richard Chavez, Cesar Chavez, Eliseo Medina, Phillip Veracruz, Gilbert Padilla, Marshall Ganz, Pete Velasco. *Source:* Walter P. Reuther Library, Wayne State University Archives

leadership circle included the general counsel, Jerry Cohen, Hartmire, and other allies, accountability rested with the only locus of political power in the union—the board.

As the growers and the Teamsters tried to consolidate their gains in the fields, the UFW expanded its boycott across the United States and Canada on a far larger scale than before. The Roman Catholic Church, whose mediators the growers and Teamsters had rebuffed, provided new levels of support. A Louis Harris poll released in October 1975 reported that 12 percent of those interviewed said that they were boycotting grapes, 11 percent were boycotting lettuce, and 8 percent were boycotting Gallo wines. Some 17 million Americans were participating in the boycott.[137] Despite the fact that the UFW's 1974 dues income had been cut in half to $515,000, it more than made up for it by raising $2.3 million in contributions. At the same time, it had to spend $2.4 million to support 600 full-time strikers and boycotters.[138] It was touch and go. When the Teamsters hired a staff of 75 and began to spend $100,000 a month to service them, the UFW organized wildcat strikes across the state.[139] The costs of overtime pay to deputy sheriffs and for the jury trials that the UFW demanded for each person who had been arrested the previous summer pushed some rural counties close to bankruptcy.[140]

Early in 1975, the conflict came to a head when Democrat Jerry Brown replaced Reagan as governor and declared his major goal to be the "restoration of peace" in the fields.[141] The legislature changed as well. In 1966, the U.S. Supreme Court ordered a reapportionment that did away with the systematic rural overrepresentation that had been in place since the 1920s. And among the new legislators were farm worker supporters Richard Alatorre of East Los Angeles and Howard Berman of Los Angeles's liberal west side.

With the political leadership of Brown, Berman, and Alatorre—and turmoil in the fields and at the supermarkets—the time was right for a legislative initiative. Although the UFW resisted legislation that would ban the boycott or rely on Reagan appointees for enforcement, times had changed. Chavez and others became convinced that the right kind of law, if enforced by Brown appointees, could give the UFW a second bite at the apple. The boycott persuaded the supermarket industry to become advocates of a legislative solution, just as the fiscal pressure turned rural county governments into legislative advocates.[142] The WCT, under the new leadership of M. E. Anderson, a younger man of 49 who had replaced Mohn the year before, seemed confident that it would enjoy the advantages of being the incumbent in union elections.[143] Growers believed that a new law could curb the boycott and, in any event, their workers would not vote for the UFW.[144]

So in May 1975, after 10 years of strife in the fields, the parties struck a deal to enact the Agricultural Labor Relations Act (ALRA).[145] It would take effect in three months, on August 28, the fifth anniversary of the Salinas lettuce strike. To lead the Agricultural Labor Relations Board (ALRB), Brown appointed Bishop Roger Mahoney. The four other members represented the key partis: LeRoy Chatfield, a leading UFW organizer from 1966 to 1973; a representative of the growers; a lawyer drawn from the Latino community; and a jurist with a labor relations background, who was known to the Teamsters.

The new law was the product not only of political bargaining, but also of hours of deliberation as the UFW developed the strategic capacity to use a collective bargaining law to organize. Participants in the deliberations came from various quarters: lawyers, led by Jerry Cohen, farm worker organizers, legislators, AFL-CIO labor officials, church leaders, and Chavez. Among the innovations they devised was the provision that employers must recognize and bargain in good faith with any union their workers chose in a secret ballot election. Unlike the NLRA, however, the bargaining must *only* be with a union so chosen. To retain its contracts, as well as win new ones, a union was required to prove that it represented a majority of the workers. Although the UFW had to defend 12 contracts, the Teamsters had to defend over 100.[146]

Another innovation was the provision that elections were to be held within seven days of the submission of cards signed by 50 percent of the employees. And, because the work was seasonal, the fact that elections were permitted only when at least 50 percent of the peak workforce was working kept them from being held at times when only the hand-picked year-round workers were employed.

Finally, it promised elections free of employer intimidation and set up procedures to process complaints, which was linked to a program of worker education. If a union won an election but failed to get a contract, it was free to strike or boycott. If the failure to get a contract was due to bad-faith bargaining, the law provided a "make whole" remedy that required the offending party to make restitution to the other for any losses that resulted.

The UFW, the Teamsters, and the growers all claimed to speak for farm workers. Now they would have to prove it.

The UFW Strikes Back: The Agricultural Labor Relations Act

Translating the ALRA into a successful organizing campaign required the UFW to once again radically redeploy its resources. While organizing representation elections across California, it also needed to maintain a strong enough boycott to turn victories into contracts. The Teamsters relied on professional organizers, crew supervisors, and the advantages of incumbency. By contrast, the UFW recruited an army of over 200 volunteer farm worker organizers, who left their jobs to work full time for subsistence wages. The UFW proved able to field enough organizers to defend its contracts, target employers under contract with the Teamsters, and target unorganized growers in major agricultural valleys across the state. As organizing began, the parties negotiated appointments to the ALRB, argued over the regulations governing implementation, including terms of access to the employers' camps and fields, sought to influence the hiring of 100 new state personnel, and debated the locations and number of regional offices. Chavez did a 1,000-mile *caminata*, or walk, up the California coast and down the Central Valley to mobilize support.

UFW winning over Teamsters

On September 2, the ALRB opened its doors, and 30 election petitions were filed that covered 8,000 workers: the UFW filed 28 and the Teamsters filed 2.[147] On September 5, the first election was held at the Molera Agricultural Group, an artichoke farm with a Teamster contract near Salinas. The UFW won 17–5.[148]

When the first round of voting ended in February 1976, 47,000 ballots had been cast in 425 elections. The UFW gained a second wind, and the WCT leadership began to doubt they had a future in the fields.[149] The Teamster leaders expected to trounce the UFW. However, in the 147 elections in which the UFW and the Teamsters went head to head, the UFW won 76 to the Teamster's 71. By casting a wide net, the UFW also won 153 elections in which it was the only union on the ballot. When it was all over, the UFW won 214 elections with 23,010 voters. The Teamsters won 115 elections with 11,459 voters. And "no union" won 33 elections with 7,665 voters.[150]

Among the growers, who thought the UFW was a dead letter, the results created such consternation that they convinced their legislative allies to allow the ALRB to run out of money on February 8, shutting down ALRB offices across the state.[151] But when the UFW gathered 729,000 signatures to qualify for a state ballot initiative to place the law in the state constitution, recalcitrant legislators restored funding.[152] Nevertheless, the UFW pursued the ballot initiative, Proposition 14, but lost 46 percent to 54 percent.[153] When union elections resumed in November, however the Teamsters decided to withdraw.[154]

Defending his predecessor's fight became far too costly for Anderson, the new WCT chief, who had spent at least $10 million with little to show for it.[155] The Teamsters lost far too many elections at ranches where they had been incumbents for three years or more. Since either party could file objections to an outcome they believed to be tainted by the misconduct of the other party, both sides objected to almost every election. Unsurprisingly, the hearings, briefs, and depositions required an army of lawyers. Although the UFW was represented by lawyers who worked for modest salaries or by trained volunteer legal workers, the Teamsters paid top dollar for every minute of legal time.[156] With as many as 40 to 50 hearings in a single day, the legal costs mounted. Most important, an antitrust suit that the UFW had filed in 1970 to challenge the Salinas contracts wound its way through the courts and grew into a legal behemoth.[157] Engaging dozens of lawyers, the suit generated legal costs of hundreds of thousands of dollars, and held damage potential in the tens of millions of dollars.[158] Along with strikes, boycotts, and legislative politics, the UFW learned how to turn its legal resources into a source of power as well.[159]

On March 10, 1977, negotiations between the UFW and the Teamsters concluded a five-year jurisdictional agreement based on a division of the turf similar to that agreed upon in 1967. The lawsuits were dropped, and the UFW found itself once again with the field all to itself, as it had 10 years before when it defeated the first growers-Teamsters alliance.[160]

The UFW won recognition from 151 employers, signed many new contracts, brought its membership back up to 30,000, and within a year was enjoying a dues income of $1.5 million. Although membership remained below the 1971 peak, it was more secure, more diverse, and more stable due to the ALRA. And the new collective bargaining law was secure for at least six more years, assuming Brown's reelection. Not only had Sacramento politics aligned with the UFW's interests, but with the election of President Jimmy Carter, national politics had as well. Growers across the country began to wonder which state would be next.[161]

CONCLUSION

The UFW's successes were due to much more than a single good call, luck, or a propitious environment. The repeated development of effective strategy was not due to any one choice but was the result of the strategic capacity that the UFW continued to develop over time. Each of the moments of victory—at Schenley, DiGiorgio, Perelli-Minetti, and beyond—had the quality of a breakthrough event that altered the environment so much that the outcomes depended to an unusual extent on the actors' strategic choices. Furthermore, the actors competed to interpret the meaning of each outcome. Victories turned out to be moments when the next move mattered most—not a time to rest on one's laurels, but a time to make something of one's success.

At these moments, the capacity to decide not only wisely but also quickly helped union leaders to retain the initiative. Keeping the initiative allowed them to choose the time, place, and means of engagement to maximize their resources, while minimizing those of their opponents. The NFWA reacted to AWOC's initiative in calling the grape strike, but regained the initiative by calling the Schenley boycott and organizing the march. The initiative passed to the employers when DiGiorgio called for elections, causing the NFWA to react, and again, when the Teamsters came on the scene. The NFWA regained the initiative by outflanking them with the governor and winning control of the electoral process. When the NFWA won this battle, however, it lost the initiative to the Teamsters at Perelli-Minetti. But by driving the Teamsters from the fields in the summer of 1967, UFWOC regained the initiative fully enough to bring the entire table grape industry under contract in July 1970, another moment at which victory brought with it the greatest challenge yet. After losing the initiative once again in 1973—and suffering through two years of sharp reverses—the UFW seized the initiative yet again with passage of the ALRA in 1975. By 1977, the UFW once again had claimed the field; it turned out, however, that that moment brought with it the greatest challenge to the UFW yet.

Epilogue

S O HOW DID it all turn out? Did the UFW go from victory to victory, establishing itself as a major force in California agriculture, labor, and politics? Did the California farm workers transform their rural ghettoes into healthy communities that afforded them economic, political, and social equality with other American workers? What has been the legacy of the struggle recounted here?

Although we have seen how David can sometimes win, remaining David, as the biblical David discovered when he became king, can be even more challenging than becoming David in the first place. Although Californians celebrate Cesar Chavez Day, Cesar Chavez streets, parks, libraries, and schools dot the Southwest, and Cesar Chavez stamps deliver the U.S. mail, the living and working conditions of California farm workers are little better at the beginning of the twenty-first century than when he began organizing in the early 1960s. The organization he led for 31 years now anchors a network of nonprofits in which farm worker organizing plays a minor role.[1]

In real dollars, the nearly 400,000 farm workers employed today by California's $30 billion agricultural industry earn wages 20–25 percent below those paid in the late 1970s.[2] In 2006, the most recent year for which such figures are available as of this writing, the average California farm wage of $9 per hour was less than half of the average wage in construction.[3] Annual farm worker earnings of $7,000–$8,000 were a quarter of factory worker earnings of $30,000–$35,000.[4] The abusive labor contracting system that was in decline throughout the 1970s has made a major comeback and accounts for some 43 percent of farm jobs today. Most farm workers are still new immigrants, many of whom arrived long after the UFW stopped organizing and at least 60 percent of whom lack a legal status that could offer even minimal protection.[5] Access to affordable housing, health care, and education remains far behind that of other workers, and with a public no longer effectively challenged to pay attention, the harsh reality of their daily lives is rarely noted.

Although the Agricultural Labor Relations Act remains the only collective bargaining law to encourage farm worker unionization in the continental United States, the organization that made it work is a shadow of its former self. It represents no more than 5,000 workers and holds some 33 contracts as compared with the 60,000–70,000 workers that it once represented and the 200 contracts that it held in the late 1970s.[6] Although other unions now also represent farm workers—the United Food and Commercial Workers Local 5 and Teamsters Local 890—they have even fewer members.[7] Most of the recent successes in farm organizing have been won outside California by organizations that have drawn inspiration from the UFW but operate independently of it: the Farm Labor Organizing Committee[8] in Ohio and North Carolina and the Coalition of Immokalee Workers in Florida, for example.[9]

The UFW no longer functions primarily as a farm workers union. Rather, it anchors a network of 14 nonprofit entities with combined assets of $42 million, collectively run by the Chavez family.[10] For the most part, these assets were capitalized during the 1970s and 1980s with funds generated under union contracts, $1.7 million in public grants from the Carter administration, direct mail marketing, and a growing portfolio of investments. The National Farm Workers Service Center, Inc., with assets of $24.6 million, coordinates entities that operate nine radio stations, build and operate affordable housing in four states, and memorialize Chavez, who died in 1993.[11] In addition, the Juan De La Cruz Farm Workers Pension Fund in 2004 held $102.7 million in assets, from which it provided benefits to only 2,411 farm worker retirees. Similarly, the Robert F. Kennedy Medical Plan held $7.9 million in assets, but insured less than 3,000 workers.[12] As shown in figure E.1, although the UFW still enjoys an annual income of over $6 million, over 60 percent comes from fundraising rather than the dues of members, including a $700,000 grant from Change to Win, the union group that broke away from the AFL-CIO.[13]

From the late 1960s to the early 1980s, the UFW had a major impact on the lives of farm workers—and the Latino community in general. Farm worker wages, benefits, and working conditions steadily improved as the UFW won contracts and as non-union employers made improvements to preempt the union.[14] Public advocacy by the UFW spurred the enactment of rural education, health, training, and legal assistance

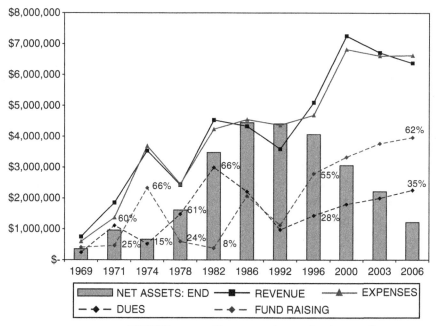

FIGURE E.I. UFW Income, Expenses, Assets (1969–2006)

programs. The UFW's readiness to demand accountability from public officials won the enforcement of local, state, and federal statutory protections and elected more responsive officials. Opportunities for farm workers' access to job, educational, and political mobility improved and at the same time facilitated a growing Latino political influence.[15] And the UFW contributed know-how, inspiration, and alumni to the broader progressive movement, including union, civic, and political leaders who learned their craft in the UFW and whose networks encourage organizing in California and elsewhere to the present day.[16]

Once again, however, a moment of victory became a moment of danger. In the past, the threat came from outside the union. In turn, the UFW responded strategically, and it prevailed. This time, however, the threat came from within and it was not overcome. Within just four years, the UFW stopped organizing, drove out most of its experienced leaders, and entered into a decline from which it has not recovered.[17] Although its economic resources continued to grow, due in large part to the stability created by the ALRA, its strategic capacity was decimated. The growers recognized this weakness, refused to renew contracts, and the UFW turned again to fundraising to sustain itself. By 1992, a year before Chavez's death, dues accounted for only 27 percent of its income, the lowest ebb since 1974.

WHAT HAPPENED?

Some explain the UFW's transformation in the same way they explain its earlier success: changing times. They argue that Republican governors, a less responsive ALRB, smarter growers, and waves of immigration halted the UFW's momentum.[18] Although these changes posed real challenges, the timing assumed by this argument doesn't work.

For one thing, many of the UFW's greatest successes came when Reagan was governor of California and Nixon was president. The UFW decided to stop organizing in 1977, when the union was at its peak of political influence and a full six years before the Republicans reassumed the California governorship in 1983. The new organizing that did occur was almost entirely in reaction to worker demand rather than union initiative. And the sharpest increases in unauthorized immigration came in the 1990s, long after the union had turned away from organizing.[19]

Others argue that social movement organizations like the UFW are inherently unstable. Led by zealots who are poor administrators, they pursue ideological goals, interpret dissent as disloyalty, and splinter or collapse like religious sects.[20] They may influence thousands of individuals and create a cultural legacy, but rarely do they institutionalize firmly enough to survive the death of their charismatic founder. On the other hand, if they are successful, their character changes as they acquire the administrative staff needed to manage the fruits of success.[21] According to this well-known "iron law of oligarchy," as staff members gain control of organizational resources, they lose their accountability and supplant members' goals with their own.[22]

Despite frequent claims by critics that Chavez had more interest in leading a movement than in building a union, he did not ignore the formidable administrative challenges the UFW faced. He and his allies, however, did not create an organizational infrastructure to meet these challenges. Instead, in the name of preserving the movement, Chavez consolidated his internal political control so he could respond to these challenges on his own terms. Chavez's later moves stifled creative internal deliberation as he began to replace experienced UFW leaders with a new, younger cadre, for whom loyalty was the essential qualification. The full-time staff, including Chavez, ultimately did use their control of organizational resources to supplant members' goals with their own. But it was the result of an attempt to meet political needs, not administrative ones. Chavez and his allies accomplished this transformation of the UFW in the five years between 1976 and 1981. Sadly, it left the union denuded of the strategic capacity that had been the source of its success for its first 15 years.[23]

Ironically, the economic, political, and cultural resources generated during the UFW's glory years allowed it to survive and even prosper as it lost membership. Revenue grew throughout the 1980s, and although dues income peaked at $4.5 million in 1982, when it constituted 66 percent of the union's income, assets peaked at $6.7 million in 1992, a year before Chavez's death. Union contracts continued to generate dues because the ALRA prevented the kind of wholesale loss of contracts that had occurred in 1973. When dues income did decline as growers failed to renew their contracts or as workers decertified the union, the UFW made up for the losses by fundraising. Membership declined, financial resources grew, and the UFW claimed to continue to speak for farm workers, but it no longer served as a significant vehicle for their organization.

While the transformation of the UFW may not seem to be part of the story of David and Goliath, it is. It shows just how hard it can be to remain David if one trades one's resourcefulness for the control of resources. I do not argue that changes in the political, economic, and social environment did not matter in the transformation of the union. They did. But, as in the earlier years, the consequences of these changes resulted from the ways that UFW leaders chose to engage with them.

TRANSFORMATION (1977–1981)

During the winter of 1975–1976, while most UFW leaders focused on consolidating the gains under the ALRA, Chavez struggled with the growing administrative and political complexity of the union.[24] Restlessness with the volunteer system that had been in force since the beginning of the grape strike began to emerge among the staff. And Chavez's personal demons, whatever their source, began to gnaw at his self-confidence, humor, and resilience.[25]

In search of models, Chavez renewed his relationship with Charles Dederich, the founder of Synanon, a Los Angeles drug treatment program that had evolved into a cult and had declared itself a "religion" a few years earlier.[26] Unfortunately for himself, the UFW, and the farm workers, Chavez came to believe that Dederich's strategy of organizational transformation was the answer. This required turning the UFW into a community of unpaid cadre, loyal to a single leader, governed by groupthink rituals, and enjoying the apparent efficiency of unquestioning obedience.[27] It is unclear how Chavez hoped to reconcile Dederich's vision with that of a democratically accountable union organized to represent farm workers—especially when the UFW thrived on diversity, contentiousness, and creativity. In fact, he could not.

Whether moved more by Dederich's model or by what psychologist Rod Kramer calls "political paranoia," or both, in 1977 Chavez began to replace the UFW leadership, transform its deliberative processes, and insulate it from the accountability that had kept it adaptive in the past.[28] He scrapped the strategic capacity that the UFW had taken years to develop.

As Chavez became absorbed in transforming the UFW, he disengaged from the challenges of organizing, negotiating contracts, and building a union.[29] Focused on ferreting out "agents"—in Dederich's words, "assholes"—Chavez initiated the first of many staff purges right after the fight for Proposition 14, in November 1976. As is the case with purges, however, blaming problems on the wrong causes only makes the problems worse, which in turn requires more purges.

In early 1977, when the UFW reached its agreement with the Teamsters, Chavez scheduled the next national Executive Board meeting at the Synanon headquarters high in the hills above Fresno. At this February meeting, strategic choices were to be made regarding how to take advantage of this unique moment. The vegetable industry remained partially organized, creating an unstable dynamic between union and non-union growers. The table grape industry remained largely unorganized and, by all accounts, posed a very difficult challenge. And the citrus, nursery, and mushroom industries had never been organized. Freed of the competitive accountability enforced by the Teamsters, however, Chavez now introduced the national Executive Board to his new organizational model and, specifically, to the Synanon game.

Dederich developed the game as an intensely political kind of group therapy. In emotionally aggressive sessions with 10–15 persons, participants verbally attacked each other to air problems. The attack was considered an expression of love, compelling self-examination by enabling people to see themselves as others did. A "game master" served as moderator and used ridicule, cross-examination, and hostile attack to advance a session that could last from one to three hours. Putting a particular person on the "hot seat" and singling out one of their own for attack by the group was an important aspect of this play. The game was key to Dederich's governance of his community. Its members were expected to follow the rules established in the sessions. Material and social rewards, such as personal prestige or occupational mobility, rewarded compliance. When "in the game," one was to criticize others and reveal personal conflicts. But when "out of the game," one was to be happy, pleasant, and cooperative.[30]

By importing the game, Chavez transformed UFW deliberations into a controlled, exclusive, and judgmental process in which one's loyalty was constantly on the line. Over the course of the next two years, Chavez tried to make the game as central to the practice of the union as it was to Synanon. In the spring of 1978, over 200 staff members traveled each Saturday from throughout the state to La Paz to play the game, even if it took five hours on the road each way.

What of the UFW's accountability mechanisms?

In terms of external accountability, the Teamster withdrawal ended a competition that had served the UFW well—and the organization of farm workers in general. The fact that the UFW's political allies in Sacramento and Washington made federal funding available to invest in expanding its nonprofit entities actually reduced the union's dependence on contract-generated revenue from its membership.[31] At the same time, however, income generated by new contracts funded the union's medical, pension, social service, and political programs. This contract income freed the UFW from its dependence on the institutional support of other unions, churches, and other groups and individuals. As one consequence, despite the objections of religious leaders, Chavez visited the Philippines in 1977, as a guest of the authoritarian Marcos regime.[32] His visit led to the resignation of UFW vice president Phillip Veracruz, a former AWOC leader and a long-time opponent of that regime.[33]

More important, internal accountability mechanisms broke down. Within the national Executive Board. The breakdown grew out of the structural reality—established at the 1973 convention when the future of the UFW hung in the balance—that control over resources had become so centralized that no venues were created within which a loyal opposition could organize the political influence necessary for accountability.

Board members focused on their individual responsibilities and expected a certain eccentricity from Chavez. Given his idolization by the farm workers and the public, they tolerated a great deal in order to avoid challenging him directly. When divisions emerged among board members in the normal course of things, they were exploited rather than mediated by Chavez, especially after the ALRB elections distinguished board members who were "winners" from those who were "losers"; the winners tended to be younger people who had built a base outside the grape industry while the losers tended to be older people whose base remained within the grape industry. Board members elected at the convention every four years were the only leaders who enjoyed the legitimacy—and the authority—of election and who operated above the level of a single farm. Local ranch committees were elected at local ranches, but were coordinated by a field staff accountable to a field office director who was appointed by the national union.

During the next four years, Chavez's drive to transform the UFW set the agenda. Only external events that could not be ignored, such as contract expirations or wildcat strikes, drew the union's attention elsewhere.

In 1977, after suffering reverses in an ill-conceived campaign to reestablish a base in the grape industry, the UFW board formally decided to stop organizing.[34] This halted a strategic advance into new industries and, because of labor market competition, made it harder to retain contracts in industries that were only partially organized. Most subsequent organizing, such as a 1978 campaign among Oxnard citrus workers, occurred in reaction to worker initiatives, not as a result of strategic choice.

In 1978, Chavez fired the UFW legal department of 17 full-time lawyers and 44 legal workers and interns, scuttling the union's ability to manage the ALRA.[35] Although lawyers had been exempted from the volunteer system since the early days of the union and earned modest salaries of $7,200 per year, Chavez reacted to a request for an increase of salary by insisting they become volunteers. When the national Executive Board balked, Chavez threatened to resign and only then prevailed in a 5–4 split. As figure E.1 shows, the salary crisis was not due to a shortage of funds. In fact, the UFW would use the funds with which it had paid in-house lawyers to contract out its legal work, but on a smaller scale, to less experienced advocates. This approach was far less productive.

Dismayed that Chavez's agenda was trumping the organizing, bargaining, and contract administration, vice president Eliseo Medina resigned within a month. The three other board members in opposition—Mack Lyons, Jessica Govea, and I—followed within the next two years, as did Gilbert Padilla, one of Chavez's original team, who served as secretary-treasurer. Three of the five officers who left had served as the union's organizing directors.

In 1979, in large measure due to inadequate preparation for bargaining with the entire vegetable industry, the UFW found itself in a protracted strike that cost one farm worker—Rufino Contreras—his life.[36] The strike further polarized the union internally, especially over the role of farm workers in it. Farm worker leaders insisted on continuing the strike when Chavez wanted to shift to a centrally controlled boycott, but were vindicated when growers signed landmark contracts that raised the minimum hourly wage from $3.70 an hour to $5 an hour.[37] Employers also accepted a "paid rep" system that was modeled on the UAW's shop committee representatives; workers would be elected to be paid full time to do the work of union representation. The paid reps were the first full-time elected officials in the UFW other than the national Executive Board itself.

By the opening of the UFW convention in August 1981, a majority of the elected national Executive Board members had already been replaced by Chavez appointees, none of whom had played a leadership role in the union—in bargaining, boycotts, or organizing—before 1977. In addition to the dismissal of the legal department, the purges led to the departure of experienced organizers, negotiators, and administrative staff as well. Only one piece remained to complete the transformation: farm worker leaders themselves.

In anticipation of the 1981 convention, the 20 paid reps—veterans of the 1979 vegetable strike who were frustrated with the UFW's lack of attention to their concerns, especially the union medical plan—caucused to nominate their own farm worker candidates for the board: Jose Renteria of Watsonville and Rosario Pelayo of Calexico. When they arrived at the convention, Chavez denounced them as traitors, drove them from the hall, and, within a month, had them fired from their positions.[38] And although a federal district court ruled late in 1982 that Chavez had acted illegally in removing these elected officials, the UFW no longer held contracts with their employers so they could not be restored to their jobs.[39] There were no further farm worker challenges to Chavez's authority.

Between 1977 and 1981, Chavez undid the UFW's strategic capacity. The changes irrevocably altered the character of the UFW leadership. Instead of a diverse team with both strong and weak ties to multiple constituencies, it became a narrow circle of people with strong ties, often Chavez family members or dependents. Access to a fresh tactical repertoire no longer came from a diverse leadership team but via paid direct marketing experts such as assembly speaker Willie Brown's consultant, Richard Ross.[40] And in lieu of relying on resources generated by doing the work of organizing—in the fields or in the cities—the UFW now relied on dues, direct-mail fundraising, and grants.

Chavez and his new team thus became accountable only to themselves, and the freewheeling deliberative process that had characterized the rise of the UFW was replaced by the stifling dynamics of the Synanon game. Venues of organizational creativity were replaced by groupthink. Access to relevant information was constricted by a culture of suspicion that suppressed inconvenient truths, while dissent became construed as disloyalty. Ironically, Chavez's determination, which had expressed itself in risk taking, confidence, and a spirit of hope that animated the early movement, now turned into a sullen stubbornness, which was a poor substitute for commitment. That the UFW could survive was evidence no longer of its resourcefulness, but rather of the depth of the political, economic, and cultural resources it had acquired during its heyday.

DECLINE (1981–1993)

During the 12 years between the 1981 convention and Chavez's death in 1993, the UFW went into steady decline. The organizing successes of the mid-1970s generated dues income for a time. Chavez compensated for the leadership deficit he had created, however, by relying on tactics he could manage centrally, such as direct marketing.

With the help of consultants, Chavez tried to use direct mail to conduct boycotts and television ads to recruit farm workers—in lieu of the organizing for which the UFW had become so well known.[41] The UFW spent lavishly on political contributions, notably a gift of $750,000 to assembly speaker Willie Brown in 1982.[42] And while this turn to direct marketing contributed little economic or political muscle that could enable the UFW to organize workers, win contracts, or build boycotts, it fueled a formidable fundraising operation that traded—and continues to trade—on the mythic status that Chavez and the UFW acquired during the 1960s and 1970s.[43]

In 1983, when Republican George Deukmejian became governor, the UFW could no longer count on a sympathetic ALRB general counsel, a gubernatorial appointee, even though it held a majority of supporters on the board itself. Although this development was not responsible for the decline in organizing during the previous five years, it made using the law to obtain contracts more difficult, especially given the UFW's enfeebled legal resources. What this political change did, however, was allow UFW leaders to rhetorically shift responsibility for the union's decline from themselves to the Republicans.[44]

Confronted with escalating grower resistance, a hostile administration, and a growing proportion of the workforce that arrived years after the organizing had stopped, the UFW no longer possessed the strategic capacity to fight back. Thus, it turned to public advocacy in lieu of organizing. By 1992, the UFW's annual revenue fell from a 1982 peak of $4.6 to $3.5 million. More significantly, dues now accounted for only 27 percent of its revenue, while 60 percent derived from various forms of fundraising. Although the number of contracts the union retained is uncertain, its membership had fallen to 5,000, down from 50,000 only 10 years before.

THE NEXT GENERATION (1993–2006)

When Chavez died in 1993, UFW leadership passed to his son-in-law Arturo Rodriguez, 44, a native of San Antonio, Texas, and a graduate of the University of Michigan School of Social Work. In 1974, Rodriguez joined the Detroit boycott, where he met a Chavez daughter, Linda. When they married in 1975, Rodriguez was reassigned to California, where he began to learn organizing. At the 1981 convention, as part of the Chavez slate, he was elected to the union's national Executive Board.

Upon assuming the helm, Rodriguez made a brief effort to resume organizing. In doing so, he faced a major challenge: atrophy in the UFW's strategic capacity. Not only did few experienced organizers remain, but the practice of organizing itself—the UFW's early strength—had become a lost art. The remaining leaders' dependence on Chavez's reputation for their fundraising, political needs, and personal legitimacy made it hard for them to acknowledge the sources of the union's decline. In this light, it was hard to take the steps needed to rebuild.

Nevertheless, during the UFW's first year back in the fields, it won eight elections, and during the next three years, it signed seven new contracts in mushrooms, roses, and lettuce.[45] The cost of obtaining these contracts in the union's weakened state, however, was a two-tier system that limited benefits to full-time workers and in many cases excluded seasonal workers hired by labor contractors entirely. This reduced employer opposition yet made the union far less attractive to seasonal workers, who still made up the majority of field workers.

In the summer of 1996, Rodriguez's big chance came as a result of the previous year's election of John Sweeney to lead the AFL-CIO. Eager to show organizing success among new, immigrant, low-income workers, Sweeney committed over $1 million in funds and staff to support Rodriguez's campaign to organize 15,000 Watsonville strawberry workers. Rodriguez focused his efforts on Coastal Berry, a major grower with outside economic interests, which the AFL-CIO had persuaded to refrain from opposing the union.[46] But after three years, the effort collapsed when the UFW was defeated by an independent union, 646–577, in May 1999.[47] Also backed by the AFL-CIO, a similar effort to organize the Washington apple industry was abandoned without results in 2001.[48] Yet another effort, this one a return to the table grapes which was funded by $700,000 from the AFL-CIO rival Change to Win union coalition, showed a similar lack of success in 2006.

Because its return to farm worker organizing was so spotty and tough, the UFW shifted its attention to greener pastures where the reputation of its founder, its fundraising capacity, and the myth of what it once had been could serve it well. In 2000, the UFW refocused on the broader Hispanic community. As Chavez's son Paul said, "If we look at growth, the Latino urban community is where it's at."[49] At the same time, the UFW amended its constitutional mission by replacing the "organizing" of farm workers with "protecting and insuring" their rights. It expanded its housing, social services, and communications enterprises. More recently, it received a $5 million state of California grant to establish a Chavez Center at the union headquarters in Keene.[50]

Perhaps the UFW's most effective efforts in the twenty-first century thus far have been in politics, where it benefits from a dramatic increase in the size of the Latino electorate coupled with the coming of age of a generation of Latino political leaders who grew up in the movement. In 2002, for example, in the last days of Governor Gray Davis's tenure, the UFW won passage of an amendment to the ALRA that provides for compulsory mediation in the event that contract negotiations break down. This victory was won after spending a total of $336,000 on lobbyists. As of 2005, however, it had only been used twice and only once by the UFW itself.[51]

As the UFW became an advocacy group, the professionalization of its staff proceeded apace. By 2000, Rodriguez ended the volunteer system and increased spending on staff salaries and benefits from $500,000, a figure unchanged since the late 1970s, to more than $2 million in

2006. Staff costs accounted for 35 percent of union expenditures as compared with 15 percent in Chavez's day—even as the number of full-time staff declined from 445 in 1979 to just 59 in 2006.

Similarly, Rodriguez boosted expenditures on legal, lobbying, and professional services—which had been about $200,000 at the time of Chavez's death—to $600,000 in 2000. By 2006, the figure hovered close to $1 million. Officers' compensation grew from $50,000 a year to $482,000 a year. In 2006, Rodriguez earned $82,000, compared with Chavez's $5,000.[52]

In the midst of these changes, the UFW had lost the capacity to operate as a union. By building on their resources—Chavez's name, the organization's tax-exempt funds, and its network of relationships— UFW leaders moved into the kind of advocacy, services provision, and public policy work that other nonprofits had done for years. Even though they were trading on Chavez's reputation, they moved further away from the organizing that created his reputation in the first place. David can indeed sometimes win, and a heroic story it can be. It can also become a tragedy, though, if David becomes Goliath and comes to rely on the very resources he overcame in the first place.

CONCLUSION

I began this book with three questions: How can the powerless sometimes challenge the powerful successfully? How can strategic resourcefulness compensate for lack of resources? And how can we exercise leadership to turn what we have into what we need to get what we want? Learning from the attempts to organize California farm workers may point us toward some answers.

From 1900 to 1950, tight labor markets created an opportunity for farm workers to leverage their labor market resources to better their conditions. Three major attempts failed to achieve more than seasonal improvements: no multiyear contracts, no sustainable farm workers union, and no reform of the rules governing the farm labor market. Recognizing the more powerful position of the growers, organizers quickly learned that no matter how well organized they were locally, they had to win outside support to make even short-term gains. Organizers of new immigrant groups used whatever modest support was available from the governments of their countries of origin. Radicals drew on national networks for legal, financial, and political support. Furthermore, the AFL, often organizing only in reaction to the radicals, backed up its efforts with union support. At times, this support took the form of secondary boycotts. None of these tactics got very far before the growers took advantage of a mobilization for war to suppress the organizing, rebuild their workforce, and strengthen their control of labor market institutions.

It was not until the 1960s when a tight labor market, the result of the end of the *bracero* program, created another opportunity to organize farm workers. This time, however, ethnic community leaders, radical organizers, and the AFL-CIO came to play roles in a common endeavor. Newly legitimate racial justice claims both weakened barriers that kept earlier efforts from joining forces and enhanced claims of economic justice as a basis for public support. At the same time, state institutions that the growers had used to consolidate earlier successes now offered farm worker organizers new venues for public mobilization. This opportunity, like David's stones, would be of little value to those who could not figure out how to take advantage of it.

So how did they take advantage of it? And why did some prove able to take greater advantage than others?

First of all, strategy matters. Opportunities and resources matter as well of course. Yet it is the ability to capitalize on opportunities by turning the resources one has into the power one needs which transforms possibility into results—what I call strategic capacity. We can create strategic capacity by the skillful assembly of a leadership team and the careful structuring of its interactions among its members, constituents, and environment. To the extent that this results in a combination of deep motivation, access to relevant information, and ongoing learning, one can make good strategy more likely.

The foundation, as we have seen, is depth of commitment—what I call motivation. David's commitment to challenge Goliath did not depend on figuring out a good strategy. On the contrary, good strategy grew out of his commitment to fight. Similarly, the UFW's commitment to the cause was a key source of its continually evolving strategy. Its rivals, on the other hand, with a marginal commitment to the project at best, did what they knew how to do. When that didn't work, they had little interest in risking novel approaches.

Commitment isn't the whole story, however. It also takes access to the right kind of information—about one's constituency, about other actors, and about the opposition. Of course, the motivation to seek out sources of information also goes back to commitment. David realized the futility of a conventional approach when he found that he couldn't move in Saul's armor. Pressed to scan the environment for an answer, he noticed the five smooth stones and recognized that he possessed just the skills needed to put them to good use. Similarly, we have seen how the UFW wove together its connections with the farm worker world, *Networking* the churches, the unions, the civil rights movement, and the political domain in widely diverse ways. These connections gave rise to a series of surprisingly effective—and often quite novel—tactics. Again, its rivals, with little access to the kind of information they would have needed to devise effective tactics, stuck to what they knew. And even when they tried to imitate the UFW's tactics, as the Teamsters did for a brief period, it didn't work because they lacked the means to generate tactics that could work for *them*, not for the UFW.

Finally, it's about learning—with curiosity, exploration, humor, and *willing to learn* the courage to risk failure as well as success. When David undertook his mission, he wasn't clear how he was going to get it done, but he had the confidence—or faith—that he could figure out how to get it done. When one approach didn't work, he tried another. Then, surprised that Goliath's arrogance blinded him to what David was planning, David struck the fatal blow. When Cesar Chavez used to say "power makes you stupid," this is what he meant: you come to rely on an overwhelming resource advantage, which is exactly what creates opportunity for the Davids of the world. Of the three components of strategic capacity, this may be the most fragile. It requires managing the tension between generating ideas and making choices, between creative dissent and organizational unity, between change and continuity. For the period analyzed in this book, the UFW pulled this off remarkably well. Chavez took particular pleasure in getting people together to figure things out, to respond to moves with countermoves, to find ways, as he would say, to "kill two birds with one stone and keep the stone." It was the breach in this kind of learning—and the practice of open deliberation required to nurture it—that most clearly indicated the new path the UFW would take.

In representative associations, such as unions, finding ways to renew leadership can be difficult for current leaders to accept because it requires creating new leadership opportunities, the incorporation of new constituencies, and leadership turnover. When success brings access to conventional resources, it may seem irresponsible to resist relying upon them; reliance, however, can quickly turn into dependence. Perhaps most critical are organizational structures through which leaders can hold themselves accountable to changing constituencies. In the UFW's early years, the accountability to farm workers and supporters was real. They held resources without which the project could not go forward. Competitive accountability to the Teamsters kept UFW leaders on task, contesting the Teamsters' turf by organizing workers. But as the UFW freed itself of external competition and came to rely on resources generated internally by highly centralized means, such as direct mail, the failure to create structures that could sustain pluralism, encourage debate, and invite challenge proved to be a disaster. Control over resources at the top and the absence of any intermediate levels of political accountability—districts, locals, or regions—meant that potential challengers could never organize, build a base, or mount a real challenge to incumbents.

As we have seen, changing environments generate opportunities and challenges. The significance of these opportunities emerges, however, from the hearts, heads, and hands of the actors who develop the means of putting them to work. People can generate the power to resolve grievances not by relying on those who hold power to use it on their behalf, but by developing the capacity to outthink—and outlast—their opponents; these are matters of leadership and organization. As students of street smarts have long understood, resourcefulness can sometimes compensate for a lack of resources. Although learning how the environment influences our choices can help us to understand the world, learning how our choices influence the environment can help us to change it.

Appendix

TABLE A.1. Labor Market

Year	Hired Farm Workers	Irrigated Acreage	Ratio	Year	Hired Farm Workers	Irrigated Acreage	Ratio
1870	16,231	58,273	3.6	**1900**	**67,493**	**1,567,913**	**23.2** *
1871	16,994	85,084	5.0	1901	72,549	1,689,712	23.3
1872	17,756	111,896	6.3	1902	77,606	1,811,511	23.3
1873	18,519	138,707	7.5	1903	82,662	1,933,310	23.4
1874	19,281	165,518	8.6	1904	87,718	2,055,109	23.4
1875	20,044	192,330	9.6	1905	92,775	2,176,908	23.5
1876	20,806	219,141	10.5	1906	97,831	2,298,707	23.5
1877	21,569	245,952	11.4	1907	102,887	2,420,506	23.5
1878	22,331	272,764	12.2	1908	107,944	2,542,305	23.6 *
1879	23,094	299,575	13.0	1909	113,000	2,664,104	23.6 *
1880	23,856	370,041	15.5	1910	120,000	2,819,598	23.5
1881	26,624	440,507	16.5	1911	126,000	2,975,091	23.6 *
1882	29,391	510,972	17.4	1912	134,000	3,130,585	23.4
1883	32,159	581,438	18.1	1913	141,000	3,286,078	23.3
1884	34,926	651,904	18.7	1914	148,000	3,441,572	23.3
1885	37,694	722,370	19.2	1915	155,000	3,597,066	23.2
1886	40,462	792,836	19.6	1916	166,000	3,752,559	22.6
1887	43,229	863,301	20.0	1917	172,000	3,908,053	22.7
1888	45,997	933,767	20.3	1918	171,000	4,063,546	23.8
1889	48,764	1,004,233	20.6 *	**1919**	**174,000**	**4,219,040**	**24.2** *
1890	51,532	1,048,421	20.3	1920	187,000	4,271,799	22.8

(*Continued*)

Year	Hired Farm Workers	Irrigated Acreage	Ratio	Year	Hired Farm Workers	Irrigated Acreage	Ratio
1891	53,128	1,092,609	20.6	1921	191,000	4,324,558	22.6
1892	54,724	1,136,797	20.8	1922	193,000	4,377,318	22.7
1893	56,320	1,180,985	21.0	1923	196,000	4,430,077	22.6
1894	57,916	1,225,174	21.2	1924	196,000	4,482,836	22.9
1895	59,513	1,269,362	21.3	1925	200,000	4,535,595	22.7
1896	61,109	1,313,550	21.5	1926	196,000	4,588,354	23.4*
1897	62,705	1,357,738	21.7	1927	201,000	4,641,114	23.1
1898	64,301	1,401,926	21.8	1928	206,000	4,693,873	22.8
1899	65,897	1,446,114	21.9	1929	206,000	4,746,632	23.0*
1930	208,000	4,699,624	22.6	1951	246,000	6,682,214	27.2
1931	187,000	4,652,616	24.9	1952	242,000	6,804,159	28.1
1932	163,000	4,605,609	28.3	1953	241,000	6,926,104	28.7
1933	153,000	4,558,601	29.8	1954	236,000	7,048,049	29.9
1934	143,000	4,511,593	31.5	1955	231,000	7,117,553	30.8
1935	**136,000**	**4,464,585**	**32.8 ***	1956	232,000	7,213,278	31.1
1936	137,000	4,417,577	32.2	1957	226,000	7,309,002	32.3
1937	159,000	4,370,570	27.5	1958	227,000	7,404,727	32.6 *
1938	150,000	4,323,562	28.8 *	1959	232,000	7,395,570	31.9
1939	149,000	4,276,554	28.7	1960	228,000	7,436,196	32.6
1940	**150,000**	**4,411,821**	**29.4 ***	1961	230,000	7,476,821	32.5
1941	159,000	4,547,089	28.6	1962	216,000	7,517,447	34.8
1942	167,000	4,682,356	28.0	1963	205,000	7,558,072	36.9
1943	171,000	4,817,624	28.2	**1964**	**190,000**	**7,598,698**	**40.0 ***
1944	172,000	4,952,891	28.8	1965	190,000	7,526,985	39.6
1945	176,000	5,249,978	29.8	1966	187,000	7,455,271	39.9
1946	176,000	5,547,064	31.5	**1967**	**170,000**	**7,383,558**	**43.4 ***
1947	184,000	5,844,151	31.8	1968	190,000	7,311,844	38.5
1948	188,000	6,141,237	32.7	1969	187,000	7,240,131	38.7
1949	**190,000**	**6,438,324**	**33.9 ***	1970	197000	7,341,847	37.3
1950	247,000	6,560,269	26.6				

Note: Major peak years for the ratio of irrigated land to workers are indicated in boldface, with box and asterisk. Minor peaks of the ratio are indicated with box and asterisk.

Source: California irrigated acreage reported in U.S. Census 1870–1949 at 10-year intervals, subsequently at 5-year intervals. Intervening years are extrapolated. California hired farm workers 1870–1900 based on U.S. Census data at 10-year intervals reported by Fuller, "Supply of Agricultural Labor," table 33. Intervening years are extrapolated. Subsequent figures on hired labor were reported yearly by the California Agricultural Statistics Service, U.S. Department of Agriculture, California Department of Food and Agriculture, Agricultural Statistics Branch, Sacramento, CA.

TABLE A.2. Biographical Information

AWOC LEADERSHIP

Name	Age	Race/Ethnicity	Religion	Regional Background	Position
George Meany	66	White Irish American	Roman Catholic	New York, DC	President, AFL-CIO
John Livingston	52	White	Protestant	St. Louis, Detroit, DC	Director of Organizing
Norman Smith	62	White	Protestant	St. Louis, Detroit, DC	AWOC Director
C. Al Green	60	White	Protestant	Modesto	AWOC Director
Walter Reuther	52	White German American	Lutheran	West Virginia, Detroit	Vice President, AFL-CIO President, UAW

AWOC STAFF

Name	Age	Race/Ethnicity	Religion	Regional Origins	Position
Ernesto Galarza	54	Mexican	Roman Catholic	Nayarit, Mexico; Sacramento; DC	Assistant Director

AWOC LEADERSHIP

Family Background	Family	Education, Work, Organizing Experience	FW Organizing Interest	Networks	Repertoires
construction union officials	M, 3C	high school; elected officer, Plumbers, Building Trades, AFL	occupational	AFL-CIO, Democrats, Roman Catholics	union politics, legislative lobbying, national politics
Missouri farm family	M	high school; organizer, elected official, UAW	occupational	UAW, Democrats	CIO 1930s-1940s, auto organizing, union politics
Missouri farm family	S	high school (?); organizer, UAW, industrial supervisor	occupational	UAW, Democrats	CIO 1930s, auto organizing
	S	high school (?); elected officer, Plasterers; director, California COPE	occupational	building trades, Democrats	building trades, COPE
German immigrant, skilled trades	M	Wayne State, Brookwood; organizer, negotiator, elected officer, UAW, CIO	vocational	UAW, ADA, Democrats, liberals, Kennedy, farm worker advocacy	organizing, bargaining, legislative national politics, union politics

AWOC STAFF

Family Background	Family	Education, Work, Organizing Experience	FW Organizing Interest	Networks	Repertoires
immigrated from Mexico	M, 2C	Occidental College, Stanford, Columbia Ph.D.; researcher, Pan American Congress, NFLU	personal, vocational	NFLU, farm workers, labor, Chicanos, farm worker advocacy	research, advocacy, organizing

(*Continued*)

AWOC STAFF

Name	Age	Race/Ethnicity	Religion	Regional Background	Position
Clive Knowles	48	White	Unitarian	Pennsylvania, New England Iowa, California	UPWA organizer
Dolores Huerta	30	Mexican American	Roman Catholic	New Mexico, Stockton	organizer
Henry Anderson	32	White		Menlo Park, Berkeley	AWOC Research Director
Larry Itliong	46	Filipino	Roman Catholic	Philippines, Stockton, Delano	organizer, business representative
DeWitt Tannehill	45	White	Protestant	Oklahoma, California	organizer, business representative
Maria Moreno	35?	Mexican American	Roman Catholic	Tulare County	organizer
Fr. Tom McCullough	37	White Irish American	Roman Catholic	Bay Area, Stockton	volunteer organizer

Family Background	Family	Education, Work, Organizing Experience	FW Organizing Interest	Networks	Repertoires
coal miner	M	Bates College, University of Chicago, Harvard Divinity School; minister, Unitarians; organizer, CIO	vocational	UPWA, socialists, liberals, farm worker advocacy	ministry, political and union organizing
mining family, father (New Mexico) small business family, (Stockton)	M	College of Pacific; teacher; organizer, CSO	personal, vocational	CSO, liberals, farm workers, Democrats, farm worker advocacy	community organizing, lobbying
professional	M	Pomona College, Stanford, UC Berkely, Ph.D; researcher, UC Berkeley	vocational	liberals, students, farm worker advocacy	research, advocacy
Philippines, small farming	M	sixth grade; organizer, CAIWU, UCAPWA, ILWU; Filipino community organizations	personal, vocational	Filipino community, union organizers, crew leaders	union, community organizing
Mexican immigrant farm workers	M	Oklahoma migrants M high school (?); farm worker, organizer, AWOC	personal, vocational	Anglo farm workers	farm work
farm work	M	high school (?); Texas, migrant farm workers F farm work	personal, vocational	Mexican farm workers	farm work
blue collar, trade union	S		vocational	Missionary apostolate, farm workers, CSO community organizers	religious community, mutual benefit assn.

(*Continued*)

TEAMSTER LEADERSHIP

Name	Age	Race/Ethnicity	Religion	Regional Background	Position
Raul Aguilar	?	Mexican American	Roman Catholic	Stockton	organizer business representative
Ben Gines	?	Filipino	Roman Catholic	Philippines, Stockton, Delano	organizer business representative
James Hoffa	48	White German Irish	Roman Catholic	Indiana, Detroit	International Brotherhood of Teamsters, President
Einar Mohn	55	White Norwegian American	Lutheran	Washington, California	President, Western Conference of Teamsters
Peter Andrade	55?	White Portuguese American	Roman Catholic	San Francisco, Salinas	Director, Cannery Division
William Grami	40	White Italian American	Roman Catholic	Kentucky, Italy, San Jose	Director of Organizing, Western Conference of Teamsters

TEAMSTER LEADERSHIP

Family Background	Family	Education, Work, Organizing Experience	FW Organizing Interest	Networks	Repertoires
farm work	S	high school (?); farm workers, organizer, NAWU, AWA	vocational	NAWU, Mexican farm workers	advocacy, community organizing
Philippines, small farming	M	high school (?); farm workers, contractor	personal, professional	Filipino community, crew leader	union, community leadership
blue collar	M	ninth grade; organizer; President, Local 299, Central Conference, Vice President, Teamsters	occupational	Teamsters, Democrats, business associates	organizing, negotiating, politics
minister, teacher	M	University of Washington; microbiologist, organizer, negotiator, officer, Teamsters	occupational	Teamsters, Democrats, business associates	organizing, negotiating, politics
blue collar	M	high school; truck driver, organizer, business representative, Local 85; president, local 890	occupational	Teamsters, Democrats, produce industry	organizing, negotiating, politics
Italian immigrant, small business, police	M	Santa Clara College, Law School; U.S. Army; organizer, Local 912; president, local 624	occupational	Teamsters, Democrats, produce industry	negotiating, politics, organizing, military

(*Continued*)

TEAMSTER STAFF

Name	Age	Race/Ethnicity	Religion	Regional Origins	Position
Al Brundage	46	White	Jewish	Bay Area	General Counsel, Western Conference of Teamsters
Bud Kenyon	50?	White		Salinas	President, Local 890
Jim Smith	50?	White		Salinas, Modesto	organizer
Oscar Gonzales	37	Mexican American	Roman Catholic	San Jose	President, Local 964
Albert Rojas	28	Mexican American	Roman Catholic	Tulare County, Oxnard	Vice President, Local 964

UFW LEADERSHIP
(1962–1965)

Name	Age	Race/Ethnicity	Religion	Regional Background	Position
Cesar Chavez	35	Mexican American	Roman Catholic	Yuma, San Jose, Delano	General Director, FWA, NFWA, UFWOC; Board Member, Credit Union

TEAMSTER STAFF

Family Background	Family	Education, Work, Organizing Experience	FW Organizing Interest	Networks	Repertoires
professional	M	UC, Berkeley, BA, MA; University of Chicago, Law School; Member, War Labor Board, Pacific Labor Bureau	occupational	labor lawyers, Teamsters, Democrats	negotiations, representation, politics
		high school; business representative, Local 890	occupational	Salinas produce industry, cannery local, Teamsters	negotiations, organizing
		high school (?); president, UPWA Local 78; organizer, Teamsters	occupational	Salinas, Modesto produce industry, cannery locals	negotiations, representation, organizing
Mexican immigrants	M	high school (?); autoworker; community activist, cursillo member, farm worker associations	personal, occupational	*Cursillo*, Roman Catholics, farm workers, OEO network	religious community, mutual benefit assn., some union organizing
Mexican immigrant farm workers	M	high school; city worker; community organizer	personal, occupational	farm workers, Roman Catholics, OEO network, community organizers	community organizing, community work, some union organizing

UFW LEADERSHIP
(1962–1965)

Family Background	Family	Education, Work, Organizing Experience	FW Organizing Interest	Networks	Repertoires
immigrant small farmers, farm workers	M, A, 8C	eighth grade; farm worker; U.S. Navy; laborer; organizer, CSO	personal, vocational	family, farm workers, CSO, Roman Catholics, Democrats, farm worker advocacy, Chicanos	community organizing, political organizing, farm work, military

(Continued)

UFW LEADERSHIP
(1962–1965)

Name	Age	Race/Ethnicity	Religion	Regional Background	Position
Dolores Huerta	33	Mexican American	Roman Catholic	New Mexico, Stockton	Vice President, FWA, NFWA, UFWOC; Board Member, Credit Union
Antonio Orendain	35	Mexican	Roman Catholic	Jalisco, Mexico; Hanford	Secretary-Treasurer, FWA, NFWA, UFWOC; Board Member, Credit Union
Gilbert Padilla	35	Mexican American	Roman Catholic	Los Banos, Hanford	Vice President, FWA, NFWA, UFWOC; Board Member, Credit Union
Manuel Chavez	37	Mexican American	Roman Catholic	Yuma, San Ysidro, Delano	Secretary-Treasurer, FWA; organizer, NFWA, UFWOC
Rodrigo Terronez	28	Mexican American	Roman Catholic	Mexico, Corcoran	Vice President, FWA; Board Member, Credit Union
Julio Hernandez	41	Mexican	Roman Catholic	Sonora, Mexico; Corcoran	Vice President, FWA, NFWA, UFWOC; Board Member, Credit Union
Chris Hartmire	29	White	Presbyterian	New York, Los Angeles	Director, CMM
Jim Drake	24	White	UCC	Oklahoma, Indio, New York	organizer, CMM

UFW LEADERSHIP
(1962–1965)

Family Background	Family	Education, Work, Organizing Experience	FW Organizing Interest	Networks	Repertoires
miners (NM), small business (Stockton)	M, D, 6C	College of Pacific, teacher, organizer, CSO, AWA, AWOC	personal, vocational	family, CSO, Democrats, Chicanos farm worker advocacy	community organizing, political lobbying
	M, A, 2C	sixth grade; farm worker, construction worker, organizer, CSO	personal, vocational	family, farm workers, CSO	community organizing, farm work
farm workers	M, 4C	sixth grade; farm worker, U.S. Army, small business, organizer, CSO	personal, vocational	family, farm workers, CSO	community organizing, farm work, military
immigrant small farmers, farm workers	M, D, 3C	fifth grade; farm worker, U.S. Navy, produce sales, car sales, prison	personal, occupational	family, farm workers, business associates	business, sales, farm work, military
	M, 2C	high school (?); farm worker, organizer, CSO	personal	family, farm workers, CSO	farm work, community organizing
barber, carpentry, farming	M, A, 9C	high school (?); barber, carpenter, contractor, organizer, CSO	personal	family, farm workers, CSO	farm work, labor contractor, community organizing
professional	M, 2C	Princeton; Union Theological Seminary, U.S. Navy, minister, East Harlem Churches; organizer, California Migrant Ministry	vocational	CMM, church leadership, UTS, farm worker advocacy	seminary, community organizing, military
professional, ministry, teaching	M, A, 2C	Occidental College; Union Theological Seminary, minister, organizer, California Migrant Ministry	vocational	CMM	seminary, community organizing

(Continued)

UFW LEADERSHIP
(1966–1967)

Name	Age	Race/Ethnicity	Religion	Regional Background	Position
Fred Ross	56	White	Agnostic	Los Angeles	Organizing Director, NFWA, UFWOC
LeRoy Chatfield	31	White	Roman Catholic	Colusa County, Bakersfield, San Francisco	Director, NFWSC
Larry Itliong	34	Filipino	Roman Catholic	Philippines, Stockton, Delano	Vice President, UFWOC; Board Member, Credit Union
Andy Imutan	35?	Filipino	Roman Catholic	Philippines	Vice President, UFWOC; Board Member, Credit Union
Phillip Veracruz	62	Filipino	Agnostic	Philippines, Washington, Chicago, Delano	Vice President, UFWOC; Board Member, Credit Union
Jerry Cohen	26	White Irish Jewish		Upper South, California, Washington, Tokyo, DC	General Counsel, UFWOC

UFW LEADERSHIP
(1966–1967)

Family Background	Family	Education, Work, Organizing Experience	FW Organizing Interest	Networks	Repertoires
professionals	M, 3C	University of Southern California; community worker, Farm Security Administration; organizer, Civic Unity League, CSO	vocational	Alinsky, CSO, liberals	organizing, training organizers
farmers, business	M, A	St. Mary's College, Christian Brother, teacher, vice-principal	vocational	Catholic religious, liberals	religious community, teaching
Philippines small farming	M	fifth grade; farm worker; organizer, CAIWU, UCAPWA, ILUW, Filipino community organizations	personal, vocational	Filipino community, union organizers, crew leaders	union, community organizing
Philippines	M, A, 3C	high school; U.S. Army, organizer, AWOC	personal, professional	Filipino community, AWOC	military, AWOC
Philippines small farming	S	Gonzaga University; cannery worker, farm worker, restaurant worker; organizer, NFLU; crew leader, AWOC	personal, vocational	Filipino community	crew leader, union organizing
professional, medical, military	M, 1C	Amherst College, UC Berkeley Law School; lawyer, California Rural Legal Assistance	vocational	legal activists, lawyers	legal advocacy, antiwar protests, student organizing

(Continued)

UFW LEADERSHIP
(1966–1967)

Name	Age	Race/Ethnicity	Religion	Regional Background	Position
William Kircher	51	White German Irish	Roman Catholic	Ohio, California, DC, Michigan	Organizing Director, AFL-CIO

UFW Volunteers

Name	Age	Race/Ethnicity	Religion	Regional Background	Position
Helen Chavez	35	Mexican American	Roman Catholic	Delano	Administrator, Credit Union
Wendy Goepel	25	White	Protestant	New York	Administrator, FWA, NFWA
Bill Esher	25?	White	Roman Catholic	Oakland	Editor, *El Malcriado*
Alex Hoffman	35?	White	Jewish	Berkeley	Lawyer, NFWA
Eliseo Medina	18	Mexican	Roman Catholic	Zacatecas, Mexico; Delano	organizer/boycotter, NFWA, UFWOC; Board Member, Credit Union

UFW LEADERSHIP
(1966–1967)

Family Background	Family	Education, Work, Organizing Experience	FW Organizing Interest	Networks	Repertoires
professionals	M, 2C	Ohio State University; journalist, education director, organizer, administrator, UAW; organizing director, AFL-CIO	vocational	AFL-CIO, UAW, Democratic politics	union education, organizing, union politics, national politics

UFW Volunteers

Family Background	Family	Education, Work, Organizing Experience	FW Organizing Interest	Networks	Repertoires
immigrant farm workers	M, A, 8C	high school; farm worker	personal	family, farm workers, CSO	bookkeeping, farm work
professional	S	Mt. Holyoke, UC Berkeley, Stanford; researcher	vocational	students, CFL, SCAL	grant writing, academic research
	S	high school; Catholic Worker, Citizens for Farm Labor	vocational	Oakland Catholic Worker, CFL	editing publications, writing
	S	UC, Berkely Law School; Free Speech Movement, lawyer	vocational	legal activists, lawyers, socialists	legal advocacy, antiwar protests
immigrant farm workers	S	eighth grade; farm worker	personal, vocational	family, farm workers	farm work

(*Continued*)

UFW Volunteers

Name	Age	Race/Ethnicity	Religion	Regional Background	Position
Marcos Munoz	23	Mexican	Roman Catholic	Mexico, Bakersfield	organizer/ boycotter, NFWA, UFWOC
Roberto Bustos	25?	Mexican American	Roman Catholic	Delano	organizer/ boycotter, NFWA, UFWOC
Maria Saludado	22	Mexican American	Roman Catholic	Delano	organizer/ boycotter, NFWA, UFWOC
Tony Mendez	22	Mexican American	Roman Catholic	Delano	organizer/ boycotter, NFWA, UFWOC
Luis Valdez	23	Mexican American	Roman Catholic	Delano, San Jose	Teatro Campesino
Marshall Ganz	22	White	Jewish	Bakersfield	service provider, NFWSC; negotiator, boycotter, NFWA, UFWOC
Jessica Govea	18	Mexican American	Roman Catholic	Bakersfield	organizer, social services boycotter

Notes: Age = time at which persons undertook farm worker organizing. For and at 33, when she began working with the UFW. Family abbreviations: children).

Sources: Anderson 1996, Brown 1972, Chatfield 1996, Cohen 1995, Daniel London and Anderson 1970, Mathiessen 1969, Medina 1998, Meister and 1989, Scharlin and Villanueva 1992, Smith 1987, Taylor 1975.

		UFW Volunteers			
Family Background	Family	Education, Work, Organizing Experience	FW Organizing Interest	Networks	Repertoires
immigrant farm workers	M, 1C	sixth grade (?); farm worker	personal	family, farm workers	farm work
immigrant farm workers	M, 1C	high school; farm worker	personal	family, farm workers	farm work
immigrant farm workers	S	seventh grade; farm worker	personal	family, farm workers	farm work
farm workers, labor contractor	M, A	Seminary; farm worker	personal	family, farm workers	farm work
farm workers, laborers	S	San Jose State; organizer, SNCC; artist, SF Mime Troop	personal, vocational	family, student activists, liberals	student organizing, community theater
professional, ministry, teaching	S	Harvard; organizer, SNCC	vocational	civil rights groups, student groups	civil rights organizing
bracero, immigrant railroad, farm workers	S	Bakersfield College; community worker, CSO	personal, vocational	family, CSO	CSO

example, Huerta is listed twice: at 30, when she began working with AWOC, M (married); A (active spouse); S (single); D (divorced); and C (number of

1987, Drake 1997, Fink 1974, Hartmire 1996, Jenkins 1985, Levy 1975, Loftis 1977, Mitchell 1979, Nelson 1966, Padilla 1999, Reuther 1976, Ross

TABLE A.3. UFW Financial Information

YEARS	1969	1971	1974	1978	1982
ASSETS:START	$ 195,962	$ 590,046	$ 1,032,266	$ 1,779,990	$ 5,189,238
ASSETS:END	$ 352,548	$ 961,591	$ 792,535	$ 1,702,790	$ 4,878,835
LIABILITIES: START	$ 1,314	$ 133,508	$ 159,045	$ 133,686	$ 1,683,653
LIABILITIES END	$ 707	$ 2,847	$ 129,690	$ 93,225	$ 1,404,832
NET ASSETS: START	$ 194,648	$ 456,538	$ 873,221	$ 1,646,304	$ 3,505,585
NET ASSETS: END	$ 351,841	$ 958,744	$ 662,845	$ 1,609,565	$ 3,474,003
NET GAIN/LOSS	$ *157,193*	$ *502,206*	$ *(210,376)*	$ *(36,739)*	$ *(31,582)*
	81%	*110%*	*–24%*	*–2%*	*–1%*
REVENUE	$ **745,151**	$ **1,852,405**	$ **3,533,485**	$ **2,426,535**	$ **4,527,951**
DUES	$ 238,551	$ 1,109,453	$ 515,281	$ 1,477,348	$ 2,990,568
Dues%	32%	60%	15%	61%	66%
FEES		$ -	$ -	$ 150	$ -
	0%	0%	0%	0%	0%
FUNDRAISING	$ 403,154	$ 461,898	$ 2,332,375	$ 594,373	$ 378,230
Fundraising%	54%	25%	66%	24%	8%
SALE OF SUPPLIES	$ -	$ 6,046	$ 179,398	$ 2,607	$ -
	0%		5%	0%	0%
OTHER	$ 103,446	$ 275,008	$ 506,431	$ 352,057	$ 1,159,153
	14%	15%	14%	15%	26%
EXPENSES	$ **593,569**	$ **1,368,670**	$ **3,685,917**	$ **2,455,927**	$ **4,233,422**
PERSONNEL	$ 203,725	$ 490,292	$ 2,352,310	$ 586,360	$ 648,346
PERSONNEL	34%	36%	64%	24%	15%
PROFESSIONAL	$ -	$ 41,076	$ 73,031	$ 42,076	$ 202,260
PROFESSIONAL	0%	3%	2%	2%	5%
OFFICERS	$ 21,248	$ 29,982	$ 21,182	$ 20,270	$ 49,606
OFFICERS	4%	2%	1%	1%	1%
PRESIDENT	$ 1,992	$ 2,371	$ 2,260	$ 3,070	$ 7,445
# officers	$ 8	$ 8	$ 9	$ 9	$ 9
AVERAGE	$ *2,656*	$ *3,748*	$ *2,354*	$ *2,252*	$ *5,512*
ADMINISTRATIVE	$ 1,158	$ 285,377	$ 868,996	$ 781,800	$ 1,753,515
	0%	21%	24%	32%	41%
PER CAPITA	$ 2,859	$ 42,300	$ 29,259	$ 55,079	$ 96,927
Dues%	1%	4%	6%	4%	3%
OTHER	$ 364,579	$ 479,643	$ 341,139	$ 970,342	$ 1,482,768
	61%	35%	9%	40%	35%
Off, Prof, Adm	4%	26%	26%	34%	47%

	1986	1992	1996	2000	2003	2006
	$ 5,394,662	$ 6,629,563	$ 3,656,656	$ 3,129,133	$ 2,794,978	1,904,729
	$ 4,810,615	$ 5,517,847	$ 4,351,346	$ 3,439,847	$ 2,752,690	1,829,042
	$ 569,878	$ 1,839,899	$ 292,065	$ 243,304	$ 418,926	541,980
	$ 362,443	$ 1,108,619	$ 291,325	382,458	$ 537,136	611,173
	$ 4,824,784	$ 4,789,664	$ 3,364,591	$ 2,885,829	$ 2,376,052	$ 1,362,749
	$ 4,448,172	$ 4,409,228	$ 4,060,021	3,057,389	$ 2,215,554	1,217,869
	$ (376,612)	$ (380,436)	$ 695,430	$ 171,560	$ (160,498)	$ (144,880)
	–8%	–8%	19%	6%	–7%	–11%
	$ 4,331,036	$ 3,587,898	$ 5,093,260	$ 7,252,944	$ 6,711,849	6,373,269
	$ 2,208,802	$ 971,849	$ 1,429,838	$ 1,797,558	$ 2,001,466	2,261,405
	51%	27%	28%	25%	30%	35%
	$ -	$ 99,189	$ 515,484	$ 1,476,281	768,234	12,849
	0%	3%	10%	20%	11%	0%
	$ 2,064,062	$ 1,121,640	$ 2,785,619	$ 3,327,141	$ 3,762,939	3,960,207
	48%	31%	55%	46%	56%	62%
	$ -	$ 1,150,748	$ 100,005	$ 397,671	124,875	111,095
	0%	32%	2%	5%	2%	2%
	$ 58,172	$ 244,472	$ 262,314	$ 254,293	54,335	27,713
	1%	7%	5%	4%	1%	0%
	$ 4,545,195	$ 4,363,756	$ 4,688,013	$ 6,819,840	$ 6,607,587	6,624,551
	$ 527,629	$ 581,016	$ 1,215,585	$ 1,900,311	$ 1,723,146	2,295,165
	12%	13%	26%	28%	26%	35%
	$ 173,036	$ 216,059	$ 419,148	$ 663,976	$ 1,042,693	976,071
	4%	5%	9%	10%	16%	15%
	$ 53,934	$ 49,562	$ 108,720	$ 328,625	375,421	481,918
	1%	1%	2%	5%	6%	7%
	$ 5,140	$ 5,767	$ 11,347	32,882	77,704	82,082
	$ 9	$ 5	$ 8	11	$ 8	9
	$ 5,993	$ 9,912	$ 13,590	$ 29,875	46,928	$ 53,546
	$ 2,010,653	$ 1,425,657	$ 2,026,532	$ 2,313,446	$ 2,137,030	2,555,126
	44%	33%	43%	34%	32%	39%
	$ 81,587	$ 103,317	$ 138,471	$ 159,505	169,827	125,707
	4%	11%	10%	9%	8%	6%
	$ 1,698,356	$ 1,988,145	$ 779,557	$ 1,453,977	1,159,470	190,564
	37%	46%	17%	21%	18%	3%
	49%	39%	54%	48%	54%	61%

Notes

Preface

1. Brueggemann, *Prophetic Imagination*.

Chapter 1

1. Levy, *Cesar Chavez*, 207.
2. Morin, *Organizability of Farm Labor*; and Fisher, *Harvest Labor Market*.
3. "Radical" refers to unions with a revolutionary, socialist orientation.
4. In January 1964, the Farm Workers Association changed its name to the National Farm Workers Association (NFWA).
5. Seasonal agreements signed during earlier organizing attempts did not reorder power relations because they reflected the labor market conditions during a particular season, but failed to create new institutional arrangements that could influence those conditions in subsequent seasons.
6. Majka and Majka, *Farm Workers, Agribusiness and the State*, 136–199; Jenkins and Perrow, "Insurgency of the Powerless," 429–468; Jenkins, *Politics of Insurgency*, 137–144.
7. Snow et al., "Frame Alignment Processes," 464–481; Davis, "Narrative and Social Movements"; Ganz, "Power of Stories in Social Movements."
8. Brown, "United Farm Workers Grape Strike," 190–221; Majka and Majka, *Farm Workers, Agribusiness and the State*, 172–199; Jenkins, *Politics of Insurgency*, 162–172.
9. Nelson, *Huelga*; Dunne, *Delano*; Mathiessen, *Sal Si Puedes*.
10. Although often viewed as a personality attribute, charisma is better understood as the interactions between a leader and his or her constituents. Max Weber attributes the "charismatic" authority of religious leaders to their followers' experience of the "divine" sources of their authority in "The Types of Legitimate Domination," vol. 1, 215–216, 241–245, and "Charisma and Its Transformation," vol. 2, 1111–1157, of *Economy and Society*. Emile Durkheim describes the role of mythic leaders, or "civilizing heroes," as communal symbols in *Elementary Forms*

of Religious Life (New York: Macmillan, 1964 [1915]), 319–322. Randall Collins argues in "On the Microfoundations of Macrosociology" that charismatic leaders are "the focal point of an emotion-producing ritual that links together a large coalition; their charisma waxes and wanes according to the degree to which the aggregate conditions for the dramatic predomination of that coalition are met." And Rajandini Pillai links their emergence to a group's experience of crisis in "Crisis and the Emergence of Charismatic Leadership in Groups." Conger and Kanungo provide a complete discussion of research in organizational contexts in *Charismatic Leadership in Organizations*.

11. On the effects of charismatic leadership, see Hollander and Offermann, "Power and Leadership in Organizations"; and House, Spangler, and Woycke, "Personality and Charisma in the U.S. Presidency."

12. Stark and Bainbridge, *The Future of Religion*, report that in 1978 California hosted 167 of the nation's 450 cults, most of which had charismatic leaders. Carlton-Ford, "Charisma, Ritual, Collective Effervescence and Self-Esteem," reports that 22 of the 44 urban communes studied had charismatic leaders.

13. Tushman and Murmann, "Organization Responsiveness to Environmental Shock."

14. This concept of power derives from Weber's view of stratification as power relations that emerge from competition and collaboration among actors within economic, status, and political markets in *From Max Weber*, 180–195. Ralf Dahrendorf articulates another version in *Class and Class Conflict in Industrial Society*. Although resources are often construed in narrow economic terms, Weber's multidimensional view is echoed in Michael Mann's account of the ideological, economic, military, and political sources of power in *The Sources of Social Power*, vol. 1: *A History of Power from the Beginning to A.D. 1760*, 1–33; Pierre Bourdieu's analysis of "cultural capital" in *Distinction*, 11–96; and Rodney Bruce Hall's "Moral Authority as a Power Resource," 591–622. The role of resource mobilization in a social movement's influence was introduced by Anthony Oberschall in *Social Conflict and Social Movements*, 1–29; and Charles Tilly in *From Mobilization to Revolution*, 52–97. The institutionalized power relations with which social movements contend is explained by Lukes in *Power: A Radical View*. At the micro level, Richard Emerson argues that power grows out of exchange relations among individuals in terms of interests and resources in "Power-Dependence Relations," 31–44. To conceptualize power relations within organizations, I draw on a tradition going back to Michels in *Political Parties*; and, more recently, Gary Salancik and Jeffrey Pfeffer, who link organizational power to those with control over critical resources in "Who Gets Power."

15. Herodotus, *The Histories*, 551–555.

16. Cohen, March, and Olsen, "A Garbage Can Model of Organizational Choice."

17. Skocpol, "Emerging Agendas and Recurrent Strategies," 356–391; Lofland, *Social Movement Organizations*, 190–191; Sewell, "Three Temporalities," 245–280; Weick, "Sensemaking in Organizations," 10–37; Gersick, "Pacing Strategic Change," 499–518. On community, identity, and liminality, see

Turner, *The Ritual Process*. On identity formation in social movements, see Jasper, *Moral Protest*, 69–99. For distinguishing between moments of cultural continuity and change, see Smelser, *Theory of Collective Action*, 109–120; Turner and Killian, *Collective Behavior*; Swidler, "Culture in Action," 273–286; and Morris, "Birmingham Confrontation Reconsidered."

18. Alinsky, *Rules for Radicals*.

19. Gamson, *Strategy of Social Protest*, 1–13, 28–37; Skocpol, "Bringing the State Back In," 3–37.

20. Psychologist Albert Bandura contrasts this "emergent interactive agency" with "pure autonomous agency" and "mechanistic agency" in "Human Agency in Social Cognitive Theory," 1175–1184.

21. Van de Ven et al., *The Innovation Journey*, 95–124.

22. Hackman and Walton, "Leading Groups in Organizations," 72–119; Bartunek, "Multiple Cognition," 337–343.

23. Porter, "Making Strategy," 61–77.

24. Hutchins, "Social Organization of Distributed Cognition," 283–307.

25. I am indebted to Theresa Amabile's fine work on creativity presented in "A Theoretical Framework," 81–130. Her work links the micro behaviors to the macro outcomes I explain. In adapting her work, I substitute "salient knowledge" for "domain-relevant skills" to capture the critical importance of environmental information to strategic thinking, and I consider a broader range of motivational sources.

26. Research on this question at the intersection of psychology and sociology is summarized by DiMaggio in "Culture and Cognition," 263–287.

27. Deci and Ryan, "Empirical Exploration."

28. Amabile summarizes this research, including her own, in *Creativity in Context*, 131–152.

29. Taylor, *Sources of the Self*.

30. Weber, *Protestant Ethic*, 75–94.

31. Conti, Amabile, and Pokkak, "Problem Solving among Computer Science Students."

32. Zaltman, Duncan, and Holbeck, *Innovations and Organizations*.

33. Amabile, "A Theoretical Framework," describes these processes as breaking set during problem solving, understanding complexity, keeping response options open, suspending judgment, using wide categories, breaking out of "scripts," and being playful with ideas. Basil Bernstein relates the development of wider cognitive categories to creative thinking in "Social Class, Language and Socialization," 170–189. James March and Johan Olsen emphasize playfulness, or a "technology of foolishness," in *Ambiguity and Choice in Organizations*.

34. The role of analogical thinking in creative problem solving is discussed by Lakoff and Johnson, "Metaphorical Structure," 195–208; Gentner, "Mechanisms of Analogical Learning," 199–239; Langer, *Mindfulness*, 115–171; and Strang and Meyer, "Institutional Conditions for Diffusion," 100–112. "Bricolage," combining old elements in new ways, was first described as a means of problem solving by Claude Levi-Strauss in *The Savage Mind*.

35. The relationship between innovative thinking at the individual level and encounters with diverse points of view is discussed in Kasperson, "Psychology of the Scientist," 691–694; Langer, *Mindfulness*, 115–171; Rosaldo, *Culture and Truth*, 196–217; and Piore, *Beyond Individualism*, 140–167. The relationship between innovative thinking and diversity at the group level is discussed by Nemeth in "Differential Contributions of Majority and Minority Influences," 22–32; Weick, *Social Psychology of Organizing*, 1–23; Senge, *The Fifth Discipline*; Rogers, *Innovations*, 371–404; DiMaggio, "Culture and Cognition"; and Van de Ven et al., *The Innovation Journey*, 67–94.

36. Langer, *Mindfulness*, 61–80; Weick, *Social Psychology of Organizing*, 1–23.

37. Campbell, "Blind Variation," 380–400; Simonton, "Creativity, Leadership and Chance," 386–426.

38. Lipsky, "Protest as a Political Resource," 1144–1158; Gamson, *Strategy of Social Protest*; McAdam, "Tactical Innovations and the Pace of Insurgency," 735–754.

39. Weick, *Social Psychology of Organizing*, 1–23; Rogers, *Innovations*, 371–403; and Van de Ven et al., *The Innovation Journey*, 3–20, 125–148, 149–180.

40. Bruner, *Acts of Meaning*, 106–116.

41. Bernstein, *Class Codes and Control*, 170–189.

42. Chong, *Collective Action*, 31–72, identifies important reputational reasons for which people join movements.

43. William Gamson links strong and weak ties in a social movement context in *Strategy of Social Protest*, 145–180. Rogers links them to a business context in *Innovations*, 371–401.

44. Moore, *Creating Public Value*; Hamel, "Strategy as Revolution," 69–78; Alinsky, *Rules for Radicals*, 127.

45. Weick, "Sensemaking in Organizations," 10–37. Weber views organizational structures as mechanisms for the legitimate exercise of authority in *Economy and Society*, vol. 1, 12–15, 48–52, 212–301. Organizations as power structures is emphasized by Emerson, "Power-Dependence Relations," 31–44; Salancik and Pfeffer, "Who Gets Power," 2–21; and Charles Perrow, *Complex Organizations*. March and Olsen, *Ambiguity*, focus on organizations as venues for deliberation and decision making.

46. For the relationship of organizational form to founders' choices, see Child, "Organizational Structure," 1–22; Oliver, "Collective Strategy Framework," 543–561; Eisenhardt and Schoonhoven, "Organizational Growth," 504–529; Weick, "Sensemaking in Organizations," 10–37; and Clemens, "Organizational Form," 205–226. For the influence of organizational structure on innovation, see Zaltman et al., *Innovations and Organizations*; and Damanpour, "Organizational Innovation," 555–590. For the relationship of structure to strategy, see Chandler, *Strategy and Structure*, 1–18, 283–323.

47. Zaltman, Duncan, and Holbeck, *Innovations and Organizations*.

48. Duncan, "Multiple Decision Making Structures," 273–292; Hackman and Walton, "Leading Groups in Organizations," 72–119; Ruscio, Whitney, and Amabile, *Motivation and Task Behaviors*.

49. On formal procedures, see Osborn, *Applied Imagination*. On the influence of multiple sources of resources and authority, see Levinthal, "Three Faces of Organizational Learning," 167–180. On decision making by negotiation, see Nemeth and Staw, "Tradeoffs of Social Control"; and Bartunek, "Multiple Cognition," 337–343.

50. Nemeth and Staw, "Tradeoffs of Social Control," 722–730; McCleod, "Ethnic Diversity"; Hutchins, "Social Organization of Distributed Cognition," 283–307; Hackman and Walton, "Leading Groups in Organizations."

51. Bartunek, "Multiple Cognition," 337–343.

52. Van de Ven et al., *The Innovation Journey*, 95–124.

53. Oliver and Marwell, "Mobilizing Technologies for Collective Action," 251–272.

54. Pfeffer and Salancik, *External Control of Organizations*; Knocke and Wood, *Organized for Action*.

55. Powell, "Institutional Effects," 115–136.

56. Chambers, "Relating Personality and Biographical Factors"; MacKinnon, "Personality and the Realization of Creative Potential," 273–281.

57. Von Hippel, *Sources of Innovation*; J. M. Utterback, "The Process of Technological Innovation within the Firm," *Academy of Management Journal* 14 (1971): 75–88.

58. Weick, *Social Psychology of Organizing*, 1–23.

59. Lewis, Lange, and Gillis, "Transactive Memory Systems," 581–598.

60. Thomas Schelling clarifies the relationship of strategy to outcomes by distinguishing among games of chance, skill, and strategy in *The Strategy of Conflict*. In games of chance, winning depends on the luck of the draw. In games of skill, it depends on behavioral facility like hitting a ball. In games of strategy, it depends on cognitive discernment—in interaction with other players—of the best course of action, as in the game of Go. In most games, all three elements come into play. Poker involves chance (deal of the cards), skill (estimating probabilities), and strategy (betting decisions). Although chance may be dispositive in any one hand, or even one game, in the long run skill and strategy distinguish excellent players—and their winnings—from others. Similarly, environmental changes can be seen as "chance" insofar as any one actor is concerned. But, in the long run, some actors are more likely to achieve their goals than others because they are better able to take advantage of these chances. Environmental change may create opportunities for social movements to emerge, but their outcomes and legacies have more to do with the strategies that actors devise to turn these opportunities to their purposes, thus reshaping their environment.

Chapter 2

1. The historical material on which this chapter is based is drawn primarily from the following sources: for general California history, I use Rolle, *California*; Starr, *Inventing the Dream*; and Starr, *Endangered Dreams*. A political overview is provided by Delmatier, McIntosh, and Waters in

The Rumble of California Politics. Phillip Taft provides background on the AFL in *Labor Politics American Style*; and Donald Garnel provides a uniquely useful account of the Teamsters in *The Rise of Teamster Power*. The faculty and staff of the University of California have assembled an overview of California agriculture in *A Guidebook to California Agriculture*, edited by Ann Foley Scheuring. Lawrence J. Jelinek provides a brief but useful history of the industry in *Harvest Empire*. A history of farmer organizations is offered by Chambers in *California Farm Organizations*. Carey McWilliams provides an invaluable analytic history in *California: The Great Exception*, a special focus on agriculture in his classic *Factories in the Field*, and an early history of Mexican immigration in *North from Mexico*, which was updated by Matt S. Meier in 1990. For farm labor organizing, the fundamental work was done by Jamieson in *Labor Unionism*. Also indispensable are Cletus E. Daniel's *Bitter Harvest*; Devra Weber's *Dark Sweat, White Gold*; and Donald Fearis's "The California Farm Worker." Although the history of California's ethnic minorities has only begun to be written, a good account of Asian immigrant farm workers is offered in Takaki, *Strangers from a Different Shore*. With respect to Mexican immigration, Elac, *Employment of Mexican Workers*, is helpful. And Kiser and Kiser, *Mexican Workers in the United States*, brings together a wide-ranging set of essays and original documents. A useful account of the role of Italian immigrants in California agriculture is provided by Andrew F. Rolle in *The Immigrant Upraised*.

2. McWilliams, *Factories in the Field*, 48–65; Rolle, *California*, 148–158; Jelinek, *Harvest Empire*, 39–46; Pfeffer, "Social Origins," 540–562.

3. Takaki, *Strangers*, 84–85.

4. The federal Naturalization Law of 1790 reserved naturalization to "free white persons" who had resided in the United States for at least two years. It was upheld despite repeated challenges on behalf of Japanese and Indian immigrants and remained in force until the 1952 McCarran-Walter Immigration Act nullified its racial restrictions. See Takaki, *Strangers*, 82, 113, 207, 298, 413, 419.

5. Taylor and Vasey, "California Farm Labor," 108–122; McWilliams, *Factories in the Field*, 66–72; Fuller, "Supply of Agricultural Labor," 19803–19811; Fisher, *Harvest Labor Market*, 21–24; Daniel, *Bitter Harvest*, 26–30; Takaki, *Strangers*, 88–92.

6. McWilliams, *Factories in the Field*, 72–80; Daniel, *Bitter Harvest*, 28–32; Jamieson, *Labor Unionism*, 46–50; Delmatier et al., *California Politics*, 70–98; Mink, "Meat v. Rice (and Pasta)"; Takaki, *Strangers*, 92–131.

7. Olmstead and Rhode, "Overview of the History of California Agriculture," 1–27.

8. Taylor and Vasey, "California Farm Labor," 281–295; McWilliams, *California*, 103–126; Jelinek, *Harvest Empire*, 47–61; Daniel, *Bitter Harvest*, 33–39.

9. My principal sources for historical statistics on California agriculture and farm workers prior to 1940 are University of California labor economists Paul S. Taylor and Varden Fuller. See Taylor and Vasey's essay "Historical Background of California Farm Labor." Fuller's "The Supply of Agricultural Labor as a Factor in the Evolution of Farm Organization in California" was published in *Senate Hearings: Subcommittee of Committee on Education and Labor* 73

Congress, 3 Session (1940), pt. 54. The data used in table 1 and chart 5 appear in appendix A, table 25, 1983. Estimates of the average number of hired farm workers have been reported yearly since 1909 and monthly since 1925 by the U.S. Department of Agriculture, Agricultural Marketing Service. Before 1909, reports were made every 10 years, so estimates for the intervening years are extrapolated. The average number of hired farm workers is a better approximation of the number of "jobs" than of the total number of individuals who filled those jobs in the course of a year. Since large numbers of individuals worked for very short peak seasons, the number of jobs is a better reflection of the size of the core farm labor force—those who made their living primarily from farm work—than is either the number of individual workers who ever set foot on a farm or the peak level of employment.

10. McWilliams, *Factories in the Field*, 72–80; Daniel, *Bitter Harvest*, 28–32; Jamieson, *Labor Unionism*, 46–50; Delmatier et al., *California Politics*, 70–98; Mink, "Meat v. Rice (and Pasta)"; Takaki, *Strangers*, 92–131.
11. Taylor and Vasey, "California Farm Labor," 291; McWilliams, *Factories in the Field*, 105; Fuller, "Supply of Agricultural Labor," 1983.
12. Taylor and Vasey, "California Farm Labor," 291; McWilliams, *Factories in the Field*, 116–119; Takaki, *Strangers*, 302–306.
13. McWilliams, *Factories in the Field*, 103–133; McWilliams, *California*, 103–126; Takaki, *Strangers*, 179–229, 294–314.
14. McWilliams, *Factories in the Field*, 104–116; Jamieson, *Labor Unionism*, 50–54; Takaki, *Strangers*, 179–229; Daniel, *Bitter Harvest*, 74–75.
15. Jamieson, *Labor Unionism*, 50–54; Takaki, *Strangers*, 179–229; Fearis, "California Farm Worker," 56–68.
16. Fearis, "California Farm Worker," 60.
17. *Oakland Tribune*, April 1, 1903, cited in Almaguer, "Racial Domination and Class Conflict," 183–207.
18. Taft, *Labor Politics*, 11–33.
19. Almaguer, "Racial Domination and Class Conflict," 183–207; Takaki, *Strangers*, 197–200.
20. Fearis, "California Farm Worker," 62–63.
21. Daniel, *Bitter Harvest*, 3, 76.
22. Dubofsky, *We Shall Be All*, 81–87.
23. Ibid., 173–197; Starr, *Endangered Dreams*, 30–38; Daniel, *Bitter Harvest*, 81–86.
24. Daniel, *Bitter Harvest*, 79.
25. Taft, *Labor Politics*, 34–40; Daniel, *Bitter Harvest*, 77–82; Jamieson, *Labor Unionism*, 55–58.
26. McWilliams, *Factories in the Field*, 162; Daniel, "Labor Radicalism," 40–93.
27. Daniel, *Bitter Harvest*, 88–91; Starr, *Endangered Dreams*, 38–44.
28. Starr, *Endangered Dreams*, 44–46; Daniel, *Bitter Harvest*, 91–100.
29. Dubofsky, *We Shall Be All*, 313–318.
30. Jamieson, *Labor Unionism*, 63–65; Daniel, "Labor Radicalism," 75–80.
31. Cardoso, "Labor Emigration," 17–18; La Follette Hearings, 1940, pt. 54, 19848, cited by Jamieson, *Labor Unionism*, 63; Daniel, *Bitter Harvest*, 66–70.

32. Elac, *Employment of Mexican Workers*, 34.

33. Martin, *Promises to Keep*, 57; Kiser and Kiser, *Mexican Workers*, 4.

34. Martin, *Promises to Keep*, 58; Weber, *Dark Sweat, White Gold*, 55.

35. Perlman and Taft, *History of Labor*, 402.

36. Brody, *In Labor's Cause*, 40.

37. Daniel, *Bitter Harvest*, 87–91.

38. Bernstein, *Lean Years*, 144–189; Perlman and Taft, *History of Labor*.

39. Daniel, *Bitter Harvest*, 82–83.

40. Fuller, "Supply of Agricultural Labor," 1986.

41. Elac, *Employment of Mexican Workers*, 34–35.

42. These census figures are cited by Taylor and Vasey in "California Farm Labor," 291. They explain that "Mexican" includes persons born both in Mexico and in the United States. Because of undocumented immigration, however, estimates of Mexican immigrants are low.

43. Taylor and Vasey, "California Farm Labor," 288–293.

44. Weber, *Dark Sweat, White Gold*, 35; Fuller, "Supply of Agricultural Labor," 19862, 19871.

45. Weber, *Dark Sweat, White Gold*, 57–61.

46. Ibid., 61, 67–68.

47. Ibid., 71–72.

48. Weber, *Dark Sweat, White Gold*, 69–78; Fisher, *Harvest Labor Market*, 31–38, 42–90.

49. Jamieson, *Labor Unionism*, 74.

50. Taylor and Vasey, "California Farm Labor," 291, 293; Takaki, *Strangers*, 316–321.

51. Takaki, *Strangers*, 315–324.

52. Ibid., 101–102, 330–334. California's 1880 anti-miscegenation law barred issuance of licenses authorizing marriage of a white person with a "Negro, mulatto, or Mongolian." Mexicans were considered "white," but Filipinos were considered "Mongolian." When the 1933 California Court of Appeals ruled that the law did not apply to Filipinos because they were "Malays," the California legislature amended the law, adding "Malay race" to the restricted categories. In 1948, the U.S. Supreme Court found the law to be unconstitutional in *Perez v. Sharp*.

53. Among these Filipino immigrants were AWOC leaders Larry Itliong (1929) and Phillip Vera Cruz (1926).

54. Takaki, *Strangers*, 318–324; Fisher, *Harvest Labor Market*, 38–41; Fearis, "California Farm Worker," 82–83.

55. Jamieson, *Labor Unionism*, 71–72; Fisher, *Harvest Labor Market*, 98–102; Weber, *Dark Sweat, White Gold*, 38–42.

56. McWilliams, *California*, 123–126; Jelinek, *Harvest Empire*, 61–77; Fearis, "California Farm Worker," 6–18; Garoyan, "Marketing," 285–299.

57. Fearis, "California Farm Worker," 16; Rolle, *California*, 150–152.

58. Scheuring and Rochin, "Organizations in Agriculture," 245–250.

59. Chambers, *California Farm Organizations*, 21–30.

60. McWilliams, *California*, 210–213; Chambers, *California Farm Organizations*, 174–176.

61. McWilliams, *California*, 123.

62. Taylor and Vasey in "California Farm Labor" cite U.S. census data that, of the 196,812 California farm laborers in 1930, 41,191 were Mexican, 16,100, were Filipino, 14,569 were Japanese, 2,191 were Chinese, and 122,761 were white. Most of an estimated 160,000 year-round workers, however, were white, while most of the estimated 96,000 seasonal workers were not. These estimates of year-round and seasonal workers add up to more than the total farm workers because they are based on jobs, not people.

63. On the Mexican "repatriation," see Kiser and Kiser, *Mexican Workers*, 33–66.

64. Sam Adams Darcy, for example, the leader of their effort, was a 27-year-old Ukrainian immigrant from New York who had learned organizing in the needle trades, the Young Communist League, and the Lenin Institute. For more, see Daniel, *Bitter Harvest*, 130–134.

65. On the TUUL and CAIWU, see McWilliams, *Factories in the Field*, 211–219; Jamieson, *Labor Unionism*, 19–21, 80–88; Fearis, "California Farm Worker," 91–98; Daniel, *Bitter Harvest*, 105–140; Weber, *Dark Sweat, White Gold*, 83–88; Starr, *Endangered Dreams*, 61–74.

66. Daniel, *Bitter Harvest*, 167–178; Jamieson, *Labor Unionism*, 88–100.

67. Jamieson, *Labor Unionism*, chapter 3, table 117; and appendix D, table 3, 427.

68. Ibid., 87.

69. My account of the Imperial Valley strike is based on McWilliams, *Factories in the Field*, 224–226; Jamieson, *Labor Unionism*, 105–110; Bernstein, *Turbulent Years*, 160–168; Daniel, *Bitter Harvest*, 222–257.

70. On the success of the Associated Farmers' campaign, see McWilliams, *Factories in the Field*, 226–229 and 231–263; Jamieson, *Labor Unionism*, 113–115; Chambers, *California Farm Organizations*, 70–81; Bernstein, *Turbulent Years*, 168–170; Starr, *Endangered Dreams*, 81–83 and 156–194.

71. Jamieson, *Labor Unionism*, 116–133, provides the best account of the ethnic unions and their successes, which are absent from subsequent histories of the period. He provides examples of contracts won in 1934 by these unions in appendix G, "Strawberry Agreement," 430, and appendix H, "San Diego County Agreements," 430–432. The agreements are between Japanese growers associations and, in the strawberries, a Filipino union, and in San Diego, a Mexican union. The San Diego agreement was witnessed by the U.S. commissioner of conciliation, E. H. Fitzgerald. Takaki provides a brief account of the Filipino Labor Union in Takaki, *Strangers*, 322–324.

72. On the exclusion of agricultural workers from the National Labor Relations Act, a signal case of grower influence over federal labor policy, see Morris, "Agricultural Labor and NLRA"; and Finegold and Skocpol, *State and Party in America's New Deal*, 141–147.

73. Although boycotts had played an important role in labor organizing in the late nineteenth century, prosecutions under the Sherman Antitrust Act in 1890 discouraged their use during the first quarter of the twentieth century. The 1932 Norris-LaGuardia Act restored their legality, making them available to transport unions and others to use. See Miller, "Legal and Economic History," 751–759.

74. On the San Francisco general strike, see Bernstein, *Turbulent Years*, 252–298; Nelson, "The Big Strike," 225–264; Starr, *Endangered Dreams*, 84–120. On its impact on the CSFL, see Taft, *Labor Politics*, 87–110. On the longshoremen, see Kimeldorf, *Reds or Rackets?*

75. Garnel, *Teamster Power*, 64–91, 92–142.

76. Leiter, *Teamsters Union*, 100–102.

77. Garnel, *Teamster Power*, 64–91; Jamieson, *Labor Unionism*, 134–164; Taft, *Labor Politics*, 111–126.

78. On Bridges and Beck, see Minton and Stuart, *Men Who Lead Labor*, 172–202; Garnel, *Teamster Power*, 142, 158–159; Leiter, *Teamsters Union*, 47–55.

79. Garnel, *Teamster Power*, 72–76.

80. Ibid., 76–77; Gillingham, *Teamsters Union on the West Coast*, 6.

81. Jamieson, *Labor Unionism*, 144–145.

82. Taft, *Labor Politics*, 111–126.

83. Jamieson, *Labor Unionism*, 145–147; Taft, *Labor Politics*, 114–117; McWilliams, *Factories in the Field*, 268–273; Fearis, "California Farm Worker," 248–250.

84. Jamieson, *Labor Unionism*, 151–152; McWilliams, *Factories in the Field*, 268–273; Fearis, "California Farm Worker," 250–252.

85. Gilb, *Einar Mohn*, 378. The packing sheds were a different story. A focal point of strikes in the lettuce industry (1934, 1935, and 1936), their NLRA status was less clear. As litigation proceeded on whether agricultural workers did a certain kind of work, did it in a certain place, or did it for a certain employer—a matter not really resolved until the Santa Cruz Packing case in 1939—growers were not ready to concede the point. In July 1937, they formed the Agricultural Producers Labor Committee, chaired by W. E. Spencer, a director of Sunkist and the Associated Farmers, to gain an exception for packing shed workers from the NLRA. The 1937 Sugar Act also created a mechanism for setting the wages of field workers in sugar beets. The measure meant little in the absence of collective bargaining, however. In sum, the growers contested unionization in the courts, the legislature, and the fields.

86. Jamieson, *Labor Unionism*, 152–153; Zieger, *The CIO*, 71–75.

87. On the consequences of the dustbowl migration, see McWilliams, *Factories in the Field*, 305–225; McWilliams, *Ill Fares the Land*, 30–50; Weber, *Dark Sweat, White Gold*, 137–161; Starr, *Endangered Dreams*, 223–245; Fearis, "California Farm Worker," 158–198. On the topic of national attention to the plight of migrants, see Starr, *Endangered Dreams*, 246–271. On page 47 of McWilliams, *Ill Fares the Land*, the author offers insight into the impact of Steinbeck's *The Grapes of Wrath* on congressional debates on the resolution creating the Tolan Committee in May 1940: "Representative Lyle H. Boren of Oklahoma denounced *The Grapes of Wrath* as a 'dirty, lying, filthy manuscript'": and Representative Alfred Elliott of California referred to it as "the most damnable book that ever was permitted to be printed and put out to the public to read." Then along came Mrs. Roosevelt a few weeks later, and, after visiting the migrant settlements in California, she blandly announced that the novel did not exaggerate the conditions. This was apparently too much for Congress, and the resolution quickly passed.

88. Weber, *Dark Sweat, White Gold*, 162–179; Fearis, "California Farm Worker," 199–239; Rogin and Shover, *Political Change in California*, 119–124. McWilliams's account of this election includes the growers' response to McWilliams's appointment as chief of the Division of Immigration and Housing in *Ill Fares the Land*, 40–47. *Factories in the Field* was published just six months after his appointment.

89. McWilliams, *Factories in the Field*, 283–304; Weber, *Dark Sweat, White Gold*, 132–136; Starr, *Endangered Dreams*, 245–254. Cesar Chavez's mentor Fred Ross was introduced to farm unionism while an administrator of the FSA's Arvin camp, south of Bakersfield, which was used in the film version of *The Grapes of Wrath*. To the extent this influenced his later work with Chavez, growers may have been correct to suspect the "subversive" consequences of the FSA camps.

90. Jamieson, *Labor Unionism*, 179–186.

91. Ibid., 188.

92. Ibid., 179–186.

93. Ibid., 189–192.

94. Ibid.

95. "Man Refusing to Picket Beaten," *Los Angeles Times*, February 23, 1941, 14.

96. Chambers, *California Farm Organizations*, 105–107.

97. On the Associated Farmers' campaign, see McWilliams, *Factories in the Field*, 226–229 and 231–263; Jamieson, *Labor Unionism*, 113–115; Chambers, *California Farm Organizations*, 70–81; Bernstein, *Turbulent Years*, 168–170; Starr, *Endangered Dreams*, 81–83 and 156–194.

98. Taft, *Labor Politics*, 137–138.

99. On the origins and evolution of the wartime *bracero* program, see Wayne D. Rasmussen's "History of the Emergency Farm Labor Supply Program." The following are also useful: Craig, "Interest Groups and the Foreign Policy Process"; Galarza, *Merchants of Labor*; Kirstein, "Anglo over Bracero"; Calavito, *Inside the State*.

100. Rasmussen, "History of Emergency Farm Labor," 20–23.

101. Ibid., 199–233.

102. Data are from U.S. Congress, Senate Subcommittee on Immigration and Naturalization of the Committee on the Judiciary, Hearings, Control of Illegal Migration, 83rd Cong,, 2nd sess., 1954, 14. Since the figures on apprehensions are for the entire United States, they show the general trajectory of illegal immigration more than its relationship to the California labor market.

103. Gamboa, *Mexican Labor*, 1–31.

104. U.S. Department of Labor, *Migrant Labor*.

105. Hawley, "Politics of the Mexican Labor Issue," 97–99; Elac, *Employment of Mexican Workers*, 22–27; Galarza, *Merchants of Labor*, 58–71; Kirstein, "Anglo over Bracero," 133–172; Craig, "Interest Groups and the Foreign Policy Process," 86–100.

106. Gilb, *Einar Mohn*, 379.

107. Takaki, *Strangers*, 406–411; Meister and Loftis, *Long Time Coming*, 59–70.

108. On the origins of the NFLU, see Mitchell, *Mean Things Happening*, 214–231; Grubbs, "Prelude to Chavez," 453–469; Jenkins, *Politics of Insurgency*,

86–90. For Mitchell's history of conflict with the Communist Party, Henderson, and the UCAPAWA, see Dyson, "Southern Tenant Farmers Union," 230–252.

109. See http://freepages.genealogy.rootsweb.com/~nsbear/surnames/becker/Bill_Becker.html.

110. NFLU, "Plans for Organization of Agricultural Labor," cited in Grubbs, *National Farm Labor Union*, 456.

111. La Follette Hearings, 1939, pt. 48, 17479, 17714–17721; and La Follette Hearings, 1940, pt. 62, 22784–22785.

112. Mitchell, *Mean Things Happening*, 251–252; Jenkins, *Politics of Insurgency*, 93.

113. Mitchell, *Mean Things Happening*, 253–256; Jenkins, *Politics of Insurgency*, 93–96.

114. Jenkins, *Politics of Insurgency*, 93–96.

115. Taft, *Labor Politics*.

116. On public support for the DiGiorgio strike, see Mitchell, *Mean Things Happening*, 254–257; Jenkins, *Politics of Insurgency*, 96–99; Taft, *Labor Politics*, 192–193.

117. Hawley, "Politics of the Mexican Labor Issue," 97–99; Elac, *Employment of Mexican Workers*, 22–27; Galarza, *Merchants of Labor*, 58–71; Kirstein, "Anglo over Bracero," 133–172; Craig, "Interest Groups and the Foreign Policy Process," 86–100.

118. Hawley, "Politics of the Mexican Labor Issue," 97–99; Elac, *Employment of Mexican Workers*, 22–27; Galarza, *Merchants of Labor*, 58–71; Kirstein, "Anglo over Bracero," 133–172; Craig, "Interest Groups and the Foreign Policy Process," 86–100.

119. National Labor Relations Board, *Decision and Order*; Mitchell, *Mean Things Happening*, 257; Jenkins, *Politics of Insurgency*, 99–100.

120. Grubbs, "Prelude to Chavez," 460–463.

121. Mitchell, *Mean Things Happening*, 257–258; Jenkins, *Politics of Insurgency*, 99.

122. Scharlin and Villanueva, *Phillip Vera Cruz*, 13–16.

123. Kirstein, "Anglo over Bracero," 133–172; Hawley, "Politics of the Mexican Labor Issue," 97–99; Mitchell, *Mean Things Happening*, 233–234.

124. Chaired by Maurice T. Van Hecke, professor of law at the University of North Carolina and chair of Region 4 of the NWLB from 1942 to 1945, the commission included Archbishop Robert E. Lucey, chair of the Bishops' Committee for the Spanish Speaking People of the Southwest; William M. Leiserson, former chair of the National Mediation Board and former member of the NLRB; Peter H. Odegard, president of the American Political Science Association; and Noble Clark, the assistant director of the Agricultural Experiment Station of the University of Wisconsin and former deputy director general of the United Nations Food and Agricultural Organization. Executive secretary Varden Fuller, a respected University of California agricultural economist, had provided much of the economic context for the public's understanding of California farm labor in testimony before the La Follette Committee.

125. President's Commission on Migratory Labor, *Migratory Labor in American Agriculture*, 37–67.

126. Hasiwar says that Beck had a "hot cargo" bill in the legislature and made a deal to withdraw support from the strike in return for blocking the bill.

127. On the Imperial Valley melon strike, see Mitchell, *Mean Things Happening*, 264–269; Jenkins, *Politics of Insurgency*, 106–112.

Chapter 3

The "Resolution Establishing Agricultural Workers Organizing Committee" epigraph is from Watson, "Hidden War"; Einar Mohn is quoted in Taylor, *Chavez*, 323–324; Cesar Chavez is quoted in Goepel, "Viva la Causa," 25.

1. "Mitchell Hits at Conditions of American Farm Workers," *IUD Bulletin*, March 1959, 15.

2. Craig, "Interest Groups and the Foreign Policy Process," 243–246.

3. Hawley, "Politics of the Mexican Labor Issue," 105–110; Phillip Martin and David S. North, "Nonimmigrant Aliens in American Agriculture," in *Seasonal Agricultural Labor Markets in the U.S.*, edited by Robert Emerson (Ames: Iowa State University Press, 1984), 168–193.

4. National Sharecroppers Fund Conference, "Proceedings: Migratory Labor and Low Income Farmers"; Jenkins, *Politics of Insurgency*, 115; "Mitchell Hits at Conditions of American Farm Workers," *IUD Bulletin*, March 1959, 15.

5. Hawley, "Politics of the Mexican Labor Issue," 11.

6. Carmines and Stimson, *Issue Evolution*, xi–xv.

7. Delmatier et al., *California Politics*, 328–341; Jacobs, *Rage for Justice*, 71–75.

8. Mitchell, *Mean Things Happening*, 332–333.

9. *Monthly Labor Review* 82, no. 4 (April 1959): 396–398.

10. Much of the story of the origins of the Mexican-American "civil rights" movement remains to be written, but see Camarillo, *Chicanos in California*, especially 69–103; Skerry, *Mexican-Americans*; Burt, *History of MAPA*.

11. Veterans in the NFWA leadership included Cesar Chavez, Manuel Chavez, and Gilbert Padilla.

12. On Alinsky, see Horwitt, *Let Them Call Me Rebel*.

13. On Alinsky and Ross, see ibid., 212–238. On Ross, see Fred Ross, Jr., "Fred Ross: August 23, 1910 to September 27, 1992"; and Arax, "UFW Memorial Honors Lifelong Activist Fred Ross." Also see Tjerendsen, *Education for Citizenship*; Levy, *Cesar Chavez*.

14. Escobar, "Bloody Christmas and the Irony of Police Professionalism," 171–199. This case was portrayed in James Elroy's *LA Confidential* (New York: Mysterious Press, 1995).

15. Mathiessen, *Sal Si Puedes*, 43.

16. The foundation was established by Chicago philanthropist Emil Schwartzhaupt in collaboration with University of Chicago sociologist Louis Wirth to promote "citizen education." It funded much of Alinsky's work in this period.

17. For further information on the "California mission band," see page 159.

18. Although little has been written about Cesar Chavez's early years, his own account is given in Levy's *Cesar Chavez*, 3–96. Cletus Daniel offers a thoughtful perspective in "Cesar Chavez and the Unionization of California

Farm Workers," 350–382. Susan Ferris and Ricardo Sandoval tell the story in *The Fight in the Fields*, 10–35.

19. A uniquely detailed account of the work of Ross, Chavez, and CSO is provided by Tjerandsen in *Education for Citizenship*, 77–138.

20. Green, *Churches, Cities and Human Community*, 1–22; Ellwood, *Fifties Spiritual Marketplace*, 1–62.

21. Pratt, *Liberalization of American Protestantism*.

22. Steinle, "Retreat, Reentry, and Retrenchment," 212–234; Hartmire, interview.

23. Anderson, "Notes toward a Typology of Worker Organizations," 7–18. Published from 1963 to 1967, *Farm Labor* reported on events, perspectives, and news coverage of interest to those supportive of farm worker organizing.

24. Levy, *Cesar Chavez*; Taylor, *Chavez*; Meister and Loftis, *Long Time Coming*; Smith, *Grapes of Conflict*; Drake, interview; Hartmire, interview; Tjerendsen, *Education for Citizenship*.

25. Tjerandsen, *Education for Citizenship*, 116–119. On the Migrant Ministry, see Smith, *Grapes of Conflict*, 32–41.

26. Perella, "Roman Catholic Approaches," 179–211.

27. Ibid., 91–92; Horwitt, *Let Them Call Me Rebel*, 256–274.

28. London and Anderson, *So Shall Ye Reap*, 79–98.

29. Franz Daniels, assistant director of organization, AFL-CIO, cited in ibid., 46.

30. Gorman, "The Forgotten Farm Worker," 31.

31. Mitchell, *Mean Things Happening*, 340–343; Meister and Loftis, *Long Time Coming*, 93; Lichtenstein, *Walter Reuther*, 366–367; Zieger, *The CIO*, 360–369.

32. On Reuther, see Lichtenstein, "Walter Reuther," 280–302; Cormier and Eaton, *Reuther*; Barnard, *Walter Reuther*.

33. Lichtenstein, *Walter Reuther*, 334; Reuther, *The Brothers Reuther*; Cormier and Eaton, *Reuther*; Barnard, *Walter Reuther*.

34. On Meany, see Zieger, "George Meany," 324–349; Fink, *Biographical Dictionary of American Labor Leaders*, 239–240; Robinson, *George Meany*.

35. Zieger, "George Meany," 342.

36. Mitchell, *Mean Things Happening*; London and Anderson, *So Shall Ye Reap*; Fink, *Biographical Dictionary*; Zieger, "George Meany."

37. On Livingston's appointment, see Zieger, *The CIO*, 365–367; Fink, *Biographical Dictionary*, 206.

38. On Alinsky and Helstein, see Horwitt, *Let Them Call Me Rebel*, 212–215.

39. On Alinsky, Helstein, and Chavez, see Levy, *Cesar Chavez*, 125–131. For Ross's account, see Ross, *Conquering Goliath*.

40. Watson, "Hidden War."

41. Ibid.

42. Lichtenstein, *Walter Reuther*, 352–353; Meister and Loftis, *Long Time Coming*, 92–95.

43. London and Anderson, *So Shall Ye Reap*, 48; Mitchell, *Mean Things Happening*; Meister and Loftis, *Long Time Coming*; Jenkins, *Politics of Insurgency*; Anderson, interview.

44. London and Anderson, *So Shall Ye Reap*, 46–47.
45. Thompson, "Agricultural Workers' Organizing Committee," 83.
46. Anderson, interview.
47. Meister and Loftis, *Long Time Coming*, 127–128; Anderson, interview; Watson, "Notes on Larry Itliong Files"; Watson, e-mail communication with author, November 2, 1999.
48. London and Anderson, *So Shall Ye Reap*, 91; Levy, *Cesar Chavez*, 145–146.
49. London and Anderson, *So Shall Ye Reap*, 89–95.
50. Anderson, interview.
51. Levy, *Cesar Chavez*, 146.
52. Franz Daniels to John Livingston, December 9, 1960; Cannon, "Farm Labor Organizes," 1–34.
53. Mitchell, *Mean Things Happening*, 290–295.
54. Anderson, interview.
55. Thompson, "Agricultural Workers' Organizing Committee," 84–90.
56. Ibid.
57. Anderson, interview.
58. Ibid.
59. Ibid.
60. Williams held hearings from August 1959 through July 1960 in Washington, DC, Michigan, Wisconsin, Minnesota, New Jersey, New York, Pennsylvania, Florida, and California. See U.S. Senate, *The Migratory Farm Labor Problem in the United States*.
61. U.S. Department of Labor, *Mexican Farm Labor Program*. The report was prepared by Edward J. Thye, a former senator from Minnesota; George C. Higgins of the National Catholic Welfare Conference; Glenn E. Garrett of the Good Neighbor Commission; and Rufus B. von Kleinsmid of the University of Southern California.
62. U.S. Department of Labor, *Mexican Farm Labor Program*.
63. Craig, "Interest Groups and the Foreign Policy Process," 206–211.
64. Ibid., 211–221.
65. Anderson, interview; Thompson, "Agricultural Workers' Organizing Committee," 90–92.
66. 20 CFR 602.2(b).
67. Public Law 78, TIAS 2331, 2 UST 1940.
68. Thompson, "Agricultural Workers' Organizing Committee," 92–99; Bardacke, *Beneath the California Sun*, 1–22.
69. Thompson, "Agricultural Workers' Organizing Committee," 100–134.
70. In the course of 1960 and 1961, AWOC was involved in 151 labor disputes in which 10,447 employees took part, according to Thompson, "Agricultural Workers' Organizing Committee," 89.
71. Ibid., 159.
72. My account of AWOC's Imperial Valley strike draws on ibid., 135–163; Meister and Loftis, *Long Time Coming*, 101; Jenkins and Perrow, "Insurgency of the Powerless," 123–130; Kushner, *Long Road to Delano*, 109–114; and Bardacke, *California Sun*, 1–22.
73. Watson, "Story of a Contract."

74. Bardacke, *California Sun*, 4–5; Kushner, *Long Road to Delano*, 110.

75. Thompson, "Agricultural Workers' Organizing Committee," 135.

76. Ibid., 141–143.

77. Ibid., 148–149.

78. Ibid.

79. Bardacke, *California Sun*, 12.

80. Ibid.

81. Ibid.

82. Thompson, "Agricultural Workers' Organizing Committee," 149–154.

83. Kushner, *Long Road to Delano*, 113.

84. Watson, "Story of a Contract."

85. Anderson, interview; Bardacke, *California Sun*, 13.

86. Leiter, *Teamsters Union*, 127–131.

87. James and Dinerstein, *Hoffa and the Teamsters*, 19–22. The McClellan hearings initiated a feud between Hoffa and Robert Kennedy, who served as general counsel to the committee, which did not end until the imprisonment of one (1967) and death of the other (1968). Both became involved in the farm worker conflict.

88. Romer, *International Brotherhood of Teamsters*.

89. Troy and Sheflin, *U.S. Union Sourcebook*.

90. Watson, "Story of a Contract."

91. Ibid.

92. Glass, "Conditions Which Facilitate Unionization," 110–112, 129–130; Walsh and Craypo, "Union Oligarchy and the Grassroots," 269–293; Watson, "Story of a Contract."

93. Glass, "Conditions Which Facilitate Unionization," 129–130. The Jim Mapes Company of Brentwood, a small lettuce shipping region near Stockton, was the only employer to follow suit.

94. Glass, "Conditions Which Facilitate Unionization," 131.

95. *Los Angeles Times*, August 20, 1963, 1.

96. Romer, *International Brotherhood of Teamsters*, 8–11; Gillingham, *Teamsters Union on the West Coast*, 88; Leiter, *Teamsters Union*, 104–105; Garnel, *Teamster Power*, 150–151.

97. Garnel, interview; Gilb, *Einar Mohn*, 387.

98. Brundage, interview; Garnel, interview.

99. On Mohn, see Gilb, *Einar Mohn*; Fink, *Biographical Dictionary*, 251–252; Al Brundage, general counsel for the Western Conference of Teamsters, 1957–1968, interview by author, November 1998; Garnel, *Teamster Power*, 177.

100. Garnel, *Teamster Power*, 64–91.

101. Watson, "Story of a Contract."

102. Ibid.; Brundage interview.

103. Taylor, *Chavez*, 323–324.

104. James and Dinerstein, *Hoffa and the Teamsters*, 76–78.

105. Neuberger, *Our Promised Land*, 182.

106. Brundage, interview.

107. Romer, *International Brotherhood of Teamsters*.

108. The Antle contract came when Meany and Hoffa were involved in a complicated set of maneuvers regarding the relationship of the Teamsters with the AFL-CIO. Meany was adamantly opposed to reaffiliation or even mutual cooperation agreements as long as Hoffa was president, but he also resisted advocates of raiding the Teamsters. Hoffa's search for allies brought him into an ironic new alliance with the independent ILWU, which had been expelled from the CIO in 1950 for Communist influence, and Beck's archrival, Harry Bridges. See Romer, *International Brotherhood of Teamsters*, 128–139.

109. U.S. Senate, *Migratory Farm Labor Problem*, 12.

110. Thompson, "Agricultural Workers' Organizing Committee," 159–160; London and Anderson, *So Shall Ye Reap*, 52–56; Meister and Loftis, *Long Time Coming*, 102–106; Reuther, *The Brothers Reuther*, 368.

111. Bardacke, *California Sun*, 19.

112. Craig, "Interest Groups and the Foreign Policy Process," 221–235.

113. Williams, "Recent Legislation Affecting the Mexican Labor Program," cited by Craig, "Interest Groups and the Foreign Policy Process," 234.

114. Anderson, interview; London and Anderson, *So Shall Ye Reap*, 57–59.

115. Anderson, interview.

116. Ibid.; London and Anderson, *So Shall Ye Reap*, 57–59.

117. Huerta claimed that this was her proposal to the conference. See Levy, *Cesar Chavez*, 146.

118. Thompson, "Agricultural Workers' Organizing Committee," 161. In late 1961, a Stockton judge also awarded the DiGiorgio Fruit Corporation damages of $150,000 to be paid by AWOC for showing the film the NFLU had made about DiGiorgio. This was three-fifths of AWOC's annual organizing budget.

119. Craig, "Interest Groups and the Foreign Policy Process," 239–243.

120. Hawley, "Politics of the Mexican Labor Issue," 112.

121. Ibid.

122. Anderson, interview; London and Anderson, *So Shall Ye Reap*, 59; Thompson, "Agricultural Workers' Organizing Committee," 161–162.

123. For Fred Ross's account, see *Conquering Goliath*. Chavez's account is given in Levy, *Cesar Chavez*, 125–131, 132–137, and 138–144. Also see Horwitt, *Let Them Call Me Rebel*, 212–215.

124. Bardacke's research on the Oxnard campaign found little evidence of "several thousand" picketing Mitchell as had been mentioned in the Levy account. E-mail communication with author, October 17, 1999.

125. Ross, *Conquering Goliath*.

126. Tjerendsen, *Education for Citizenship*, 100.

127. Levy, *Cesar Chavez*, 143.

128. Ibid., 87.

129. Jacobs, *Rage for Justice*, 78–79.

130. Gilbert Padilla, vice president, United Farm Workers, 1962–1973; secretary-treasurer, UFW, 1973–1980, telephone interview with author.

131. Hartmire, interview.

132. Ibid.

133. Tjerendsen, *Education for Citizenship*, 112.

134. Padilla, interview; Hartmire, interview.

135. Metzler, "The Farm Worker," 17–24, 90.

136. Hartmire, interview.

137. It was eventually accepted and used to fund the Oxnard Service Center, which was independent of the FWA. Padilla, interview.

138. Mathiessen, *Sal Si Puedes*, 56.

139. Padilla, interview; Tjerendsen, *Education for Citizenship*, 77–116.

140. Rosaldo, *Culture and Truth*, 196–217.

141. Hartmire, interview; Jim Drake, minister-organizer, California Migrant Ministry, 1962–1965; boycott coordinator, UFW, 1965–1966; administrative assistant to Cesar Chavez, 1966–1968; New York boycott director, 1969–1971; organizing director, 1971–1972; New York boycott director, 1973–1975; organizer, 1975–1977. Interview with author, Boston, June 1997.

142. Levy, *Cesar Chavez*, 157–158; Taylor, *Chavez*, 107–108.

143. Padilla, interview.

144. Taylor, *Chavez*, 113–114; Levy, *Cesar Chavez*, xxi–xxv.

145. Hartmire, interview.

146. My account of the founding convention is based on Farm Workers Association, "Agenda, Founding Meeting at Fresno, California, September 30, 1962"; Farm Workers Association, "Minutes, First Organizational Meeting, Fresno, California, September 30, 1962"; Padilla, interview; Hartmire, interview; Levy, *Cesar Chavez*, 173–178.

147. Identifying accurate numbers is a recurring problem, especially because FWA leaders often used numbers more for motivation than analysis. Where records are available, I have used them, such as the LM-2 reports to the Department of Labor that began in 1967. Where not available, I compared the numbers given by the union, the press, the opposition, and other observers and, taking the interests of each party into consideration, have used the best estimate I can. In this case, 25,000 is based only on Chavez's report.

148. Farm Workers Association, "Acta Oficial"; Padilla, interview.

149. Farm Workers Association, "Acta Oficial."

150. Farm Workers Association, "Constitution."

151. Farm Workers Association, "Acta Oficial."

152. Horwitt, *Let Them Call Me Rebel*, 174–175.

153. Padilla, interview.

154. Mathiessen, *Sal Si Puedes*, 53.

155. Goepel, "Viva la Causa," 25.

156. Ibid.; Nelson, *Huelga*, 51; Padilla, interview.

157. Hartmire, interview; Drake, interview; Padilla, interview.

158. Goepel, "Viva la Causa"; Hartmire, interview; Drake, interview.

159. Levy, *Cesar Chavez*, 160.

160. Nelson, *Huelga*, 19–21; Hartmire, interview; Drake, interview.

161. Smith, *Grapes of Conflict*, 42–59; Hartmire, interview; Drake, interview; Padilla, interview.

Chapter 4

Green is quoted in Brown, "United Farm Workers Grape Strike," 168.

1. The following periodicals were particularly helpful in documenting farm labor organizing developments: *Farm Labor* was published from 1963 to 1967 in Berkeley, California, by Citizens for Farm Labor and edited by Henry Anderson. The *Valley Labor Citizen* is the official publication of the Fresno-Madera Labor Council, Fresno-Madera Building Trades Council, Tulare-Kings Building Trades Council, and Tulare-Kings Labor Council; it is published in Fresno, California, and edited by George Ballis. *El Malcriado* was the official publication of the Farm Workers Association, was published by the Farm Worker Press, Delano, California, beginning in January 1965, and was edited by William Esher. The *California Farmer*, published in San Francisco, is a conservative voice of California agriculture; the *Southern California Teamster* is the official organ of Joint Council 42, International Brotherhood of Teamsters, Los Angeles, California. These publications reported the news from the perspective of the supporters of farm worker organizing, the local AFL-CIO, the Farm Workers Association, the growers, and the southern California Teamsters.

2. Craig, "Interest Groups and the Foreign Policy Process," 239–264; Hawley, "Politics of the Mexican Labor Issue," 111–114.

3. *Oakland Tribune*, January 15, 1964.

4. *San Francisco Examiner*, February 23, 1964.

5. California Assembly Committee on Agriculture, "The Bracero Program and Its Aftermath."

6. *Farm Labor* 1, no. 4 (March 1964).

7. Ibid.

8. *Stockton Record*, March 11, 1964.

9. *Valley Labor Citizen* 59, no. 40 (March 20, 1964).

10. *Valley Labor Citizen* 60, no. 2 (November 26, 1965); *Los Angeles Times*, October 25 and 27, 1964.

11. *Farm Labor* 2, no. 5 (December 1964).

12. Harrington, *The Other America*.

13. Gitlin, *The Sixties*; Cowan, *Making of an Un-American*; Miller, *Democracy Is in the Streets*; Gamson, "Commitment and Agency," 27–50.

14. *Farm Labor* 1, no. 2 (November–December 1963).

15. Interview of John Soria by Kirke Wilson, appearing as "The Oxnard Farm Workers Service Center." The Emergency Committee to Aid Farm Workers funded a farm worker service center in Oxnard, which was staffed by John Soria and Jose Rivera. A forerunner of service centers soon to be established with OEO support, it offered social services like those offered by the CSO. During 1962 and 1963, it reported that 800 workers contributed $3 per month to keep it going. The emergency committee also set up a 400-member service center in the Imperial Valley run by UPWA organizers Ralph Perez and Joe Retes.

16. *Farm Labor* 1, no. 1 (September 1963).

17. Ibid.

18. Smith, *Grapes of Conflict*, 113–116.

19. Hartmire, interview.

20. Thompson, "Agricultural Workers' Organizing Committee," 161–162; Taylor, *Chavez*, 101–102; AWOC, Minutes.

21. Taylor, *Chavez*, 101–102; Meister and Loftis, *Long Time Coming*, 106–108; Anderson, interview.

22. AWOC, Memorandum to All Business Representatives from C. Al Green, January 31, 1964.

23. Fisher, *Harvest Labor Market*, 31–38, 42–90.

24. Taylor, *Chavez*, 101–102; Meister and Loftis, *Long Time Coming*, 105–108; AWOC, Memorandum to All Business Representatives; AWOC, Memo to Stockton Labor Contractors from C. Al Green, March 18, 1964; Anderson, interview.

25. Taylor, *Chavez*, 101–102, 125.

26. London and Anderson, *So Shall Ye Reap*, 59; Meister and Loftis, *Long Time Coming*, 106–108; AWOC, "Minutes of the First AWOC Meeting."

27. Meister and Loftis, *Long Time Coming*, 105–108; Anderson, interview.

28. The FWA newspaper, *El Malcriado*, depicted the labor contractor as "Don Coyote."

29. Taylor, *Chavez*, 101–102.

30. Scharlin and Villanueva, *Phillip Vera Cruz*, 29–30.

31. Meister and Loftis, *Long Time Coming*, 126–128.

32. Mathiessen, *Sal Si Puedes*, 56; Goepel, "Viva la Causa."

33. Ibid.

34. Mathiessen, *Sal Si Puedes*, 56; Goepel, "Viva la Causa."

35. Tjerendsen, *Education for Citizenship*, 98–100.

36. Ibid.; Goepel, "Viva la Causa"; Wilson, "The Oxnard Farm Workers Service Center"; Brown, "United Farm Workers Grape Strike," 259–260; Ross, *Conquering Goliath*; Padilla, interview.

37. Ross, *Conquering Goliath*; Levy, *Cesar Chavez*, 125–144.

38. Goepel, "Viva la Causa"; Taylor, *Chavez*, 111; Ganz, oral history interview.

39. Brown, "United Farm Workers Grape Strike," 258–259; Padilla, interview; Ganz, oral history interview.

40. Goepel, "Viva la Causa"; *El Malcriado*, no. 1, January 1965.

41. Taylor, *Chavez*, 111.

42. Ferris and Sandoval, *Fight in the Fields*, 74–75.

43. Brown, "United Farm Workers Grape Strike," 259.

44. Eliseo Medina, organizer, United Farm Workers, 1966–1977; Chicago boycott director, 1967–1970 and 1973–1975; national Executive Board member, 1973–1977; vice president, 1977–1978. Interview with author.

45. Padilla, interview.

46. Ibid.

47. Morris, "Probation Report concerning Manuel Chavez," June 8, 1964.

48. Padilla, interview.

49. Ibid.

50. Drake, interview.

51. Taylor, *Chavez*, 116.

52. *San Francisco Examiner*, February 27, 1964.

53. Smith, *Grapes of Conflict*, 50–59; Hartmire, interview; Drake, interview; Padilla, interview.
54. Adair, oral history interview.
55. Medina, interview.
56. Adair, oral history interview.
57. Mathiessen, *Sal Si Puedes*, 58–59; Taylor, *Chavez*, 131.
58. Taylor, *Chavez*, 129–130; *El Malcriado*, no. 1, January 1965.
59. *El Malcriado*, no. 6, March 19, 1965.
60. Padilla, interview.
61. *El Malcriado*, no. 1, January 1965.
62. Translation by the author.
63. *Los Angeles Times*, April 20, 1965.
64. *San Francisco Chronicle*, February 20, 1965.
65. *Farm Labor* 3, no. 2 (July 1965).
66. *Los Angeles Times*, February 14, 1965.
67. *San Francisco Examiner*, March 23, 1965.
68. *San Jose Mercury News*, April 16, 1965. The California Farm Labor Panel was chaired by Benjamin Aaron, the director of the Institute of Industrial Relations, UCLA, and included Daniel G. Aldrich, Jr., the chancellor of the University of California at Irvine, and Arthur M. Ross, a professor of business administration at Berkeley. It served from April 1965 to December 1965.
69. *San Francisco Chronicle*, April 25, 1965.
70. *Farm Labor* 3, no. 2 (July 1965).
71. *Sacramento Bee*, June 18, 1965; *Monterey Bay Labor News*, June 24, 1965.
72. *Farm Labor* 3, no. 3 (August 1965).
73. *Sacramento Bee*, July 31, 1965; *Farm Labor* 3, no. 4 (September 1965).
74. *Sacramento Bee*, April 4, 1965.
75. *Farm Labor* 3, no. 1 (May 1965); no. 2 (July 1965).
76. *Patterson Irrigator*, January 14, 1965.
77. *San Francisco News-Call Bulletin*, March 24, 1965.
78. *Farm Labor* 2, no. 1 (May 1965).
79. *San Francisco Examiner*, March 25, 1965.
80. *San Francisco Chronicle*, March 26, 1965; *Salinas Californian*, March 26, 1965.
81. *San Francisco Examiner*, March 28, 1965.
82. *California Farmer*, April 17, 1965.
83. *Farm Labor* 2, no. 4 (September 1965).
84. Taylor, interview.
85. *Farm Labor* 3, no. 5 (July 1965).
86. Ibid.
87. Adair, oral history interview.
88. *Farm Labor* 3, no. 5 (July 1965).
89. "Green to William De Paoli, Manager, California Asparagus Association, March 18, 1965," *Farm Labor* 3, no. 1 (May 1965).
90. "Green to Wirtz, March 24, 1965," *Farm Labor* 3, no. 1 (May 1965).
91. Ibid.
92. Burt, *History of MAPA*.
93. Padilla, interview.
94. Ibid.

95. *El Malcriado*, no. 11, May 1965.

96. *Sacramento Bee*, April 1, 1965.

97. *Valley Labor Citizen*, no. 44 (April 16, 1965); *Farm Labor* 3, no. 1 (May 1965).

98. Adams, "The Grape Industry."

99. Nelson, *Harvesting and Handling*, 12.

100. *Valley Labor Citizen* 60, no. 51 (June 4, 1965).

101. Ibid., June 5, 1965. Lionel Steinberg would also be the first table grape grower to sign with UFWOC as a result of the table grape boycott in 1970.

102. *Valley Labor Citizen* 60, no. 51 (June 5, 1965).

103. *El Malcriado*, no. 11, June 11, 1965.

104. Goepel, "Viva la Causa"; *El Malcriado*, no. 10, May 14, 1965; Taylor, *Chavez*, 119; Meister and Loftis, *Long Time Coming*, 124–125.

105. Ferris and Sandoval, *Fight in the Fields*, 82–83.

106. Taylor, *Chavez*, 119; Hartmire, interview; Drake, interview; Padilla, interview.

107. Taylor, *Chavez*, 119; Hartmire, interview.

108. *El Malcriado*, no. 11, May 28, 1965; Levy, *Cesar Chavez*, 179–181.

109. Taylor, *Chavez*, 121–122.

110. Padilla, interview.

111. *Farm Labor* 3, no. 3 (August 1965); no. 4 (September 1965).

112. Ronald B. Taylor, farm labor reporter for the *Fresno Bee*, 1959–1975, and the *Los Angeles Times*, 1975–1990, telephone interview by the author, March 1999.

113. Padilla, interview.

114. Ibid.

115. *Valley Labor Citizen* 30, no. 6 (July 23, 1965).

116. *El Malcriado*, no. 14, July 9, 1965.

117. Translation by the author.

118. *Valley Labor Citizen* 30, no. 6 (July 23, 1965); *Farm Labor* 2, no. 3 (August 1965); the *Movement*, publication of the Student Non-Violent Coordinating Committee, San Francisco, August 1965; Taylor, interview. I first read about the FWA in the August 1965 *Movement* account of the rent strike.

119. Brown, "United Farm Workers Grape Strike," 122.

120. Levy, *Cesar Chavez*, 181.

121. In addition to sources on the civil rights movement mentioned above, the following provide useful background on this period: Edsall and Edsall, *Chain Reaction*; Goodwin, *Remembering America*; Margolis, *Last Innocent Year*.

122. *Valley Labor Citizen*, no. 40 (March 19, 1965).

123. *El Malcriado*, no. 11, May 28, 1965.

124. Padilla, interview.

125. Smith, *Grapes of Conflict*, 117–118.

126. Padilla, interview.

127. Ibid.

128. Taylor, *Chavez*, 130.

129. *El Malcriado*, no. 17, August 20, 1965.

130. Hartmire, interview.

131. Padilla, interview.

132. *El Malcriado*, no. 16, August 6, 1965; no. 17, August 20, 1965; no. 18, September 3, 1965.
133. Taylor, *Chavez*, 130; Padilla, interview.
134. *El Malcriado*, no. 19, September 17, 1965.
135. Ganz, oral history interview.

Chapter 5

1. For documentation on the California table grape industry, I rely on the following sources: Allmeddinger, *California Grape Industry*; Adams, "The Grape Industry"; Jamison, *California Fresh Deciduous Fruit Industry*; Federal-State Market News Service, *Marketing California Grapes*.
2. Dunne, *Delano*, 105; Meister and Loftis, *Long Time Coming*, 131–133; Vucinich, "Yugoslavs in California," 287–309; Marshall Ganz to Jack Minnis, SNCC Research Director, November 4, 1965, in personal collection of author.
3. Dunne, *Delano*, 105.
4. Brown, "Fruit and Nut Crops," 147–152.
5. Nelson, *Harvesting and Handling*, 107–108. By the 1980s, most wine grape harvesting had been mechanized while table grape harvesting remains as labor intensive today as in the 1960s.
6. Metzler, "The Farm Worker," 47.
7. Ibid., 17–24.
8. Allmedinger, *California Grape Industry*; Adams, "The Grape Industry."
9. Brown, "United Farm Workers Grape Strike," 110–111; Meister and Loftis, *Long Time Coming*, 131–133; Blum, "The Other Delano Grape Growers"; Dunne, *Delano*, 109–110.
10. Allmedinger, *California Grape Industry*; Adams, "The Grape Industry." According to Garoyan, "Marketing," 290–291, since the enactment of the California Marketing Act of 1937, growers of a particular commodity can vote to impose a tax on themselves to establish mechanisms to regulate production, set standards, conduct research, market their products, and so forth.
11. DiGiorgio Corporation, *Securities and Exchange Commission Report*; Geier, "Three Case Studies in Agri-Industry," 10–11.
12. Altman, "Financial Survey of Schenley Industries," 41–60.
13. Schenley Industries, "Letter to Stockholders," Annual Report 1941, 7, and 1942, 16.
14. Schenley Industries, Annual Report, Form 10-K, Securities and Exchange Commission; Dunne, *Delano*, 127.
15. Chairman Lewis Rosenstiel and President Lester Jacobi, in Schenley's "Letter to Stockholders," May 22, 1940, declare: "In its relations with employees your company has from the beginning been guided by modern and liberal conceptions" (5). In their November 12, 1941, letter, they report: "Schenley Plants operate under regulations established by union contracts. Negotiations between representatives of the company and the union members have been amicable and cooperative in every instance" (10–11). And in their August 31, 1948, letter they report: "During the past fiscal year,

agreements were signed with approximately 100 locals of the AF of L, CIO and other unions" (17).

16. Anderson, interview; Scharlin and Villanueva, *Phillip Vera Cruz*, 28–29.

17. Wattell, "Lewis Solon Rosenstiel," 701–703; *Who Was Who*, Lewis Solon Rosenstiel, 352.

18. Taylor, *Chavez*, 124; *Valley Labor Citizen*, no. 14 (September 17, 1965); no. 15 (September 24, 1965).

19. Taylor, *Chavez*, 124–125; *Valley Labor Citizen*, no. 14 (September 17, 1965).

20. AWOC, "Delano Grape Strike Calendar."

21. Taylor, *Chavez*, 124.

22. Ibid.; *Fresno Bee*, September 10, 1965.

23. Padilla, interview.

24. Nelson, *Huelga*, 20–23; Taylor, *Chavez*, 125–126. Nelson provides a first-person account of the first 100 days of the grape strike from his perspective as a UFW volunteer organizer, a role in which he served from 1965 to 1967.

25. Medina, interview.

26. Padilla, interview.

27. Nelson, *Huelga*, 20–22.

28. Levy, *Cesar Chavez*, 183–185; Nelson, *Huelga*, 22–24; Drake, interview; Hartmire, interview; Padilla, interview; Taylor, *Chavez*, 126.

29. Levy, *Cesar Chavez*, 183–185; Taylor, *Chavez*, 126–128.

30. Hartmire, interview; Levy, *Cesar Chavez*, 185.

31. Chatfield, interview; Padilla, interview.

32. Levy, *Cesar Chavez*, 185.

33. Medina, interview.

34. Levy, *Cesar Chavez*, 183–185; Nelson, *Huelga*, 24–28; Drake, interview; Hartmire, interview; Medina, interview; Padilla, interview.

35. Padilla, interview; UFW Chronology, September 19, 1965.

36. *El Malcriado*, no. 19, September 1965.

37. Brown, "United Farm Workers Grape Strike," 168.

38. Levy, *Cesar Chavez*, 186.

39. Hartmire, interview.

40. *Valley Labor Citizen*, no. 15 (September 24, 1965); Ann Draper, "Grapes of Wrath, 1965 Vintage," *Farm Labor* 3, no. 5 (October 1965); Nelson, *Huelga*, 31–32, 74–75.

41. Nelson, *Huelga*, 33–43; Taylor, *Chavez*, 129–140; Meister and Loftis, *Long Time Coming*, 134–136; Drake, interview; Padilla, interview.

42. Brown, "United Farm Workers Grape Strike," 168–188.

43. Taylor, *Chavez*, 146–147.

44. Hartmire, interview; Drake, interview.

45. Hartmire, interview.

46. Meister and Loftis, *Long Time Coming*, 135.

47. *California Farmer*, November 20, 1965.

48. *San Francisco Chronicle*, October 11, 1965.

49. Taylor, *Chavez*, 151.

50. *Farm Labor* 3, no. 6 (November 1965).

51. Hirschman, "Against Parsimony," 89–96.

52. Brown, "United Farm Workers Grape Strike," 264–265.
53. Ibid., 255, 265–268.
54. Ibid., 264–265.
55. Ibid., 261; Ganz, oral history interview.
56. Mathiessen, *Sal Si Puedes.*
57. Medina, interview.
58. Ibid.
59. Rojas, interview.
60. AWOC, minutes of AWOC strike meetings.
61. Mathiessen, *Sal Si Puedes.*
62. Taylor, *Sources of the Self.*
63. Dunne, *Delano*, 24.
64. Nelson, *Huelga*, 59–60.
65. Taylor, *Chavez*, 142–143; Nelson, *Huelga*, 96–97.
66. Brown, "United Farm Workers Grape Strike," 160–161; Nelson, *Huelga*, 97–99, 101–105; Drake, interview.
67. Hartmire, interview.
68. Brown, "United Farm Workers Grape Strike," 161; Levy, *Cesar Chavez*, 192–193.
69. Levy, *Cesar Chavez*, 196–197.
70. Dunne, *Delano*, 110.
71. Meister and Loftis, *Long Time Coming*, 133.
72. As recounted in chapter 2, the Agricultural Labor Bureau played a key role in the 1930s strikes.
73. Taylor, interview.
74. *California Farmer*, October 2, 1965.
75. *California Council of Growers Newsletter*, November 1, 1965.
76. *San Francisco Examiner*, November 9, 1965.
77. Dunne, *Delano*, 106.
78. Ibid., 104.
79. Taylor, interview.
80. Ibid., 110–113.
81. Taylor, *Chavez*, 160–162; *Valley Labor Citizen*, no. 30 (January 28, 1966).
82. Taylor, interview.
83. Dunne, *Delano*, 103.
84. Taylor, *Chavez*, 152–153.
85. Padilla, interview.
86. *San Francisco Chronicle*, November 18, 1965.
87. Ibid., November 29, 1965.
88. Ibid., December 17, 1965.
89. Ganz to Minnis, November 4, 1965; Drake, interview.
90. *San Francisco Chronicle*, October 12, 1965.
91. *NFWA Boycott Newsletter*, December 17, 1965, in possession of author; Drake, interview.
92. "List of Boycott Centers, National Boycott Schenley Liquors and Delano Grapes, Memo #1, January 1966," in possession of author. Of 25 boycott centers, 6 were CORE contacts, 4 were SNCC contacts, 2 were SDS

contacts, 2 were CMM contacts, 1 was a Mississippi Freedom Democratic Party contact, and 10 listed no formal affiliation. Centers outside California were in New York, Chicago, Washington, DC, Boston, Detroit, Cleveland, Philadelphia, Baltimore, Newark, Hoboken, Atlanta, and New Orleans. California centers were located in Los Angeles, San Francisco, Marin County, Contra Costa County, the Mid-Peninsula, San Jose, Davis, Sacramento, Modesto, Fresno, and Bakersfield.

93. "List of Boycott Centers, National Boycott Schenley Liquors and Delano Grapes, Memo #1, January 1966," in possession of author.

94. *Valley Labor Citizen*, no. 26 (December 17, 1965).

95. "Don't Buy Roma" leaflet, in possession of author; Drake, interview.

96. Smith, *Grapes of Conflict*, 136.

97. AFL-CIO, Resolution No. 221, Proceedings of the Sixth Constitutional Convention of the AFL-CIO, San Francisco, December 14, 1965.

98. Schrade, e-mail; Meister and Loftis, *Long Time Coming*, 138–139.

99. Ibid.

100. Taylor, interview.

101. Ganz, oral history interview.

102. *Valley Labor Citizen*, no. 27 (December 24, 1965); Taylor, *Chavez*, 155.

103. Taylor, *Chavez*, 155.

104. Ganz, oral history interview.

105. Herman Levitt, secretary-treasurer, Hotel and Restaurant Employees Union, Los Angeles Council, 1960–1996, interview by author; *Valley Labor Citizen*, no. 28 (January 7, 1966).

106. Ibid., 153.

107. Taylor, *Chavez*, 152–154.

108. *San Francisco Chronicle*, December 22, 1965.

109. *Movement*, January 20, 1966.

110. Ibid.

111. *Valley Labor Citizen*, no. 34 (January 18, 1966).

112. *Los Angeles Times*, December 24, 1965.

113. Taylor, *Chavez*, 155–157.

114. *Movement*, January 20, 1966.

115. Morris, "Agricultural Labor and NLRA"; *California AFL-CIO News*, February 18, 1966.

116. *Schenley Boycott Newsletter*, February 20, 1966, in possession of author.

117. *El Malcriado*, no. 30, February 28, 1966.

118. Ibid., no. 25, December 15, 1965.

119. Ibid., no. 30, February 28, 1966.

120. Chatfield, interview.

121. Ibid.

122. Drake, interview; Ganz, "Notes on the March to Sacramento."

123. Ganz, "Notes on the March to Sacramento."

124. *Los Angeles Times*, January 6, 1966.

125. Levy, *Cesar Chavez*, 206–207.

126. *Valley Labor Citizen*, no. 40 (March 19, 1965).

127. Wilson, *The Amateur Democrat*; Jacobs, *Rage for Justice*, 97–98.
128. *Farm Labor* 4, no. 2 (March 1966).
129. Ibid.
130. Schrade, e-mail; Reuther, *The Brothers Reuther*, 368.
131. Schrade, e-mail; Edelman, e-mail.
132. Dunne, *Delano*, 83.
133. Taylor, *Chavez*, 159.
134. Ibid., 160–161.
135. Ibid., 165–167.
136. Brown, "United Farm Workers Grape Strike," 161–162; Ganz, oral history interview.
137. Levy, *Cesar Chavez*, 208–209.
138. Ibid.; Ganz, oral history interview.
139. Meister and Loftis, *Long Time Coming*, 144–145.
140. *El Malcriado*, no. 33, April 10, 1966.
141. Brown, "United Farm Workers Grape Strike," 168.
142. Levy, *Cesar Chavez*, 208–209; Ganz, oral history interview.
143. Levy, *Cesar Chavez*, 208–213; Ganz, oral history interview; Chatfield, interview.
144. *Sacramento Bee*, March 19, 1966; *San Francisco Chronicle*, March 23, 1966; UFW Chronology, April 8, 1966.
145. *San Francisco Chronicle*, March 24, 1966.
146. Ibid., March 26, 1966.
147. Ibid., March 25, 1966.
148. Ibid., March 26, 1966.
149. Ibid., March 31, 1966.
150. Valdez, "Tale of the Raza," 40–43.
151. Thomas Kircher, labor lawyer, Cincinnati, Ohio, and son of William Kircher, AFL-CIO organizing director, interview by author.
152. Reuther, *The Brothers Reuther*, 368.
153. Taylor, *Chavez*, 157.
154. Kircher, interview.
155. Ibid.; *Who's Who: The American Catholic*, "William L. Kircher," 402; *Who's Who in Finance and Industry*, "William L. Kircher," 402; *Who's Who in the South and Southwest*, "William L. Kircher," 406.
156. Kircher, interview.
157. Taylor, *Chavez*, 158–159.
158. Ibid.
159. Ibid., 171.
160. Ibid., 172.
161. Levy, *Cesar Chavez*, 147.
162. Ganz, oral history interview.
163. Levy, *Cesar Chavez*, 213.
164. Ibid.; Taylor, *Chavez*, 173.
165. Levitt, interview; Padilla, interview.
166. Woolsey, "Statement of Schenley Industries, Inc.," 7.

167. Weinstein, "Sidney Korshak"; Robert McG. Thomas, Jr., "Sidney R. Korshak, 88, Dies."

168. Levitt, interview; Taylor, *Chavez*, 175–177.

169. Levy, *Cesar Chavez*, 215–217; Levitt, interview; Hartmire, interview; Taylor, *Chavez*, 176–177.

170. Levitt, interview.

171. William Grami, director of organizing, Western Conference of Teamsters, 1960–1979, transcript of filmed interview conducted by Tejada-Flores; Brundage, interview.

172. Levy, *Cesar Chavez*, 215–217; Hartmire, interview; Taylor, *Chavez*, 176–177. Schenley had already raised the wages from the prestrike minimum of $1.25 to $1.40 per hour.

173. Levy, *Cesar Chavez*, 215–217.

174. Ganz, oral history interview.

175. Ibid.

176. Taylor, *Chavez*, 178.

177. *San Francisco Chronicle*, April 8, 1966.

178. Ibid., April 9, 1966.

179. *Sacramento Bee*, April 11, 1965.

180. Ganz, oral history interview.

181. Somers, "Narrative Constitution of Identity," 605–649.

182. Chong, *Collective Action*; Kim and Bearman, "Structure and Dynamics of Movement Participation," 70–93; James Coleman, *Foundations of Social Theory*; Rochon, *Culture Moves*.

183. Meister and Loftis, *Long Time Coming*, 137.

184. Brown, "United Farm Workers Grape Strike," 180–182.

185. Ibid., 168–172.

186. Rose, "Woman Power"; Saludado, oral history interview.

187. Levy, *Cesar Chavez*.

188. Hartmire, interview; Chatfield, interview; Drake, interview.

189. Jerome Cohen, general counsel, UFW, 1968–1981; interviews by author, 1995 and 1998; Chatfield, interview; Padilla, interview.

190. Brown, "United Farm Workers Grape Strike," 170–180. In this section, Brown offers an excellent analysis of the strike community under the heading of "The Style of la Causa." He documents the practice of the norms of "virtuous behavior" expected of *huelguistas* and the "egalitarian community" in which they participated.

191. The role of "charismatic communities" in identity formation—and "re-formation"—is discussed by Turner, *The Ritual Process*; Gamson, "Commitment and Agency," 27–50; Verta Taylor and Nancy E. Whittier, "Collective Identity in Social Movement Communities," 104–130; and Peterson, *Maps of Meaning*, 216–232.

192. George Ballis in *Farm Labor* 3, no. 5 (October 1965).

193. Taylor, *Chavez*, 186; Brown, "United Farm Workers Grape Strike," 157–159.

194. Henry Anderson in *Farm Labor* 4, no. 3 (April 1966).

195. Medina, interview.

Chapter 6

The Grami quote is from the interview by Tejada-Flores. The Chavez quote is from Dunne, *Delano*, 153. Dunne's account is particularly useful for the period of the DiGiorgio organizing drive during which he visited Delano. His report is based on first-person observation and interviews.

1. *San Francisco Chronicle*, April 8, 1966; Taylor, *Chavez*, 178.
2. Hartmire, interview; Levy, *Cesar Chavez*, 221–223.
3. *San Francisco Chronicle*, April 9, 1966.
4. Robert DiGiorgio Obituary, *San Francisco Chronicle*, February 15, 1991; *Business Wire*, "Obituary," February 14, 1991; *Who's Who in Finance and Industry*, "Robert DiGiorgio," 214.
5. Padilla, interview; Taylor, *Chavez*, 184–186.
6. Although Chavez continued to correspond with Ross, he became less of a presence in 1963, when his work took him to Arizona to form the Guadalupe Organization, a community group modeled on CSO. In late 1964, Warren Haggstromn, a social work professor at the University of Syracuse and a collaborator of Alinsky's, got $314,000 in OEO funds approved for a demonstration project in community organizing and recruited Ross to direct the field work. The project was terminated a year later due to "political controversy." See Horwitt, *Let Them Call Me Rebel*, 256–274.
7. Levy, *Cesar Chavez*, 223.
8. UFW, "Minutes of UFW General Meeting," April 19, 1966; *El Malcriado*, no. 35, May 5, 1966.
9. AFL-CIO Executive Council, "Statement on Boycott of DiGiorgio Products"; *El Malcriado*, no. 36, May 19, 1966.
10. UFW Chronology, May 19, 1966.
11. *El Malcriado*, no. 36, May 19, 1966; no. 37, June 2, 1966.
12. UFW Chronology.
13. *El Malcriado*, no. 35, May 5, 1966; UFW Chronology.
14. Taylor, *Chavez*, 184.
15. *Fresno Bee*, May 16, 1966.
16. *El Malcriado*, no. 36, May 19, 1966.
17. UFW, DiGiorgio Chronology, May 14, 1966.
18. Dunne, *Delano*, 143.
19. Ibid.
20. Brundage, interview.
21. Ibid.; Taylor, *Chavez*, 188–190.
22. Brundage, interview.
23. Ibid.; Derek Grami, telephone interview with author.
24. D. Grami, interview; Brundage, interview; Grami Obituary.
25. Brundage, interview.
26. Dunne, *Delano*, 141–143; Brundage, interview.
27. Brundage, interview.
28. Ibid.
29. Taylor, *Chavez*, 188–190.

30. Levy, *Cesar Chavez*, 223–224; *El Malcriado*, no. 36, May 19, 1966; Taylor, *Chavez*, 187–188.
31. Levy, *Cesar Chavez*, 225–226.
32. Ibid., 226–227.
33. Ganz, oral history interview.
34. W. Grami, interview.
35. Taylor, *Chavez*, 190.
36. Ibid., 189.
37. *Fresno Bee*, May 25, June 2, 1966.
38. *San Francisco Chronicle*, June 8, 1966; *Valley Labor Citizen*, no. 50 (June 10, 1966); *Southern California Teamster* 26, no. 27 (June 22, 1966); *Fresno Bee*, June 7, 1966.
39. *Fresno Bee*, June 7, 1966.
40. Taylor, *Chavez*, 190; *Fresno Bee*, June 8, 1966.
41. UFW, DiGiorgio Chronology, June 14, 1966.
42. UFW Chronology, June 10, 1966.
43. Ibid., June 17, 1966; *Valley Labor Citizen* 26, no. 27 (June 22, 1966).
44. UFW Chronology, June 17, 1966.
45. Ibid., June 18, 1966.
46. Taylor, *Chavez*, 190–191; Levy, *Cesar Chavez*, 228–229.
47. UFW, "Minutes," June 22, 1966; UFW Chronology, June 22, 1966; Levy, *Cesar Chavez*, 228–229.
48. Taylor, *Chavez*, 189–190.
49. Taylor, interview.
50. Taylor, *Chavez*, 191–192.
51. Ibid., 192; Levy, *Cesar Chavez*, 229–230; *San Francisco Chronicle*, June 23, 1966; UFW Chronology, June 22, 1966.
52. Taylor, *Chavez*, 192–193; Levy, *Cesar Chavez*, 230–231.
53. Taylor, *Chavez*, 193; Levy, *Cesar Chavez*, 231; *San Francisco Chronicle*, June 25, 1966; *Fresno Bee*, June 25, 1966.
54. Letter, Cesar Chavez to Sen. Harrison Williams," Fred Ross Papers; *El Malcriado*, no. 39, June 30, 1966.
55. Taylor, *Chavez*, 193–194; Levy, *Cesar Chavez*, 231.
56. UFW Chronology, June 29, 1966.
57. UFW, "Minutes," June 28, 1966; Hartmire, interview; Taylor, *Chavez*, 194–195.
58. Levy, *Cesar Chavez*, 231–234; UFW Chronology, June 30, 1966.
59. UFW Chronology, June 29, 1966.
60. UFW, "Minutes," June 28, 1966; *El Malcriado*, no. 39, June 30, 1966.
61. *El Malcriado*, no. 39, June 30, 1966; *Los Angeles Times*, July 10, 1966.
62. *San Francisco Chronicle*, July 1, 1966; UFW Chronology, July 1, 1966; Taylor, *Chavez*, 194.
63. Haughton, "Report and Recommendations"; *Los Angeles Times*, July 15, 1966.
64. Dunne, *Delano*, 147–150; Levy, *Cesar Chavez*, 234.
65. Brown, "United Farm Workers Grape Strike," 191–192.

66. Levy, *Cesar Chavez*, 234.

67. Saludado, oral history interview.

68. Medina, interview.

69. Dunne, *Delano*, 158.

70. Taylor, interview.

71. UFW Chronology, August 21, 1966; Dunne, *Delano*, 157–159.

72. *El Malcriado*, no. 41, July 28, 1966.

73. W. Grami, interview.

74. Taylor, *Chavez*, 197–198.

75. Medina, interview; Taylor, *Chavez*, 199–200; Levy, *Cesar Chavez*, 234–235; Brown, "United Farm Workers Grape Strike," 182–185.

76. Brundage, interview.

77. Ross, "El Mosquito Zumbador," May 24–August 30, 1966; Saludado, oral history interview.

78. Medina, interview; Taylor, *Chavez*, 199–201; Levy, *Cesar Chavez*, 234–235.

79. Medina, interview; Taylor, *Chavez*, 199–201; Levy, *Cesar Chavez*, 234–235.

80. Medina, interview.

81. Levy, *Cesar Chavez*, 234.

82. Dunne, *Delano*, 157.

83. Levy, *Cesar Chavez*, 236–237.

84. Medina, interview; Dunne, *Delano*, 154–167; Taylor, *Chavez*, 198–199.

85. Medina, interview.

86. *El Malcriado*, no. 42, August 11, 1966.

87. Dunne, *Delano*, 151; Levy, *Cesar Chavez*, 235–236.

88. Taylor, *Chavez*, 195–197.

89. Senate Fact Finding Committee on Agriculture, *Special Report*, 26.

90. *Los Angeles Times*, July 28, 1966; Taylor, *Chavez*, 197.

91. Taylor, *Chavez*, 197.

92. *Southern California Teamster* 26, no. 35 (August 17, 1966); Scharlin and Villanueva, *Phillip Vera Cruz*, 40.

93. Padilla, interview; *El Malcriado*, no. 42, August 11, 1966; Levy, *Cesar Chavez*, 243.

94. *El Malcriado*, no. 42, August 11, 1966.

95. Levy, *Cesar Chavez*, 237–238.

96. Taylor, *Chavez*, 200.

97. *Southern California Teamster* 26, no. 35 (August 17, 1966).

98. Ibid., no. 36 (August 24, 1966).

99. Levy, *Cesar Chavez*, 236–237.

100. *El Malcriado*, no. 42, August 25, 1966.

101. Levy, *Cesar Chavez*, 244.

102. Ibid., 244–245.

103. Dunne, *Delano*, 164–165.

104. Medina, interview.

105. Ibid.

106. *Los Angeles Times*, September 1, 1966; Taylor, *Chavez*, 202.

107. Dunne, *Delano*, 166.

108. Taylor, *Chavez*, 195.
109. Ibid.
110. Saludado, oral history interview.

Chapter 7

1. Taylor, *Chavez*, 197; Levy, *Cesar Chavez*, 239–240.
2. Ibid., 240.
3. Levy, *Cesar Chavez*, 240–242.
4. Ibid., 239.
5. Ibid., 240.
6. Ibid., 239–242.
7. UFWOC, "Constitution," Article V, section 2.
8. AWOC, Rules and Regulations of A.W.O.C., Articles I and II.
9. Taylor, *Chavez*, 197.
10. Dunne, *Delano*, 93.
11. Levy, *Cesar Chavez*, 242–243.
12. Ibid., 242.
13. *El Malcriado*, no. 37, June 2, 1966; no. 53, January 13, 1967.
14. Taylor, *Chavez*, 202–203; Ganz, oral history interview.
15. *El Malcriado*, no. 37, June 2, 1966; no. 38, June 16, 1966; no. 40, July 14, 1966; no. 42, August 11, 1966; Taylor, *Chavez*, 204–205.
16. *El Malcriado*, no. 53, January 13, 1967; no. 60, May 10, 1967.
17. *Valley Labor Citizen* 62, no. 15 (October 7, 1966); *El Malcriado*, no. 46, October 7, 1966; UFW Chronology, October 2, 1966.
18. Chatfield, interview; Schrade, e-mail; *El Malcriado*, no. 50, December 2, 1966; Taylor, *Chavez*, 205, 216.
19. Taylor, *Chavez*, 203.
20. Ibid.
21. *El Malcriado*, no. 45, September 23, 1966.
22. Ibid.
23. W. Grami, interview.
24. *El Malcriado*, no. 45, September 23, 1966.
25. Levy, *Cesar Chavez*, 257–258.
26. *UFWOC Newsletter*, January 19, 1967; Cella, *California Wine Pioneers*.
27. UFW Chronology.
28. Levy, *Cesar Chavez*, 258.
29. *El Malcriado*, no. 46, October 10, 1966.
30. Ganz, oral history interview.
31. Levy, *Cesar Chavez*, 249.
32. Alinsky, *John L. Lewis*, 71.
33. Levy, *Cesar Chavez*, 247–250; *El Malcriado*, no. 48, November 4, 1966.
34. Levy, *Cesar Chavez*, 250–251; *El Malcriado*, no. 48, November 4, 1966.
35. UFW Chronology, October 27, 1966.
36. *San Francisco Examiner*, December 4, 1966; *Farm Labor* (January 1967).
37. UFW Chronology, November 5, 1966; *El Malcriado*, no. 49, November 18, 1966.
38. Taylor, interview.
39. *El Malcriado*, no. 47, October 21, 1966; UFW Chronology, October 16, 1966.

40. *El Malcriado*, no. 47, October 21, 1966; no. 48, November 4, 1966; no. 49, November 18, 1966; UFW Chronology, November 16, 1966.

41. *El Malcriado*, no. 48, November 18, 1966.

42. Ibid., November 4, 1966.

43. *El Malcriado*, no. 46, October 7, 1966; no. 47, October 21, 1966; no. 48, November 4, 1966; Rabbi Albert Vorspan, Letter to Manischewitz Kosher Winery; *San Francisco Examiner*, December 18, 1966.

44. Medina, interview.

45. *El Malcriado*, no. 56, March 15, 1967.

46. UFW Chronology, February 27, 1966.

47. *El Malcriado*, no. 56, March 15, 1967.

48. UFW Chronology, March 4, 1967.

49. *Southern California Teamster* 26, no. 47 (November 9, 1966).

50. Ibid., 27, no. 4 (January 11, 1967).

51. Padilla, interview; *Southern California Teamster* 27, no. 4 (January 11, 1967).

52. *East Bay Labor Journal*, October 10, 1966.

53. *San Francisco Chronicle*, October 21, 1966.

54. *El Malcriado*, no. 57, March 15, 1967; no. 58, April 12, 1967.

55. Cohen, 1998 interview.

56. Ibid.; Chatfield, interview.

57. Cohen, 1998 interview.

58. Ibid.

59. Ibid.

60. UFW Chronology, September 16, 1966.

61. *San Francisco Chronicle*, October 25, 1966.

62. *El Malcriado*, no. 38, June 16, 1966.

63. Ibid., no. 3, January 15, 1965.

64. Levy, *Cesar Chavez*, 258.

65. UFW Chronology, November 29, 1965.

66. Alberto Rojas, United Farm Workers Union (Teamsters), board member, 1966–1967; United Farm Workers, organizer, 1967–1977. Interview by author.

67. Ibid.

68. Ibid.

69. *El Malcriado*, no. 45, September 23, 1966.

70. UFW Chronology, September 3, 1966.

71. Rojas, interview.

72. W. Grami, interview.

73. Rojas, interview; Levy, *Cesar Chavez*, 259.

74. *El Malcriado*, no. 63, June 20, 1967.

75. Brundage, interview.

76. UFW Chronology, January 13, 1967.

77. Ibid., January 21, 1967; *El Malcriado*, no. 32, February 3, 1967; Gibbons, Confidential Memorandum to James R. Hoffa.

78. Dunne, *Delano*, 172.

79. Steven Brill, *The Teamsters* (New York: Simon and Schuster, 1978), 183; Watson, "Notes on Larry Itliong Files."

80. Brundage, interview.

81. *Southern California Teamster* 27, no. 6 (April 5, 1967).

82. *El Malcriado*, no. 61, May 24, 1967.

83. Brown, "United Farm Workers Grape Strike," 134; Levitt, interview; Levy, *Cesar Chavez*, 260; *El Malcriado*, no. 59, April 26, 1967.

84. Taylor, *Chavez*, 204.

85. *El Malcriado*, no. 60, May 10, 1967.

86. Ibid., no. 59, April 26, 1967.

87. Ibid., no. 61, May 24, 1967.

88. Medina, interview.

89. Rojas, interview.

90. *Valley Labor Citizen* 62, no. 39 (March 24, 1967).

91. UFW Chronology, May 11, 1967; *El Malcriado*, no. 61, May 24, 1967.

92. UFW Chronology, April 28, 1967.

93. *El Malcriado*, no. 60, May 10, 1967.

94. Ibid., no. 61, May 24, 1967.

95. Byfield, Boyle, and Glaser, Letter to A. Perelli-Minetti & Sons.

96. UFW Chronology, February 16, 1967.

97. Rabbi Joseph B. Glaser, Letter to Fred Perelli-Minetti, Cesar Chavez, Bill Grami, Fr. Eugene Boyle, Rev. Richard Byfield, Dr. Richard Norberg, April 21, 1967, UFW Papers.

98. Glaser, Memorandum of Meeting on April 28.

99. Cohen, Notes on the Meeting with the Teamsters of Friday, May 19, 1967.

100. Rojas, interview.

101. Ibid.

102. Levy, *Cesar Chavez*, 260.

103. Cohen, "Rabbi Glaser Phone Conversation," June 16, 1967, UFW Papers.

104. Richard White, Letter to Rabbi Joseph B. Glaser, June 16, 1967; Letter, Glaser to White, June 20, 1967; Letter, White to Glaser, June 22, 1967; Letter, Glaser to White, June 25, 1967, all in UFW Archives.

105. UFW Chronology, July 11, 1967.

106. *Los Angeles Times*, July 12, 1967.

107. Cohen, 1998 interview; Levy, *Cesar Chavez*, 261.

108. Cohen 1998 interview; Levy, *Cesar Chavez*, 261; Taylor, *Chavez*, 208.

109. *Los Angeles Times*, July 25, 1967.

110. *Valley Labor Citizen* 62, no. 39 (March 24, 1967); no. 41 (April 7, 1967); Taylor, *Chavez*, 216.

111. *El Malcriado*, no. 42, April 14, 1967.

112. Gibbons, "Finances of the United Farm Workers of America 1967–1974," LM-2 reports filed with the U.S. Department of Labor, Research Bulletin, International Research Department, International Brotherhood of Teamsters, August 5, 1975, Gibbons Papers.

113. Taylor, *Chavez*, 214.

114. Brown, "United Farm Workers Grape Strike," 134.

115. Ganz, oral history interview.

116. *Fighting for Our Lives*, a 1975 film, documented the 1973 strike described here.

117. In addition to references specified below, the following historical account is based on these sources: Taylor, *Chavez*; Ferris and Sandoval, *Fight in the*

Fields; Ganz, oral history interview; Levy, *Cesar Chavez*; Daniel, "Cesar Chavez and the Unionization of California Farm Workers."

118. Steven V. Roberts, "Fear and Tension Grip Salinas Valley in Farm Workers' Strike," *New York Times*, September 6, 1970, 32.

119. "Farm Union Signs a Contract with Lettuce Grower on Coast," *New York Times*, August 31, 1970, 27.

120. All of UFWOC's first contracts were signed with growers who were not only economic or political outsiders to the local grower community, but were also ethnic outsiders. Rosensteil of Schenley, Lionel Steinberg of the David Freedman Company, and Eli Black of Interharvest were all Jewish.

121. "Court Enjoins Chavez Union," *New York Times*, September 17, 1970, 55. Brazil had served as the district attorney during the 1936 Salinas lettuce strike and was infamous for deputizing growers as vigilantes and ordering the high school woodshop to produce clubs with which they could "discipline" the strikers.

122. "Chavez Calls Lettuce Boycott," *New York Times*, September 18, 1970, 11.

123. For example, "Chavez Reaches Pact in Florida," *New York Times*, March 1, 1972, 1; "Chavez Fasting to Protest Arizona Farm Labor Law," *New York Times*, May 15, 1972, 23.

124. "Conservative Groups Mount Campaign against Chavez Union," *New York Times*, March 26, 1972, 48; Leroy F. Aarons, "Opponents Try Legislation to Halt Chavez," *Washington Post*, August 29, 1972, A1. Legislation at the federal level was a dead letter as UFWOC leaders opposed any procedure that would substitute the NLRB's dysfunctional bureaucracy for the freedom to conduct secondary boycotts. And for most growers, the problem was not in their face enough to make them willing to cede any collective bargaining rights to their workers at all.

125. For example, "Governor of Oregon Vetoes Bill Regulating Farm Labor Unions," *New York Times*, July 2, 1971, 50.

126. UFW Office of the President: Cesar Chavez Collection, boxes 1, 18, and 36, Wayne State Archives.

127. In December 1970, for example, the NFWSC received a $225,000 grant from the Center for Community Change, a Washington, DC, foundation established by Reuther and others; *New York Times*, December 14, 1970, 28.

128. "Farm Workers Accepted as Union by AFL-CIO," *New York Times*, February 22, 1972, 22.

129. Tim O'Brien, "Lettuce: A Boycott Blossoms; Democrats, TV Give Union Drive a Boost: Lettuce Boycott Bolstered," *Washington Post*, July 16, 1972, A1.

130. "Letter from Cesar Chavez," *New York Review of Books* 21, no. 17 (October 31, 1974).

131. "Teamsters End a Truce with Chavez's United Farm Workers," *New York Times*, December 15, 1972, 33.

132. "Teamsters Gain California Farms: Growers Shift from Chavez: Boycott Threatened, Walkout Planned, Contract Not Made Public," *New York Times*, April 16, 1973, 40.

133. Philip Shabecoff, "Labor Votes Fund for Chavez Union: $1.6-Million Will Be Used in Fight with Teamsters: Purpose of Funds," *New York Times*, May 10, 1973, 22.

134. Leroy F. Aarons, "Farm Union Fights for Life under a Hot Desert Sun," *Washington Post*, June 24, 1973.

135. "Chavez Is Starting a Fast to Affirm Nonviolence," *New York Times*, August 20, 1973, 10.

136. George Baker, "UFW Convention Is Facing Troubles," *Washington Post*, September 24, 1973, A4.

137. Majka and Majka, *Farm Workers, Agribusiness and the State*.

138. Full-time volunteer figures provided by Kathleen Schmeling, interim associate director, Walter P. Reuther Library, College of Urban, Labor and Metropolitan Affairs, Wayne State University.

139. Winthrop Griffith, "Is Chavez Beaten," *New York Times Magazine*, September 15, 1974, 258.

140. Interview with Jerome Cohen, 2005.

141. Salzman, "Has Brown's Ambition Kept the ALRB Bankrupt?" 68.

142. Wells, *Strawberry Fields*, 295–297.

143. Harry Bernstein, "L.A. Teamster Named to Head Union's Western Conference," *Washington Post*, January 6, 1974, 3.

144. Daniel, "Cesar Chavez and the Unionization of California Farm Workers," 350–365.

145. Ronald Taylor, "Farm Union Peace Seen on Coast," *New York Times*, May 8, 1975, 85; William Wong, "Fruitful Harvest," *Wall Street Journal*, May 30, 1975, 30; Henry Weinstein, "Coast Farm Vote May End Labor Feud," *New York Times*, August 17, 1975, 40.

146. Cohen, 2005 interview; Wells, *Strawberry Fields*, 297–299.

147. Larry Stammer, "Petitions Filed for Farm Worker Union Election," *Los Angeles Times*, September 3, 1975, 1.

148. ALRB 75-RC-15-M, 1 ALRB no. 4.

149. Former UFW general counsel Jerome Cohen reported an initial call from Brown, indicating an approach from the Teamsters in April 1976.

150. Agricultural Labor Relations Board, *First Annual Report*, 9–18.

151. Les Ledbetter, "Demise of Labor Board Perils Agricultural Truce in California," *New York Times*, February 18, 1976, 78.

152. "California Legislature Passes Record Budget Totaling $12.86 Billion," *New York Times*, July 2, 1976, 5.

153. "A Fighting Proposition," *Wall Street Journal*, November 11, 1976, 20.

154. Lee Dembart, "Teamsters Meet with Chavez Unit," *New York Times*, June 12, 1976, 21; "Teamster Officials, Chavez Hold Talks," *Washington Post*, December 24, 1976.

155. Bill Richards, "Teamsters-UFW Jurisdictional Pact Reported," *Washington Post*, January 8, 1977, 1; "Peace in the Fields and Vineyards," *New York Times*, March 16, 1977, 53.

156. William Wong, "Chavez Union Wins Long Fight with Teamsters," *Wall Street Journal*, March 11, 1977, 7.

157. *Chavez v. Fitzsimmons*, filed in January 1973, U.S. District Court, Northern District of California.

158. William Carder, former UFW attorney, interview by author.

159. For documentation of the preceding paragraph as well as the most insightful and complete account of the UFW's strategic use of legal resources, see Gordon, "Law, Lawyers and Labor."

160. Wallace Turner, "Chavez and Teamsters Sign Accord," *New York Times*, March 11, 1977, 41.

161. Donald Janson, "Farm Leaders Map Strategy on Unions," *New York Times*, July 20, 1977, 10.

Epilogue

1. The recent organizational, financial, and political picture of the UFW and related entities has been carefully documented by Miriam Pawel in a four-part series, "UFW: A Broken Contract," in the *Los Angeles Times*, January 8–11, 2006; and by Matt Weiser in a three-part series, "Inside the UFW," in the *Bakersfield Californian*, May 10–12, 2004.

2. Kahn, Martin, and Hardiman, *California's Farm Labor Market*; Greenhouse, "U.S. Survey Find[s] Farm Workers Pay Down for 20 Years," A1.

3. Farm Labor, Agricultural Statistics Board, National Agricultural Statistics Service, U.S. Department of Agriculture, "Hired Workers: Annual Average Wage Rates by State, 2005–2006" (November 17, 2006), 15; U.S. Department of Labor, Bureau of Labor Statistics, "May 2006 State Occupational Employment and Wage Estimates: California," available at www.bls.gov.

4. Phillip Martin, "Labor Relations in California Agriculture" (University of California Institute for Labor and Employment, 2001).

5. Ibid.

6. My estimate of UFW membership is based on the *2006 LM-2 Report*, filed with the U.S. Department of Labor, March 29, 2007. It reports a membership of 5,504, of whom 4,592 work under contract, 874 are retired, and 38 are "in service to the union." Also, the 2003 report of the Juan De La Cruz Pension Fund indicated employer contributions on behalf of 3,536 workers. In the peak months of 2004, the Robert F. Kennedy Farm Workers Medical Plan covered only 3,000 workers, as reported in "Linked Charities Bank on the Chavez Name," *Los Angeles Times*, January 8, 2006. The number of UFW contracts is reported in Miriam Pawel, "For UFW, Contracts Are Give and Take," *Los Angeles Times*, March 20, 2006.

7. UFCW Local 5, the successor of an earlier independent union, represents 1,950 farm workers according to its 2002 LM-2 report while Teamsters Local 890, holder of the Bud Antle contract, represents some 4,000 farm workers, according to Martin, 81.

8. Steven Greenhouse, "Growers' Group Signs the First Union Contract for Guest Workers," *New York Times*, September 17, 2004.

9. Eric Schlosser, "A Side Order of Human Rights," *New York Times*, April 6, 2005.

10. Miriam Pawel, "Linked Charities Bank on the Chavez Name," *Los Angeles Times*, January 9, 2006; IRS 990 forms, U.S. Department of Labor's LM-2 Labor Organization Annual Report and Form 5500, Annual Return/Report

of Employee Benefit Plans; Matt Weiser, "UFW, Affiliates Are a Family Affair," *Bakersfield Californian*, May 9, 2004.

11. Matt Weiser, "A Union of Nonprofits," *Bakersfield Californian*, May 9, 2004.

12. Labor Secretary Ray Marshall granted the UFW $500,000 to teach migrants English; see "Federal Contract Signed to Teach Migrants English," *New York Times*, January 12, 1978, A14. The Community Service Agency granted $600,000 to develop a microwave communication system for the UFW; see "Building Constituencies," *Wall Street Journal*, February 1, 1979, 16. The Farm Bureau objected to a Community Service Agency grant of $125,000 to support development of the UFW credit union; see Ward Sinclair, "Community Services Agency Burglarized of Last-Minute Grant Data," *Washington Post*, January 24, 1981, A3.

13. U.S. Department of Labor, *2006 LM-2 Report*.

14. Phillip L. Martin and J. R. Abele, "Unions: Their Effect on California Farm Wages," *California Agriculture* 44, no. 6 (1990): 28–30.

15. Cheryl Miller, "The UFW: Faded Glory?" *California Journal* 36, no. 10 (October 1, 2004): 20.

16. For example, on May 11, 2005, some 4,000 people attended the funeral of Los Angeles Federation of Labor secretary-treasurer Miguel Contreras. Contreras, 52, grew up in a farm worker family, and his father served as the ranch committee president at a company under union contract from 1970 to 1973. After joining the picket lines in 1973, he volunteered full time with the UFW for four years. After leaving the UFW in 1977, he became a full-time union organizer, eventually becoming the first Latino to head the L.A. County Labor Federation. Former UFW Executive Board member Eliseo Medina now serves as a national executive vice president of the Service Employees International Union (see Miriam Pawal, "Former Chavez Ally Took His Own Path," *Los Angeles Times*, January 11, 2006).

17. Robert Lindsey, "Glory Days Are Fading for Chavez and UFW," *New York Times*, December 23, 1984, E4.

18. Martin, 75–80.

19. "U.S. Official Blames Farmers for Worker Shortage in West," *New York Times*, June 21, 1987, 24; Ward Sinclair, "Immigration Uncertainties Pinch Flow of Farm Workers; U.S. Growers Bidding against Each Other: U.S. Growers Vie for Migrant Laborers: Immigration Uncertainties Pinch Farmers," *Washington Post*, July 3, 1987, A1; Miriam J. Wells and Don Villarejo, "State Structures and Social Movement Strategies: The Shaping of Farm Labor Protections in California," *Politics and Society* 32, no. 3 (September 2004): 291–326.

20. Zald and Ash, "Social Movement Organizations," 327–341.

21. Weber, *Economy and Society*, vol. 2, 181.

22. Michels, *Political Parties*.

23. Miriam Pawel, "Decisions of Long Ago Shape the Union Today," *Los Angeles Times*, January 10, 2006, 1.

24. "Nuts-and-Bolts Unionism; Chavez's UFW Struggling to Make Transition from Social Activism to Day-to-Day Basics: UFW Now Wrestling with Nuts-and-Bolts Unionism," *Washington Post*, January 30, 1978.

25. See Kramer, "Political Paranoia in Organizations."

26. Miriam Pawel, "Decisions of Long Ago Shape the Union Today," *Los Angeles Times*, January 10, 2006, 1; http://religiousmovements.lib.virginia.edu/nrms/synanon.html.

27. Ofshe, "Social Development of the Synanon Cult," 109–127.

28. Kramer, "Political Paranoia in Organizations."

29. Robert Lindsey, "Criticism of Chavez Takes Root in Farm Labor Struggle," *New York Times*, February 7, 1979, 16.

30. Ofshe et al., "Social Structure and Social Control in Synanon," 67–76; Yablonski, *Synanon*.

31. "Federal Contract Signed to Teach Migrants English," *New York Times*, January 12, 1978, A14.

32. Bernard Wideman, "Cesar Chavez Hails Philippines' Rule," *Washington Post*, July 29, 1977, A11; "Panel Critical of Chavez Visit to Philippines," *Washington Post*, September 23, 1977, B11.

33. Richard D. Lyons, "Philip [*sic*] Vera Cruz, 89, Helped to Found Farm Worker Union," *New York Times*, June 16, 1994, B9.

34. Cohen, "UFW Must Get Back to Organizing," 5.

35. Wayne King, "Chavez Faces Internal and External Struggles," *New York Times*, December 6, 1981, 1; Gordon, "Law, Lawyers and Labor."

36. Robert Lindsey, "Union Lettuce Worker Shot Dead in Clash with Nonstriking Pickers: Dispute Involves Wages," *New York Times*, February 12, 1979, A14.

37. Robert Lindsey, "Chavez's Farm Workers Union, Once Fighting to Survive, Senses Victory; Growers Rejected Demands," *New York Times*, September 10, 1979, A16.

38. Wayne King, "Chavez Faces Internal and External Struggles," *New York Times*, December 6, 1981, 1; Judith Cummings, "Dispute Intensifies over Chavez's Leadership of Farm Workers," *New York Times*, January 3, 1983, A8.

39. "Judge Backs 9 Farm Union Aides Who Were Dismissed by Chavez," *New York Times*, November 19, 1982, A19.

40. Robert Lindsey, "Chavez and Farm Workers Adapt Tactics to the Times," *New York Times*, July 31, 1983, 20.

41. Robert Lindsey, "Glory Days Are Fading for Chavez and U.F.W.," *New York Times*, December 23, 1984, E4.

42. Lindsey, "Chavez and Farm Workers Adapt Tactics to the Times," 20.

43. Katherine Bishop, "Chavez Takes a Smaller Union into Another Decade of Fights," *New York Times*, June 18, 1989, E4.

44. Constanza Montana and John Emshwiller, "Staying Alive: Its Ranks Eroding, Farm Workers' Union Struggles to Survive: UFW Hopes a Grape Boycott Will Rebuild Its Influence," *Wall Street Journal*, 1.

45. *Rural Migration News*, April 1, 1996; Carey Goldberg, "Farm Workers Sign Accord with Lettuce Growers, Ending a Long and Bitter Conflict," *New York Times*, May 30, 1996, A14.

46. Steven Greenhouse, "Chavez Son-in-Law Tries to Rebuild Legacy," *New York Times*, June 30, 1997, A8.

47. In 2002, the UFW won representation rights and a contract with Coastal Berry at both its Watsonville and Oxnard properties, but the momentum to organize the rest of the industry had been long dissipated. Early in 2005, Dole Food Company, an employer noted for its resistance to the UFW. *Rural Migration News*, January 19, 2005.

48. *Rural Migration News*, January 1, 2002.

49. Ibid., July 1, 2000.

50. Pawel, "Farm Workers Reap Little as Union Strays from Its Roots."

51. Ibid.

52. U.S. Department of Labor, *2006 LM-2 Report*.

References

Adair, Doug. 1995. Transcript of an oral history interview. California State University, Northridge, Provost's Committee on Chicano Labor, March 10.

Adams, Jed A. 1966. "The Grape Industry: Production and Marketing Situation." Bureau of Marketing, California Department of Agriculture, Sacramento, February 4.

AFL-CIO. 1965. "Resolution No. 221, Proceedings of the Sixth Constitutional Convention of the AFL-CIO." San Francisco, December 14.

———. 1966. "Audit Report: AFL-CIO Agricultural Workers Organizing Committee, January 1, 1965–March 1, 1966." Washington DC: mimeo. Walter Reuther Library, Archives, Wayne State University, Detroit, MI.

AFL-CIO Executive Council. 1966. "Statement on Boycott of DiGiorgio Products." May 6. Stanford University Archives, Fred Ross Collection.

Agricultural Labor Relations Board. *First Annual Report of the Agricultural Labor Relations Board for the Fiscal Years Ended June 30, 1976, and June 30, 1977.* Sacramento, CA: ALRB, January 24.

Alinsky, Saul D. 1949. *John L. Lewis: An Unauthorized Biography.* 2nd ed., New York: Vintage, 1970.

———. 1971. *Rules for Radicals.* New York: Vintage.

Allmeddinger, W. 1965. *The California Grape Industry: Some Production and Marketing Trends and Prospects.* Fermenting Materials Processors Advisory Board, July.

Almaguer, Tomas. 1995. "Racial Domination and Class Conflict in Capitalist Agriculture: The Oxnard Sugar Beet Workers' Strike of 1903." In *Working People of California*, edited by D. Cornford. Berkeley: University of California Press.

Altman, Alan. 1951. "A Financial Survey of Schenley Industries and Distillers Corporation, Seagrams Limited." M.B.A. thesis, Boston University.

Amabile, Theresa M. 1996. "A Theoretical Framework." In her *Creativity in Context.* Boulder, CO: Westview.

American Arbitration Association. 1966. "Memorandum to the Governor of California: Concerns Fact Finding Procedure with the DiGiorgio Corporation: Report and Recommendations." California State University Library. July 14.

Anderson, Henry. 1961. *To Build a Union: Comments on the Organization of Agricultural Workers*. Stockton, CA: Self-published.

———. 1964. "Notes toward a Typology of Worker Organizations." In *Farm Labor*, edited by Henry Anderson, 7–18. Berkeley, CA: Citizens for Farm Labor, April.

———. 1996. Interview by author. Tape recording. Oakland, CA, August.

Arax, Max. 1992. "UFW Memorial Honors Lifelong Activist Fred Ross." *Los Angeles Times*, October 19:A-3.

Asociación de Trabajadores Campesinos. 1963. "Acta Oficial de Convencion Constitucional." Delano, CA, January 20. UFW Archives, Walter Reuther Library, Wayne State University, Detroit, MI.

AWOC. 1960. Rules and Regulations of A.W.O.C. AWOC Papers.

———. 1962. "Minutes of the First AWOC Meeting, June 23, Oakland, California." AWOC Papers.

———. 1964a. Memorandum to All Business Representatives from C. Al Green, January 31. AWOC Papers.

———. 1964b. Memo to Stockton Labor Contractors from C. Al Green, March 18. AWOC Papers.

———. 1965a. Memo from David C. McCain, Office Manager, to Victor Van Bourg, Attorney at Law, February 2. AWOC Papers.

———. 1965b. Minutes of AWOC strike meetings, October 19–30, 1965. AWOC Papers.

———. 1966. S-O-S (Support Our Strike) Committee. "Delano Grape Strike Calendar." Delano, CA, January. AWOC Papers.

"AWOC Organizes Farm Labor." 1961. *Farm Quarterly*. UFW Archives, Walter Reuther Library, Wayne State University, Detroit, MI.

Bandura, A. 1989. "Human Agency in Social Cognitive Theory." *American Psychologist* 44, no. 9:1175–1184.

Bardacke, Frank. Forthcoming. "The River's Source." In his *Beneath the California Sun*. New York: Norton.

Barnard, John. 1983. *Walter Reuther and the Rise of the Auto Workers*. Boston: Little, Brown.

Bartunek, J. M. 1993. "Multiple Cognition and Conflicts Associated with Second Order Organizational Change." In *Social Psychology in Organizations*, edited by J. K. Murnighan. Englewood Cliffs, NJ: Prentice-Hall.

Bates College. 1996. "The Continuing Education of Clive Knowles '33." Available at www.bates.edu/pubs/mag/96-winter/knowles.html (accessed March 15, 2000).

Bernstein, Basil. 1975. "Social Class, Language and Socialization." In his *Class Codes and Control: Theoretical Studies towards Sociology of Language*, 2nd ed. New York: Schocken.

Bernstein, Harry. 1967a. "AFL-CIO, Teamsters End Battle over Farm Workers." *Los Angeles Times*, July 12.

———. 1967b. "Cleric-Union Cartel Bludgeons Farmers, Grower Council Says." *Los Angeles Times*, July 25:3, 17.

Bernstein, Irving. 1960. *The Lean Years: A History of the American Worker, 1920–1933*. Baltimore, MD: Penguin.

———. 1969. *The Turbulent Years: A History of the American Worker, 1933–1941*. Boston: Houghton Mifflin.

Blum, Ken. 1966. "The Other Delano Grape Growers." *Farm Labor* 5, no. 1 (November):10–12.

Bourdieu, Pierre. 1984. *Distinction: A Social Critique of the Judgement of Taste.* Cambridge, MA: Harvard University Press.

———. 1990. *The Logic of Practice.* Palo Alto, CA: Stanford University Press.

Brody, David. 1980. *Workers in Industrial America: Essays on the 20th Century Struggle.* New York: Oxford University Press.

———. 1993. *In Labor's Cause.* New York: Oxford University Press.

Brown, Dillon S. 1983. "Fruit and Nut Crops." In *A Guidebook to California Agriculture*, edited by Ann Foley Scheuring. Berkeley: University of California Press.

Brown, Jerald. 1972. "The United Farm Workers Grape Strike and Boycott, 1965–70: An Evaluation of the Culture of Poverty Theory." Ph.D. diss., Cornell University.

Brown, Shona L., and Kathleen M. Eisenhardt. 1997. "The Art of Continuous Change: Linking Complexity Theory and Time-Paced Evolution in Relentlessly Shifting Organizations." *Administrative Science Quarterly* 42, no. 1:34–56.

———. 1998. *Competing on the Edge: Strategy as Structured Chaos.* Boston: Harvard Business School Press.

Brueggemann, Walter. 2001. *The Prophetic Imagination.* Minneapolis, MN: Augsburg Fortress.

Brundage, Al. 1998. Telephone interview by author. Cambridge, MA, November.

Bruner, Jerome. 1990. *Acts of Meaning.* Cambridge, MA: Harvard University Press.

Burt, Kenneth. 1982. *The History of MAPA and Chicano Politics in California.* Sacramento, CA: Kenneth Burt and the Mexican American Political Association.

Byfield, Rev. Richard, Rev. Eugene Boyle, and Rabbi Joseph Glaser. 1967. Letter to A. Perelli-Minetti & Sons. Ad Hoc Committee, January 31. Joseph B. Glaser Files, Walter Reuther Library, Wayne State University, Detroit, MI.

Calavito, Kitty. 1992. *Inside the State: The Bracero Program, Immigration, and the I.N.S.* New York: Routledge.

California Assembly Committee on Agriculture. 1965. "The Bracero Program and Its Aftermath: An Historical Summary." April 1.

———. 1969. *The California Farm Workforce: A Profile.* Sacramento: California Advisory Committee on Farm Labor Research.

California Council of Growers Newsletter.

California State Senate. 1967. "Special Report on Farm Labor Disputes." Fact-Finding Committee on Agriculture. State of California Archives.

Camarillo, Albert. 1984. *Chicanos in California: A History of Mexican Americans in California.* San Francisco: Boyd and Fraser.

Campbell, Donald T. 1960. "Blind Variation and Selective Retention in Creative Thought as in Other Knowledge Processes." *Psychological Review* 67:380–400.

Cannon, Grant. 1961. "Farm Labor Organizes." *Farm Quarterly* 16, no. 1 (Spring): 1–34.

Carder, William. 2005. Interview by the author. August 17, Berkeley, CA.

Cardoso, Lawrence. 1979. "Labor Emigration to the Southwest, 1916 to 1920: Mexican Attitudes and Policy." In *Mexican Workers in the United States: Historical and Political Perspectives*, edited by George C. Kiser and Martha Woody Kiser. Albuquerque: University of New Mexico Press.

Carlton-Ford, Steven L. 1992. "Charisma, Ritual, Collective Effervescence and Self-Esteem." *Sociological Quarterly* 33, no. 3:365–388.

Carmines, Edward G., and James A. Stimson. 1989. *Issue Evolution: Race and the Transformation of American Politics*. Princeton, NJ: Princeton University Press.

CBS Television. 1960. "Harvest of Shame." *CBS Reports*, November 25.

Cella, John B., II. 1994. *California Wine Pioneers: Profiles of the State's Wine Industry Leaders*. Wine Spectator Scholarship Foundation, M. Shanken Communications.

Chambers, Clarke A. 1952. *California Farm Organizations: A Historical Study of the Grange, the Farm Bureau, and the Associated Farmers, 1929–1941*. Berkeley: University of California Press.

Chambers, J. A. 1973. "Relating Personality and Biographical Factors to Scientific Creativity." *Psychological Monographs* 78(7).

Chandler, Alfred D. 1962. *Strategy and Structure: Chapters in the History of the American Industrial Enterprise*. Cambridge, MA: MIT Press.

Chatfield, Leroy. 1996. Interview by author. Sacramento, CA.

Chavez, Cesar. 1966. Letter to Senator Harrison Williams. June 25. Stanford University Archives, Fred Ross Collection.

Child, John. 1972. "Organizational Structure, Environment and Performance: The Role of Strategic Choice." *Sociology* 6, no. 1:1–22.

Chong, Dennis. 1991. *Collective Action and the Civil Rights Movement*. Chicago: University of Chicago Press.

Clemens, Elisabeth. 1996. "Organizational Form as Frame: Collective Identity and Political Strategy in the Labor Movement, 1880–1920." In *Comparative Perspectives on Social Movements*, edited by Doug McAdam, John McCarthy, and Meyer Zald. Cambridge: Cambridge University Press.

Code of Federal Regulations. 20, 602.2(b).

Cohen, Jerome. 1967a. Handwritten notes on Teamster-UFW Negotiations, May 26. UFW Archives, Wayne State University, Detroit, MI.

———. 1967b. Notes on the Meeting with the Teamsters of Friday, May 19, 1967. UFW Archives, Walter Reuther Library, Wayne State University, Detroit, MI.

———. 1986. "UFW Must Get Back to Organizing." *Los Angeles Times*, January 15, 5.

———. 1995, 1998, 2005. Interviews by author. Carmel, CA.

Cohen, Michael D., James G. March, and Johan P. Olson. 1972. "A Garbage Can Model of Organizational Choice." *Administrative Science Quarterly* 17:1–25.

Collins, Randall. 1981. "On the Microfoundations of Macrosociology." *American Journal of Sociology* 86 (March):984–1013.

Conger, Jay A., and Rabindra N. Kanungo. 1998. *Charismatic Leadership in Organizations*. Thousand Oaks, CA: Sage.

Congressional Research Service. 1980. *History of the Immigration and Naturalization Service*. Washington, DC: U.S. Government Printing Office.

Conti, R., T. M. Amabile, and S. Pokkak. 1995. "Problem Solving among Computer Science Students: The Effects of Skill, Evaluation Expectation and Personality on Solution Quality." Paper presented at the Annual Meeting of the Eastern Psychological Association, Boston, April.

Cormier, Frank, and William J. Eaton. 1970. *Reuther*. Englewood Cliffs, NJ: Prentice-Hall.

Cowan, Paul. 1967. *The Making of an Un-American: A Dialogue with Experience.* New York: Viking.

Craig, R. B. 1970. "Interest Groups and the Foreign Policy Process: A Case Study of the Bracero Program." Ph.D. diss., University of Michigan, Ann Arbor.

Dahrendorf, Ralf. 1958. *Class and Conflict in Industrial Society.* Palo Alto, CA: Stanford University Press.

Damanpour, Fariborz. 1991. "Organizational Innovation: A Meta-Analysis of Effects of Determinants and Moderators." *Academy of Management Journal* 34, no. 3:555–590.

Daniel, Cletus E. 1972. "Labor Radicalism in Pacific Coast Agriculture." Ph.D. diss., University of Washington.

———. 1981. *Bitter Harvest: A History of California Farmworkers, 1870–1941.* Ithaca, NY: Cornell University Press.

———. 1987. "Cesar Chavez and the Unionization of California Farm Workers." In *Labor Leaders in America*, edited by Melvyn Dubofsky and Warren Van Tine. Urbana: University of Illinois Press.

Daniel, Franz. 1960. Letter to John Livingston, December 9. Box 14/30, Department of Organization, George Meany Memorial Archives, Silver Spring, MD.

Davis, J. E. 2002. "Narrative and Social Movements: The Power of Stories." In *Stories of Change: Narrative and Social Movements*, edited by J. E. Davis. Albany: State University of New York Press.

Deci, E. L., and R. M. Ryan. 1980. "The Empirical Exploration of Intrinsic Motivational Processes." In *Advances in Experimental Social Psychology*, edited by L. Berkowitz. New York: Academic.

Delmatier, Royce D., Clarence E. McIntosh, and Earl G. Waters, eds. 1970. *The Rumble of California Politics, 1848–1970.* New York: Wiley.

DiGiorgio Corporation. 1965. *Securities and Exchange Commission Report.* Washington, DC: U.S. Government Printing Office.

DiMaggio, Paul. 1997. "Culture and Cognition." *Annual Review of Sociology* 23:263–287.

Drake, Jim. 1997. Interview by author. Boston, MA, June.

———. 1999. E-mail communication to the author, November 3.

Dubofsky, Melvyn. 1988. *We Shall Be All: A History of the Industrial Workers of the World*, 2nd ed. Urbana: University of Chicago Press.

Duncan, R. B. 1973. "Multiple Decision Making Structures in Adapting to Environmental Uncertainty: The Impact on Organizational Effectiveness." *Human Relations* 26, no. 3:273–292.

Dunne, John Gregory. 1967. *Delano: The Story of the California Grape Strike.* New York: Farrar, Straus & Giroux.

Dyson, Lowell K. 1973. "The Southern Tenant Farmers Union and Depression Politics." *Political Science Quarterly* 88, no. 2 (June):230–252.

East Bay Labor Journal. Various dates.

Edelman, Peter. 1999. E-mail communication to the author, December 1.

Edsall, Thomas Byrne, with Mary D. Edsall. 1991. *Chain Reaction: The Impact of Race, Rights, and Taxes on American Politics.* New York: Norton.

Eisenhardt, Kathy M., and Claudia Bird Schoonhoven. 1990. "Organizational Growth: Linking Founding Team, Strategy, Environment, and Growth among US Semiconductor Ventures, 1978–1988." *Administrative Science Quarterly* 35:504–529.

Elac, John C. 1961. *Employment of Mexican Workers in U.S. Agriculture, 1900–1960: A Bi-national Economic Analysis*. Los Angeles: University of California. Reprint, San Francisco, CA: R and E Research Associates, 1972.

Ellwood, Robert S. 1997. *The Fifties Spiritual Marketplace: American Religion in a Decade of Conflict*. New Brunswick, NJ: Rutgers University Press.

El Malcriado. 1965–1967.

Emerson, Richard. 1962. "Power-Dependence Relations." *American Sociological Review* 27:31–44.

Escobar, Edward J. 2003. "Bloody Christmas and the Irony of Police Professionalism: The Los Angeles Police Department, Mexican Americans, and Police Reform in the 1950s." *Pacific Historical Review* 72, no. 2:171–199.

Farm Labor. 1963–1967.

"Farm Worker Organizing Urged by IUD Convention." 1961. *IUD Bulletin* (December).

Farm Workers Association. 1962a. Agenda for first organizational meeting, September 30, Fresno, CA. UFW Archives, Walter Reuther Library, Wayne State University, Detroit, MI.

———. 1962b. Minutes of first organizational meeting, September 30, Fresno, CA. UFW Archives, Walter Reuther Library, Wayne State University, Detroit, MI.

———. 1963. Constitutional Convention. "Acta Oficial, Convención Constitucional, Fecha: 20 Enero 1963, Lugar: Salón de Cristo Rey, Parroquia Nuestra Sra. de Guadalupe, Delano, California." UFW Archives, Walter Reuther Library, Wayne State University, Detroit, MI.

Fearis, Donald F. 1971. "The California Farm Worker, 1930–42." Ph.D. diss., University of California, Davis.

Federal Interagency Committee on Migrant Labor. 1947. *Migrant Labor: A Human Problem: Report and Recommendations*. Washington, DC: U.S. Department of Labor, Retraining and Reemployment Administration.

Federal-State Market News Service. 1968. *Marketing California Grapes, Raisins, Wine: 1966 Season*. Sacramento, CA.

Ferris, Susan, and Richard Sandoval. 1997. *The Fight in the Fields: Cesar Chavez and the Farmworkers Movement*, edited by Diana Hembree. New York: Harcourt Brace, 1997.

Finegold, Kenneth, and Theda Skocpol. 1995. *State and Party in America's New Deal*. Madison: University of Wisconsin Press.

Fink, Gary M. 1974. *Biographical Dictionary of American Labor Leaders*. Westport, CT: Greenwood.

Fisher, Lloyd H. 1953. *The Harvest Labor Market in California*. Cambridge, MA: Harvard University Press.

Fuller, Varden. 1939. "The Supply of Agricultural Labor as a Factor in the Evolution of Farm Organization in California." Ph.D. diss., University of California, Berkeley. Published in *Senate Hearings: Subcommittee of Committee on Education and Labor 73 Congress, 3 Session* (1940), pt. 54.

Galarza, Ernesto. 1964. *Merchants of Labor: The Mexican Bracero Story: An Account of the Managed Migration of Mexican Farm Workers in California 1942–1960*. Santa Barbara, CA: McNally and Loftin.

Gamboa, Erasmo. 1990. *Mexican Labor and World War II: Braceros in the Pacific Northwest, 1942–47*. Austin: University of Texas Press.

Gamson, William. 1975. *The Strategy of Social Protest*. Belmont, CA: Wadsworth.

———. 1991. "Commitment and Agency in Social Movements." *Sociological Forum* 6, no. 1:27–50.

Ganz, Marshall. 1965. "Boycott Newsletter." Papers in the personal collection of the author.

———. 1994a. Oral history interview by Professor Robert Brandfon. Transcript in possession of the author.

———. 1994b. "Notes on the March to Sacramento." Unpublished paper in possession of author.

———. 2001. "The Power of Story in Social Movements." Paper presented at the American Sociological Association Annual Meeting.

Garnel, Donald. 1972. *The Rise of Teamster Power in the West*. Berkeley: University of California Press.

———. 1998. Telephone interview by author. Cambridge, MA, October.

Garoyan, Leo. 1983. "Marketing." In *A Guidebook to California Agriculture*, edited by Ann Foley Scheuring. Berkeley: University of California Press.

Geier, Joel. 1965. "Three Case Studies in Agri-Industry." *Farm Labor* 4, no. 4 (August):10–11.

Gentner, Dedre. 1989. "Mechanisms of Analogical Learning." In *Similarity and Analogical Reasoning*, edited by S. Vosiadou and A. Ortony. Cambridge: Cambridge University Press.

Gersick, Connie J. 1994. "Pacing Strategic Change: The Case of a New Venture." *Administrative Science Quarterly* 29:499–518.

Getzels, J., and M. Csikszentmihalyi. 1976. *The Creative Vision: A Longitudinal Study of Problem Finding in Art*. New York: Wiley-Interscience.

Gibbons, Harold J. 1967. Confidential memorandum to James R. Hoffa concerning meeting with Bill Kircher, January 25. Harold Gibbons Papers. Archives, University of Southern Indiana, Evansville.

Gilb, Corinne Lathrop. 1974. Einar Mohn, Teamster Leader: An Oral History. Bancroft Library, University of California, Berkeley.

Gillingham, J. B. 1956. *The Teamsters Union on the West Coast*. Berkeley: University of California Press.

Gitlin, Todd. 1987. *The Sixties: Years of Hope, Days of Rage*. New York: Bantam.

Glaser, Rabbi Joseph B. 1967a. April 28 memo to Perelli-Minetti Family, Cesar Chavez, and others concerning meetings on April 28 in San Francisco, CA. UFW Archives, Walter Reuther Library, Wayne State University, Detroit, MI.

———. 1967b. Letter to Richard White, O'Melveny and Myers, Los Angeles, CA, June 20. UFW Archives, Walter Reuther Library, Wayne State University, Detroit, MI.

———. 1967c. Handwritten notes of a telephone conversation, June 16, 1967, at 6:00 p.m. UFW Archives, Walter Reuther Library, Wayne State University, Detroit, MI.

Glaser, Rabbi Joseph B. 1967d. Letter to Richard White, O'Melveny and Myers, Los Angeles, CA, June 23. Response to letter of June 22. UFW Archives, Walter Reuther Library, Wayne State University, Detroit, MI.

Glass, Judith Chanin. 1966. "Conditions Which Facilitate Unionization of Agricultural Workers: A Case Study of the Salinas Valley Lettuce Industry." Ph.D. diss., University of California, Los Angeles.

Goepel, Wendy. 1964. "Viva la Causa: Interview with Cesar Chavez." *Farm Labor* 1, no. 5 (April):25.

Goodwin, Richard N. 1988. *Remembering America: A Voice from the Sixties.* New York: Harper and Row.

Gordon, Jennifer. 2005. "Law, Lawyers and Labor: The United Farm Workers' Legal Strategy in the 1960s and 1970s and the Role of Law in Union Organizing Today." Unpublished paper.

Gorman, Patrick. 1959. "The Forgotten Farm Worker." *I.U.D. Digest* (Winter):31–37.

Grami, Derek. 1998. Telephone interview by author. Cambridge, MA, October.

Grami, William. 1995. Interview conducted by Rick Tejada-Flores. Santa Rosa, CA, July.

Granovetter, Mark. 1973. "The Strength of Weak Ties." *American Journal of Sociology* 78:1360–1380.

Green, Clifford J., ed. 1996. *Churches, Cities and Human Community: Urban Ministry in the United States, 1945–1985.* Grand Rapids, MI: Eerdmans.

Greenhouse, Steven. 1997. "U.S. Survey Find[s] Farm Workers Pay Down for 20 Years." *New York Times,* May 3, A1.

Grubbs, Donald H. 1974. "Prelude to Chavez: National Farm Labor Union in California." *Labor History* 453–469.

Hackman, J. Richard, and Richard Walton. 1986. "Leading Groups in Organizations." In *Designing Effective Work Groups,* edited by Paul Goodman, 72–119. San Francisco: Jossey-Bass.

Hall, Rodney Bruce. 1997. "Moral Authority as a Power Resource." *International Organizations* 51, no. 4 (Autumn):591–622.

Hamel, Gary. 1996. "Strategy as Revolution." *Harvard Business Review* 74, no. 69:69–78.

Harrington, Michael. 1962. *The Other America: Poverty in the United States.* New York: Macmillan.

Hartmire, Wayne C. 1996. Interview by author. Tape recording. Sacramento, CA, August.

Haughton, Ronald W. 1966. "Report and Recommendations." American Arbitration Association, San Francisco, July 14.

Hawley, Ellis W. 1979. "The Politics of the Mexican Labor Issue, 1950–1965." In *Mexican Workers in the United States: Historical and Political Perspectives,* edited by George Kiser and Martha Woody Kiser, 97–114. Albuquerque: University of New Mexico Press.

Hernandez, Julio. 1995. Transcript of an oral history interview. California State University, Northridge, Provost's Committee on Chicano Labor, March 9.

Herodotus. 1972. *The Histories,* translated by Aubrey de Selincourt, 551–555. London: Penguin.

Hirschman, Albert O. 1984. "Against Parsimony: Three Easy Ways of Complicating Some Categories of Economic Discourse." *American Economic Review* 74, no. 2 (May):89–96.

Hollander, Edwin P., and Lynn R. Offermann. 1990. "Power and Leadership in Organizations: Relationships in Transition." *American Psychologist* 45, no. 2:179–190.

Holmaas, Arthur J. 1950. *Agricultural Wage Stabilization in World War II.* Washington, DC: U.S. Government Printing Office.

Horwitt, Sanford D. 1989. *Let Them Call Me Rebel: Saul Alinsky, His Life and Legacy.* New York: Knopf.

House, Robert J., William D. Spangler, and James Woycke. 1991. "Personality and Charisma in the U.S. Presidency: A Psychological Theory of Leader Effectiveness." *Administrative Science Quarterly* 36, no. 3:364–397.

Hutchins, Edwin. 1991. "The Social Organization of Distributed Cognition." In *Perspective on Socially Shared Cognition*, edited by L. B. Resnick, J. M. Levine, and S. D. Teasley, 283–307. Washington, DC: American Psychological Association.

International Brotherhood of Teamsters. 1975. "Research Bulletin: Finances of the United Farm Workers of America, 1967–74." August 5. Harold Gibbons Papers, Archives, University of Southern Indiana, Evansville.

Jacobs, John. 1995. *A Rage for Justice: The Passion and Politics of Phillip Burton.* Berkeley: University of California Press.

James, Ralph C., and Estelle Dinerstein. 1965. *Hoffa and the Teamsters: A Study of Union Power.* New York: Van Nostrand.

Jamieson, Stuart. 1946. *Labor Unionism in American Agriculture.* Bulletin 836, Bureau of Labor Statistics, U.S. Department of Labor. Reprint, New York: Arno, 1975.

Jamison, John A. 1964. *The California Fresh Deciduous Fruit Industry: Structure, Organization, and Practices.* Davis: University of California, Division of Agriculture Sciences.

Jasper, James M. 1997. *The Art of Moral Protest: Culture, Biography, and Creativity in Social Movements.* Chicago: University of Chicago Press.

Jelinek, Lawrence J. 1979. *Harvest Empire: A History of California Agriculture.* San Francisco: Boyd and Fraser.

Jenkins, J. Craig. 1985. *The Politics of Insurgency: The Farm Worker Movement in the 1960s.* New York: Columbia University Press.

Jenkins, J. Craig, and Charles Perrow. 1977. "Insurgency of the Powerless: Farm Worker Movements in the U.S." *American Sociological Review* 42:429–468.

Kahn, Aktar M., Phillip Martin, and Phil Hardiman. 2003. *California's Farm Labor Market: A Cross-Sectional Analysis of Employment and Earnings in 1991, 1996, and 2001.* Working Paper, State of California, Employment Development Department, Labor Market Information Division, Applied Research Unit, August.

Kasperson, C. J. 1978. "Psychology of the Scientist: Scientific Creativity: A Relationship with Information Channels." *Psychological Reports* 42:691–694.

Kim, Hyojoung, and Peter S. Bearman. 1997. "The Structure and Dynamics of Movement Participation." *American Sociological Review* 62 (February):70–93.

Kimeldorf, Howard. 1988. *Reds or Rackets? The Making of Radical and Conservative Unions on the Waterfront.* Berkeley: University of California Press.

Kircher, Thomas. 1999. Interview by author. March.

Kirstein, Peter N. 1973. "Anglo over Bracero: A History of the Mexican Worker in the United States from Roosevelt to Nixon." Ph.D. diss., St. Louis University.

Kiser, George C., and Martha Woody Kiser, eds. 1979. *Mexican Workers in the United States: Historical and Political Perspectives*. Albuquerque: University of New Mexico Press.

Knocke, David, and James R. Wood. 1981. *Organized for Action: Commitment in Voluntary Associations*. New Brunswick, NJ: Rutgers University Press.

Kramer, Rod. 2000. "Political Paranoia in Organizations: Antecedents and Consequences." *Research in the Sociology of Organizations* 17:47–87.

Kuhn, Gene. 1966. "Chavez, Teamster Officials Will Meet." *Fresno Bee*, May 19.

Kushner, Sam. 1975. *The Long Road to Delano*. New York: International.

La Follette Committee. 1939. Hearings, 76th Cong., 2nd sess., pt. 48, 17479, 17714–177121.

———. 1940. Hearings, 76th Cong., 3rd sess., pt. 62, 22784–22785.

Lakoff, George, and Mark Johnson. 1980. "The Metaphorical Structure of the Human Conceptual System." *Cognitive Science* 4:195–208.

Langer, Ellen. 1989. *Mindfulness*. Reading, MA: Addison-Wesley.

Leiter, Robert D. 1957. *The Teamsters Union: A Study of Its Economic Impact*. New York: Bookman.

Levinthal, D. 1997. "Three Faces of Organizational Learning: Wisdom, Inertia, and Discovery." In *Technological Innovation: Oversights and Foresights*, edited by R. Garud, P. Nayyar, and Z. Shapira, 167–180. Cambridge: Cambridge University Press.

Levi-Strauss, Claude. 1962. *The Savage Mind*. London: Weidenfeld and Nicolson.

Levitt, Herman. 1996. Interview by author. Los Angeles, CA, August.

Levy, Jacques. 1975. *Cesar Chavez: An Autobiography of la Causa*. New York: Norton.

———. 1999. E-mail communication with author, October 17.

Lewis, Kyle, Donald Lange, and Lynette Gillis. 2005. "Transactive Memory Systems, Learning, and Learning Transfer." *Organization Science* 16, no. 6 (November–December):581–598.

Lichtenstein, Nelson. 1968. "Walter Reuther." In *Labor Leaders in America*, edited by Melvyn Dubofsky and Warren Van Tine, 280–302. Urbana: University of Illinois Press.

———. 1995. *Walter Reuther: The Most Dangerous Man in Detroit*. Chicago: University of Illinois Press.

Lipsky, Michael. 1968. "Protest as a Political Resource." *American Political Science Review* 62, no. 48:1144–1158.

Lofland, John. 1996. *Social Movement Organizations*. New York: de Gruyter.

London, Joan, and Henry Anderson. 1970. *So Shall Ye Reap*. New York: Crowell.

Los Angeles Times. Various dates.

Lukes, Stephen. 1974. *Power: A Radical View*. London: Macmillan.

MacKinnon, D. W. 1965. "Personality and the Realization of Creative Potential." *American Psychologist* 20, no. 2:273–281.

Majka, Theo J., and Linda C. Majka. 1982. *Farm Workers, Agribusiness and the State*. Philadelphia: Temple University Press.

Mann, Michael. 1986. *The Sources of Social Power*, vol. 1: *A History of Power from the Beginning to A.D. 1760*. New York: Cambridge University Press.

March, James, and Johan Olsen. 1976. *Ambiguity and Choice in Organizations*. Bergen, Norway: Universeitetsforiaget.

Margolis, Jon. 1999. *The Last Innocent Year: America in 1964, the Beginning of the "Sixties."* New York: Morrow.

Martin, Philip L. 1996. *Promises to Keep: Collective Bargaining in California Agriculture*. Ames: University of Iowa Press.

Mathiessen, Peter. 1969. *Sal Si Puedes: Cesar Chavez and the New American Revolution*. New York: Dell.

McAdam, Doug. 1982. *Political Process and the Development of Black Insurgency, 1930–1970*. Chicago: University of Chicago Press.

———. 1983. "Tactical Innovations and the Pace of Insurgency." *American Sociological Review* 48:735–754.

McCleod, P. L. 1992. "The Effects of Ethnic Diversity on Idea Generation in Small Groups." In *Best Paper Proceedings*, Academy of Management Convention, Las Vegas, NV.

McWilliams, Carey. 1939. *Factories in the Field: The Story of Migratory Farm Labor in California*. Santa Barbara, CA: Peregrine.

———. 1942. *Ill Fares the Land: Migrants and Migratory Labor in the United States*. Boston: Little, Brown.

———. 1948. *North from Mexico: The Spanish-Speaking People of the United States*. Updated by Matt S. Meier, 1990. New York: Praeger.

———. 1949. *California: The Great Exception*. Berkeley: University of California Press.

Meany, George. 1960. Letter to Norman Smith officially reconstituting the Agricultural Workers Organizing Committee (AWOC). June 7. Agricultural Workers Organizing Committee Papers, 1959–1966, UFW Archives, Walter Reuther Library, Wayne State University, Detroit, MI.

Medina, Eliseo. 1998. Interview by author. Tape recording. Los Angeles, CA, August.

Meister, Dick, and Anne Loftis. 1977. *A Long Time Coming: The Struggle to Unionize America's Farm Workers*. New York: Macmillan.

Mentasti, Rev. Ronald T., R. Kenneth Bell, and Jerome Lackner, M.D. 1967. Letter to A. Perelli-Manetti [sic] and Sons, March 4. UFW Archives, Walter Reuther Library, Wayne State University, Detroit, MI.

Metzler, William H. 1964. "The Farm Worker in a Changing Agriculture." Part 1 of *Technological Change and Farm Labor Use, Kern County, California, 1961*. Davis: California Agricultural Experiment Station, Giannini Foundation of Agricultural Economics in Cooperation with Farm Production Economics Division, Economic Research Service, U.S. Department of Agriculture, September 17–24, 90.

Michels, Roberto. 1962 [1911]. *Political Parties: A Sociological Study of Oligarchical Tendencies of Modern Democracy*. New York: Collier.

Miller, James. 1987. *Democracy Is in the Streets: From Port Huron to the Siege of Chicago*. New York: Simon and Schuster.

Miller, James J. 1961. "Legal and Economic History of the Secondary Boycott." *Labor Law Journal* (August):751–759.

Mink, Gwendolyn. 1986. "Meat v. Rice (and Pasta): Discovering Labor Politics in California, 1875–85." In *Old Labor and New Immigrants in American Political Development: Union, Party, and State*. Ithaca, NY: Cornell University Press.

Minton, Bruce, and John Stuart. 1937. *Men Who Lead Labor*. New York: Modern Age.

Mintzberg, Henry, and Alexandra McHugh. 1985. "Strategy Formation in an Adhocracy." *Administrative Science Quarterly* 30, no. 2:160–198.

"Mitchell Hits at Conditions of American Farm Workers." 1959. *IUD Bulletin* (March): 15.

Mitchell, H. L. 1979. *Mean Things Happening in This Land: The Life and Times of H. L. Mitchell, Co-Founder of the Southern Tenant Farmers Union*. Montclair, NJ: Allenheld, Osmun.

Monthly Labor Review. 1959. 82, no. 4 (April):396–398.

Moore, Mark H. 1995. *Creating Public Value: Strategic Management in Government*. Cambridge, MA: Harvard University Press.

Morin, Alexander. 1952. *The Organizability of Farm Labor in the United States*. Cambridge, MA: Harvard University Press.

Morris, Aldon. 1993. "Birmingham Confrontation Reconsidered: An Analysis of the Dynamics and Tactics of Mobilization." *American Sociological Review* 58:621–636.

Morris, Austin P., S.J. 1966. "Agricultural Labor and NIRA." *California Law Review* 54:1939–1989.

Morris, Clifton. 1964. "Probation Report concerning Manuel Chavez." Kern County Superior Court, State of California, June 8.

Movement. 1965–1966.

National Advisory Committee on Farm Labor. 1967. *Farm Labor Organizing 1905–1967: A Brief History*. New York: National Advisory Committee on Farm Labor.

National Farm Workers Association. 1963. "Constitution." UFW Archives, Walter Reuther Library, Wayne State University, Detroit, MI.

National Labor Relations Board. 1949. *Decision and Order* 87, no. 125:720–754.

National Sharecroppers Fund Conference. 1957. "Proceedings: Migratory Labor and Low Income Farmers." November 13, New York.

Nelson, Bruce. 1995. "The Big Strike." In *Working People of California*, edited by Daniel Cornford, 225–264. Berkeley: University of California Press.

Nelson, Eugene. 1966. *Huelga: The First Hundred Days of the Delano Grape Strike*. Delano, CA: Farm Worker Press.

Nelson, Klayton E. 1985. *Harvesting and Handling California Table Grapes for Market*. Oakland: University of California, Division of Agriculture and Natural Resources.

Nemeth, Charlan Jeanne. 1986. "Differential Contributions of Majority and Minority Influences." *Psychological Review* 93, no. 1:22–32.

Nemeth, C. J., and B. M. Staw. 1989. "The Tradeoffs of Social Control and Innovation in Groups and Organizations." In *Advances in Experimental Social Psychology*, vol. 22, edited by L. Berkowitz, 722–730. New York: Academic.

Neuberger, Richard L. 1939. *Our Promised Land*. New York: Macmillan.

NFLU. 1947. Confidential memorandum: Plans for Organization of Agricultural Labor. Southern Tenant Farmers' Union Papers, University of North Carolina, Chapel Hill, reel 32. Cited in Grubbs, *National Farm Labor Union*, 456.

Oberschall, Anthony. 1973. *Social Conflict and Social Movements*. Englewood Cliffs, NJ: Prentice-Hall.

Ofshe, Richard. 1980. "The Social Development of the Synanon Cult: The Managerial Strategy of Organizational Transformation." *Sociological Analysis* 41:109–127.

Ofshe, Richard, et al. 1974. "Social Structure and Social Control in Synanon." *Journal of Voluntary Action Research* 67–76.

Oliver, Christine. 1988. "The Collective Strategy Framework: An Application to Competing Predictions of Isomorphism." *Administrative Science Quarterly* 33, no. 4:543–561.

Oliver, Pamela E., and Gerald Marwell. 1992. "Mobilizing Technologies for Collective Action." In *Frontiers of Social Movement Theory*, edited by Aldon D. Morris and Carol McClurg Mueller, 251–272. New Haven, CT: Yale University Press.

Olmstead, Alan M., and Paul W. Rhode. 1997. "An Overview of the History of California Agriculture." In *California Agriculture: Issues and Challenges*, 1–27. Davis: Giannini Foundation, University of California, Division of Agriculture and Natural Resources. August.

Osborn, A. 1963. *Applied Imagination: Principles and Procedures of Creative Thinking*. New York: Scribner's.

Padilla, Gilbert. 1999. Telephone interview by author. Fresno, CA, March.

Pawel, Miriam. 2006. "Farm Workers Reap Little as Union Strays from It's [*sic*] Roots." *Los Angeles Times*, January 8, 1.

Perella, Frederick J., Jr. 1996. "Roman Catholic Approaches to Urban Ministry, 1945–85." In *Churches, Cities and Human Community*, edited by Clifford J. Green, 179–211. Grand Rapids, MI: Eerdmans.

Perlman, Selig, and Phillip Taft. 1935. "Labor Movements." In their *History of Labor in the United States, 1896–1932*, vol. 4. New York: Macmillan.

Perrow, Charles. 1986. *Complex Organizations: A Critical Essay*. New York: McGraw-Hill.

Peterson, Jordan. 1999. *Maps of Meaning: The Architecture of Belief*. New York: Routledge.

Pfeffer, Jeffrey, and Gerald Salancik. 1978. *The External Control of Organizations: A Resource Dependence Perspective*. New York: Harper and Row.

Pfeffer, Max J. 1983. "Social Origins of Three Systems of Farm Production in the United States." *Rural Sociology* 48, vol. 4:540–562.

Pillai, Rajandini. 1996. "Crisis and the Emergence of Charismatic Leadership in Groups: An Experimental Investigation." *Journal of Applied Social Psychology* 26, no. 6:543–563.

Piore, Michael. 1995. *Beyond Individualism*. Cambridge, MA: Harvard University Press.

Porter, Michael E. 1996. "Making Strategy." *Harvard Business Review* 74, no. 6:61–77.

Powell, Walter W. 1988. "Institutional Effects on Organizational Structure and Performance." In *Institutional Patterns and Organizations*, edited by Lynne G. Zucker. Cambridge, MA: Ballinger.

Pratt, Henry J. 1972. *The Liberalization of American Protestantism*. Detroit, MI: Wayne State University Press.

President's Commission on Migratory Labor. 1951. *Migratory Labor in American Agriculture*. Washington, DC: U.S. Government Printing Office.

———. 1979. "Wetback Invasion: Illegal Alien Labor in American Agriculture." In *Mexican Workers in the United States: Historical and Political Perspectives*, edited by George Kiser and Martha Woody Kiser, 131–153. Albuquerque: University of New Mexico Press.

President's 1940 Committee to Coordinate Health and Welfare. 1947. *Migrant Labor: A Human Problem: Report of the Interagency Committee on Migratory Labor*. Washington, DC: U.S. Government Printing Office.

Public Law 78. 1940. TIAS 2331, 2 UST.

Rasmussen, Wayne D. 1951. "A History of the Emergency Farm Labor Supply Program, 1943–47." Agricultural Monograph No. 13. U.S. Department of Agriculture, Bureau of Agricultural Economics.

Reuther, Victor. 1976. *The Brothers Reuther*. New York: Houghton Mifflin.

"Robert DiGiorgio: San Francisco Business Leader." 1991. *San Francisco Chronicle*. Obituary, March 15:B7.

Roberts, Steven V. 1970. "Fear and Tension Grip Salinas Valley in Farm Workers' Strike." *New York Times*, September 6, 32.

Robinson, Archie. 1981. *George Meany and His Times: A Biography*. New York: Simon and Schuster.

Rochon, Thomas. 1998. *Culture Moves: Ideas, Activism, and Changing Values*. Princeton, NJ: Princeton University Press.

Rogers, Everett. 1995. *Diffusion of Innovations*. New York: Free Press.

Rogin, Michael Paul, and John L. Shover. 1970. *Political Change in California: Critical Elections and Social Movements, 1890–1966*. Westport, CT: Greenwood.

Rojas, Alberto. 1998. Interview by author. Tape recording. San Francisco, CA, August.

Rolle, Andrew F. 1968. *The Immigrant Upraised: Italian Adventurers and Colonists in an Expanding America*. Norman: University of Oklahoma Press.

———. 1998. *California: A History*, 5th ed. Wheeling, IL: Harlan Davidson.

Roomer, Sam. 1962. *The International Brotherhood of Teamsters: Its Government and Structure*. New York: Wiley.

Rosaldo, Renato. 1989. *Culture and Truth: The Remaking of Social Analysis*. Boston: Beacon.

Rose, Margaret. 1995. "Woman Power Will Stop Those Grapes: Chicana Organizers and Middle-Class Female Supporters in the Farmworkers' Grape Boycott in Philadelphia, 1969–70." *Journal of Women's History* (Winter):6–32.

Ross, Fred. 1966a. "El Mosquito Zumbador." Mimeo series. Fred Ross Papers, Stanford University Archives, Palo Alto, CA.

———. 1966b. Letter, Cesar Chavez to Sen. Harrison Williams, June 25. Fred Ross Papers, Stanford University Archives, Palo Alto, CA.

———. 1989. *Conquering Goliath: Cesar Chavez at the Beginning*. Keene, CA: United Farm Workers.

Ross, Fred, Jr. 1992. "Fred Ross: August 23, 1910 to September 27, 1992." Memorial biography, distributed at San Francisco memorial service, October.

Rural Migration News. Available at http://migration.ucdavis.edu/rmn (accessed January 1, 2002).

Ruscio, J., D. Whitney, and T. M. Amabile. 1995. *How Do Motivation and Task Behaviors Affect Creativity? An Investigation in Three Domains.* Waltham, MA: Brandeis University Press.

Salancik, G. R., and J. Pfeffer. 1977. "Who Gets Power—and How They Hold on to It: A Strategic Contingency Model of Power." *Organizational Dynamics* 2, no. 21:2–21.

Saludado, Antonia. 1995. Transcript of an oral history interview. California State University, Northridge, Provost's Committee on Chicano Labor, June 11.

Salzman, Ed. 1976. "Has Brown's Ambition Kept the ALRB Bankrupt?" *California Journal* (June):68.

San Francisco Examiner. Various dates.

Scharlin, Craig, and Lilia V. Villanueva. 1992. *Phillip Vera Cruz: A Personal History of Filipino Immigrants and the Farmworkers Movement,* edited by Glenn Omatsu and Augusto Espiritu. Burbank, CA: Fremont.

Schelling, Thomas C. 1960. *The Strategy of Conflict.* Cambridge, MA: Harvard University Press.

Schenley Industries. 1941. "Letter to Stockholders." Annual Report, 7.

———. 1942. "Letter to Stockholders." Annual Report, 16.

———. 1965. Annual Report, Form 10-K, Securities and Exchange Commission. Washington, DC, December.

Scheuring, Ann Foley, ed. 1983. *A Guidebook to California Agriculture.* Berkeley: University of California Press.

Scheuring, Ann Foley, and Refugio I. Rochin. 1983. "Organizations in Agriculture." In *A Guidebook to California Agriculture,* edited by Ann Foley Scheuring, 245–250. Berkeley: University of California Press.

Schrade, Paul. 1984. Interview by author. Tape recording. Los Angeles, CA, July.

———. 1999. E-mail communication to the author, November 28.

Senate Fact Finding Committee on Agriculture. 1967. *Special Report.* January 9. Sacramento: Senate of the State of California.

Senge, Peter. 1990. *The Fifth Discipline: The Art and Practice of the Learning Organization.* Garden City, NY: Doubleday.

Sewell, William, Jr. 1996. "Three Temporalities: Toward an Eventful Sociology." In *The Historic Turn in the Human Sciences,* edited by Terrence J. McDonald, 245–280. Ann Arbor: University of Michigan Press.

Shroyer, John. 1967. Letter to "Dear Friend," May 17. Stanford University Libraries, Department of Special Collections and University Archives, UFWOC Collection.

Simonton, D. K. 1988. "Creativity, Leadership and Chance." In *The Nature of Creativity: Contemporary Psychological Perspectives,* edited by R. J. Sternberg, 386–426. Cambridge: Cambridge University Press.

Skerry, Peter. 1993. *Mexican-Americans: Ambivalent Minority.* Cambridge MA: Harvard University Press.

Skocpol, Theda. 1984. "Emerging Agendas and Recurrent Strategies in Historical Sociology." In *Vision and Method in Historical Sociology,* 356–391. New York: Cambridge University Press.

———. 1985. "Bringing the State Back In: Strategies and Analysis in Current Research." In *Bringing the State Back In,* edited by Peter Evans, Dietrich

Rueschemeyer, and Theda Skocpol, 3–37. New York: Cambridge University Press.

Smelser, Neil J. 1962. *Theory of Collective Action*. New York: Free Press.

Smith, Norman. 1959. Correspondence to John Livingston, May 13. Box 13/27, Department of Organization, George Meany Memorial Archives, Silver Spring, MD.

Smith, Sydney D. 1987. *Grapes of Conflict*. Pasadena, CA: Hope.

Snow, David A., E. Burke Rochford, Jr., Steven Worden, and Robert D. Benford. 1986. "Frame Alignment Processes, Micromobilization, and Movement Participation." *American Sociological Review* 51:464–481.

Somers, M. 1994. "The Narrative Constitution of Identity: A Relational and Network Approach." *Theory and Society* 23:605–649.

Southern California Teamster. 1965–1967.

Stanford University Library. 1999. Department of Special Collections, Archivist's Introductions, Ernesto Galarza Papers.

Stark, Rodney, and William Bainbridge. 1985. *The Future of Religion: Secularization, Revival and Cult Formation*. Berkeley: University of California Press.

Starr, Kevin. 1985. *Inventing the Dream: California through the Progressive Era*. New York: Oxford University Press.

———. 1996. *Endangered Dreams: The Great Depression in California*. New York: Oxford University Press.

Steinle, Donald R. 1996. "Retreat, Reentry, and Retrenchment: Urban Ministry in the United Church of Christ, 1945–1980." In *Churches, Cities and Human Community: Urban Ministry in the United States, 1945–1985*, edited by Clifford Green, 212–234. Grand Rapids, MI: Eerdmans.

Stockton Record. Various dates.

Strang, David, and John Meyer. 1994. "Institutional Conditions for Diffusion." In *Institutional Environments and Organizations*, edited by W. Richard Scott and John W. Meyer, 100–112. Beverly Hills, CA: Sage.

Swidler, Ann. 1986. "Culture in Action: Symbols and Strategies." *American Sociological Review* 51, no. 2:273–286.

Taft, Phillip. 1968. *Labor Politics American Style: The California State Federation of Labor*. Cambridge, MA: Harvard University Press.

Takaki, Ronald. 1989. *Strangers from a Different Shore: A History of Asian Americans*. New York: Penguin.

Taylor, Charles. 1989. *Sources of the Self*. Cambridge, MA: Harvard University Press.

Taylor, Paul S., and Tom Vasey. 1936. "Historical Background of California Farm Labor." *Rural Sociology* 1, no. 3(September):108–122. Reprinted in Paul S. Taylor. 1981. *Labor on the Land: Collected Writings 1930–1970*. New York: Arno.

Taylor, Ronald B. 1966a. "Teamsters Give NFWA Free Hand at DiGiorgio." *Fresno Bee*, June 7:1-B.

———. 1966b. "Teamster Chiefs Divide on Leaving DiGiorgio to Chavez." *Fresno Bee*, June 8.

———. 1975. *Chavez and the Farm Workers*. Boston: Beacon.

———. 1999. Interview by author. Telephone call. March.

Taylor, Verta, and Nancy E. Whittier. 1992. "Collective Identity in Social Movement Communities: Lesbian Feminist Mobilization." In *Frontiers in Social Movement*

Theory, edited by A. D. Morris and C. M. Mueller, 104–130. New Haven, CT: Yale University Press.

"Teamster Union, Chavez Sign Peace Accord." 1967. *Fresno Bee*, July 22.

Thomas, Robert McG., Jr. 1996. "Sidney R. Korshak, 88, Dies: Fabled Fixer for the Chicago Mob." *New York Times*, January 22:D-10.

Thompson, Mark Elliott. 1963. "The Agricultural Workers' Organizing Committee, 1959–1962." Master's thesis, Cornell University.

Tilly, Charles. 1978. *From Mobilization to Revolution*. Reading, MA: Addison-Wesley.

Tjerendsen, Carl. 1980. *Education for Citizenship: A Foundation's Experience*. Santa Cruz, CA: Emil Schwartzhaupt Foundation.

Troy, Leo, and Neil Sheflin. 1985. *U.S. Union Sourcebook*. West Orange, NJ: IRDIS.

Turner, Ralph, and Lewis Killian. 1987 [1972]. *Collective Behavior*, 3rd ed. Englewood Cliffs, NJ: Prentice-Hall.

Turner, Victor. 1966. *The Ritual Process: Structure and Anti-Structure*. Ithaca, NY: Cornell University Press.

Tushman, Michael, and Peter Murmann. 1997. "Organization Responsiveness to Environmental Shock as an Indicator of Organizational Foresight and Oversight: The Role of Executive Team Characteristics and Organization Context." In *Technological Innovation: Foresights and Oversights*, edited by Raghu Garud, Praveen Nayyoi, and Zur Shapira. New York: Cambridge University Press.

United Farm Workers. 1966. DiGiorgio Chronology. UFWOC Collection, Archives, Walter Reuther Library, Wayne State University, Detroit, MI.

———. Various dates. Minutes of UFW General Meetings. UFW Papers, UFWOC Collection, Walter Reuther Library, Wayne State University, Detroit, MI.

United Farm Workers Organizing Committee. 1960–1966. Archives, Special Collections, Stanford University, Palo Alto, CA.

———. 1965–1968. UFW Chronology of the Strike (August 6, 1965–March 11, 1968). Compiled from newspaper clippings from the *Fresno Bee*, *Los Angeles Times*, *San Francisco Chronicle*. Collected by UFWOC, Archives, Wayne State University, Walter Reuther Library, Detroit, MI (hereafter UFW Chronology).

———. 1966–1967. Handwritten "Friday Night Meeting Minutes." April–June 1966; and September 9, 1966–April 21, 1967. UFWOC Collection, Walter Reuther Library, Wayne State University, Detroit, MI.

———. 1967a. "The Case against Perelli-Minetti: An Appeal for Justice." Dear Friends Letter, January 19. UFW Archives, Walter Reuther Library, Wayne State University, Detroit, MI.

———. 1967b. "Constitution." UFWOC Collection, Walter Reuther Library, Wayne State University, Detroit, MI.

U.S. Bureau of the Census. 1968. *Census of Agriculture, 1964: Statistics for the State and Counties, California*, vol. 1, pt. 48. Washington, DC: U.S. Government Printing Office.

U.S. Department of Labor. 1947. Retraining and Reemployment Administration. *Migrant Labor: A Human Problem: Report and Recommendations*. Federal Interagency Committee on Migrant Labor. Washington DC: U.S. Government Printing Office.

———. 1959. Bureau of Employment Security. *Mexican Farm Labor Program: Consultants Report*. Washington, DC: U.S. Government Printing Office.

U.S. Department of Labor. 2007. *2006 LM-2 Report*. March 29.

U.S. Senate. 1940. Subcommittee on Senate Resolution 266 of the Committee on Education and Labor. *Hearings: Violations of Free Speech and Rights of Labor*: pt. 1, *Supplementary Hearings*. Washington, DC: U.S. Government Printing Office.

———. 1942. Committee on Education and Labor. *Employers Associations and Collective Bargaining in California*. Report no. 1150, pt. 3, 77th Cong., 2nd sess. Washington DC: U.S. Government Printing Office.

———. 1961. Subcommittee on Migratory Labor. *The Migratory Farm Labor Problem in the United States: A Report Together with Individual Views to the Committee on Labor and Public Welfare, United States Senate, Made by Its Subcommittee on Migratory Labor Pursuant to Senate Resolution 267 (86th Congress, 2nd Session)*. Washington, DC: U.S. Government Printing Office.

———. 1962. *The Migratory Farm Labor Problem in the United States: Second Report to the Committee on Labor and Public Welfare, United States Senate, Made by its Subcommittee on Migratory Labor, Pursuant to Senate Resolution 86 (87th Congress, 1st Session)*. Washington, DC: U.S. Government Printing Office.

Valdez, Luis. 1966. "The Tale of the Raza." *Ramparts* 5, no. 2(July):40–43.

———. 1995. Transcript of an oral history interview. California State University, Northridge, Provost's Committee on Chicano Labor, June.

Valley Labor Citizen. 1960–1967.

Van de Ven, Andrew H., Douglas E. Polley, Raghu Garud, and Sankaran Venkataraman. 1999. *The Innovation Journey*. New York: Oxford University Press.

von Hippel, Eric. 1988. *The Sources of Innovation*. New York: Oxford University Press.

Vorspan, Rabbi Albert. 1966. Letter to Manischewitz Kosher Winery, December 2. Fred Ross Papers, Stanford University Archives, Palo Alto, CA.

Vucinich, Wayne. 1960. "Yugoslavs in California." *Historical Society of Southern California Quarterly* 42, no. 3 (September):287–309.

Walsh, Edward J., and Charles Craypo. 1979. "Union Oligarchy and the Grassroots: The Case of the Teamsters' Defeat in Farm Worker Organizing." *Sociology and Social Research* 63, no. 2:269–293.

Watson, Don. 1998a. "Hidden War: The Packinghouse Workers (UPWA) and the Agricultural Workers (NAWU) in California Agriculture, 1954–1961." Paper presented at the Southwest Labor Studies Conference, Austin, TX, April 25.

———. 1998b. "Story of a Contract: The United Packinghouse Workers of America and the Vegetable Grower Bud Antle, 1954–1961." Paper presented at the North American Labor History Conference, Detroit, MI, October 17.

———. 1999. Notes on Larry Itliong Files. UFW Collection, Walter P. Reuther Library, Wayne State University, Detroit, MI.

Wattell, Harold. 1977. "Lewis Solon Rosenstiel." *Dictionary of American Biography*, 2nd ed. New York: Scribner's, 701–703.

Weber, Devra. 1994. *Dark Sweat, White Gold: California Farm Workers, Cotton, and the New Deal*. Berkeley: University of California Press.

Weber, Max. 1946 [1920]. *From Max Weber: Essays in Sociology*, translated and edited by H. H. Gerth and C. Wright Mills. New York: Oxford University Press.

———. 1958 [1905]. *The Protestant Ethic and the Spirit of Capitalism*. New York: Scribner's.

———. 1978 [1914]. *Economy and Society*, vols. 1 and 2, edited by Guenther Roth and Claus Wittich. Berkeley: University of California Press.

Weick, Karl E. 1979. *The Social Psychology of Organizing*. New York: McGraw-Hill.

———. 1993. "Sensemaking in Organizations: Small Structures with Large Consequences." In *Social Psychology in Organizations*, edited by J. K. Murnighan, 10–37. Englewood Cliffs, NJ: Prentice-Hall.

Weinstein, Henry. 1996. "Sidney Korshak, Alleged Mafia Liaison to Hollywood, Dies at 88." *Los Angeles Times*, January 22, A-3.

Wells, Miriam J. 1996. *Strawberry Fields: Politics, Class, and Work in California Agriculture*. Ithaca, NY: Cornell University Press.

Western Conference of Teamsters. 1974. "Teamsters Get the Canneries." In *The History of Western Conference of Teamsters*. Burlingame, CA: Western Conference of Teamsters.

White, Richard. 1967. Letter to Rabbi Joseph Glaser concerning Perelli-Minetti. June 22. UFW Archives, Walter Reuther Library, Wayne State University, Detroit, MI.

Who Was Who. Lewis S. Rosenstiel biographical sketch, 352.

Who's Who in Finance and Industry. William L. Kircher biographical sketch, 402.

Who's Who in the South and Southwest. William L. Kircher biographical sketch, 406.

Who's Who: The American Catholic. William L. Kircher biographical sketch, 402.

Williams, Lee G. 1962. "Recent Legislation Affecting the Mexican Labor Program." *Employment Security Review* 29, no. 31 (February).

Wilson, James Q. 1962. *The Amateur Democrat: Club Politics in Three Cities*. Chicago: University of Chicago Press.

Wilson, Kirke. 1964. Interview of John Soria in "The Oxnard Farm Workers Service Center." *Farm Labor* 1, no. 6 (May).

Woolsey, James G. 1966. "Statement of Schenley Industries, Inc." California Senate Fact Finding Committee on Agriculture, Delano, CA, July 20.

Yablonski, Lewis. 1967. *Synanon: The Tunnel Back*. Baltimore, MD: Penguin.

Zald, Mayer N., and Roberta Ash. 1966. "Social Movement Organizations: Growth, Decay and Change." *Social Forces* 44, no. 3 (March):327–341.

Zaltman, Gerald, Robert Duncan, and Jonny Holbeck. 1973. *Innovations and Organizations*. New York: Wiley.

Zieger, Robert H. 1987. "George Meany: Labor's Organization Man." In *Labor Leaders in America*, edited by Melvyn Dubofsky and Warren Van Tine, 324–349. Urbana: University of Illinois Press.

———. 1995. *The CIO, 1935–55*. Chapel Hill: University of North Carolina Press.

Index

CPSIA information can be obtained at www.ICGtesting.com
Printed in the USA
BVOW11s0826090814

362227BV00004B/37/P